Indians and British Outposts in Eighteenth-Century America

UNIVERSITY PRESS OF FLORIDA

Florida A&M University, Tallahassee
Florida Atlantic University, Boca Raton
Florida Gulf Coast University, Ft. Myers
Florida International University, Miami
Florida State University, Tallahassee
New College of Florida, Sarasota
University of Central Florida, Orlando
University of Florida, Gainesville
University of North Florida, Jacksonville
University of South Florida, Tampa
University of West Florida, Pensacola

Indians and British Outposts in Eighteenth-Century America

DANIEL INGRAM

University Press of Florida
Gainesville · Tallahassee · Tampa · Boca Raton
Pensacola · Orlando · Miami · Jacksonville · Ft. Myers · Sarasota

Copyright 2012 by Daniel Ingram
All rights reserved
Printed in the United States of America on acid-free paper

First cloth printing, 2012
First paperback printing, 2014

Library of Congress Cataloging-in-Publication Data

Ingram, Daniel Patrick, 1960–
Indians and British outposts in eighteenth-century America / Daniel Ingram.
   p. cm.
Includes bibliographical references and index.
ISBN 978-0-8130-3797-4 (cloth: alk. paper)
ISBN 978-0-8130-6038-5 (pbk.)
   1. Indians of North America—First contact with Europeans. 2. Fortification—United States—History—18th century. 3. Frontier and pioneer life—United States. 4. Great Britain. Army—Military life—History—18th century. 5. United States—Race relations—History—18th century. 6. Great Britain—Colonies—America—Defenses. 7. United States—History—Colonial period, ca. 1600-1775. I. Title.
E98.F39I54 2012
973.2'6—dc23   2011037511

The University Press of Florida is the scholarly publishing agency for the State University System of Florida, comprising Florida A&M University, Florida Atlantic University, Florida Gulf Coast University, Florida International University, Florida State University, New College of Florida, University of Central Florida, University of Florida, University of North Florida, University of South Florida, and University of West Florida.

University Press of Florida
15 Northwest 15th Street
Gainesville, FL 32611-2079
http://www.upf.com

For Stacey

Contents

List of Illustrations ix

Acknowledgments xi

Introduction: British Forts and Indian Neighbors 1

1. The Key to Carolina: Old Hop, Little Carpenter, and the Making of Fort Loudoun, 1756–1759 27

2. Anxious Hospitality: Loitering at Fort Allen, 1756–1761 . . 59

3. The Greatest Mart of All Trade: Food, Drink, and Interdependence at Michilimackinac, 1761–1796 88

4. A Year at Niagara: Violence, Diplomacy, and Coexistence in the Eastern Great Lakes, 1763–1764 121

5. Like Stars That Fall: Keeping Up Appearances at Fort Chartres, 1765–1772 156

Conclusion: The Mohawks' New World 193

Notes 203

Bibliography 235

Index 249

Illustrations

Maps

1.1. Fort Loudoun and Cherokee towns, 1756–1761 30
2.1. Blue Mountain region of Pennsylvania, 1755–1761 61
3.1. Forts and towns around the Straits of Mackinac, 1690s–1790s 93
4.1. Niagara River corridor, 1763 125
5.1. Fort Chartres and the western Illinois country, 1765–1771 . . 159

Figures

I.1. Examples of forts 8
I.2. Cantonment of British forces in North America, 1765 . . . 20
1.1. Seven Cherokees in London, 1730 33
1.2. Draught of Cherokee Country, 1762 42
1.3. Plan and profile of Fort Loudoun, 1757 47
2.1. Map of Fort Allen and Fort Norris region, 1759 67
2.2. Plan of Fort Allen, 1756 68
3.1. Sketch of Michilimackinac, 1765 105
4.1. Plan of Fort Niagara, 1763 137
4.2. Niagara River and portage, 1764–1765 147
5.1. Mississippi settlements between the Ohio and Kaskaskia Rivers, 1765 165
5.2. Plan of Fort Chartres ruins, 1820 189

Acknowledgments

Many people and organizations helped me shepherd this book to its final form. Work began at the College of William and Mary, and my friends and colleagues there were invaluable. James Axtell played an especially important role as an editor and friend. James P. Whittenburg, Kris E. Lane, and Michael N. McConnell provided very valuable suggestions. Thanks also to Carol Sheriff, Cindy Hahamovitch, Scott Reynolds Nelson, Kimberley L. Phillips, Dale Hoak, Marley R. Brown III, Philip D. Morgan, Ronald Hoffman, Michael McGiffert, and Roz Stearns for giving me the benefit of their valuable time and tutelage. Philip Levy, John Coombs, David Muraca, David Brown, and Robert Paulett, with whom I shared many summers digging under the unforgiving Virginia sun, have been especially good friends and colleagues. Thanks also to David Preston, Brian Geiger, Steven Feeley, Creston Long, Sharon Sauder Muhlfeld, Emily Blanck, Bill Carrigan, Ericka Thoms, Lily Richards Harwood, Jim Piecuch, Beth English, Joan Campbell, Chesley Flotten, Laurie Bauer-Coleman, Elizabeth Kelly Gray, Catherine Dann-Roeber, and David Corlett for helping to make my years in Williamsburg rewarding and entertaining.

In my home state of Michigan I met many friends who have stuck with me through the years in all kinds of weather. Thanks to Timothy Koerner, Sandra Van Burkleo, Joseph P. Ward, Howard and Linda Williams, Steve Simonson and Lisa Coon, Dudley and Gerry Smith, Paul and Deb Smith, Michael Lavoie and Emy Richardson, Matthew and Laura Spittle, and Mark Rabinowitz for much support and friendship along the way, and in the years to come.

Professional organizations and libraries have been invaluable to my work. William and Mary's Lyon G. Tyler Department of History and Graduate School of Arts and Sciences provided funding through their Historical Archaeology Apprenticeship and History Writing Resources

Center. I am proud of my association with the Colonial Williamsburg Department of Archaeological Research, where I worked as a field school instructor for several summers. The General Society for Colonial Wars provided important funding for my research through their George Washington Fellowship, for which I am very grateful. Thanks also to the staffs of the William L. Clements Library at the University of Michigan, the Burton Historical Collection at the Detroit Public Library, the American Philosophical Society, the Historical Society of Pennsylvania, the Peterson Center Library in Mackinaw City, Michigan, the Main Library at Michigan State University, the Library of Michigan, the Kresge Library at Wayne State University, the Earl Gregg Swem Library at William and Mary, and the Bracken Library at Ball State University.

At the University Press of Florida, Meredith Babb has been an obliging and understanding editor who understood the rigors involved in finishing a manuscript and starting a new job simultaneously. The UPF editors and staff have been enormously helpful in guiding me through the publication process. Colin G. Calloway and Andrew K. Frank each read the entire manuscript for the press and offered much-appreciated encouragement and suggestions. Also thanks to Jonathan Lawrence, Cynthia Nemser-Hall, and Jacqueline Kinghorn Brown.

A slightly different version of the chapter on Fort Allen appeared in the *Pennsylvania Magazine of History and Biography* in July 2009. Thanks to the journal's director, Tamara Gaskell, her staff, and their anonymous readers for their help in preparing the article and for permitting me to publish a revised version here. Thanks also to Charles Beatty-Medina, Melissa Rinehart, and the anonymous readers of the *Michigan Historical Review* for many helpful comments on other parts of the manuscript.

I have benefited vastly from my associations with two wonderful institutions: the University of South Florida, where I began my career as a history professor, and Ball State University, where I plan to finish it many years hence. During my two years as a visiting professor at USF, Fraser Ottanelli provided me with the freedom to develop new classes and the liberty to revise and refine my manuscript. I will always be grateful to the USF faculty, staff, and students who helped to make my sojourn in Tampa unforgettable. At Ball State I will have a whole career to repay my debts of gratitude. Thanks to Bruce E. Geelhoed, Kevin E. Smith, Abel A. Alves, Nicole Etcheson, Scott M. Stephan, and the rest of the faculty and staff of the BSU Department of History for bringing me to Muncie and helping me settle in.

Understanding and patient families have provided the bedrock for many book projects, and my experience is no exception. My father, Terry Ingram, taught me to love history at a very early age. My interest in forts and Native Americans began long ago with his stories of Pontiac and Tecumseh. Thomas Ingram, Jennifer Ingram, Cindy Ross, Terry Peters, Beth Long, Stewart Harris, Jeff Harris, Ray and Pat Harris, and their families have always given me the support and encouragement I needed. The Joyrich family represents my experience with extended kinship. Thanks to Myron, Ida, Nomi, Cory, Lynne, Richard, Eden, and Ava for their love and help over the years, which I try my best to reciprocate. Wendy Joyrich convinced me to continue my studies many years ago, and provided me with tremendous levels of support and friendship along the way. She did not live to read this book, but her influence marks every page.

Finally, I extend my deepest gratitude to my wife, Stacey Harris Ingram, who has seen me through this and other trials and tests. Nothing I write can adequately express the extent of her influence on every facet of my life. My personal devotion to her is complete. But she deserves notice here as a professional too. Stacey has worked as a public school teacher for almost three decades. Thousands of students are better readers, writers, and human beings because of her efforts. These efforts are too often unappreciated and overlooked, as are those of her millions of counterparts throughout the world. Stacey, then, provides me with more than encouragement, stability, and love. She is also an exemplar of professionalism that I hope I can emulate successfully in my own classroom efforts. As my wife and partner, she knows she has my thanks. As a dedicated teacher, she deserves everyone's.

Introduction

British Forts and Indian Neighbors

> As the confused and timid throng left the protecting mounds of the fort, and issued on the open plain, the whole scene was, at once, presented to their eyes. At a little distance on the right, and somewhat in the rear, the French army stood to their arms, Montcalm having collected his parties, so soon as his guards had possession of the works. They were attentive but silent observers of the proceedings of the vanquished, failing in none of the stipulated military honours, and offering no taunt or insult, in their success, to their less fortunate foes. Living masses of the English, to the amount in the whole of near three thousand, were moving slowly across the open plain, towards the common center, and gradually approached each other, as they converged to the point of their march, a vista cut through the lofty trees, where the road to the Hudson entered the forest. Along the sweeping borders of the woods, hung a dark cloud of savages, eyeing the passage of their enemies, and hovering, at a distance, like vultures, who were only kept from swooping on their prey, by the presence and restraint of a superior army. A few had straggled among the conquered columns, where they stalked in sullen discontent; attentive, though, as yet, passive observers of the moving multitude.
>
> James Fenimore Cooper, *The Last of the Mohicans*

The scene described in this excerpt from Cooper's famous novel is the British retreat from Fort William Henry in August 1757. Orderly English troops march glumly toward a bloody end they cannot foresee. French victors stand by nobly and review the vanquished redcoats as they pass through the gates of their fort for the last time. No mention is made in the passage of the many British-allied Indians accompanying the surrendered British troops, though their presence is noted in other parts of the novel. In this paragraph the author chooses to draw a contrast between the orderly European soldiers and the "dark cloud" of skulking "savages," who occupy the "sweeping borders of the woods" as if they were dangerous features of the natural environment. Their violent potential and mastery of nature is effectively demonstrated throughout the book, but here the superior French and English forces keep them in a temporary state of passivity. This oppositional structure of Indians as dark, furtive, and primeval and of Europeans as orderly, thoughtful, and culturally superior is a common feature of the romantic literature of Cooper's era. Unfortunately for the memory of Indians who actually interacted with British troops, traders, and cultural brokers near backcountry forts, this image of furtive natives waiting in the forest's shadows, overawed by orderly European personnel and imposing fortress walls, has come to typify fort-based cultural interactions in the American imagination.[1]

More than many other fixtures of American popular mythology, frontier forts and the people associated with them have been incorporated into a heroic interpretation of colonial Indian-white relations. This historical model, popularized during the nineteenth-century romantic era by writers such as Cooper and historian Francis Parkman, saw British (and to a lesser degree, French) colonizers as spreaders of advanced European civilization. In short, those who encountered and overcame the challenges of the "savage" American wilderness and its inhabitants deserved the rewards of conquest. Soldiers manning forts were nothing less than the forebears of America's republican promise. Indians, though admirable for their skills and primitive nobility, were regarded as features of America's natural world rather than social beings. They were to be subdued by more-civilized conquerors along with the forests and soil. Forts themselves were portrayed as cultural and economic entrepôts and battlegrounds of superior European civilization, overshadowing and overawing the "primitive" natives who visited them. This nineteenth-century heroic view of the frontier and its outposts fits neatly into American nationalist mythology and remained a powerful feature of history textbooks and popular culture well into the twentieth century.[2]

If this heroic view of forts and garrisons as the forerunners of empire had remained safely ensconced in the nineteenth century, I might never have approached this subject. However, this vision of forts as the intrepid cutting edges of the European imperial saw blade remained surprisingly potent in twentieth-century popular culture. People growing up in the mid-twentieth century should be familiar with this romanticized image of the relationship between fort personnel and Native Americans, though in the consensus-driven atmosphere of the 1930s–1950s the British soldiers in such forts were often portrayed as villains who sought to subvert Indians for their own imperial (and hence undemocratic) purposes. In fiction such as Walter Edmonds's *Drums along the Mohawk* and Kenneth Roberts's *Northwest Passage*, and the films based on those novels, this heroic vision influenced generations of Americans. *Northwest Passage* became a popular television show in the 1950s, taking its place beside *The Wonderful World of Disney* and *Daniel Boone* (in the 1960s) as purveyors of romantic frontier ideals set in colonial America. Hundreds of movie Westerns reinforced this heroic ideal for the nineteenth-century West as well. Of course, Cooper's *Last of the Mohicans* saw several popular film and television adaptations throughout the twentieth century. As recently as 1992, a new and quite good film version of the story reified a view of forts as places that heralded imperial change, and as places where Indians and Europeans could find nothing but conflict.

Heroism was fine for descendants of the victors in the cultural contests of the American colonial period, but not for descendants of the first Americans, whose ancestors bore the brunt of the European invasion. Twentieth-century Native Americans knew well that their ancestors participated fully in the continent's colonial-era struggles and grated at their continued relegation as secondary, romanticized figures in early American history. In the 1960s and 1970s, encouraged in part by the American civil rights movement and increased Native American activism, some historians began looking for new historical models that would amplify native agency in colonial affairs and correct some of the nationalistic, heroic depictions of white colonizers. Some historians argued for models of analysis using anthropological and archaeological methods to free the researcher from the colonialist cultural baggage that permeates much literature. Using these methods, historians could view colonial intercultural meetings as diffusions of traits rather than impositions of dominant or superior cultures over lesser ones. Global social and economic models also offered paths to locating Indians as significant actors within the North American story. In these studies Indians were shown as participants in a larger Atlantic exchange economy, either to cast them as victims of a coercive global trade system or to include them as socioeconomic actors alongside colonists and slaves. But some have criticized both anthropological "cultural invasion" models and deterministic economic frameworks for a basic teleological flaw: they often look at Native Americans' stories through the lens of their eventual loss. Still, this new emphasis on historical studies using ethnographies, anthropological and cultural theories, and archaeology alongside traditional documentary history has informed a whole generation of scholars and students. These studies, taken along with two generations of Native American activism, have led to a more powerful and nuanced view of the roles Indians played in American history. The impact of this scholarship is felt in popular history, too, as a comparison of the 1936 and 1992 film versions of *Last of the Mohicans* shows very clearly.[3]

My particular frustration with depictions of colonial fort life in both popular culture and much recent scholarship is the persistent habit of seeking ways to include Indians into nationalistic or imperial frameworks. Either as consumers, connected to and exploited by a global economic system, or as representatives of a larger indigenous nation, language group, or culture, Indians are often studied as players in a wide-ranging game. This, one supposes, is the price of inclusion in history: individuals become subsumed within larger narratives. This is especially troubling for studying backcountry fort life, because existence in such outposts was influenced as much or more by local concerns as by larger global or imperial initiatives and contingencies. A more fruitful method for analyzing the kinds of interactions that took place near military posts is to highlight Europeans' and Indians' experiences in more localized geographic or conceptual contexts. This does less well at explaining native and settler participation in global systems, but comes closer to capturing Indian-European cultural interplay as it happened at the local level. Indians did not usually consider themselves part of a global system or an extended multicultural American colonial regime. Soldiers and others in backcountry outposts understood their roles in imperial regimes, but they also adapted to the demands of the local economy, which was usually dominated by native concerns, not imperial objectives. Indians and Europeans were not simply their national imperatives writ small. In close company and at the mercy of a frequently unsympathetic natural environment, they often found cultural common ground in spite of their larger purposes and prejudices.

Some recent scholarship has embraced this local perspective on intercultural backcountry encounters, though usually with a glance toward a wider interpretive significance. For example, Richard White's *The Middle Ground*, a study that has bestrode ethnohistory like a colossus since its publication in 1991, emphasizes the local cultural accommodations that took place wherever Indians met Europeans in the Great Lakes region, redefining the entire notion of Indian-European diplomacy. However, White's subtitle, *Indians, Empires, and Republics in the Great Lakes Region, 1650–1815*, reveals the framework of a larger global narrative. Still, his structuralist interpretation of cultural exchange has become invaluable to studying local encounters. Also helpful in seeing forts as local worlds rather than peripheral imperial outposts are recent works on the importance of cultural brokers, negotiators and translators who moved easily between cultural worlds, helping to bridge the differences between Indians and Europeans at the local level in pursuit of larger colonial goals. But backcountry localism has also been studied on its own merits. Andrew R. L. Cayton and Fredrika J. Teute's 1998 collection *Contact Points* presents essays that study backcountry sites in order to redefine the concept of frontiers at the local level, identifying several physical and conceptual arenas of cultural change with diverse, permeable meanings. These studies suggest an early American world where no outcomes seemed inevitable to the participants. They reveal frontiers in persistent states of negotiation, using strategies informed both by local priorities and outside imperatives. Most importantly, they move closer to interpreting Indian-white interactions from a native, rather than a Eurocentric, vantage. This moves closer to interpreting the little worlds of forts and garrisons in ways unencumbered by popular cultural perceptions or historiographical demands for larger significances. Viewing forts and their locales from the perspectives of the Indians and garrisons that occupied and visited them emphasizes the efforts and importance of individual contact in the backcountry, the fluidity of cultural exchange and influence, the difficulties and promises fostered by mutual misunderstandings, and the degree to which backcountry contingencies could often squelch larger political, military, and economic purposes.[4]

This study examines five British forts in colonial America to emphasize the interweaving of local and general sociocultural imperatives at backcountry contact points. The question posed in each case is the following: To what degree were the activities, imperatives, and identities of these posts influenced by Native American culture instead of, or in addition to, European imperial or colonial culture? In each case, native traditions and cultural imperatives mixed with colonial military missions and everyday challenges of life in and near outposts. Imperial objectives and pan-Indian concerns run through each of these case studies. But this book moves toward a view of backcountry contact points as places where local concerns often trumped outside strategies. This often created tension between the liminal fort-based worlds and the responsibilities and goals of outside native and British societies. But for the Indians and military people who met, traded, and parleyed at forts, immediate concerns defined a kind of cultural exchange separate from outside traditions, values, and imperatives. One of the hardest parts of fort-based interactions for both British and Indian participants was negotiating the localized terms of these small arenas while still answering the pressures of outside responsibilities. In many ways, forts were their own little worlds. This study seeks to recognize elements of interaction that could take place only in backcountry contact points, instead of seeing forts merely as peripheral outposts of empire. Looking at these cases from an indigenous perspective, as much as possible, helps to prevent being led astray by the overwhelming European cultural saturation of the primary documents.

Unfortunately, this Eurocentric documentary bias is difficult to avoid when studying forts. Almost all documents from the American colonial period were recorded by Europeans, and even those documents relating Indian speech were taken down by European scribes and filtered through English and French interpreters. This problem is exacerbated by the military requirements of fort life. Commandants and Indian agents filed regular reports and wrote many letters, but almost all of them were official in nature and dealt with military matters, operations relating to their European rivals, and the everyday logistics of fort life. Indian affairs were frequent topics of these communications, but fort personnel usually recorded only "vital" information: Indian threats, amounts and costs of Indian gifts, minutes of diplomatic congresses, and other details deemed important enough to send on to military and political superiors. Reliable ethnographic information is difficult to glean from much fort-related source material.

There are notable exceptions to this dearth of useful Indian material. Raymond Demere, the South Carolina officer who commanded Fort Loudoun in what is now eastern Tennessee, seems to have spent every waking moment writing letters containing prodigious amounts of information about Indian activities. John Wilkins, the penultimate commandant of Fort Chartres in Illinois, kept a detailed journal of Indian activities at the fort during his command. These are only two examples; many more exist for British, French, and Spanish North America. But even these rich sources are laden with the biases of the writers and, though essential, are problematic sources for studying Indian activity. Unfortunately, archaeology does not ameliorate the problems of European bias in the case of military forts as much as one would hope. Fort sites have presented sparse evidence of the presence of Indians, which is surprising given our documentary knowledge of abundant Indian activity near such posts as Crown Point, Michilimackinac, Niagara, Chartres, and many others. Since all of the source material must be sifted for European bias and military and trade prerogatives, any attempt to construct actual Indian histories wholly from these sources remains problematic. What emerge from the sources are stories of the European occupation of these posts that are complicated by the ethnohistorical Indian vantage, rather than true histories of Indian participants. But even if Indians' activities at and near British forts cannot be described in rich and dependable detail, the native perspective helps us create pictures and stories of fort life that are truer to actual experience than those based upon popular mythology and concepts of empire.[5]

There was surely nothing unusual about the concept of a fort to Europeans or Indians in the eighteenth-century American backcountry. European cities of that century still sat amid their medieval walls, though many had overflowed them with extensive suburbs. In some cases civic fortifications had been rebuilt according to the latest theories in military engineering; Europe was awash in blood and sieges during the seemingly endless, grotesque wars of the seventeenth and eighteenth centuries. For European settlers and soldiers in America, building a log palisade around a settlement was fundamental for protection against both native and European foes. The same was true of many Indian villages in the more heavily populated parts of the Eastern Woodlands. Harmen Meyndertsz van den Bogaert, the New Netherlands trader who provided one of the first European descriptions of Mohawk life in the 1630s, described palisaded Iroquois villages with gates and towers; this was the norm throughout eastern North America at sedentary native settlements with larger populations.

European forts came in as many shapes and sizes as there were European purposes in the backcountry. Military, trade, and settlers' forts dotted the peripheries of colonial America by the 1750s. Large stone or earthen forts, such as the French Fortress Louisbourg guarding the mouth of the St. Lawrence River, were similar in scale and construction to those that protected European cities. Smaller impermanent structures, such as

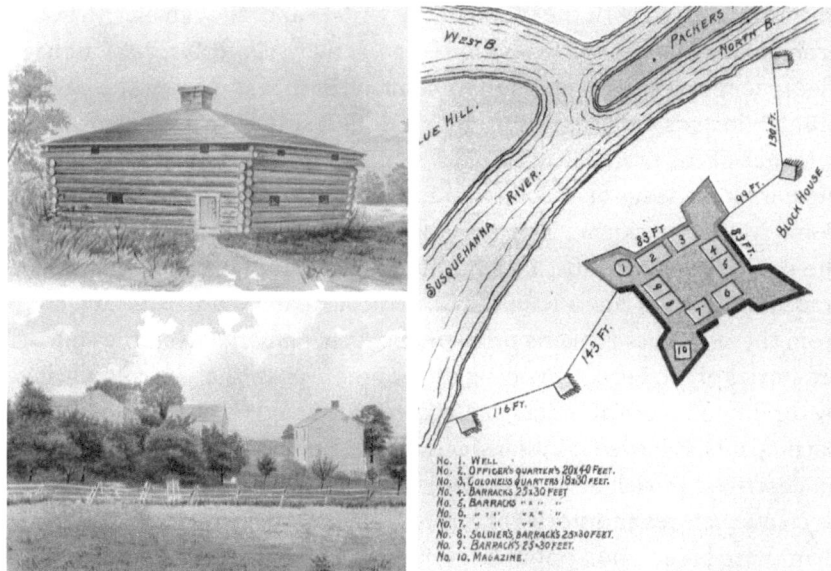

Fig. I.1. Examples of the variety of installations commonly referred to as "forts" in mid-eighteenth-century America. *Top left:* Stewart's Blockhouse on the Susquehanna River. *Bottom left:* Ralston and Brown Stockade, a farm on the Lehigh River. *Right:* Fort Augusta, a formal military fort built near the multiethnic town of Shamokin. From H. M. M. Richards, *Report of the Commission to Locate the Site of the Frontier Forts of Pennsylvania* (1896). Bracken Library, Ball State University, Muncie, Indiana.

the French (later British) Great Lakes posts, resembled colonial outposts in other parts of the world, and usually contained small, transitory garrisons. Even smaller trading posts, blockhouses, and redoubts, usually built quickly for specific contingencies, could be found guarding rivers, roads, and other vital geographic points; these would usually house only a few men for short periods. Farmhouses would sometimes have protective palisades as well. Even future colonial cities such as New York, Philadelphia, and Charlestown maintained their defensive walls well into the colonial period. But the mere existence of a log palisade or bastion is not the criterion for the forts included in this study. I am interested in military fort culture, and the kinds of forts I have chosen to study all had connections to provincial and imperial military concerns, while still existing as specific local functionaries in Indian country.

The forts in this study share some important features. First, they were all military outposts in Indian country, manned by armed combatants sent into the backcountry for specific military reasons. This is crucial, because I wish to measure their colonial and imperial missions against the rigors of their lives in the backcountry and their contact with Indians. Two of these forts were built by British colonies during wartime; three were French forts built to support the trade and administration of New France, which then passed into British hands at the end of the Seven Years' War. Second, they were substantial forts. Though some of them were quite small (Forts Allen and Loudoun, for example), they were meant to last for an extended period of occupation of at least months; all were occupied eventually by troops for at least a few years. Unlike blockhouses or stockaded farms, such forts would house, at different times, a wide range of professional and temporary soldiers, traders, and Indian agents. Third, unlike small blockhouses, these forts all became important stopping points for Native American travelers, diplomats, warriors, and hunters. This was sometimes because of their geographical locations, many of which had held importance in native cultures for centuries. Indians also came to forts like the ones in this study because British officials were there, with the power to regulate trade, conduct diplomacy, and relate news of far-off events. And of course, Indians traded at or near all of the forts in this study. Stated simply, the forts in this book had their own fort cultures that were determined by their missions, their occupants, their native visitors and neighbors, and their locations in regions dominated by Indians. In some ways each of these forts is unique, and I certainly look at different themes for each of them. But these five outposts do not come close to comprehending the vastness of backcountry experiences. They are examples, chosen carefully but with some randomness, to show features of imperial and provincial fort life that complicate the heroic image of British occupation of the backcountry.

Fort personnel always found out quickly that Indians and their lifeways would matter greatly to their missions. The initial interaction processes certainly followed pragmatic guidelines; both Indians and Europeans knew what had worked before, and they used experience and common sense to learn the "rules" of their new surroundings and neighbors. Often an experienced cultural broker, a well-traveled Indian or a European Indian agent or trader, would help with this process. Negotiating a working relationship with local and visiting Indians was vital. Soldiers, traders, and commissaries, far from the support and conveniences of European culture, had to find ways to accommodate the pressures of the natural environment in order to find food, traverse the backcountry, and conduct warfare. This necessitated establishing peaceful relations with local natives who already possessed the information and skills necessary to establish a successful outpost.

While immediate confrontation and violence could ensue from these meetings, especially in times of heightened political tensions, cooperation was often the first instinct of both natives and newcomers. Forts were places where Indians could temporarily put aside their mistrust of newcomers and receive news of far-off events and material gifts. Soldiers, traders, and craftsmen living in backcountry outposts had separated themselves from many of the rules and structures of their own societies, despite their maintenance of military rigor and discipline. In their new zone of interaction, they inhabited a cultural arena separate from their European-colonial world, where cooperation with their new neighbors meant success and survival. Indians seeking trade and other perceived benefits of European friendship entered the same arena when they interacted with fort personnel. This stage of backcountry interaction contained great promise for coexistence and mutual benefit, as long as the powerful outside pressures of European and Indian objectives allowed forts and their surrounding landscapes to remain places of cultural confluence rather than sites of opposition and conflict.

For British officers and soldiers, these outside pressures were constant, especially during wartime. Forts served a multitude of roles in colonial America. First and foremost, fortifications served as bulwarks against military incursions by European enemies or as marks of possession for Great Britain or its colonial governments. During conflicts such as the Seven Years' War, forts and garrisons were almost always on alert and armed as well as finances would allow. Carts and bateaux would traverse fragile supply lines through harsh terrain to support the posts. Still, forts and other outposts were self-sufficient to a degree corresponding with their remoteness. Soldiers worked as hunters, fishermen, woodcutters, and farmers to supply posts with food and fuel. Communication with British authorities in the East was as fragile as the supply lines; indeed, the two were identical. Fort commandants were expected to keep the peace with Indians who controlled the country and its lines of communication and to punish them if they attacked British travelers or troops.

This was especially important at smaller outposts and blockhouses, which were almost wholly at the mercy of the local populations. In larger forts like Niagara, Pitt, or Chartres, garrisons could hold off Indian attacks but were always subject to siege warfare; only trenches and European artillery could reduce a substantial stone or earthen fort. But in most places, British forts needed native help to carry out their primary mission of holding the continental interior against French and Spanish foes.[6]

Forts were also centers of trade and thus attracted Indian activity. This was especially true of French backcountry forts, most of which were small, lightly garrisoned, and lacked military structures such as barracks. When these forts passed to Britain after the Seven Years' War, British commandants strained to accommodate the economic nature of the small posts while still maintaining military readiness and marking the backcountry as part of the Empire. Though most backcountry outposts retained their status as trading centers, not all forts allowed trade activities within the walls of the palisade. Frequent Indian visitors, some of them unfamiliar and with unsure allegiances, created an unacceptable breach of security if allowed the run of the post. Instead, traders would travel to Indians' villages or operate from trading towns adjacent to the fort, as was the case at Pittsburgh, Detroit, and many other locations. Valuable loads of trade goods would often be stored in the forts for protection against theft by natives or Europeans. But the main object of forts in the Indian trade was to protect trade operations themselves. Indian consumers knew that British garrisons could launch small-scale punitive expeditions and offer refuge for traders when they angered their customers. However, it was often the Indians themselves who needed protection against disreputable traders. Fort commandants were not only guards of English interests; they were often the only representatives of English civil authority available. This made them responsible for enforcing trade agreements between the Crown or individual colonies and Indian groups. Indians never ceased to request British intercession in trade practices they considered unfair.[7]

Given the extent to which backcountry forts have been imagined as centers of dispossession and oppression, it is surprising that Indians found so much use for them. Enforcement of trade regulations was one of the reasons. Protection of Indian families against French and native aggression was another. This was especially true in Iroquoia during the Seven Years' War, when the British military sought the aid of allied Iroquois groups in their efforts against France. Iroquois leaders made it clear that their aid would never materialize unless New York agreed to build forts to protect Indian families while their men assisted in military operations. These requests for forts and blockhouses to be built near Iroquois "castles," or large villages, were frequent during the early years of the war, though colonial governments strained to provide the funding. Sir William Johnson, the Irish trader and Indian agent who later became superintendent of the Indian Department in the North, adamantly argued for the establishment of as many forts as the Iroquois requested at the outset of the Seven Years' War. In addition to the refuge that forts would offer Iroquois families, they would also invigorate the fur trade, which was often depressed during wartime because of the lack of adequate protection. The Six Nations understood their importance to British wartime objectives. They used their influence to demand forts when necessary and to control the shape and mission of forts and garrisons when possible. For example, when an Oneida speaker, Canaghquaeson, reminded Johnson of the many Oneida requests for a fort in 1756, his requests read more like polite demands. He informed Johnson of the Oneidas' "unanimous resolution of having one" and insisted on a reputable garrison that would prevent trade irregularities and excessive sales of rum.[8]

Despite native accommodation of forts and their missions into their own cultural orbits, the presence of forts and garrisons accelerated changes already taking place within native societies. Indian women found forts and their personnel useful in many ways. Eighteenth-century French commandants frequently married native women, just as fur traders had done for decades, and for the same reasons. Marrying Indian women established kinship ties between commandants, traders, and other European fur-trade functionaries and their native business partners. In some cases, as with some Great Lakes peoples, this extended kinship was fictive: a social and diplomatic connection deliberately configured as familial. In other cases, as in English or French intermarriage with Cherokee women, the kinship tie was established through the matrilineal succession of ethnic identity: a child of a Cherokee woman and a European father was as much a Cherokee as any powerful chief or war woman. For the women themselves, however, marrying Europeans provided opportunities for empowerment not available within their own cultural milieus. They became translators, negotiators, and brokers within a world usually seen by Europeans as male-dominated. These arrangements required modification under the British regime, whose Protestant commandants and officers would not marry Indian women. Many took common-law native brides, however, including William Johnson himself. British officers, soldiers, and fur traders knew the benefits of establishing kinship ties with Indian women, and women used these liaisons to travel, trade, and otherwise transcend the boundaries of their own cultural roles. Forts and trading posts became places of opportunity for women seeking out these opportunities, making such outposts centers of the transformation of gender roles already prevalent in eighteenth-century America.[9]

Indian women looked to forts for economic opportunities, too. Throughout the Eastern Woodlands, Indian women controlled the domestic economy of native agricultural societies. Native American farmers were women, and they sought markets to sell their surpluses of corn, squash, and beans. Soldiers and fort-based traders made good customers, especially in natural and human environments defined and mastered by centuries of indigenous innovations in foodways. Indians knew how to provide grain, fish, game, and tree syrup to hungry garrisons. Of these the most important lifeline was maize, the exclusive province of women in every eastern native agricultural culture. European customers provided Indian women with the opportunity to augment their domestic economies through sales of surplus grain. They also ground corn in mills, prepared processed food for fur trade and military expeditions, and produced baskets and other handicrafts for sale to military families. Men sometimes bargained with white soldiers and traders for sales of agricultural surpluses as a component of traditional intercultural gift exchanges. Still, women often did the legwork and bargaining, showing up at forts with carts full of maize, pumpkins, and other goods for sale to under-provisioned garrisons. Indian women used their control of agricultural output and domestic crafts to establish themselves as vital consumers in the growing backcountry trade alongside their hunter-husbands, and forts provided them with ready markets.[10]

Even with such opportunities, forts were not always welcome among Indian women. They became centers for the distribution of alcohol, a common source of domestic chaos in Indian life. They also brought the potential for military strife into the backcountry. Both British and French forts were locations for mustering native men into European military expeditions. This not only separated men from their families but also proliferated an ongoing tendency that had begun to alter native gender roles to women's disadvantage: the elevation of male hunters and warriors in importance in native societies. Warfare had long been an important role among Native American males. However, the frequent European wars of the eighteenth century had led to an elevation of war prowess as a marker of male identity and source of power. Hunting also took on new importance as the acquisition of pelts in the expanding fur economy turned young, prolific hunters into important market consumers. Increasingly, men who excelled at playing European economic and military games came to dominate diplomacy and leadership in their villages and nations. The rise of young warriors and hunters within native social structures came at both a functional and cultural cost to women. Their traditional roles as determiners of home life and domestic economy and as advisers on matters of peace and war came under increased pressure as the eighteenth century wore on. Forts may have provided women with material and matrimonial opportunities, but they served also as foci for important changes in gender roles that challenged women's power within their own societies.[11]

From the perspectives of native men and women, the successful accommodation of backcountry forts depended upon the cooperativeness and tractability of the European personnel inside. Indians demanded friendly and dependable garrisons and looked upon ethnically insensitive soldiers and officers with understandable disdain. This often made Indians unwilling to undertake garrison duty alongside European allies during wartime. For example, during King George's War, William Johnson pointed out to New York governor George Clinton that Iroquois men would rather fight the French directly in Canada than "keep in a Garrison among so many Christians." British regular soldiers usually possessed little experience in intercultural contact or knowledge of native customs. Provincial troops were even worse. They were occasionally settlers, serving in defense of their farms and families against French and Indian threats, but more often they were day laborers or artisans who were unfamiliar with military rigor or Indian affairs. It is not surprising, therefore, that garrisons sometimes treated Indians with less tolerance or politeness than native diplomatic and hospitality customs demanded. For example, during the Seven Years' War a young Mohawk man approached Fort Johnson in New York to welcome the newly arrived garrison. Instead of being greeted with the appropriate hospitality and gifts, he was insulted and sent away. Soon afterward some of the garrison entered the town surrounding the fort and assaulted Indians there, injuring one seriously. Several Mohawk chiefs complained angrily to Johnson, demanding that he either replace the garrison with men who were "acquainted with them and their Customs" or face the violent consequences. Threats of Indian violence were almost never made explicitly to British allies; such threats would be considered breaches of polite diplomacy. Instead, village headmen and diplomats would warn of the unstable tempers of their "young men" and how difficult it would be to keep them under control if offended. These were not just diplomatic stratagems, nor were they idle threats. Young hunters and warriors in the field were most likely to encounter soldiers, and they would bear the brunt of intolerant or culturally ignorant newcomers to the backcountry.[12]

British affronts were often simple acts of disrespect or impoliteness, which stoked suspicions that officers and enlisted men did not have the Indians' interests at heart. This was especially true in areas such as New York and Pennsylvania, where forts had been built with the permission of Indian allies. For example, in 1762 an Onondaga speaker complained that officers at frontier posts refused to listen to Iroquoian visitors or interact as friends should. "The Officers at the several Posts, when we want to Say anything to them on Business, Trade, etc. will not hear Us, or look upon Us, but tell us they have nothing to say, or do with Us, nor with the Trade," he complained to Johnson. "So that really we are in a very bad Situation, and wish that there were such Officers as wou'd behave more friendly to Us." The Onondaga speaker also wished that there were more trained interpreters available to prevent such "misunderstandings."[13] Breaches of customary politeness and hospitality offended Indians everywhere but were worse in areas where regular and provincial soldiers had been invited as guests and allies.

Indian complaints about rude transitory fort personnel may also revealed their greater fear: that backcountry forts would attract civilian settlers. Indian groups throughout eastern North America actively and consistently resisted increased settlement. "The Indians are much more dissatisfied at the appearance of Settlers, than ever at a Garrison," Johnson wrote to the British commander in chief, Thomas Gage, in 1767, "as the former increases and overspreads the country." Conflicts between Indians and backcountry colonists occurred frequently throughout the colonial period. English settlers, unlike many of their French forebears, were mainly farmers bent on clearing woods for arable land. This destroyed hunting and fishing sites and upset the environmental balance of Indian lifeways. After the devastating geographic dislocations of the seventeenth century, many Indian groups, especially those in the Ohio Valley and the Great Lakes region, were determined to oppose increased English settlements in the West. The British Proclamation of 1763, which forbade new settlements west of the Appalachian range, was intended to placate disgruntled Indians as well as to forestall individual colonies' land claims. But as Indians knew well, colonial governments needed backcountry settlements to strengthen their land claims and to profit eventually from commodities produced in the West. Only settlers and their plows could successfully transform sections of the American West into British or provincial strongholds, and Native Americans knew it. Examples of violent incidents between backcountry settlers and Indians are too numerous to require mention here. Of the five forts included as main topics in this study, four feature Indian-settler animosities as primary sources of regional conflict.[14]

Even during wartime some English-allied Indians resented forts and large garrisons, despite their potential advantages. An Onondaga delegation made this clear to the proprietors of Pennsylvania in 1756 when the province announced plans to build Fort Augusta near the multiethnic town of Shamokin. "We cannot comprehend the method of making war which is made use of, by our Brethren the English," they complained. "When we go to War, our manner is to destroy a Nation & theres an end of it. But the English Chiefly regard building Forts, which Looks as if their only Scheme was to *take possession of the Lands*." Cherokees negotiating with the French governor of Louisiana spoke of English forts as sites of oppression and scorned them as "Houses of Force" and "horred Magazines." This attitude only worsened during times of peace, when threats of French depredations decreased. Kanadiohara, a Chenussio Seneca chief, complained in April 1762 that British blockhouses built between German Flats and Oswego in New York had been represented originally as temporary wartime outposts but now looked more permanent. He outlined several abuses by officers and soldiers and asked that the forts be removed immediately, "as the French are now entirely Conquered." Iroquois speakers made the same request in the multiethnic village of Oquaga later that year and warned of imminent violence. "Some of our Warriors are foolish," they warned Johnson, "And some of our Brother's soldiers don't fear God." They pleaded that the forts be "pull'd down & kick'd out of the way" before conflict ensued. Indian acceptance of British forts was based upon necessity and the degree to which they could determine the goals, size, and permanence of the posts.¹⁵

If Indians decided that British forts did not answer their needs, the consequences could be severe, especially for smaller posts. The cost of failing to meet native expectations was made most apparent during the 1763–64 Indian uprising, inaccurately called Pontiac's Rebellion by the British. In the space of a few weeks, every Great Lakes and Ohio Valley post that France had ceded to Britain in the 1763 Treaty of Paris fell to Indian attack save the large posts at Detroit, Niagara, and Pittsburgh. Both Detroit and Fort Pitt endured months-long sieges, and Niagara's portage was attacked and held in a virtual state of siege by Chenussio Senecas. The story of this rebellion has undergone years of interpretive rigor, from Parkman's early depiction of a desperate last-ditch battle of the races to modern studies that emphasize Indian priorities, power, and geographic defense as motives. But the attacks of the Indian uprising show much from a localized perspective as well. Military reports show a remarkable level of intercultural familiarity between Indians and soldiers at small outposts. At Michilimackinac, soldiers casually enjoyed watching a game of *bag' gat' iway*, an Indian ball game, moments before the Ojibwa attackers overran the fort. Fort Miamis was taken by surprise when the British commandant, Ensign Robert Holmes, was (perhaps unintentionally) lured into a fatal trap by the native woman who shared his bed. The garrison of Fort Edward Augustus, formerly Fort La Baye in Wisconsin, listened to the warnings of their native friends from across Lake Michigan and abandoned their post before it was attacked. Despite mutual fears and distrusts that were great enough to spark a wide-scale Indian rebellion, British fort personnel and Indians maintained considerable closeness at the local level.¹⁶

Indians viewed British forts with ambivalence. They visited them frequently for trade goods, protection, and information. In some cases Indian women found European husbands in these outposts. But many Indians hated the posts, even while they found them useful. Forts provided gifts of useful goods, provisions, and rum. But they also attracted British farmers, to whom Indians were simply in the way. Fort commandants used their power to confer presents and regulate trade to treat Indian visitors as underlings and dependents, though the visitors were often less than impressed with British attempts to act tough and appear manly.

Forts were also bases for military operations, where thousands of Indians joined British and colonial military forces during the imperial wars of the eighteenth century. But when British allies failed to treat Indians as real friends and partners, Indians could easily turn against them.

British imperial and provincial authorities shared the natives' ambivalence about the outposts, but for different reasons. Colonial policy depended upon capitalizing on American natural resources and manufactures. This involved expanding the Indian fur trade and increasing agricultural output through proliferation of settlements, and both enterprises demanded military protection. Indians approved of and depended on trade, as long as it was properly regulated. But the settlements that would inevitably follow angered Indians, making most backcountry operations difficult, dangerous, and unprofitable. Threats from European enemies mandated keeping military posts throughout the backcountry. But British plans to hold the region only made sense if the expense of forts and armies in the West was justified by eventual financial profits. Private joint-stock companies that provided most of the operating capital for new colonial ventures would only invest in backcountry operations if they could be assured of military protection. However, the British Lords of Trade and provincial governors found it difficult to justify the expense of operating forts if trade revenues did not sufficiently enrich the mother country. Provincial governments found these expenses even more onerous. How devoted British policy makers remained to an image of America filled with forts flying Union Jacks depended upon whether they believed that they could profit from the continental interior.

Provincial officials often found balancing these concerns difficult. Two of the forts in this study, Fort Allen in Pennsylvania and Fort Loudoun in western South Carolina, were built by provincial governments prompted by the exigencies of the Seven Years' War. Fort Allen was constructed as part of a defensive line protecting Pennsylvania's cities and towns from French and Delaware attacks. Because the fort was a response to an emergency, its construction was not controversial or challenged by the provincial government. But as time went on and the fort seemed to offer more advantages for visiting Indians than for Pennsylvania's traders or settlers, its continued maintenance became problematic for provincial officials.

Fort Loudoun's story presented a different set of problems for South Carolina's government. The fort would be hundreds of miles from Charlestown in the Tennessee Overhills country, and it seemed to be proposed almost entirely to please the British-allied Overhill Cherokees. No emergency prompted its building except persistent rumors of imminent French incursions into the region and reports of Cherokee duplicity. But colonial officials argued that the long-term economic strength of the colony demanded that staunch Cherokee friends guard the "wild" backcountry. Of course, the personnel at a fort built largely to please Indian allies had to put Indian affairs above all other concerns. In the end, Fort Loudoun did poorly in guaranteeing South Carolina's prosperity because it failed to please its Cherokee neighbors.

Enforcing military policy in the trans-Appalachian West after 1755 fell to the British army rather than to provincial governments. This made the political balancing act even more troublesome, because military readiness mandated holding forts won from France during the Seven Years' War. But the operations were so expensive and dangerous that even Commander in Chief Gage became an ardent opponent of the fort system. Anything that annoyed Indians made little sense to Gage. Unhappy Indians undermined the fur trade and made the continental interior unprofitable. He argued that forts had proven incapable of protecting Pennsylvania, Virginia, and the Carolinas during the Seven Years' War. Because of their stationary locations, forts were unsuited to managing the Indian trade; it was preferable to have traders and Indian agents living near native population centers. In Indian country, settlers would do no better than forts to enrich the empire, because the backcountry's remoteness made any crops raised or merchandise produced there too expensive to export. Inspired by his expert on indigenous peoples, Sir William Johnson, Gage's biggest concern was Indian dissatisfaction with British encroachment. "I know of nothing so liable to bring on a serious Quarrel with the Indians, as an Invasion of their Property," Gage wrote to the Earl of Hillsborough, the British secretary of state for the colonies. "Were they drove from their Forest, the Peltry Trade would decrease, and it is not impossible that worse Savages would take refuge in them." By the early 1770s he was proposing that forts be abandoned, new settlements restricted, and Britain's Indian trading partners be left alone. "Let the Savages enjoy their Deserts in quiet, little Bickerings that will unavoidably sometimes happen," Gage recommended after many years of failing to provide Britain with a profitable backcountry.[17]

Sir William Johnson knew that maintaining former French forts would be difficult. French Indian agents, traders, and habitants had spent

Fig. I.2. *Cantonment of Forces in North America, 11th Octr. 1765.* This map shows British regular troops stationed in America, including those at Forts Chartres, Michilimackinac, and Niagara. After the Seven Years' War the trans-Appalachian backcountry became a militarized region, though the negligible troop concentrations could never do more than mark local areas as British possessions. Library of Congress, Geography and Map Division.

decades spreading stories of British native-extirpation plans. New British garrisons, usually much larger than those employed by France, seemed to many Indians a fulfillment of those threats. Backcountry forts, according to Johnson, could "in no way prevent the Invasion of the Indians," who could easily skirt the forts in small parties, elude the pursuits of garrisons, destroy and sack boats and settlements, and cut off supply routes. More importantly, the forts were increasingly seen by natives as an effort to "hem in" and check the Indians' movements, making it more likely that natives would reject the posts' advantages and attack them. Settlers were familiar with the kind of devastation and cruelty Indians could visit upon backcountry inhabitants during times of conflict, and fleeing colonists provided no advantages to Britain. Johnson believed that smaller posts, using the "French Maxim" of rewarding Indians with gifts, were the best way to maintain trade and good relations with the native masters of the trans-Appalachian country.[18]

Presents were the key to keeping Indians happy at forts because they answered the Indians' need to believe and trust in their European partners. Part of the gift exchange was functional from the Indians' perspective. They had come to depend upon presents of food, ammunition, clothing, rum, and other necessities and had incorporated gifts into their material lifeways. Restricting them caused economic harm to native groups. But even more importantly, presents were physical signs that the people giving them were truly friends. Indian notions of hospitality demanded that visitors receive good treatment and something of value from their hosts. When Indians came to forts their visits were leaps of faith, at least in part. They had no way of knowing the efficacy of British or French words. But to give valuable goods to a friend was a step toward proving one's love and trustworthiness. Indians reasonably interpreted any restriction or retrenchment of gifts as an alteration of the terms of European-Indian friendship. Such actions could have dire consequences for future amities.[19]

Indian expectations of presents made forts very expensive propositions. Sir Jeffrey Amherst, Gage's predecessor, wondered why Indians should be rewarded for simply visiting forts when other occupants of the Americas made their livings through labor and trade. During the Indian uprising in 1763, Amherst told Johnson that when hostilities ended, the Indians involved should expect a resumption of trade, and nothing more. "As to *presents*, it would certainly be the highest presumption in them to expect any," he told his Indian supervisor. "They can never be considered by us as a people to whom we owe *rewards*, and it would be madness, to the highest degree, ever to bestow favors on a race who have so treacherously, and without provocation on our side, attacked our Posts, and butchered our Garrisons." Amherst's effort to restrict presents was an important trigger of the 1763 uprising.[20]

Gage knew better than Amherst the extent to which Indians saw presents as persistent proofs of friendship, and he understood the inseparability of maintaining forts and giving gifts. "As long as there are Forts in the Indian Country," he wrote to Hillsborough, "the distant Indians accustomed to transact all Business there, will still haunt the Forts, on many Pretences, of Business with the Commanders, whether on the subjects of Trade or Negotiation, and they are never to be turned away, without some Present." Indians understood the importance of their friendship to British colonial plans, and availed themselves of the proofs of that friendship whenever they could. Indians did not see this as bribery; they knew the difference between gifts and payment for services rendered. As long as Indians equated gifts with friendship and trustworthiness, the fort system would remain expensive.[21]

One gift that troubled British fort personnel more than any other was liquor. Physical dependency was not the issue; Indians were almost never addicted to alcohol. Though it was one of the most popular trade goods plied in the backcountry, the supply was never constant or dependable enough for many Indians to succumb to alcoholism. Nor were Indians any more biologically susceptible to its intoxicating effects than anyone else in colonial America. The difference between Indians and Europeans was in how alcohol was used. To native consumers, alcohol was almost purely a means of intoxication, which had many social and cultural advantages. While intoxicated, Indians swept aside the cares and responsibilities of the world. The normal restrictions of social reciprocity did not hold for actions committed while drunk. Furthermore, intoxication was a state similar to dreaming, in which Indians could communicate with lost kin or powerful spirits. Strong drink also fulfilled native social roles, such as welcoming and mourning rituals. Indians did not share the European concept of drinking as a social pleasure or as a brace against illness or cold. But alcohol abuse brought all the same devastations to native lifeways that existed in European culture, including violence, disease, poverty, and domestic abuse. Despite attempts to control the sale and spread of liquor by both Indians and Europeans, rum and brandy became important consumables in native life. Indians would purchase it if they could, but they also expected presents of liquor when visiting their friends in French and British forts.[22]

This tendency of Indians and traders to use British forts as alcohol markets bothered British authorities, but there was little anyone could do about the problem except scold the participants. Indians expected rum at the posts and left "disgusted" if they did not receive it. Drunkenness provided a perfect excuse for native activities that the British found troubling, such as gathering intelligence and raiding settlements. Most worrisome for fort personnel was when Indians used the fort itself as a drinking establishment or store. Johnson berated Iroquois leaders for not restricting these activities. "Your People are daily coming hither with Numbers of Kegs as if this was a Trading House for Rum," he scolded Six Nations representatives at Fort Johnson. Gage observed that native leaders "constantly complain that it is brought to them," but despite their complaints "they can't refrain from drinking it and even demand it, and are angry when it is refused." Fort commandants repeatedly attempted to restrict the sale of rum, and tried to include less alcohol in their allocation of gifts. When Indians obtained alcohol near a fort, they were often required to consume it some distance away.[23]

Liquor struck at the heart of British attempts to impose mastery over a region. If Indians viewed military posts as places for entertainment and alcohol, then the forts' roles as intimidating outposts of empire would be undermined. Because liquor was one commodity that only Europeans could provide in volume, and one that the military felt the need to guard and restrict, Indians would continue to associate forts and alcohol throughout the colonial period and beyond.

For these reasons and others, Indians continued to visit British forts wherever they existed, despite their frequently held resentments. Some of those forts were built at the behest of Indians, who took care that posts not be used to subvert Indian culture or to destroy Indian lives. Other forts were strongly opposed, but native diplomats, warriors, and women did their best to ensure that the forts and garrisons would not attract settlers or endanger their people. In every case, Indians saw British backcountry forts as fixtures upon their native landscape. Forts often occupied important geographic points that Indians were bound to pass. But despite the redcoats and British colonial aspirations within, Indians did not see forts as alien. There was nothing unusual about firearms, fighting men, and wooden pales.

British fort personnel hoped that their outposts would be harbingers of the successful spread of European trade and culture. Indians had other ideas. Some used violence to advance their aims; others used friendship and diplomacy. Those who did not advocate tearing forts down immediately worked to incorporate them into their native topography and lifeways. But native acceptance of, and opposition to, military posts in the backcountry were not dichotomous features of Indian-white relations. They were connected functions in Indians' attempts to negotiate the terms of an unwanted European invasion that, by the 1750s, had clearly come to stay. The most surprising notion that continually springs from the primary documents of colonial America is the extent to which Native American priorities persistently affected, redefined, and reordered the missions of British frontier forts and their personnel. Far different from the cowering, suspicious natives of Cooper's novels and subsequent popular imagination, Indians often saw forts as Indian-European places, and they were important actors in the dramas played out in these centers of cultural confluence.

This book demonstrates this cultural confluence using five case studies. Fort Loudoun, built by South Carolinians in what is now eastern Tennessee, was built at the request and under the supervision of powerful Cherokee leaders. It is most famous for its downfall and destruction during the Cherokee War of the late 1750s. However, its construction, its maintenance, and the failure of its commandants to navigate the tricky waters of Cherokee diplomacy reveal better the complicated role English forts could play in Indian societies. Similar complications were evident in Pennsylvania during the Delaware War of 1755–1758. Provincial Fort Allen was a small link in a chain of defensive forts that was meant to spearhead an invasion of Indian country. Its personnel and Pennsylvania's provincial leaders found that native notions of hospitality would impose other priorities on the post. It became a place for rest, diplomacy, and even drunkenness—indeed, almost everything except the launching point for an invasion or a protector of local settlers. In both of these locations, a tense coexistence seemed more beneficial to local natives than conflict. This was the case even in a place like Michilimackinac, where local Odawas and Ojibwas despised their new British neighbors. There, as in other remote outposts, native foodways and British trade goods helped form an interdependent relationship between British soldiers and suspicious Indians. Coexistence was also the strategy for Chenussio Senecas, who controlled the region around the Niagara fort complex during the Indian uprising of 1763. However, their path was more contentious. Having lost their French allies, the Chenussios used their most important bargaining tool, their control of the vital Niagara River corridor, to establish their importance in local affairs. This involved Iroquois diplomatic techniques, both violent and submissive, that had maintained Iroquois power and privileges throughout the eighteenth century. Fort Chartres, a huge fort on the Mississippi River in Illinois country, presented a thornier problem for Britain in the years after the uprising. The Illinois region's native groups knew that logistical problems and geographic unfamiliarity would hamper any British attempt to hold their newly won western holdings. Consequently, many Indians resisted the notion of peaceful coexistence at Fort Chartres more than in other parts of North America. Chartres was no "middle ground." British troops there were hopelessly out of their depth in dealing with hostile, demanding, or overbearing local chiefs, grumbling French habitants, and the constant financial demands of keeping up such a remote fort. In the Illinois country of the mid-1760s, nothing could have convinced local natives that descendants of these sickly, hapless British occupiers would someday dominate the continent.

These five forts and their native visitors illustrate the complicated texture of backcountry cultural encounters and relations. They share several attributes. In each location, British authority is revealed as malleable and open to negotiation, despite the firm imperatives of provincial governments and Britain's American military command. Trade availability was a primary concern for Indians, but fairness and sound regulation emerge as more important factors. Indians held fort commandants responsible for managing disreputable traders. In each location, Indians expected their cultural practices to be followed, or at least respected. They also understood the trepidation with which British fort personnel held their French enemies, and used that fear to demand presents, gun and tool repairs, and interpreters to prevent trade inequities. In none of these cases did Indians feel that forts and military personnel endangered their lifeways or control of their territories. At worst, they feared that forts would bring civilian encroachment. Large armies such as John Bradstreet's punitive expedition into the Ohio Valley in 1764 caused much more native consternation than permanent posts, which Indians felt they could overpower through attack or siege if necessary. Most importantly, Indians were involved in just about every aspect of fort operations: scouting, staging military operations, provisioning, diplomacy, and even fort planning and construction. Even at Fort Chartres, where Illinois and Wabash-region Indians did not fear or, in some cases, even respect the British regime, Indians were heavily involved in British fort life. In these five locations, and throughout the North American backcountry, forts were Indian as well as European places.

Despite the occasional appearance of British incompetence and ineffectiveness, this study is not intended as a critique of the British fort system or military regime in North America. In Indian country, just as in Ireland, Africa, and India, British colonial outposts were implanted with multiple objectives. The first was to create a "mark of possession" in a remote and possibly hostile natural and cultural environment. But negotiation followed; especially in America, colonial conquest was a series of dialogical or multilogical puzzles that involved mutual understandings, revelatory misunderstandings, brash hauteur, and pragmatic solutions to unforeseen complications. In this sense, forts and garrisons could not conquer Indian country at all. They could only hope to hold their positions long enough to negotiate agreements with their native neighbors before their military mission ended, bureaucrats withdrew their funds, or Indians ran out of patience. But a fort's success was not always measured by how well it secured a region militarily for Britain or one of its colonies. In military posts from the Mississippi to the Susquehanna, success was often decided by how well British forts pleased Indians. Natives' considerable effectiveness in defining fort-based cultural relations and determining the means of life and death in the backcountry made them indispensable and unavoidable fixtures of everyday colonial military life. The wooden pales and earthen breastworks of British backcountry forts did cast lasting shadows over the West, but for Indians their shadows blended with those cast by familiar trees and hills. Like European cities, societies, and trade, backcountry forts were changes to the countryside that Indians understood. Fort culture reflected this, and activities within these little intercultural worlds present a complicated view of empire at the local level.

1

The Key to Carolina

Old Hop, Little Carpenter, and the Making of Fort Loudoun, 1756–1759

In July 1753, South Carolina governor James Glen met with Cherokee and Creek emissaries to prevent further fighting between the two nations and to establish a firm alliance between his colony and prominent Cherokee leaders based in the important Overhill town of Chota. This was the governor's first meeting with Little Carpenter, nephew and deputy of Overhill leader Old Hop, and their short conversation exemplified English-Cherokee parlance in the 1750s. Little Carpenter opened by reminding Glen that he had met personally with King George II in London in 1730 and that the monarch had promised to supply the Cherokees with guns and ammunition to avenge themselves against their enemies. If they were to quit fighting the Creeks, Little Carpenter insisted, the order must come from the king himself.[1]

Glen suggested that Little Carpenter had forgotten the particulars of the 1730 treaty and that the Cherokee leader should agree to accept his words as "the great King's Talk." Little Carpenter refused and asked to be allowed to travel to England and reaffirm the treaty with the king in person. Glen claimed that the Cherokees could not spare such a great sachem in those dangerous times. "There are other Countries and Places to go to England from besides this," warned Little Carpenter. Glen held firm, insisting that the king would never meet with the Cherokee emissary without the royal governor's authorization. Little Carpenter immediately shut down the talk, telling Glen, "We can not do any Thing without the

Consent of Old Hop." This came as a surprise to Glen, who had organized the conference months before and had assumed that Little Carpenter's delegation had been given full authority to negotiate peace. Glaring at the Cherokee leader, Glen fumed to his own delegation, "I have been 10 Years here and never saw this Man before." But, despite the flaring tempers, the tension had already passed. Little Carpenter had established his status with the governor and, handing Glen a pipe sent by Old Hop, smoked with the South Carolinian delegation and continued the talks.[2]

Little Carpenter's meeting with Glen anticipated the style of negotiations that would dominate Cherokee-British relations throughout the mid-1750s. From the colonists' perspective, the Cherokees were valuable allies, necessary to the vital deerskin trade and protectors of the exposed Virginia-Carolina backcountry. But Cherokee leaders did not intend to provide their friendship for free. Dependent on European trade goods by the middle of the eighteenth century, they needed British protection of trade routes and regulation of traders and prices. At the same time, they fought to preserve their status among their own people and their influence and dignity in the face of British allies and European and Native American enemies. Little Carpenter pointed out to Glen that he was the governor's equal. He had met and treated with King George II, walked London's streets and parks, and wished to be acknowledged as the king's good servant. He reminded the governor that other colonies and countries desired the Cherokees' favor as trading partners and military protectors. Finally, as an additional stalling tactic, he demonstrated the fractious and, to Britons, confusing nature of Cherokee village politics by feigning his insufficient authority to conclude diplomatic agreements. After establishing his power and status, he and Glen continued to discuss trade from a position of strength and equanimity.

Cherokees dominated the Carolina backcountry in the mid-eighteenth century, and despite their numbers and importance in the region their existence was fraught with anxiety. Already allied with the British and immersed in the European deerskin trade for three decades by the 1750s, the westernmost group of Cherokees in the Overhill region still felt isolated and threatened by the French and their Indian allies to the north and south. Cherokee leaders such as Little Carpenter and Old Hop knew that colonial governments desired backcountry forts to protect settler communities and trade, and they hoped that British forts in Cherokee country might also answer many of their own needs. Forts brought status and respect in the eyes of their French-allied enemies and other Cherokees living in the Lower and Middle regions. British garrisons could provide regulation of the skin trade and prevent the abuses of unscrupulous Indian traders. Outposts could also serve the social and material needs of Cherokee men and women by creating safe marts of commerce. Cherokee women especially desired new forts as places where they could sell surplus crops and handicrafts, and, in some cases, find husbands. Those Cherokee motives fit well within British colonial plans to fortify the backcountry.

Trader and Indian agent Edmond Atkin insisted that to obtain permission for such fort building, British authorities needed to establish favorable and fair trade practices with Native Americans, a process he described as "building Forts in their hearts." But Atkin may not have counted on the conceptual fortresses already guarding Cherokee hopes and ambitions. Defensive Overhill Cherokees, adjusting to life in a new Indian-European consumer economy and involved unhappily in European political entanglements, needed more than just physical bulwarks and sentries. To obtain true prestige and status among friends and foes alike, Cherokee leaders forced Europeans to build forts on Cherokee terms, in the places they chose, to guard their own goals and purposes. They used all the diplomatic means at their disposal to force the South Carolinians to build a fort in the Overhills according to their wishes. This fort, named for the British commander in chief, Lord Loudoun, represented the first line of contact between Native Americans and the governments of Virginia and the Carolinas in the heart of southern Appalachia. As such, its short history provides an example of the extent to which Native American priorities intruded upon provincial military and expansion goals. Far from a mere outpost of empire, Fort Loudoun became a vital link in Cherokee lifeways and diplomacy, and its construction and operation said as much about Cherokee intercultural expectations as it did about provincial objectives. Eventually, Fort Loudoun's failure to satisfy these expectations led to its downfall.[3]

By the 1750s, Cherokees played a vital role in South Carolina's expansion plans. They had established themselves as protectors of British backcountry interests during the Yamasee War in 1715, when a British-Cherokee alliance helped save Charlestown from possible destruction. Military cooperation and dramatic increases in deerskin trade revenues during the 1730s and 1740s made the Cherokees vital to the continued health and happiness of the province. Glen described the Cherokee nation as the "key

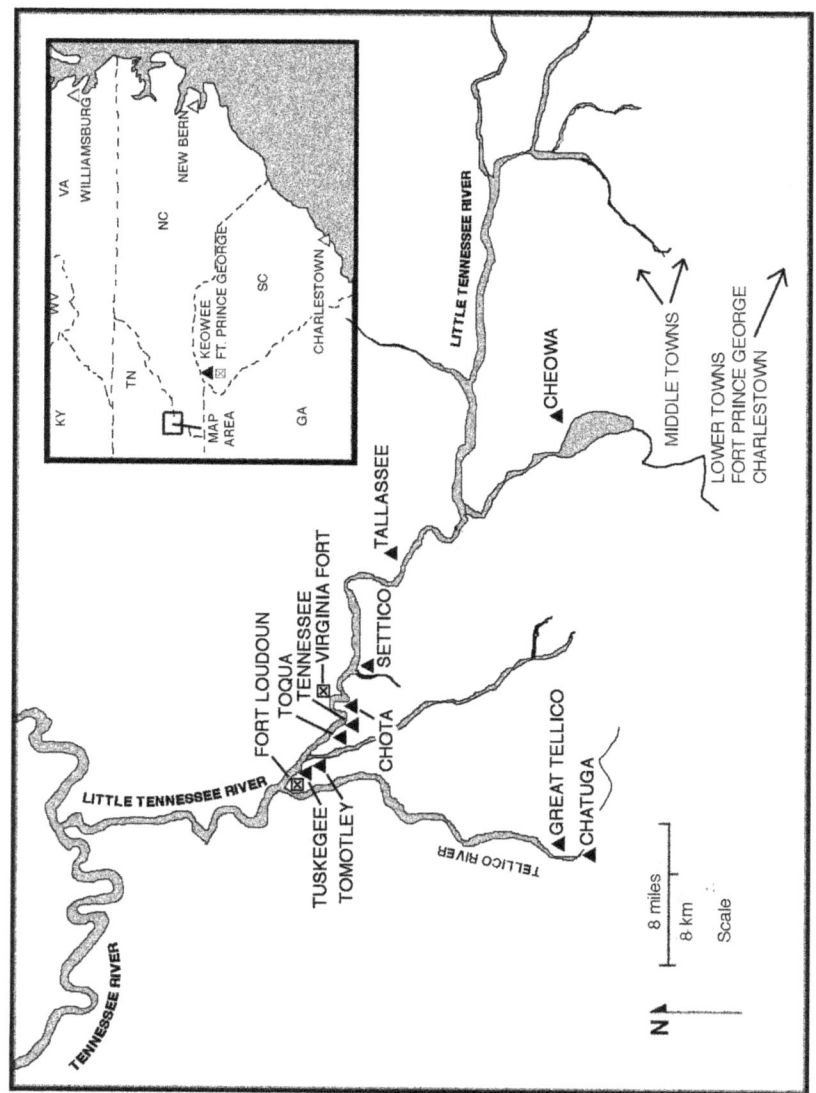

Map 1.1. Fort Loudoun and Cherokee towns in the Overhills region, 1756–1761.

to Carolina," a "natural Fortification thrown around us, as a Bulwark to our Backs." He understood that Cherokee friendship had been beneficial in the past, but he also knew well the great danger that would ensue if they were to become enemies. The Cherokees were a large nation, "far more numerous than all the Six Nations [Iroquois] together," claimed Glen in 1755. Should they become enemies, they were well situated to attack the Carolina backcountry without fear of pursuit over the rugged mountains they called home.[4]

Construction of Fort Prince George near the Lower Cherokee town of Keowee in 1753 helped guard the passes from the South Carolina backcountry into the mountains. Trader Atkin, who would later serve briefly as Indian superintendent for the Southern District, knew that a single lower-country fort would be insufficient. If the British would not provide an Overhill fort, he argued, the French inevitably would do so, and that would move important Cherokee leaders closer to French interests and domination. Trader Ludovic Grant agreed, arguing to Glen that an Overhill fort would be as much an encouragement to the Cherokees in the mountains as Fort Prince George had been for the Lower towns. With the fort to protect their women and children, Cherokee men would be more likely to venture out against South Carolina's enemies. If the Cherokees were the key to Carolina, an Overhill fort seemed to be the key to establishing a strong South Carolina–Cherokee alliance.[5]

In order to achieve his diplomatic objective, Glen would have to win over the Overhill headmen, especially Old Hop and Little Carpenter, two emerging leaders seeking to buttress their status and authority in the face of constant challenges from within and without. For decades Cherokee numbers had been diminished by disease and war with Creeks and other Indian groups in the region. In the face of such pressures, the structure of Cherokee village authority ensured that headmen faced challenges from their own people as well, especially young men who took a less indulgent approach to European expansion. As in most Eastern Woodland societies, it was only by the acclimation of their own people that Old Hop and Little Carpenter maintained their positions and status, and that approval could be withdrawn at any time. This status anxiety made it necessary for village headmen to temper their accommodation of British objectives with demands for British favors. For example, in an April 1752 talk addressing rumors that Cherokees were planning to attack English settlers, Old Hop started by assuring the South Carolinians of his importance, claiming that despite his old age "he is much looked upon in this Nation." He assured the British delegation that he had notified all the Overhill towns "to be careful of the white People and not to hurt any of them." He then left it to another Cherokee leader, Tacite, to relate the long, "tedious" list of trade goods that would be required to ensure the Cherokees' protection and favor. Such demands for respect were necessary: a village headman like Old Hop depended upon favorable British trade relations to establish the reputation for wisdom and acumen that was requisite for leadership. This reputation could be challenged at any time, in public places or behind the scenes. Even Old Hop's kinsman Little Carpenter challenged him at times; he later told Fort Loudoun's commandant, Raymond Demere, that Old Hop would treat with anyone who brought him presents. Another Cherokee later told Demere's brother Paul that Old Hop was not to be trusted and that while his speech seemed "very fair," the "old Rogue" spoke with "two tongues." Even with the benefit of age and wisdom, Old Hop needed to constantly reaffirm his status with Cherokees and Englishmen alike.[6]

Because he had met the king personally, Little Carpenter possessed an unusual advantage in his dealings with British elites. In 1730 he was one of seven Cherokees who accompanied traveler Alexander Cuming to London to meet King George II and to be awed by the spectacle of one of the world's largest cities. The delegation agreed to a treaty of perpetual friendship between the Cherokees and the English, which was often cited in subsequent years by Cherokee diplomats. For example, Old Hop reminded Glen that when "his People was in England" they had personally talked with the king and that the agreement made with him "was still in their Town House." Because of the king's assurance of friendship, Old Hop insisted that the Cherokees "would always love the English as Brothers that sucked one Mother." Little Carpenter might have been the last of that delegation still alive in the 1750s. He enjoyed reminding Glen and others that he had met, eaten with, and parleyed with the king, an honor and connection many elite Britons craved but which few ever enjoyed. Little Carpenter did not hesitate to use the 1730 meeting as a trump card, just as any British courtier would. In 1753 he asked to see the true copy of the treaty given to him personally by "the great King George." When Glen said he lacked the original, Little Carpenter insisted that it did not matter, as he had committed "the great King's Talk" to memory. Little Carpenter continued to emphasize his royal connections with Glen's successor as governor, William Henry Lyttelton. In 1756 he put Lyttelton on notice:

Fig. 1.1. Engraving showing the seven Cherokee leaders who accompanied Alexander Cuming to London in 1730. Little Carpenter (Attakullakulla) is on the far right. His visit with King George II became a lifelong diplomatic advantage for the Overhills leader. © Trustees of the British Museum.

"Tis been 26 Years since I was in England, but (I) still remember our Father King George's Talk and hope to hear from him by you." He liked to remind Lyttelton that South Carolina was bound to provision the Cherokees whenever they were in need, because when he was in London the king had promised to supply them with "every thing that would be necessary." Royal governors and influential traders liked to feel as autonomous as possible in their dealings with influential native leaders. Little Carpenter knew this, and used his personal connection with the monarch to undermine that autonomy whenever possible. However, direct congress with the king was more than a mere bargaining tool for Little Carpenter. It conferred status on the Cherokee leader that few English people and only a handful of living Indians enjoyed.[7]

Status and authority in the eyes of British leaders helped ensure continued and equitable trade, which by the 1750s had become a mainstay of Cherokee village life. Native men and women of the region were shrewd and practiced consumers and traders, and they sought fair prices and quality goods from the traders who lived in their villages. If traders cheated them or offered substandard goods, Cherokees could travel to Virginia or North Carolina for better bargains or deal covertly with French traders. But South Carolina's traders were the Cherokees' most direct source for their "necessaries," and Cherokee headmen always sought to maintain strict regulation of trade and fair prices.[8]

Trade was made difficult by traders' frequent manipulations of prices and supply. Because of alcohol's great profit potential, some would sell only liquor for deerskins, causing some customers to fall into poverty after having "drinked all their Skinns." Shortages of supplies, often instituted deliberately by traders to keep prices high, were frequent sources of conflict. To counter this, Cherokees always encouraged colonial governors to license and send as many well-supplied traders as possible, because the added competition would decrease prices and increase supply. This was made difficult by the traders' influence with provincial elites and the inherent territoriality of the fur trade. Old Hop complained in October 1755 that only one trader, John Eliott, served the needs of the seven towns in his locale, and asked Glen to send others. Glen promised Old Hop that he would find more traders to send, but he reminded the Cherokee leader that more traders would only encourage more indebtedness. The best way to ensure plentiful trade and a healthy consumer economy, he told Old Hop, was for Cherokees to become more industrious trappers and resist the temptations of easy credit. Cherokees increasingly engulfed in a system of credit and consumer exchange required responsible on-the-spot oversight and regulation of trade. Their alternatives were traveling to better markets or undertaking violent regulation themselves, and neither would encourage honest traders to visit them.[9]

Meager supplies of goods were a frequent complaint against traders and English trade policy, but these shortcomings were compounded when traders deliberately cheated their Native American customers. Little Carpenter complained that traders used faulty weights and measures to swindle his people. Glen supplied Cherokee village leaders with measuring sticks and weights authorized by the provincial assembly, but this did little to ameliorate the situation. "Do what we can, the white People will cheat us on our Weights and Measures, and make them less," Little Carpenter protested. "What is it a Trader can not do? They cheat us in the Measure of our Powder. Some of the white Men borrowed my Yeard [measuring stick] and cut it, and then gave it back for which I was blamed." Ludovic

Grant confirmed these practices, and claimed that despite colonial statutes to regulate trade and measures, "there has not been one single Article observed by a Trader." He described the traders' use of "fals Stilliards [scales], short Yards, and little Measures" and noted that the official standard measuring devices sent upcountry for the Cherokees' use often never arrived, "the Traders pretending they had no punctual Orders to carry them." Mankiller of Tellico, an Overhill Cherokee leader from one of the largest towns in the region, knew the value of trade goods and what he and his people should pay for them. However, his knowledge of goods and prices was worthless if traders continued to "impose" on his people "with their Stilliards." Regulation of traders and their methods was a constant Cherokee demand and a necessary prerequisite to friendly Indian-British relations throughout North America.[10]

In their efforts to maintain status and protect their people from belligerent enemies and unscrupulous traders, Overhill Cherokee leaders had long sought an expanded British military presence in the region, albeit a Cherokee-regulated expansion. According to Atkin, as early as 1746 Cherokee agents had asked that two forts be built in the Overhill region "for the protection of their Families, and to enable them to keep out the French." Cherokees would help build and garrison the forts, they promised, and provision it for two years. Cherokee diplomats knew well how to play the British against their European foes. Cherokee affections would naturally move toward the British if they provided proper forts and friendly garrisons, but if the French were able to build there first, "then every thing would be as *they* pleased."[11]

Glen had long argued in the South Carolina Assembly for an Overhill fort. At a conference in Saluda Old Town in the spring of 1755, he promised Little Carpenter and a large assembly of Cherokee headmen that he would build them one soon, in exchange for their cession of all Cherokee lands to the British. Little Carpenter took Glen's promise seriously enough that throughout the following year he and his fellow sachems continually demanded immediate action on the project. They understood the extent to which their numbers and mastery of their terrain impressed Glen, and used it to induce the governor to build a fort quickly or risk losing Cherokee protection. "We expect that you will perform your Promise," warned Little Carpenter in October 1755, "But if you don't let us hear anything from you we shall think you have forgot us, and we shall have our own Thoughts." Glen begged off as best he could, complaining that the king had not yet authorized the fort's construction and that he could not set a building date. In fact, it was not the king or the provincial council that stood in the way, but the province's Lower House of Assembly and the frightful cost of the proposed mountain outpost.[12]

Funding the construction of a fort in the Overhill country brought the friendly competition between Virginia and South Carolina into the fore. Both colonies were eager to gain Cherokee support in protecting and facilitating trade in the backcountry and with military campaigns against the French and their Native American allies. George Washington's failed 1754 campaign in Pennsylvania and the outbreak of open hostilities with the French made the construction of a defensive fort in the Cherokee backcountry even more vital. Backcountry rumors of French incursions into Cherokee country ran rampant in 1754–55, and an Overhills fort could help provide a base to encourage Indian allies and Carolina settlers alike. In October 1754 the Crown appropriated £20,000 in credit and specie to Virginia governor Robert Dinwiddie to form an expedition against the French and construct necessary defenses, and instructed him to assist South Carolina in constructing an Overhills Cherokee fort as soon as possible. But Dinwiddie was willing to part with only £1,000 to help Glen with the project. In March 1755 the Committee on Indian Affairs in South Carolina's Upper House proposed that South Carolina issue the necessary funds immediately and worry about reimbursement later. The full Upper House agreed, but the Lower Assembly did not see why their colony should bear the brunt of the expense. After all, they argued, Glen had promised them in 1751 that they would never be burdened with funding an Overhill fort, and they considered it "a matter of doubt" whether the Cherokees could be considered British subjects. Besides, the previous year they had appropriated £5,000 to build Fort Prince George near the Lower towns, and balked at another huge capital outlay for a questionable enterprise hundreds of miles away in the mountains. Glen was disappointed, and so was Dinwiddie, who chided the South Carolina governor for his inability to fund the project despite South Carolina's professed "Oppulency and Riches."[13]

After making his promises to the Cherokees at the Saluda conference, Glen tried again to extract funding for the proposed fort. He reminded the Assembly, "When a public & positive Promise is made to Indians, they are very impatient to have it perform'd." He also noted that since the conference the Cherokees had sent letters "in very strong Terms" to discover the progress Glen was making in funding the project. "So eager were they to have a Fort," Glen continued, that the Overhill leaders had commissioned a delegation led by Little Carpenter to travel to Charlestown to lobby for the fort's immediate construction. Glen again asked for funding, and promised again that the king would reimburse it, but the Assembly still hesitated and asked for more documentation from the king and further proofs of fealty from the Indians.[14]

When Glen supplied the necessary paperwork, the Assembly assented to funding the fort, which they agreed should be "a Place of strength, & such a One as may be capable to defend our Allies, the Indians, & strike a Terror into our Enemies, the French." But they still issued only an additional £1,000 for the project, despite continued urging from both Glen and Old Hop. Glen argued that for a good, solid fort he would need at least £4,000 to £5,000, and for £1,000 extra he could construct "a regular Fort, with a good large Fasse [a surrounding ditch], & a solid Rampart & Parapet." Glen continued to lobby, citing the expense of constructing remote forts. As an example of the spectacular costs of undertaking such a large project almost five hundred miles from Charlestown in the rugged mountainous terrain, he noted that the initial cost for provisioning and garrisoning the fort might be as much as £6,000. Finally, Glen borrowed £2,000 personally for the project and waited while the Assembly argued over passage of a funding tax bill. Only after the accession of Glen's replacement, William Henry Lyttelton, did the Assembly agree to provide £3,000 for the Overhill fort, this time without promise of reimbursement, but instead as an outright gift from the colony to the Crown.[15]

While South Carolina's governor and Assembly negotiated terms for building the new fort, Cherokee leaders used the animosity and competition between Virginia and South Carolina to hurry the project along. In September 1755 several Cherokee representatives led by one of Old Hop's sons met with Dinwiddie in Williamsburg. Dinwiddie had wondered why they did not honor his requests for Cherokee warriors to join in General Edward Braddock's failed expedition that summer. They told the Virginia governor that they had fully intended to but were stopped by a letter from Glen urging them to meet with him at the Congaree trading post instead. Dinwiddie was furious and accused Glen of never seriously pressing the Indians at Saluda to aid the Virginia expedition.[16]

With the first year of war going against the British, Dinwiddie needed Cherokee military aid desperately. Over the ensuing months he decided to take over the Overhills fort project. He placed the blame for Cherokee intransigence on Glen's inability to fund the project, and feared that Overhills men would join the French if the fort were not built that summer. "The Cherokees propose send'g in 600 Men, if we build them a Fort in the Upper Cherokee Co'try," Dinwiddie promised George Washington. Virginia had waited long enough. Dinwiddie announced that he planned to send Major Andrew Lewis and sixty men to Chota immediately to build the fort. Dinwiddie instructed Lewis to tell the Cherokees that Virginians were building them a fort to protect their women and children while their men went to war, and the governor clearly expected the Cherokees' help in planning and constructing the fort. "They will assist You with their young Men," Dinwiddie told Lewis, and ordered him to leave behind a small cannon and garrison if the Indians so desired, though he hoped that the South Carolinians would arrive and supply those. Dinwiddie's hopes of backcountry success against the French and their numerous native allies depended fully on Cherokee aid, and he despaired that without the help of the Overhill men the Virginia provincial troops would "not be able to defeat the Enemy, who are chiefly Ind[ian]'s."[17]

Lyttelton continued on with South Carolina's fort project, unaware of Dinwiddie's initiative and Lewis's commission. By June 1756 the expedition began staging at Fort Prince George. The party's commander, Captain Raymond Demere, promised Overhill headmen that he would lead his men to Chota soon to begin building the fort. Old Hop and Little Carpenter lost no time in sending word that the Virginians had beaten South Carolina to the punch. "The Virginia People promised us a Fort the other Day and are now here a building it," the Cherokee leaders wrote to Demere, and urged him to quickly send his company up and begin building a separate fort. Demere understood the Cherokees' nuance of a promise made and kept by the Virginians as a rebuke to the South Carolinians for their delays, and so did Lyttelton. Old Hop wrote the governor to tell him that the Cherokees and the Virginians lived at Chota as loyal subjects of King George, "together as Brothers." He asked Lyttelton for one hundred men from Virginia and the same from South Carolina, "no more nor no less," to garrison the fort, though he also promised that Cherokee men would help them if any enemies showed up. This request for a separate fort surprised Dinwiddie, who hoped that Lewis's Chota fort alone would spur an immediate outpouring of Cherokee military help and that Lewis's vital company would be able to return to Virginia soon. "We never tho't of send'g a Garrison to it as it is so great a Distance," Dinwiddie wrote Lyttelton, but he promised to put it before his Assembly immediately and to send a few men in the meantime. Dinwiddie also tried to elicit twenty-five men from North Carolina for garrison duty. "Every Thing sho'd be done to keep 'em in good Temper," Dinwiddie told North Carolina's governor, Arthur Dobbs. Forts alone could lend prestige and protection to Cherokee villages and leaders, but to gain the Cherokees' help against French foes the colonies would have to supply more than logs and bulwarks.[18]

Andrew Lewis understood better than the colonial governors the extent to which the Cherokees influenced Virginia's fort project. When he suggested to the Chota headmen that South Carolina and Virginia combine their efforts to build one substantial fort, the chiefs would not hear of it. "They insisted on our Building them a fort at Chota and told me that they had Layed off a Spot (for) the Carolina People to Build another, and to Satisfy them I was obliged to Comply," Lewis complained to Demere. Despite Lewis's best efforts to enlist Overhill fighting men for Virginia's campaigns, most Cherokee men would not budge until Virginia's fort was garrisoned. Little Carpenter also requested more guns, ammunition, and trade goods, and apparently he told Dinwiddie that if the Cherokees did not receive them, "they should be obliged to tell the White People to leave their Nation they being of no Service to them." Old Hop was even more direct, telling Dinwiddie that if they did not send traders and a garrison for the fort, it would be a blatant sign that the Virginians did not value them as allies. He also told Dinwiddie that the French threatened to occupy the empty Chota fort, and he promised to hold the governor responsible. "If we should get hurt by the French," he warned Dinwiddie, "I shall Lay all Blame on you for Ever, for This is the second time I have sent to you about it." Virginia's Overhills fort was clearly not having the effect Dinwiddie desired.[19]

While the Virginians worked to ease Cherokee disappointment, the South Carolinians faced their own pressures. Since early June, when the fort expedition left Charlestown for Fort Prince George, rumors had sent ripples of fear through the backcountry. Fort Prince George's commander, Thomas Harrison, started the rumor mill grinding. "Some Days past we had a great Talk," Harrison wrote to Lieutenant William Shrubshoal, commander of the expedition. "The Indians was going to kill all the White People, but I think it is over for this Time and when you come it will give a great deal of Easiness to the Indians which really are Friends to the

English." He noted that there were certainly many younger Cherokees who might wish to attack the British, but he remained confident that they could be kept in check through "Fear of the few which will not agree to it."[20]

Four days later he was not so sure. Harrison wrote again to Shrubshoal to report daily rumors that Indians intended to kill all whites in Cherokee country, stating that only Old Hop and five others stood against rebellion. Apparently, some Indians had spread a rumor that the fort expedition actually intended to kill all the Cherokee men in the region and to enslave the women and children. Little Carpenter suggested that Lyttelton himself come to Keowee to assure the young men that the English were their friends and would protect them. Ominously, Harrison reported that Cherokee messengers had been sent to Chota to discover Old Hop's sentiments. If the old leader gave the order, the Indians near Keowee would kill all the white people in Fort Prince George, a post the Cherokees believed to be so inconsequential and easy to besiege that they regarded it as "nothing." Seemingly not all Cherokees desired an Overhill fort or an expanded English presence in the region, and even Old Hop, the most assiduous fort proponent, might have had his doubts.[21]

Despite the grim warnings of Cherokee disaffection, Demere's arrival at Fort Prince George offered him plenty of evidence that Cherokees desired forts for their own purposes. Upon his arrival, Demere experienced the bountiful hospitality that Cherokee women customarily bestowed upon visitors. Three hundred Cherokees from both Keowee and the Middle towns performed a "formal ceremony" that consisted of feasting and a dance given by the "Ladies of the Town." As Demere would discover later, Cherokee women had good reason to welcome the South Carolinians: British garrisons and forts offered them ready markets for surplus corn. As part of the welcoming ceremony at Fort Prince George, Keowee's women lavished presents upon Demere in a great showing of their food production capabilities as well as their generosity. In return for some "refreshment" that Demere had sent to their town the day before, the women gave him "a great Number of Cakes of Bread of their own make and green Peas and Squashes," despite their professed lack of provisions. This food shortage would be temporary; corn grew in great abundance near Keowee. Demere noted that the garrison of Fort Prince George had produced seven to eight hundred bushels the previous year, and expected to exceed that amount in the fall. Indian women hoped that the busy men at the new Overhills fort would not be as productive, at least in the beginning, and would be happy to purchase their corn surpluses. Demere later found that Indian women would be indispensable to the success of his fort and that the fort offered women attractive social possibilities.[22]

Contrary to reports of imminent Indian aggression, Demere and his men found no hostile Cherokees at Fort Prince George, only some "old stayed men" from the Lower villages who promised to serve Governor Lyttelton and remain loyal to King George. After the welcoming celebration was over, the fort party began consolidating the food and materials that they would need to lug over the mountains, while curious Cherokees prodded them for information. On July 12 an Overhill delegation including Little Carpenter and the brother of Oconostota, the Great Warrior of Chota, arrived at the fort to ascertain the expedition's progress. Demere noted happily that the headmen did not seem interested in talking business, but instead "only great Compliments did pass from either Side." The two Cherokees regretted that they could not meet personally with Lyttelton in Charlestown, as both Demere and the governor had requested. Traveling and scheduling were too difficult in the summertime, and they preferred to stay at Keowee to observe the expedition's preparations.[23]

On July 20, Little Carpenter decided that the time for compliments was over. He assembled some of his chiefs and demanded to know when Demere would proceed to the Overhills, and seemed satisfied to learn that the expedition would set out in a few days. He also suggested that the fort be built near his own town, Tomotley, which was only a couple of miles from Chota. But the next day Little Carpenter and his chiefs returned and demanded that the force proceed at once. When Demere claimed that he was not yet ready, Little Carpenter flew into a rage, calling him a "great Lyar" and characterizing the British captain as more a "little Boy" than a potent warrior. Demere believed the abrupt change stemmed from an old grudge, specifically James Glen's broken promise to supply Little Carpenter with rum, but he was not taking any chances. He ordered his men to take up their arms, and that seemed to satisfy Little Carpenter for the moment.[24]

Demere hoped that Little Carpenter's hostile behavior was an isolated personal outburst rather than a serious indication of general Cherokee frustration. On July 25 Little Carpenter returned and apologized to Demere, blaming the outburst on rum. "I take him to have a great deal of Deceit in him even when sober," Demere wrote to Lyttelton, adding that

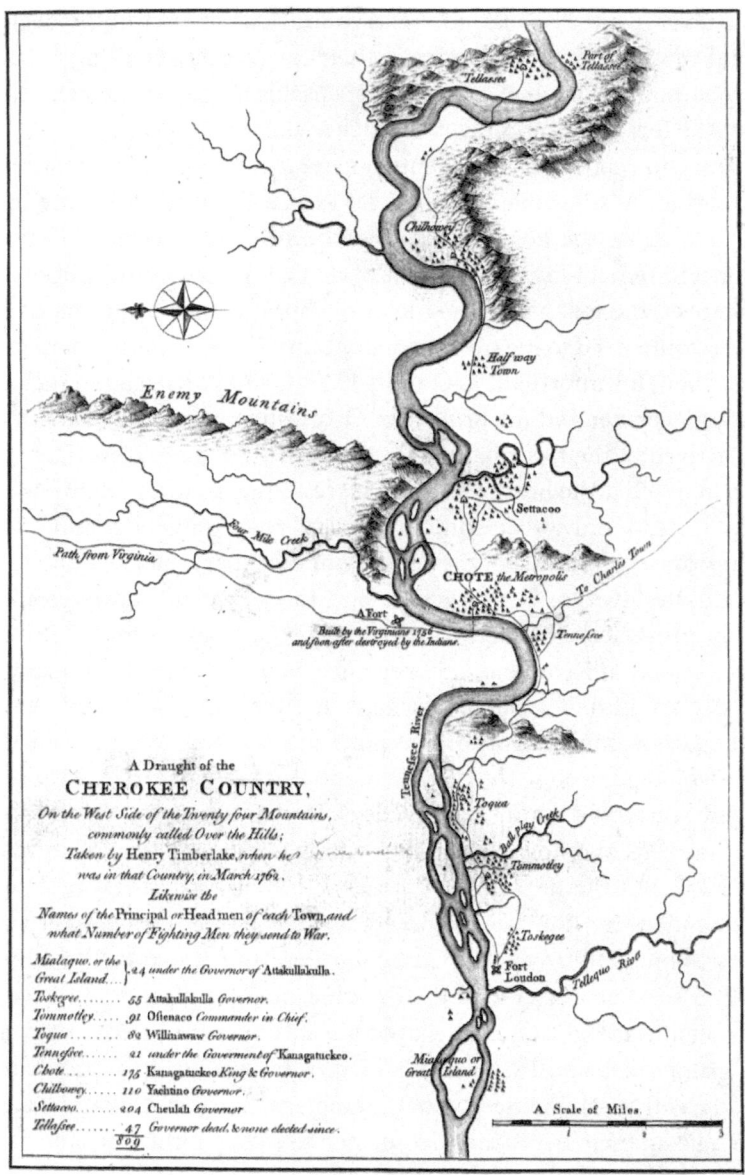

Fig. 1.2. Lieutenant Henry Timberlake prepared his "Draught of the Cherokee Country" during a diplomatic visit in 1762. The map shows Fort Loudoun along with several principal Overhill towns. His depiction of the Overhills themselves as "enemy" mountains indicates the contentious nature of Cherokee-British relations at the end of the Seven Years' War. From Thomas Jefferys, *A General Topography of North America*. Library of Congress, Geography and Map Division.

Keowee's Cherokees sometimes worried about Little Carpenter's behavior "when in Drink." But Little Carpenter's frustration may have been more a serious indication of Cherokee fear, impatience, and mistrust than an alcohol-induced impropriety. Old Hop apparently shared his nephew's impatience with the expedition's lack of progress, and he began to take steps to hurry Demere along. On August 3 he informed Demere that an Overhill Cherokee hunting party had encountered a large force of enemy Savannah Indians in the area. Demere concluded that this alarm was deliberately designed to frighten and spur on the fort expedition.[25]

When Demere's advance surveying group arrived at Tomotley, they confirmed that Old Hop intended to frighten the British into action and to play off South Carolinians against Virginians. The old chief told Sergeant William Gibbs, commander of the survey party, that he suspected the South Carolina fort would never be built. The party found little evidence of Savannah incursions into the Overhill towns, despite Old Hop's frequent warnings that they continually stirred up trouble among the Creeks and Choctaws. As time went on, Old Hop became more impatient and angry. The old chief wrote to Dinwiddie that "the Carolina Men . . . have promised us a great many Things but we cannot find one Word of Truth in any thing they say or promise us," knowing that the accusation would migrate back to Lyttelton. By August 28 Old Hop was furious at the lack of progress and sent word to Demere that he regarded the captain's continued promises as "nothing but Lies."[26]

Demere continued to offer a number of excuses for not proceeding to the Overhills, including a lack of reinforcements for Fort Prince George and a dearth of provisions, but others felt that Cherokee manipulation might have been a cause. Cherokees in the Lower towns were in no hurry to lose the fort-building party, as long as they had provisions and gifts to share. Engineer William Gerard De Brahm, who had been lured from his job as surveyor general of Georgia to plan and build the Overhill fort, claimed that Indians and traders worked to capitalize on English insecurities. "Every Day is another Day appointed to set off, Every Traider & pack horse man has his peculiar Friend among the Indians, of whom he brings great and bad new intelligences," the engineer informed Lyttelton, "After which the Indians are ask'd to give there Ta[l]ks, which are taken as memorandum, Sent Down to Town, Your Excellency, ye Council & publick Set in uneasiness." He claimed that these rumors were "but inventions and compositions of old & new histories mixt together" and served no purpose "but to get a Caske of Rum or Some Shearts."[27]

Meanwhile, Old Hop continued his plan to frighten the English into action. In early September he sent a letter to the headmen of Keowee, asking if the garrison of Fort Prince George had "used them and their Women ill" and had barred them from trading at the fort. Demere told Lyttelton that the people of Keowee remained perfectly happy with the garrison. He feared that Old Hop had begun to "embrace the French interest" and was trying to lay the groundwork for a Cherokee rebellion. Andrew Lewis, nearing his completion of the Chota fort, suspected that Little Carpenter planned to foment an uprising. The promised Cherokee military aid to Virginia had still not materialized, and Lewis suspected that Little Carpenter may have been involved in French plans to build a fort near Great Tellico. "Little Carpenter, who has the ruleing of this Nation, is a great Villain and will do every thing in his Power to serve the French," Lewis wrote to Lyttelton, confirming British fears even as De Brahm sought to debunk them.[28]

When Demere finally arrived at Tomotley on October 1 he received a friendly reception from Old Hop, surrounded by two hundred Cherokees in full regalia. The old chief was enthusiastic about the arrival of the fort expedition and hoped that "all the bad Talks and every thing that was passed might be forgot and remembered no more." Demere finally understood the Overhill Cherokees' frustration with British delays. Curtailment of trade had driven them into a state of genuine and fearful poverty—they were "very poor and all naked," according to Demere—and he understood why they would "embrace any Proposal made to them to get Relief." But after the initial diplomatic presentation of Cherokee goodwill, Old Hop returned to matters of business. He promised to comply with any of the king's and the new governor's wishes, and seemed happy at the change in government in South Carolina, since his "friend" Glen's promises for a fort had turned out to be "nothing but Lies." Old Hop then spoke of his desires regarding "his" forts. "I have one Fort at Chote," he told Demere, referring to the still unmanned Virginia fort. "I want another one here," he asked, "Then do you fix on a Spot to build one for yourself that a Gun being fired at one may alarm all three." Three forts? Demere had no funding, authority, or intention to build any other forts, but he welcomed Old Hop's promises of help after months of rumors and threats. He even induced Old Hop to admit that he had been talking with French-allied

Indians, though the old Cherokee claimed unconvincingly that he "did not do it with any Intent to hurt the Carolinians, or the Virginians." But Demere was even more impressed with Little Carpenter's promises to prevent the French from building at Great Tellico or anywhere else among the Overhills. "He has got at this present Time more Power and Influence over the Indians than Old Hopp," Demere claimed, and he hoped that with Little Carpenter's help the fort could be built and manned quickly.[29]

Old Hop and Little Carpenter further established their authority by determining the final location of the fort. On October 4 they accompanied Demere and De Brahm to examine the engineer's chosen site, which was one mile farther from Tomotley than surveyed previously. Demere suspected that the temperamental engineer's change in location was "more for Contradiction's sake than any Thing else," but he and the two Cherokees humored De Brahm initially. Once they saw the site, Old Hop and Little Carpenter vetoed the new location immediately. It was "almost a desert" without good planting ground for corn, they insisted, and they knew it to be frequented by "lurking" enemies. But their main objection was that it was too far from their towns to be of any economic or military use. When De Brahm insisted on the location because of its strategic position at a fork in the Tennessee River, the Cherokee leaders denied this advantage, claiming that only insignificant canoes could navigate the river safely. Agreeing gently with the Cherokee position that the ground was too sandy for the garrison to plant corn, Demere suggested that they should try to keep the Indians happy, though he still left the decision up to De Brahm. Angered at the captain's implicit preference for the Indians' input, De Brahm handed his pistol to Demere and asked him to "shoot him through the Head" if he would not listen to expert advice. Angry and frustrated, Demere suggested that the engineer "blow up his own Brains himself" if he so wished. This tempestuous display alarmed the two Cherokees, who had endured De Brahm patiently thus far but had finally had enough. They demanded outright that the fort be built at the original location near Tomotley, and after more "discussion" the engineer consented. Old Hop knew how to behave diplomatically, but he and Little Carpenter would not consent to have "their" fort built in a place that would not serve their needs for protection and status. Old Hop had a fort near his town, and Little Carpenter required one just as close to Tomotley.[30]

De Brahm's supervision of the fort's construction, which began on October 4 right after the site argument, can only have increased Cherokee anxieties about the value of their alliance with the British. On the one hand, De Brahm went right to work, issuing stern commands to Demere's soldier-workers without even allowing them time to build adequate shelters. However, despite early progress on the fort, the engineer's mercurial management style caused morale to drop quickly. "He fanceys himself a verry great Monarch and wants the whole Command to himself," complained Demere. De Brahm had bigger goals than fort building; unknown to Demere, he hoped to win an appointment as surveyor general of South Carolina. When this did not materialize, he became insolent and threatened to return to Georgia, "where he should be thank'd for his Service." By November the strain had begun to show in the lack of progress on the fort. Soldiers still had not been allowed to construct houses for themselves, while De Brahm had moved into a Cherokee house in Tomotley after hearing a rumor about a possible French attack on their camp.[31]

With Demere and De Brahm at loggerheads and the fort project stalled, Old Hop turned again to spreading rumors to spur on the bickering British. He told Demere that Indians from Great Tellico, the largest Overhill town, had been among the French eliciting support for an attack on the Tomotley camp by French, Creek, Choctaw, and Savannah forces and that the new fort must be made defensible immediately. Demere ordered De Brahm to finish the palisades, and for once the engineer agreed and set to work. Though these rumors turned out to be grounded in reality, they also reflected Old Hop's fear of losing his health, status, and influence over the young men. The old headman believed he would die soon, and told Demere to trust only Oconostota and Old Hop's brother. Surprisingly, he did not recommend any of his many sons or any other headmen, including his nephews Little Carpenter and Willanawa, because he did not know how they would "behave" after his passing.[32]

The dispute between Demere and De Brahm did not abate with the arrival of winter. When the engineer decided that the fort was nearly complete, he tried to turn the provincial troops' sympathies away from Demere and almost provoked a mutiny. As for the fort, Demere professed his astonishment at the lack of progress: "Can you call this a fort, no Guns or Platforms, no Barracks, no Guard, no necessary Houses or Drains so requisite for the Health of the Garrison, no Houses for the Officers, but miserable Hovels built at their own Expences . . . in short Nothing as yet to be seen deserving the Name of a Fort." Still, De Brahm declared his job complete, left instructions for finishing the fort, and deserted the

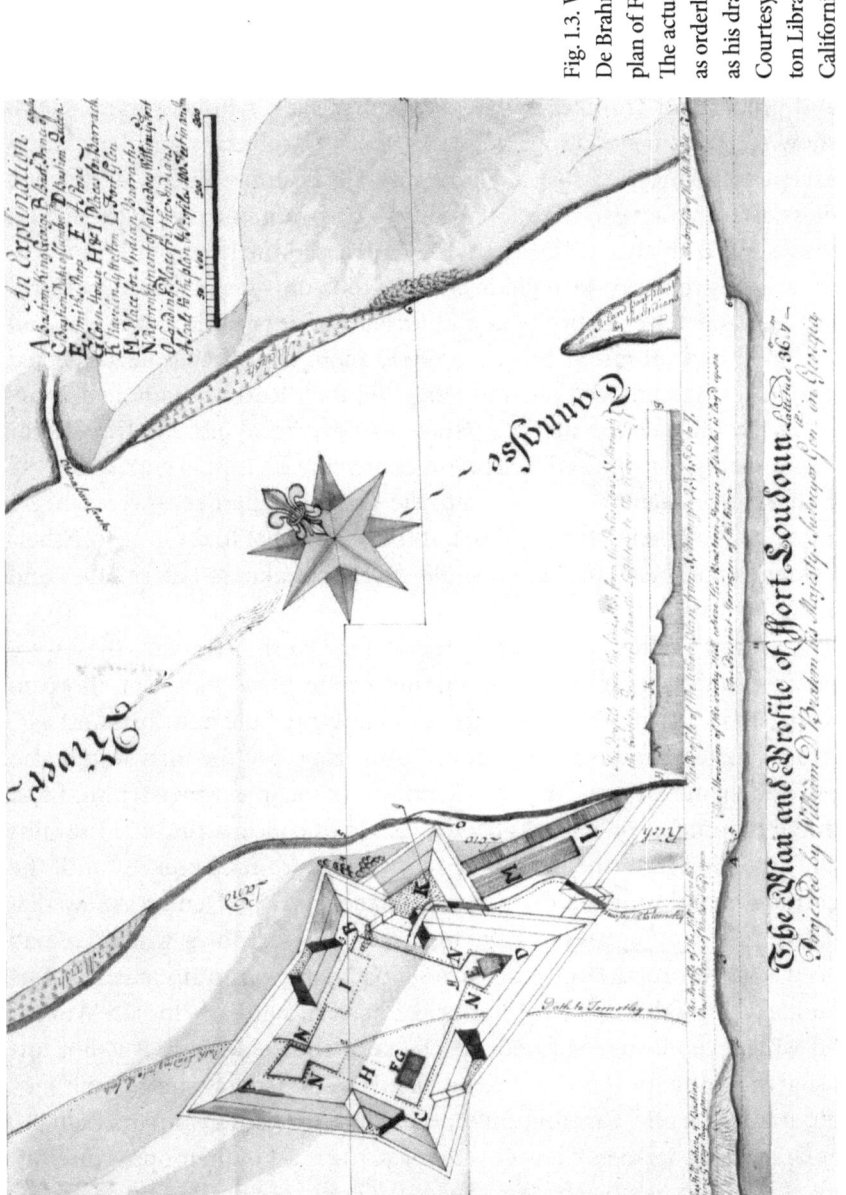

Fig. 1.3. William Gerard De Brahm's projected plan of Fort Loudoun. The actual fort was never as orderly or immaculate as his draft promised. Courtesy of the Huntington Library, San Marino, California.

operation. With the project's two principal British representatives locked in combat over the fort's progress, the Cherokee headmen were less than enthusiastic. Old Hop continued to warn of possible Savannah incursions and to press for completion of the fort.[33]

Growing divisions among Overhill Cherokees regarding their alliance with South Carolina may have prompted Old Hop's anxiousness, but his immediate purpose was to encourage Demere to finish the fort quickly and prepare for trouble. By late November the Cherokees had little to show for their negotiations with the South Carolinians and Virginians except an unmanned fort at Chota and De Brahm's watery, unfinished mess at Tomotley. No additional traders had come to supply them, and the renewed alliance with Britain only increased their danger. When Andrew Lewis returned to Williamsburg he took only seven Cherokee fighting men, far fewer than the one hundred warriors Little Carpenter and Old Hop had promised. Dinwiddie told them angrily that he suspected the French had induced them to renege on their treaty, but his anger only served to indicate the depth of Cherokee leverage. Unfazed, the Cherokees once again promised to send more men once Virginia garrisoned the Chota fort. As later events showed, the Overhill Cherokees were sincere about helping their British allies, but they knew that to do so before their demands had been answered would display weakness before allies and enemies alike.[34]

To make matters even more urgent for Overhill leaders, they were probably facing pressure from another group they could not afford to disregard or disappoint. Cherokee women wanted the new forts and garrisons as protection for their families and crops, but the forts would also provide them with small but vital amounts of income. Provisioning a fort in the mountains had always been a source of concern, and the Carolinians intended from the beginning to buy food from Cherokees until the garrison could produce their own. By January 1757, Demere knew that native provisioning would have to sustain the fort for a while. He had been able to procure only five canoe loads of corn to nourish the fort builders through the winter, and was forced to send an "Indian Wench" off with several wagons to buy all the corn she could find. It is not unusual that Indian women would be called upon as merchants, even if they did it infrequently. Farming and home economy were a woman's domain, and Cherokee women knew how to make the most of their opportunities, much to Demere's frustration. Because Cherokees desired trade goods, both necessities and "trifling Things," they would charge the garrison as much as they could for their crops. "We are obliged to pay very dearly for Corn," Demere complained to Lyttelton. Because traders brought "no Goods proper for the purchasing of Corn," women wished only for goods that the troops had brought with them. Until more traders came to the Overhills region to trade for skins, and until they brought the right kinds of commodities, Cherokee women would have to depend on the new fort and its garrison for the goods they needed.[35]

Some Cherokee women depended on the fort for more than economic benefits. Soon after the garrison settled itself at Tomotley, some native women married soldiers. Such intercultural marriages were not unusual, though they often took the form of common-law unions. Traders and Indian agents had long valued native wives, especially because being adopted by a Native American family gave white men special status and connections for trade and diplomacy. The benefits for Cherokee women were also substantial. As the wives of traders and soldiers, Cherokee women could become important cultural go-betweens and increase their own level of status. Children of such intermarriages remained Cherokees, because kinship was determined by matrilineal succession. Such children often grew to become influential in both white and native societies, increasing the value of intermarriage for Cherokee women and their kin. But these were not merely marriages of convenience or practicality. Cherokee women often sided with their soldier-husbands against their own leaders, providing Demere with reliable intelligence and bringing food to the fort when provisions were low or threatened. British forts and personnel sometimes offered Cherokee women levels of social autonomy and economic security that were unattainable in their own society.[36]

Internecine Cherokee animosities created yet another problem for the fort project. Overhill headmen had argued for a fort near their homes partly because of their competition with the Keowee people after Fort Prince George's construction. With new forts guarding Chota and Tomotley, jealousy among leaders from other Upper towns was predictable. In November, Demere learned that Mankiller and others from Great Tellico had visited the French at Fort Toulouse on the Alabama River, and rumors spread that the Tellico people had agreed to abandon their village and move to Hiwassee Old Town, where the French planned to build a new fort. When Demere confronted Mankiller in December, the Tellico headman convinced him that Old Hop and Little Carpenter had ordered him to go to Fort Toulouse and that when he met with the French he still had "Old Hop's Commission," a string of beads, hanging from his neck. Demere was delighted that Mankiller, a headman who had "been always disafected to the English," had been so easily brought over to the British interests.[37]

Subsequently, Demere was sorely disappointed to hear in January that some of Tellico's people had indeed moved to Hiwassee. Lieutenant Robert Wall went to Tellico to investigate, and he met there with a "throng" of Indians still living in the town and eager for trade. Wall gave them presents sent by Demere and promised that trade would soon return to the village. Meanwhile, at Chota, Old Hop and Great Warrior eagerly pressed Demere for information about what had transpired with Mankiller. Demere told them he would placate the Tellico people with presents but that he would never again reward the "very deceitful Villain" Mankiller. When Wall reported back he confirmed that as long as trade goods were in such a short supply in Tellico and nearby villages that "those Towns will always be uneasy and dissatisfied." Mankiller confirmed this, making it clear to Demere that until a regular trader came to Tellico, he would have nothing more to say to the English.[38]

By January 1757, Cherokees began to learn how much their aspirations for an expanded British military presence among them would interfere with their own goals rather than encourage them. James Glen and other fort proponents had always stressed that maintaining good relations with key Cherokees was reason enough to fortify the backcountry. However, with the onset of the Seven Years' War, Britain needed native fighters as well as amicable Cherokee elites. Fort Loudoun, as the Overhill fort would soon be named, represented an extension of British military policy in the remote mountainous region. Indians there who hoped for increased trade, better regulation of traders, and more status and authority among their own people would have to take on British geopolitical motives along with their own. This involved Cherokee promises to participate in far-flung military ventures such as the 1758 Forbes campaign in Pennsylvania, but provincial war objectives also infused British-Cherokee relations closer to home. Fort Loudoun and the policies that accompanied it quickly became more trouble than they were worth for Overhill leaders.

Cherokees would not readily fight nearby French soldiers and their Indian allies without pay, and enemy scalps soon joined woven baskets and deerskins as hot commodities in the Overhill towns. At the end of

January 1757, Demere had little with which to impress the Cherokees. Fort Loudoun had been hastily palisaded after De Brahm's abrupt desertion and cannot have been a very attractive inducement to Cherokee cooperation. With trade goods sparse in the region, Demere turned to direct payment for Cherokee participation in the war. "Nothing is more valuable amongst brave Men and Warriors than Trophies of Victory," he told the headmen at Chota. "Nothing is more worthy Acceptance than the Scalps of our Enemies; I want some and hope that some of you will soon bring me some French Scalps, or some Indian Scalps that are in Friendship with the French." He promised to give the equivalent value of thirty pounds of leather in exchange for each scalp.[39]

South Carolina's Assembly supported the scalp bounty initiative, agreeing to defray the cost of "a Gun, one Pound Powder, three Pounds of Bullets, a Matchcoat, a Blanket, a Flap, a Check Shirt, a laced Hat, a Knife & two Ounces of Vermillion" for each enemy scalp brought in from remote areas. Even larger rewards would be granted for killing enemy interlopers in the Cherokee towns themselves. Scalp bounties were nothing new in British North America, but their increased use among the Cherokees led to trouble almost immediately. In August a group of young Cherokee men brought five scalps to Fort Loudoun, supposedly taken from enemy Savannahs, and asked for their reward. Little Carpenter knew immediately that the scalps were from friendly Chickasaws, and warned that the error was likely to cause trouble with longtime friends. He blamed the new English policy for causing the mistake. "I can think of nothing that induced them to do this Action, but their hurry to return home to receive the reward," he complained to Demere, upset that a group of upstanding young men had "returned like Thiefs With a Lye in their Mouths." He asked Demere to stop the scalp bounties immediately. His Cherokees preferred open and honest trade to blood rewards.[40]

With most of the Seven Years' War action far away from the smoky hills of Cherokee country, Demere looked for any opportunity to make his fort, his garrison, and his Cherokee allies useful. In June 1757 he found an opportunity. Beneath constant rumors of French-Cherokee machinations swirling through the Overhills, Demere heard that seven French-allied Savannahs had been seen visiting Tellico. Demere told Old Hop, Standing Turkey, and other Cherokee headmen that killing the Savannahs would prove conclusively their allegiance to the king. Old Hop wondered skeptically why Demere thought seven Savannahs represented such a dire threat, and the captain replied that they would be enough "to make a start with." The Cherokee leaders resisted creating such a provocation. Old Hop liked to keep his options open with the French, and did not wish to endanger anyone at Tellico. He asked if they might wait and kill the conspirators after they left town. While the headmen retired overnight to think about the proposal, Demere remained adamant that the Savannahs be killed "some Way or other" and organized a party composed of provincial volunteers and two Indians to attack the enemy. They succeeded in killing three of the seven Savannahs, much to Demere's delight. "The Blow is now given," he proclaimed to Lyttelton, sure that the Cherokees' participation in the raid would force them into an open war with the French-allied Savannahs. He publicly rewarded the two Cherokees, hoping to inspire regret among nonparticipants. But the Overhill headmen did not enjoy being forced into such a confrontation by Demere, whom they had hoped would bring more trade goods to the region rather than increased bloodshed. Demere finally convinced Old Hop, Standing Turkey, and another chief, the Smallpox Conjurer, to agree that the killings were justified, but only after bribing them with new matchcoats and promises of more ammunition and trade goods for their towns. Still, Demere's rash action did nothing to allay Cherokee disappointments, and it worsened relations with the Savannahs and Tellico.[41]

At the bottom of growing Cherokee disaffection was the issue of trade, which the headmen had hoped would be improved by an official South Carolinian presence in the region. On February 5, Old Hop angrily accused the British of reneging on their 1755 Saluda agreement. South Carolina had built them a fort and manned it with a small garrison, but traders still charged prices far above those to which Glen had agreed, making Old Hop regard Charlestown's promises as "Nothing but Lies." He was particularly upset about Chota's principal trader, John Elliot, whom Demere admitted sold goods at a "most exorbitant Price." A week later, Old Hop apologized for his anger but argued that his people would make poor bulwarks against the French without decent guns and ammunition. Demere agreed, knowing that the Cherokees' guns were old and in bad repair, and told Lyttelton that Old Hop could hardly be expected to "send his People to fight with their Fists."[42]

Cherokees could not wait indefinitely for Lyttelton to act in such dangerous times, and used every lever they possessed to improve trade practices. Well aware that the garrison needed corn grown by Cherokee women, they withheld it to pressure the fort's commissary to negotiate equitable trading terms and prices. They also knew that the British feared a French-Cherokee alliance above all, and reminded Demere and other British authorities that the French had always promised them an abundance of trade in exchange for an alliance. Demere was forced to take that threat seriously when proof of a late-1756 French-Cherokee agreement emerged. In April 1757 a recently signed document, "Articles of Peace and Friendship concluded between the French Governor (of Louisiana) & certain Deputies from the Cherokee Nation," was found aboard a captured French merchant ship, the *Revanche*. Lyttelton hurriedly urged the Assembly to improve the trade situation in the Overhills so as to "remove, as far as possible, all cause of Discontent in the Minds of the Indians." Despite these efforts, traders continued to charge exorbitant prices for vital trade goods.[43]

Fort Loudoun's presence did as little to instill ethical practices among backcountry traders as it did to enforce fair prices. In July 1757, Little Carpenter asked that John Elliot be recalled from the Overhills. Elliot had never stopped cheating Indians with faulty weights and measures, and he refused to bring sufficient quantities of useful goods to the towns. According to Little Carpenter, this caused "so many Talks" among the Cherokees and was a direct source of their disaffection. Little Carpenter warned Demere outright that without trade improvements they would soon be forced to resort to "the French at Tuskegee," and that the quicker Lyttelton corrected the situation, the less the Overhill Cherokees would plot and complain. Cherokee impatience stemmed from actual poverty, but status and conspicuous consumption also played a role. Old Hop and Little Carpenter continued to press for the guns and ammunition they needed for hunting and protection, but Elliot brought only food and rum, commodities that could be sold to Indians and troops alike. At a Fort Loudoun meeting with Elliot and Demere, Cherokee headmen complained, "the Creeks does Laugh at em for being not well Supplyed with them as they are them selves." Little Carpenter and Old Hop agreed to give Eliott the benefit of the doubt if he would start supplying the arms and tools they needed instead of more rum and flour, but less-accommodating Cherokees were beginning to grumble.[44]

With Fort Loudoun failing to provide the consumer equity and social status Cherokees expected, new rumors of schemes and alliances began to fly throughout the region. In April 1757, Indian Superintendent

Edmond Atkin reported to Lyttelton that Cherokees had attacked a few western Virginia settlements. He further suspected that Little Carpenter had become Britain's "Secret Enemy" and had concluded an alliance with the French-allied Shawnees. Indian agent and trader John Stuart also reported a "visible Alteration in the Behaviour of the Indians" after Little Carpenter returned from a visit to Charlestown, but he assured Lyttelton that the headman remained firmly attached to British interests and maintained his status among the Overhill Cherokees. The following month a new rumor emerged that involved an Iroquois-Cherokee alliance to attack Fort Loudoun from both without and within and to kill the entire garrison. By August, British personnel throughout the region chimed in with their reports on the reliability of the Overhill leaders, with Little Carpenter's reputation for reliability growing and Old Hop's receding.[45]

Mistrust of Old Hop may or may not have been misplaced, but it is understandable given the old leader's continued manipulations of Cherokee-British relations, machinations among the French, and inflated assertions of authority. Old Hop continued to insist that his voice was necessary to maintain the British alliance, and he demonstrated this to his own people by asserting his power over Demere. For example, in July 1757 Old Hop had forced Demere to purchase one of his "slaves," "a French Deserter that has been Some time in this Nation & his own Property." Demere could not refuse, fearing that if he did so, Old Hop would throw the French captive in the River "for the fish to eat." In the increasingly unsure political arena of the Overhills, with French agents and anti-British Cherokee nativists vying for his people's allegiance, Old Hop needed to reaffirm his power and influence over the British commandant. But such loyalty tests only increased British doubts about Old Hop's influence and reliability. With official opinions about Old Hop's and Little Carpenter's loyalties shifting constantly, Fort Loudoun's situation grew increasingly precarious.[46]

Reports of possible Cherokee plots came amid other unsettling news at Fort Loudoun. Little Carpenter reported in July 1757 that the French had built a new fort on the Savannah River. Demere offered to send to Charlestown for help, but Little Carpenter felt they should act immediately because "Things are Generally too Long before they are Determined in Carolina," and he proposed an immediate British attack. While deciding how much of his garrison he should risk, Demere learned that Old Hop had been conspiring at Chota with French John, a trader in league with the Creeks and Savannahs. Little Carpenter sought to dispel Demere's distrust of the old chief, saying the "old fool" would listen to anyone who "brought him a small String of Beads." Demere was relieved when fifteen Cherokees brought in a French scalp taken near Fort Toulouse; this, he hoped, might finally provoke his long-anticipated Cherokee-French war. But the commandant could not disregard French John, a known enemy treating with headmen practically under the fort's walls. Demere put a bounty on him equal to five hundred pounds of leather, but killing the conspirator would be a delicate matter because he was under Old Hop's protection. When the trader learned about the bounty and ran off to Tellico for protection, Demere tried to contract Mankiller's help. Mankiller agreed to kill French John and his friend Savannah Tom secretly and tactfully within twenty days. Amid the general confusion created by Demere's meddling, Savannah Tom allegedly killed a white woman at Tellico. This finally prompted Cherokee declarations of war against the Savannahs—a convenient victory for Demere but a tragedy for the Overhill people. In less than one year as commandant of Fort Loudoun, Demere had disrupted relations between Overhill towns, contracted a Cherokee leader to act as a covert assassin, and drawn the Cherokees into European conflicts they would have preferred to avoid.[47]

In August 1757, Paul Demere replaced his brother Raymond as commander of Fort Loudoun, but Cherokee frustrations and complaints about trade continued. The new commandant reminded Cherokee leaders that Choctaws and Savannahs complained constantly about their treatment at the hands of their French allies and that Cherokees had never obtained anything from the French but promises. He urged them to be patient with Elliot, by then the sole trader in the Fort Loudoun region. Overhill leaders had little choice but to complain and hope for the best, hating trade abuses but afraid to lose their only trader. Complaints intensified over the next two years as John continued using faulty measures, watering down his rum, and charging prices that ensured Cherokee poverty and damaged their leaders' status.[48]

Disappointed though the Overhill leaders may have been, their new promises to oppose the French still provided an excellent opportunity for them to demand vital gifts and supplies. In October 1757, Little Carpenter prepared to set out with a small party to destroy the new French fort on the Savannah. Paul Demere was dismayed at the headman's requests for guns, hatchets, ammunition, and war paint, but he could do nothing but comply after his brother had urged them on for so long. Demere reported being "tormented" on a daily basis with Indian requests for gifts of food and repairs for their guns, hatchets, and tools. Little Carpenter and Old Hop were happy to learn in December that a trading post was planned for Chota. All the Overhill towns would be supplied, including Tellico, despite their recent fraternizing with the French.[49]

But new Cherokee campaigns against the French meant an increased use of scalp bounties, which put even more pressure on undersupplied traders. In January 1758, Little Carpenter's party took fifteen French scalps, and the headman wrote to Demere to put in his order: "I hope you will have white Shirts made ready against we come. Make them large. Our Paint is gone. Please send to me two Pounds of Paint by the Bearer and four Bottles of Rum. I hope you have kept four Keggs of Rum." With dozens of Cherokees pledged to Forbes's spring campaign against Fort Duquesne in Pennsylvania, such demands would only increase. "They expect to be entairten'd when they go to War, and when they come back, and Every time they come to give a Talk in the Fort, and on other Meeting," despaired Demere, who, because he was "on the Spot" and knew the dangerous consequences for refusing, had no choice but to accede. By April, Cherokees had sent men north to help the Virginians, and a huge force prepared to set out against the French to the south. Demere depleted his stores outfitting the Cherokee parties and feared that when they returned he would have no goods to give them.[50]

Constant warfare and inability to maintain sufficient supplies of trade goods strained relations between the Overhill Cherokees and Fort Loudoun's garrison throughout 1758. As young Cherokee men agitated against British authority, their leaders became hesitant to proffer their promised military aid and feigned lack of authority to hedge against uncertain outcomes. In March, Little Carpenter refused a request from Lyttelton to bring a French prisoner to Charlestown because "the young Man was not willing," and the Overhill leader insisted that he would "never force his Inclination" on another. The following month Old Hop refused to help Demere capture a trader, Samuel Jarron, who was wanted for an unnamed crime, either sedition or conspiring by letter with the French. "He has done Nothing but writing," complained Old Hop. Since Jarron had lived among them for many years, the Cherokees considered him a relative and would not give him up. In June, Old Hop and Standing Turkey refused a reward of three hundred pounds of leather to send men after two deserters, claiming that the fugitives "had too much the start" and that "the Path was too Bloody and dreadfull." When Lyttelton accused Overhill Cherokees from the village of Settico of attacking settlers in Halifax and Bedford Counties, Old Hop protested his helplessness in the matter. "I told them ... to be kind to the White People," he insisted, "But some will be Rogues, and we have too many amongst us, Especially the lower Towns." When Demere reminded him that the Settico people were from the Overhills, not the Lower towns, Old Hop claimed that he was helpless. He had lost his authority over his own people, he asserted, because he refused to speak badly of the British. As Old Hop knew very well, authorities in Virginia and South Carolina could do nothing but forgive such minor, unfriendly Cherokee actions. Fort Loudoun had not altered the Cherokee-British balance of power among the Overhills at all, and its failure to answer Cherokee needs only weakened the older accommodationist leaders' status and influence and encouraged anti-British nativist sentiments.[51]

Throughout the following year, Demere's influence with Overhill leaders diminished as new reports of Cherokee disaffection in the region made Fort Loudoun more a lightning rod for dissatisfaction than a beacon of hope. Some of this may have been caused by Demere himself, whom Little Carpenter claimed was "not so attentive to the Indians & so kind to them" as his brother Raymond had been. More tension resulted from Lyttelton's unmerited efforts to brand Little Carpenter a deserter after he withdrew his men from the Forbes expedition without leave, an action well within Cherokee fighting traditions. But by early 1759, general British-Cherokee relations had already deteriorated beyond the control or influence of Fort Loudoun. In April 1759, Cherokees of Settico, eager to avenge earlier deaths at the hands of Virginia settlers, raided settlements in western North Carolina, killing dozens of settlers and spreading fear throughout the backcountry. Lyttelton's plan to use Cherokees as foot soldiers in a general southern campaign disintegrated as a frightened South Carolinian populace demanded that the government control their Indian allies. Lyttelton ordered trade suspended at Settico in August 1759 and stopped sales of arms to the Overhills altogether.[52]

For Indians already dissatisfied with trade and always in need of ammunition and guns for hunting, this was a giant step backward in their relations with the colonies. But Lyttelton cared little for Cherokee complaints, having already decided that only military intimidation could compel the Cherokees to meet their treaty obligations. Ignoring a last-minute Cherokee peace delegation to Charlestown in September,

Lyttelton declared them to be in open rebellion; sent letters to all surrounding colonial governors and the headmen of the Chickasaws, Creeks, and Catawbas; and prepared South Carolina for open war with the Cherokee Nation. This was an outcome few could have foreseen only a few years before, when Glen had demanded and won an Overhill fort to guard the "key to Carolina."[53]

Fort Loudoun would eventually meet its end at the Cherokees' hands in August 1760 when they besieged the fort and forced its capitulation, despite Little Carpenter's sincere efforts at moderation. Indian wives of British soldiers showed great courage in sneaking food into the fort and arguing for leniency, but to little avail. As for Old Hop, by then his shifting loyalties no longer mattered. The old headman had succumbed to disease earlier that year, and nativists led by Standing Turkey and Oconostota held authority in the Overhill region. After the garrison's surrender, Cherokees killed Paul Demere and thirty-two of the fort's men, and enslaved or adopted the rest.[54]

But the making of the fort revealed as much about the Cherokees' lives and desires as did the fort's breaking during the Cherokee-British War. Cherokee leaders desperately wanted forts near their towns to regulate trade and conspicuously define their status among Indians and Europeans alike. They exercised their influence to have forts built on sites of their choice, where they would serve Cherokee interests best. They knew that Glen was right to characterize them as the key to South Carolina's success, and they understood that the colonists needed them more than they needed the Virginians or the Carolinians.

Contrary to Cherokee expectations, allowing forts in their country also brought British military operations and expansionist policies closer to home. Old Hop, Little Carpenter, and other Cherokee leaders finally realized their desire for a provincial Overhill fort, but then they had to live with it. The result was increased tension between pro-French nativists and pro-British accommodationists among their own people, as well as conflicts with ever-encroaching settlers in the colonial backcountry. Native American dispossession should seldom, if ever, be seen as the Indians' own fault, especially when their leaders tried their best to navigate the waters of the new Indian-European world to their peoples' best advantage. But the making of Fort Loudoun is as good an example as any to show that people under pressure should choose their wishes carefully.

2

Anxious Hospitality

Loitering at Fort Allen, 1756–1761

Of the many occupations Benjamin Franklin pursued during his storied life, one of the less acclaimed was that of a frontier fort builder. Franklin's achievements in philosophy, politics, diplomacy, and science are so significant that his contributions to Pennsylvania defense during the late-1750s Delaware War have paled in biographical comparison. But given the unexpected developments at Franklin's Fort Allen, it is fitting that it was planned and built by an individual known more for his diplomatic legacy than for his martial expertise. Constructed as part of a chain of defensive outposts to protect Pennsylvania's towns and cities from Indian threats, Fort Allen became instead a diplomatic way station, a moderately successful trading post, and even a rum-soaked watering hole. In fact, the fort became many things, but it never really fulfilled its original purpose in Pennsylvania's frontier-defense plans. Fort Allen's mission, like that of Fort Loudoun and other forts scattered throughout British North America, was defined not only by those who planned and built it but also by its occupants and visitors. Fort Allen was not exceptional in this regard. It does, however, provide an excellent example of how the collision of provincial military imperatives, backcountry settlement ambitions, and Native American cultures helped define and complicate an outpost's mission.

Much of the tension that defined Fort Allen's brief existence on the northern slope of Pennsylvania's 150-mile-long Blue Mountain ridge stemmed from its frequent Indian guests. Situated aside the Lehigh River near a vital passage through the ridge, the fort was sure to attract native passersby. It was especially well placed as a stopping point for Indian diplomatic visitors to the Lehigh Valley towns of Easton and Bethlehem. During such visits, native travelers expected the full hospitality of the fort's garrison and commandant, as they would of any hosts throughout Indian country. Fort Allen's importance as a native diplomatic checkpoint and resting place eventually outweighed its original function as a frontier base for punitive expeditions against belligerent Delawares. With hundreds of Indians visiting each year, and with a garrison that never exceeded one hundred men and seldom exceeded fifty, it is understandable that Indian visitors helped define the identity and nature of the small wooden stockade. Meant to reassure local settlers and to bring stability to the liminal geography that divided the upper Susquehanna River Indian country and British Pennsylvania, Fort Allen produced unexpected and ironic results. Instead of keeping Delawares away from the Blue Mountain region and its European settlers, it attracted them. Instead of regulating unscrupulous British traders, it helped bring them a ready, native customer base. Fort Allen became ultimately an Indian place as well as an English one, where the most famous resident was not Franklin or some other provincial celebrity but the renowned Delaware chief Teedyuscung. Colonial exigencies and anxieties merged with native notions of hospitality and reciprocal obligation at Fort Allen, producing a place of anxious hospitality for both Europeans and Indians.[1]

Northampton County in the mid-1750s might have seemed a place of both promise and tension to many Pennsylvanians. Rapid demographic expansion and ethnic and religious diversity characterized the region; indeed, Northampton County itself was relatively new, as were many of the towns south of Blue Mountain. A boom in town building had created a minor white population explosion in the Blue Mountain region after 1730, though most of this urbanization was located west of Reading and the Schuylkill River. In Northampton County the principal towns were the new county seat of Easton, founded by Pennsylvania's proprietary Penn family in 1752, and the German Moravian spiritual capital of Bethlehem, established in 1741. Easton lay at the fork of the Delaware and Lehigh Rivers, about sixty miles north of Philadelphia. It was a planned town, laid out in a grid pattern surrounding a central square, similar to the design of recently established Reading. The strategic spot had been settled since the 1730s, and the town already had hundreds of inhabitants at its inception, including English, Scots-Irish, and German immigrants. Easton's position

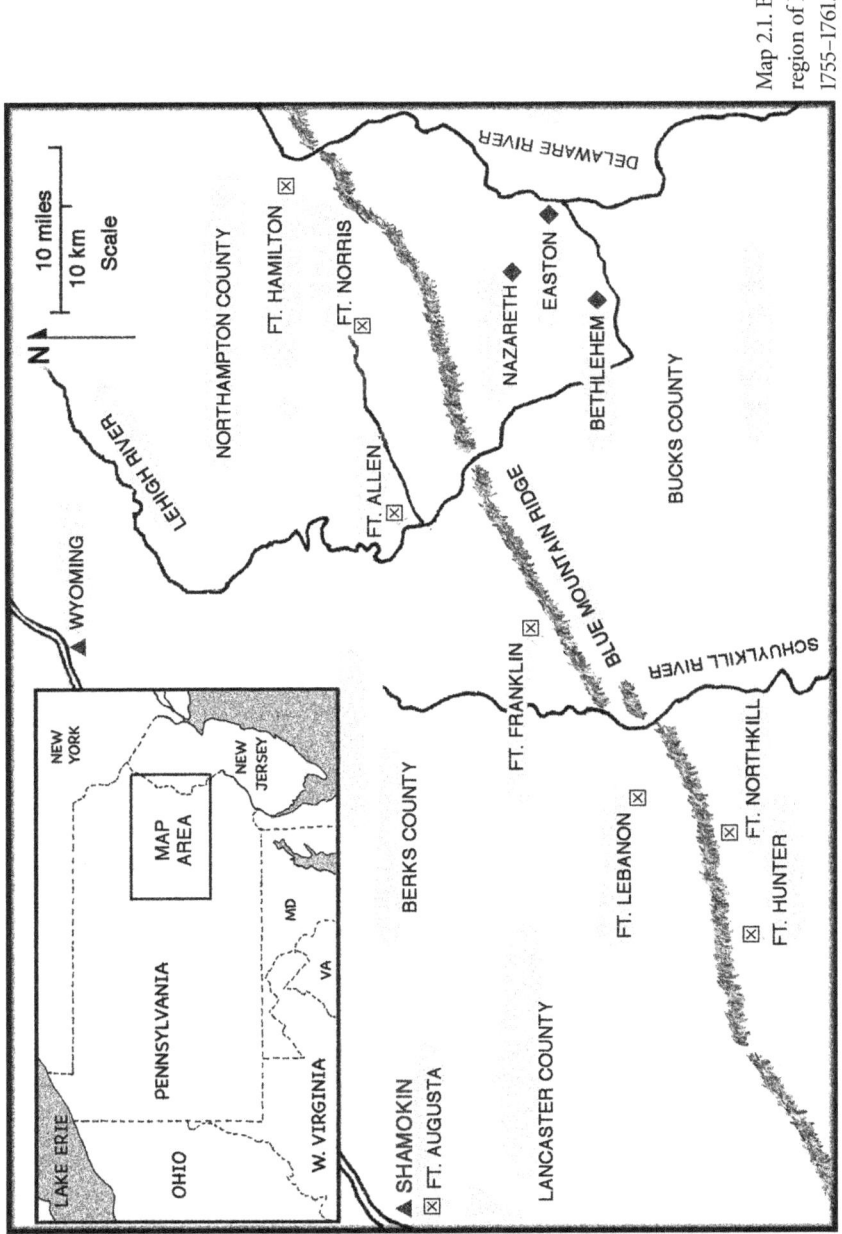

Map 2.1. Blue Mountain region of Pennsylvania, 1755–1761.

at the fork of two major waterways made it a natural trade center for goods moving into Pennsylvania from New Jersey, though it would take several decades for the town to find commercial success. Twelve miles to the west lay Bethlehem, another planned town with several hundred residents. But Bethlehem's municipal design concerned its society as well as its shape. Its population was ordered into "choirs" divided by gender, age, and marital status as part of a utopian, communal "General Economy" designed to maximize social and spiritual education. In contrast to Easton's polyglot ethnic population, Bethlehem's was relatively homogeneous: Moravian, German-speaking, communal, and almost uniformly literate. From Bethlehem one could travel west, past small settlers' farms, toward the towns of Northampton and Reading, or northeast to Bethlehem's sister town of Nazareth, about ten miles distant. Or a traveler could take the northern path parallel to the Lehigh River and head toward the river's water gap through the stony face of Blue Mountain. Thirty miles north of Bethlehem, on the north side of the ridge, lay Gnadenhütten, the most important of several Moravian-Indian mission towns scattered throughout the region.[2]

Gnadenhütten probably represented the zenith of ethnic diversity in Northampton County. Established in 1746 as a home for the Moravians' Mahican refugee-converts from New York, the town quickly became a center of Moravian and Native American activity. The town provided separate sections for its German, English, Mahican, and Delaware inhabitants. Its idyllic setting and tidy town plan and architecture probably did make it feel like the "little sylvan utopia" described by historian Anthony F. C. Wallace, except when its frequent European and Indian visitors complicated the town's communal idealism. Gnadenhütten's Christian Indian townsfolk did not give up their kinship ties or friendships with Native Americans throughout the region and far beyond. Because of this, both Christian and non-Christian Indians made Gnadenhütten their home, or at least a regular resting place. Owing to its location at a vital pass through the mountains, the site hosted passing traders and native visitors from many backgrounds. A newcomer to the region might be surprised to find a diverse multiethnic crowd at Gnadenhütten, gathered around a Moravian "love-feast," listening to sermons extolling vividly the glories of Christ's blood, or enjoying a trombone recital played expertly by resident Brethren. As the anchor of several Moravian mission towns, Gnadenhütten figured prominently in the order's proselytizing efforts. But with the outbreak of the Seven Years' War both the mission towns north of Blue Mountain and white settlements to the south would feel the sting of decades-old Delaware-white animosities.[3]

The Seven Years' War began in 1754 with Virginia's inability to remove expansionist French forces from the forks of the Ohio and Monongahela Rivers in western Pennsylvania. This immediately imposed crises of allegiance upon native groups from the Delaware River to the Great Lakes. Delawares themselves—British allies and supposed tributaries of the Six Nations Iroquois—were immediately disappointed with Lieutenant Colonel George Washington's blunders at Fort Necessity in 1754 and General Edward Braddock's disastrous expedition into the heart of Pennsylvania in 1755. Besides failing to challenge the French establishment of Fort Duquesne, Braddock further alienated Indian allies by arrogantly refusing their help and repeatedly insulting them. Many Delawares' allegiance to Pennsylvania was already stretched thin by years of trying to navigate the turbulent waters of diplomacy coursing between provincial officials, Iroquois diplomats, and fearful, suspicious white settlers while still trying to maintain the European trade upon which they had come to depend. By 1755, Britain and Pennsylvania had displayed only a pitiful lack of power and a total inability to protect their friends from the French and their native allies. Several Delawares responded by striking out in anger against their best targets of opportunity: the white settlers scattered throughout the Pennsylvania backcountry. In 1755 and 1756 Delawares raided white farms and settlements both north and south of the Blue Mountain ridge. Fearful traders refused to journey into the Susquehanna region. Trade ground to a halt, infuriating belligerent Indians further and impoverishing those who chose peace rather than war. Ineffective against the French threat in the Ohio Valley, Pennsylvanians now faced an uprising of their closest neighbors.[4]

As Susquehanna-region Delawares grew increasingly attached to French interests and threatened British settlements, those Delawares still allied with Pennsylvania requested that forts and trading posts be constructed near the multicultural Susquehanna towns of Shamokin and Wyoming to guard and supply those increasingly important population centers. In this request they found common cause with Pennsylvania's white settlers south of Blue Mountain, who also petitioned the province repeatedly for forts and troops to protect them against real or rumored Indian threats. Pennsylvania's remaining Delaware allies would be disappointed. The province was not yet willing to fund military outposts deep in Pennsylvania's interior in 1755. However, escalating Indian attacks forced the Assembly to consider providing frontier fortifications and troops to protect white settlements closer to Philadelphia. Northampton and Berks Counties' small towns and farms, perched precariously between Philadelphia and the Blue Mountain ridge, lacked sufficient arms and experienced military leaders to organize effective local militias. Panic and rumors spread quickly throughout the frontier, inflaming settlers' anti-native animosities. By November 1755 both white settlers and English-allied Indians were demanding greater provincial protection and a resumption of trade in the Blue Mountain region. As events would have it, one of the first forts to be built would serve both constituencies, albeit unexpectedly.[5]

Of immediate concern to the inhabitants of Easton and Bethlehem were reports of unfamiliar Indians seen near Gnadenhütten. Some of the town's native inhabitants and Moravian missionaries reported rumors that Delawares would soon attack the settlement, sending waves of fear throughout the region. Gnadenhütten's Indian converts had long been a source of suspicion for non-Christian Delawares living in Pennsylvania's interior, who saw the Moravian Indians as too closely allied to English settlement ambitions and too eager to reject native culture for European lifeways. Gnadenhütten's residents took the rumors and warnings seriously and planned to take refuge in Bethlehem until the danger passed, but tragedy struck before they could evacuate their village. On November 24, 1755, a large band of French-allied Munsee Delawares attacked Gnadenhütten, killing several inhabitants and partially burning the village. By attacking the mission town, the Munsees hoped to establish their ability to kill allies of the English and thwart provincial plans quickly and easily. Local white settlers began fleeing their homes and farms for the larger towns south of the mountains. Munsees attacked Gnadenhütten again on January 1, 1756, after a provincial militia company under the command of Captain William Hays arrived to protect the townspeople's corn stores and remaining property. Twenty of Hays's seventy-two men died in the attack, and more deserted after fleeing the town, reducing the company to only eighteen. Gnadenhütten itself was burned. The defeat of Hays's troops sent the region into full-blown panic. On January 3 a handful of Indians attacked settlers near Allemangel, a few miles from Gnadenhütten, and set the entire population of seventy people fleeing for their lives over Blue Mountain. With backcountry tensions at the breaking point, Philadelphians feared that these attacks on a peaceful mission town would bring the Delaware uprising into the populated heart of the province.[6]

If Gnadenhütten's attackers had hoped to drive a wedge between Christian Indians and their European friends, they must have been disappointed by the results. Terrified and impoverished by the loss of their village, and with few options open to them, Gnadenhütten's Delaware and Mahican residents sought refuge among the Moravians in Bethlehem and assured Governor Robert Morris of their loyalty to Pennsylvania and Britain. Morris commended the refugees and promised that they would receive aid commensurate with their status as Pennsylvanians. He also promised to build and garrison a fort at Gnadenhütten to help the refugees reclaim and guard their property, offering them "equal Security with the white people" on the frontier. Morris's goals were modest. "The Fort intended to be built will only be a Wooden one," Morris told the Bethlehem Moravians, "Or a Stockade thrown round the Buildings there, as shall be found most convenient." Pennsylvania's Assembly had already authorized a grant of £60,000 for frontier defense on November 26. Economy was essential: the fort at Gnadenhütten would be just one in a line of forts stretching along Blue Mountain from the Delaware River in the north to Maryland's border in the south. The original plan was to have the missionaries construct the fort on Moravian-donated land near the ruins of Gnadenhütten, but the Brethren had other ideas. Although they had already begun to fortify and arm Bethlehem to a degree unusual for pacifists, they claimed little expertise in fort construction and asked Easton's Justice William Parsons to undertake the project. Several members of Pennsylvania's assembly fanned out across the backcountry in December to help erect the new forts. The January attack on Hays's company accelerated their efforts.[7]

Benjamin Franklin arrived in Bethlehem in January 1756 to organize the Gnadenhütten fort-building expedition, and was appalled at the chaos in the Blue Mountain region and in the Moravian capital. Hundreds of white and native refugees had poured into Bethlehem, doubling the town's population. "We found this place fill'd with Refugees," Franklin wrote to Morris, "the Workmen's Shops, and even the Cellars being crouded with Women and Children." He warned the governor that all the regions' settlements were requesting additional troops. Lehigh Township had been entirely deserted after Hays's defeat. Refugees from the Irish settlement on the Lehigh promised to retreat from the area entirely unless thirty men could be sent to guard them and their property. Franklin was hesitant to begin moving troops around at the whim of panicked residents, especially refugees who had chosen to flee rather than to "behave like Men." He immediately ordered local magistrates to raise troops or risk losing their settlements and authorized a bounty of forty dollars per enemy Indian scalp. He also set out for Gnadenhütten with his fort-building party of 130 men and suggested to Morris that the province hurry in completing the "Ranging Line of Forts" as soon as possible. The thirty-mile march to Gnadenhütten was terrifying and intimidating for Franklin's detachment; much of the route was a desolate and frightening scene of burned farms and unburied bodies. Despite the risk to the exposed party from Delawares who had already proven their ability and inclination to attack large bodies of troops, the expedition arrived safely in Gnadenhütten on January 16 and began burying the dead, laying out their fort, and cutting palisades.[8]

Nine days later, Franklin declared the fort finished and named it for his friend William Allen, Pennsylvania's chief justice. The finished fort was 125 feet long and 50 feet wide, with triangular bastions, a twelve-foot-high palisade, a surrounding trench, and three buildings for the garrison. "We had one swivel Gun, which we mounted on one of the Angles," Franklin wrote later in his autobiography, "And fired it as soon as fix'd, to let the Indians know, if any were within hearing, that we had such Pieces, and thus our Fort (if such a magnificent Name may be given to so miserable a Stockade) was finished in a Week." He hoped that the "contemptible" fort would still be "a sufficient Defence against Indians who have no cannon." Despite his uncomplimentary description, the small fort was a substantial symbol for the chaotic Lehigh region. It was fairly well built despite its speedy construction, unlike Fort Franklin, the next fort down the defensive line, which would stand only for a few months. With a proper garrison, Fort Allen could serve to anchor the province's defense of the Lehigh region.[9]

Procuring and provisioning garrisons proved more difficult than building forts. By early February 1756 the project had nearly devoured the £60,000 authorized by the Assembly. Lack of experienced officers and proper measures for establishing military law and discipline also threatened the enterprise. Fort Allen's original garrison consisted of

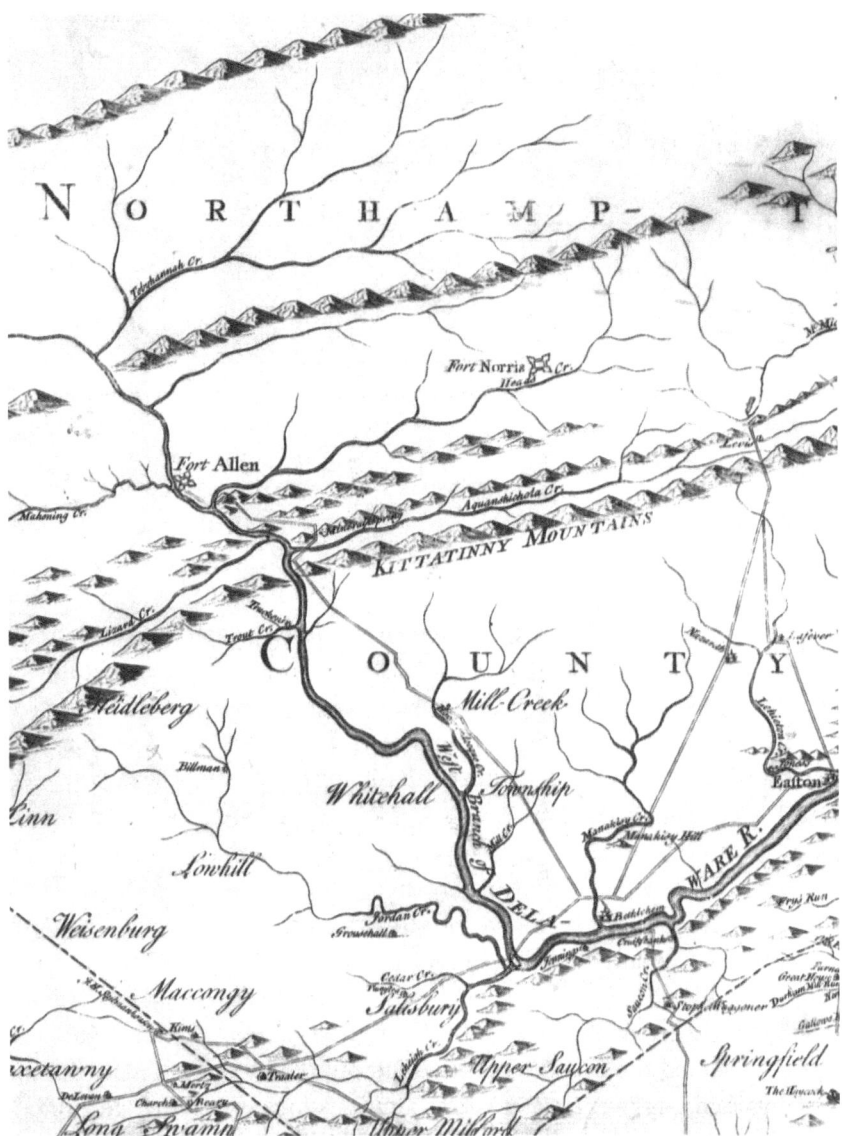

Fig. 2.1. This detail from Nicholas Scull's 1759 map of Pennsylvania shows Forts Allen and Norris, two of the outposts on the 1756 fort line. It also reveals the divided nature of Northampton County, with British settlements located mainly south of Blue (Kittatinny) Mountain. Fort Allen was a liminal space both culturally and geographically. Library of Congress, Geography and Map Division.

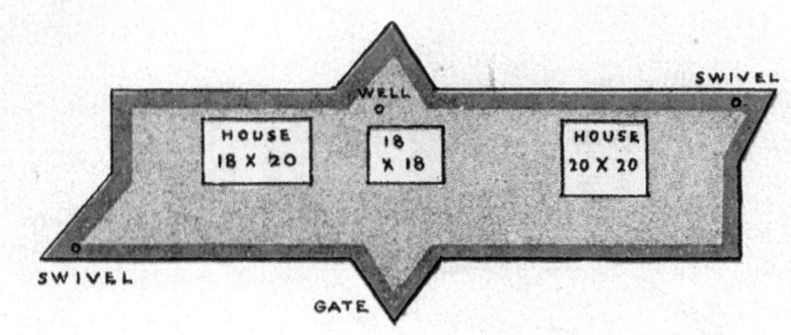

Fig. 2.2. Benjamin Franklin's plan of Fort Allen, 1756. From H. M. Richards, "The Indian Forts of the Blue Mountains" (1896). Courtesy of Bracken Library, Ball State University, Muncie, Indiana.

50 men under Captain Isaac Wayne, and the combined garrisons on the fort line totaled only 389 men. Many of them spent much of their time away from their forts, escorting wagon trains and friendly Indians, ranging the frontier, and protecting settlers if requested. Such duties stressed the undermanned militia units to their limits. Without sufficient numbers of well-trained soldiers and officers, the fort line garrisons were stretched too thin to guard against Indian incursions. Furthermore, it was increasingly clear that the original strategic basis for the fort line was unworkable. Pennsylvania's commissioners had hoped that after the frontier was secured and its women and children possessed safe refuges, provincial troops could invade the Susquehanna country. But settlers and militiamen were hesitant to join forays into Indian country, preferring to guard their own homes and towns. Attempts to motivate colonial raiding parties with scalp bounties failed. Settlers living under the constant threat of attack had little desire to further infuriate Munsees or other hostile natives, and they valued the fort line for the defense it offered them rather than for its role in any overall strategic scheme. As long as soldiers remained nearby, settlers were satisfied to wait out the situation and hope for the best.[10]

By the summer of 1756, Fort Allen had already fallen into a state of mismanagement and confusion. When James Young, Pennsylvania's commissary general of the musters, inspected the fort in June he found only fifteen men present and no one commanding the post. The rest of the garrison was scattered throughout the country between Fort Allen and Bethlehem, escorting friendly Indians and Moravian missionaries. Jacob Meis, the fort's commanding lieutenant, was in Easton petitioning for soldiers' back pay. Young could not even find most of the fort's provisions, though he noted seeing a "large Quantity of Beef very ill Cured." When Fort Allen's new commandant, Captain George Reynolds, arrived in late June, he reported the poor condition of the garrison and a shocking lack of decent arms and ammunition, "not above fifteen Gunes any ways Good." He asked Parsons for permission to raid Bethlehem's armories for decent munitions, but other, more farsighted fort commanders in the region had already coveted and confiscated some of the Moravian Brethren's best weapons. After six months the Blue Mountain forts had done little to improve the province's position in the ongoing Delaware war, and they seemed barely capable of maintaining their own garrisons and protecting the region.[11]

However ill-suited Fort Allen may have seemed as a protector of the region's settlers, it soon emerged as an inviting meeting place for Indians. In May 1756 an Iroquois delegation led by Seneca headman Kanuksusy, an influential British ally, arrived at the fort and settled in to await additional native ambassadors. Kanuksusy had asked several Indians to meet at Bethlehem during the summer to begin peace deliberations. The Moravian capital had been drowned in white and native refugees since the beginning of the year. "Most of our Rooms have been obliged to lodge 20 or 25 Persons and Seventy of our Indians have lived in one Small House where they had but 2 Rooms," wrote a Bethlehem resident in April. But many of the region's native denizens still preferred the cramped quarters of Bethlehem or the spartan confines of Fort Allen to the uncertainties of the Susquehanna region. For example, two Moravian Delawares, Nicodemus and his son Christian, had tried moving to the multicultural native town of Tioga near the New York border. When they learned that French-allied Munsees dominated the town, they fled back to the safety of Fort Allen and the protection of Kanuksusy. The influential Iroquois ambassador, along with Shawnee sachem "King" Paxinosa, persuaded both Bethlehem Moravians and Fort Allen militiamen to ensure the safety of visiting native ambassadors in preparation for a major peace conference to be held in Easton. However, that town had already become a haven for disgruntled refugee settlers and a major center of anti-Indian animosities. Vigilantes from New Jersey had crossed the Delaware River and set up shop in Easton, eager for confrontations with native visitors. With little but trouble awaiting them at Easton, native delegates lodged at Fort Allen were in no hurry to move on to the county seat. As the summer wore on, more native visitors continued to prefer the hospitality of Bethlehem or the Fort Allen area to the intolerant atmosphere of Easton.[12]

It is not unusual that Indians would expect comfort and hospitality from a fort built to defend the province against belligerent native interlopers. Hospitality toward visitors was a long-standing and fundamental fixture of Eastern Woodland Indian life. Throughout eastern North America, Indians felt obligated to extend generosity to their guests, and friendly visitors expected polite treatment when visiting allies or kin. This type of reciprocal social exchange helped prevent destructive conflicts between native groups and made traveling far from home bearable. Such effusive hospitality and forbearance was sure to create friction when tested against less patient Europeans. When Indians made extended visits to European towns and forts, their hosts sometimes complained, to other Europeans at least, about native "loitering." These descriptions pepper British documents of the period and point out a basic incongruity between native and European conceptions of manners and meetings in the colonial American woods. What was loitering for Europeans was an essential expectation in native culture. Indians would have found frustration with the length of a guest's stay disrespectful and offensive.[13]

In Pennsylvania, hospitality was planted firmly in native culture and was typically extended to Indian and European visitors alike. Moravian missionary David Zeisberger experienced Delaware hospitality personally after his arrival in Pennsylvania in the 1740s. He observed that it was a host's duty to "care for the wants of a guest as long as he may choose to remain and even to give him provisions for the journey when he does make up his mind to go." Food was always provided immediately to weary travelers. According to Zeisberger, "If the guests are from a distance and are very good friends, the whole kettle of food is set before them, they are given dishes and spoons and allowed to help themselves first to as much as they wish." Zeisberger's friend and fellow missionary John Heckewelder noted that on "more than one hundred instances" he had experienced this effusive brand of hospitality, and that it was not reserved exclusively for Indian guests: "A person is never left standing, there are seats for all; and if a dozen should follow each other in succession, all are provided with seats, and the stranger, if a white person, with the best." Heckewelder insisted that these favors were given out of a sense of social responsibility and that hosts would expect the same treatment themselves. But reciprocal hospitality did not imply a simple quid pro quo relationship, according to Heckewelder: "I have seen a number of instances in which a return was out of the question, where poverty would not admit of it, or distance of abode put it out of the power of the visitor to return the same civilities to his host; when white people are treated in this way, with the best entertainment the house affords, they may be sure it is nothing else than a mark of respect paid to them, and that the attentions they receive do not proceed from any interested view." Hospitable treatment became doubly important when guests were diplomats. Ambassadors on diplomatic missions usually enjoyed the comforts of a chief's house, and nothing would be spared to make such delegates feel welcome. To do otherwise would degrade a village headman's reputation and power among other villages or nations and weaken his status among his own people.[14]

Presenting guests with gifts was also an important component of native hospitality. Presents served as physical examples of generosity that went beyond supplying visitors with food and drink, which was expected of everyone. In Pennsylvania's native societies, where material goods and abstract favors were deemed to exist in a constant state of reciprocal redistribution, the exchange of presents served as a concrete example of love, alliance, and peaceful intentions. These obligations were especially important in times of great danger, as when help in battle was requested and given. Indian notions of generosity, hospitality, and reciprocal exchange permeated dealings between native groups and between Indians and Europeans. Such favors were not to be refused among friends. Presents and hospitable treatment were the glue that held friends together in the face of natural challenges and human belligerence. Pennsylvania's Delaware and Iroquoian allies had every reason to expect hospitable treatment at Fort Allen, especially those who risked life and limb by acting as go-betweens in the province's Indian-white conflicts.[15]

Fort Allen was perfectly situated for native visits. Its strategic location made it a familiar locale for travelers. Indians visiting the fort did not have to worry about interactions with local white settlers, most of whom kept their settlements south of Blue Mountain. Indeed, Fort Allen's location was a major source of contention with the white population of Northampton County; settlers preferred that the line of forts be located south of the ridge among their homes and farms. Perhaps because of the fort's location, maybe because of its frequent Indian visitors, or possibly because of the fort's relatively short existence, no white settlement or garrison community grew up near the fort. This was also a welcome development for native visitors, who detested the growth of white settlements much more than they did the establishment of forts. Instead of settlers' farms, temporary Indian shelters surrounded Fort Allen for much of its existence. There is little indication that the fort played host to female camp followers or white families, as was the case at larger British army forts like Ligonier and Pitt, at least in its first three years of service. Traders probably did not operate close to the fort before 1758, most likely because of the ongoing threat of native violence in backcountry during the Delaware uprising. But with Bethlehem and Easton only a day or two's journey away, provisions and supplies were easy to obtain when needed. Provincial troops were probably never crowded in the small fort, since the entire garrison was seldom present; troops were always away escorting travelers, protecting farmers' homesteads, or ranging the countryside. In many ways, Fort Allen was the kind of outpost that visiting Indians liked best: able to provide provisions and presents without the threat of permanent settler farms or overwhelming troop strength.[16]

If traveling Indians expected hospitable treatment at Fort Allen, their expectations were doubled for the upcoming Easton conference, where the presence of important provincial officials and hundreds of native delegates would ensure their safety and comfort. The provincial government and their Iroquois allies had called for the Easton conference as a way to stop Delawares' attacks and discover the sources of their animosities. As the date of the conference approached, Morris decided to concentrate as many displaced friendly Indians in the county seat as possible. He ordered that all Indian refugees and visitors be moved to Easton from Bethlehem to relieve crowding in the Moravian town and allow the province to aid the displaced natives. It devolved upon Parsons, as Easton's chief magistrate and the region's military commander, to prepare the town for their arrival. Easton must have been quite a sight during such treaty conferences. The Penns' idyllic, neatly surveyed county seat was near to bursting with townspeople, traders, white and Indian refugees, native ambassadors and their retinues, and armed New Jersey vigilantes. Morris asked Parsons to post plenty of guards to ensure that the Indians remained safe "from the Insults of the People," but also to watch the Indians themselves, "in case they should not be so Friendly as they pretend." In addition to those worries, Parsons needed to maintain order among the guards themselves. Easton's tavern keepers loved new customers and sold rum to Indians, townsfolk, and soldiers alike. With Indians, civilians, and soldiers "being all drunk," as Parsons complained, the town would be "in the Utmost Confusion and Danger" during the conference.[17]

On July 18 the guest of honor arrived. Teedyuscung, a Munsee headman living at Tioga whom the English sometimes called "King of the Delawares," had led a few violent forays against white settlements during the preceding months. His influence throughout the Susquehanna country, much of it a result of his own aggressive self-promotion, made his participation vital to securing peace. After carefully weighing the benefits that might accrue from alliances with the French or the British, Teedyuscung had decided that a British alliance was the best way for Pennsylvania Delawares to retain enough power to survive the complicated international contest for control of the region. However, his reputation as a drinker and reveler was as well known in the region as his status as a diplomat and headman. When he arrived in Easton he lost no time in taking advantage of the hospitality commonly offered at peace conferences. No traders had traveled up the Susquehanna for some time, and Teedyuscung hoped that he would find plenty of presents and rum available at the conference. Upon arrival he told Parsons that his journey from Tioga was a long way to go without any rum, and he continued hinting until Parsons supplied the chief with two small bottles. As the conference wore on the merriment continued, frustrating the conference's organizers but providing rare wartime entertainment for the native delegates. Morris's secretary, Richard Peters, reported that Teedyuscung and his "wild Company" started the conference off "perpetually Drunk, very much on the Gascoon [bragging], and at times abusive to the Inhabitants" of Easton. Peters found the "King of the Delawares" to be a formidable figure, describing the Munsee chief as a "lusty rawboned Man, haughty and very desirous of Respect and Command," who could supposedly "drink three Quarts or a Gallon of Rum a Day without being Drunk."[18] Even the experienced trader and diplomat Conrad Weiser had his hands full keeping Teedyuscung and other native diplomats on task during the conference.

The July 1756 Easton conference was only a preliminary meeting, designed to lay the groundwork for more substantive talks later in the fall. In the meantime, native diplomats clearly intended to take advantage of all the customary accoutrements of friendly diplomacy while they lasted.

Morris began to wonder if Easton, with its taverns and temperamental residents, might not be a poor place to conduct Indian diplomacy. But when the governor suggested moving the proceedings to Bethlehem or some other more placid location, Teedyuscung was indignant. He was having a good time in Easton and did not wish to be shuttled "from place to place like a Child." Morris relented and continued the conference at Easton. In the end, Teedyuscung and Kanuksusy agreed to convince other influential Delawares to meet again at Easton later in the year. But the summer conference's completion did not mean the end of the delegates' appetite for revelry. By then, Easton's townsfolk were ready for some peace and quiet, and Bethlehem still stretched at the seams with refugees. Luckily for Teedyuscung's retinue, another familiar, entertaining location lay just across the Blue Mountains.[19]

By early August, Teedyuscung had concluded his talks with Morris and had started his journey back to Wyoming and Tioga to convince rebellious Delawares to make peace with the province. On the way he stopped at Fort Allen to wait for his baggage train to catch up, and he enjoyed the garrison's hospitality so much that he settled in for a short stay. Teedyuscung was no stranger to the location; indeed, he was a past resident. From 1750 to 1754 he had lived (unhappily) as a Moravian convert at Gnadenhütten under the Christian name Gideon. Richard Peters was alarmed at news of Teedyuscung's "loitering" at the fort and insisted that the chief be sent on his way in order to convince Tioga's delegates to come to Easton before winter. Teedyuscung apologized and agreed to send two men to Tioga in his place, implying that he was comfortable where he was. He promised that when the men returned he would "make all Dispatch" in bringing the talks to a successful conclusion. Morris was surprised that Teedyuscung kept "loitering at a fort in so shameful a manner when he knows the necessity there is of his speedy Return to his People." He sent Parsons a string of wampum for the chief to urge him on his way. "Remind him how much he has to do and how little a time it is before the Winter will set in," Morris prodded Parsons impatiently. But trouble was brewing at Fort Allen. When Morris referred to Teedyuscung's "shameful" manner, Parsons thought he was referring to the chief's lack of dispatch. He would soon find that the matter was more complicated.[20]

Teedyuscung stayed at Fort Allen because of the availability of liquor there, and the corrupt conduct of the fort's temporary commandant, Lieutenant Miller. According to Teedyuscung's interpreter, Ben, the "villainous" lieutenant made good profits selling liquor to Indians and whites alike. "As long as the Indians had money," Ben told Parsons, "the Lieutenant sold them Rum, so that they were almost always drunk." Miller had also cheated the drunken Teedyuscung out of some deerskins, which had been intended as a present for Governor Morris. The prospect of a provincial officer cheating and delaying an important Indian delegate at such a critical point in peace negotiations was bad enough, but Parsons learned soon that the context of Teedyuscung's loitering was even more troubling. When Captain Reynolds returned to Fort Allen, he wrote to Parsons of having had some trouble with the visiting Indians. "I am resolved to let no more of them into ye fort for ye are So unruly that there is no Liveing with them," he reported. He added perfunctorily that while he was away in Philadelphia, some of the soldiers "got a little mery with the Liquor." Reynolds was gifted at understatement. That merriness was actually a full-fledged mutiny, prompted by a corporal, Christian Weyrick, and uncontrolled liquor availability.[21]

On August 5, Teedyuscung brought three women into the fort. While he "kept one as his own," according to Reynolds, the other two joked and cavorted with Miller and his sergeants. Jealous of the officers, the drunken Weyrick tried to have the women ejected from the fort. When Miller refused, the corporal assaulted him. Weyrick and two other men proceeded to behave "very undecently" with the women, washing their genitals with rum afterwards to prevent "Getting Sum Distemper of ye Squas." The mutineers then went on a full-fledged alcohol-fueled rampage, firing guns into the fort's walls and encouraging their comrades to take over the post and kill the several Reading militiamen who had sided with Miller. After hearing about the uprising, Parsons sent Captain Jacob Wetterhold to Fort Allen to arrest Weyrick for inciting the mutiny and Miller for not doing enough to suppress it. Upon his arrival, Wetterhold reported that the fort's ensign, who had also been absent, had already returned and brought the situation under control.[22]

Wetterhold confirmed that liquor was the probable engine of the dispute. Parsons responded by ordering the Indians' rum allowance lowered to one-quarter of a pint per day and restricting them to temporary shelters built outside the fort. He immediately informed Morris that the post's officers had apparently "turn'd ye Fort to a Dram Shop." Northampton County's justice of the peace, Timothy Horsfield, confirmed Parsons's report. "I've been told that Capt. Reynolds has had one hogshed of rum after another and sold it to his Men and Doubly to ye Indians and Every one that would give Money for it," he told Parsons. Fort Allen had gone from providing rum as Indian gifts and militia provisions to selling it as a commodity. From the provincial perspective, the danger to Pennsylvania's defensive and military imperatives was obvious. From Teedyuscung's cultural vantage, it was unacceptable to be barred from the fort and have his liquor restricted as if the mutiny had been his fault. He stormed away from Fort Allen in a huff. His role in the episode should not be idealized; he had "loitered" at the fort partially because liquor could be had there, apparently at affordable prices and in good supply. Still, he considered himself an ambassador on official provincial business and expected politeness and hospitality from the fort's commandant. Teedyuscung needed no correction or punishment, as Horsfield knew well. The fort's garrison and officers had failed in their mission to guard the province and support its diplomatic efforts. Teedyuscung needed to be hurried upon his way, but Horsfield also understood that the situation required tact and understanding of the Munsee headman's point of view.[23]

Unrest at Fort Allen threatened to upset the province's peace plans, and Pennsylvania's Assembly acted quickly to clean up the mess. The Provincial Council recommended that Conrad Weiser and Parsons be sent to Fort Allen to punish Lieutenant Miller, reestablish order, and urge Teedyuscung on his way. Morris, no longer governor but still in attendance at the council (he had been succeeded by William Denny in the interim), suggested that Kanuksusy be sent to the Six Nations to ask what their leaders thought of Teedyuscung's loitering and rumored acts of sedition. Denny immediately ordered Weiser to look into the affair and make any inquiries and arrests he deemed necessary. After spending over £60,000 on frontier defenses, Pennsylvania's government could not allow one of its own forts to endanger the peace of the region it had been charged to protect.[24]

As the governor and council tried to minimize the diplomatic damage caused by the mutiny, Horsfield arrived at Fort Allen and set about placating an ill-tempered Teedyuscung. He caught up with the chief (who had angrily left the fort) and apologized for the misunderstanding, promised to punish Miller, and agreed to forward the controversial deerskins to Morris. Appreciative of Horsfield's efforts, Teedyuscung agreed to accompany him back to the fort and then to hurry on with his mission to Wyoming. When they arrived at Fort Allen, they found that Reynolds and his ensign had abandoned the fort (again) and that the post was under the temporary command of the "sober and prudent" Lieutenant Geiger of Wetterhold's company. By then Horsfield had confirmed that Reynolds and Miller had "made a Tippeling House of the Fort," writing to Morris that "Several of the Men after a Deduction of all their pay remain 14 or 15 [pounds] indebted to their Capt. for Liquor." Horsfield promised to restrict all rum and punch sales indefinitely, hoping that this would take care of the lack of discipline. Weiser and Parsons decided to go further; apparently, the officers' malfeasance had sunk too deeply into the garrison's structure. They determined that Fort Allen's entire complement of troops must be removed to alleviate the culture of corruption. Their solution was to switch garrisons with one of the nearby forts. Reynolds and his whole garrison ended up at nearby Fort Norris, and that fort's complement, led by Captain Jacob Orndt, arrived at Fort Allen just in time to host Teedyuscung and his retinue one last time before he returned to the north.[25]

Teedyuscung wasted little time in finishing his business at Tioga and Wyoming. On October 9 he sent word to Orndt and Reynolds that he was waiting at Wyoming and that he would soon deliver several white prisoners to comply with treaty obligations. But Teedyuscung had heard rumors that if he brought a large party to Fort Allen or Easton, the English would kill them all, so he thought it prudent to send one Indian with one prisoner to Fort Allen to make sure his people would be safe. Orndt, who expected a large number of Delawares and Iroquois to pass by his fort on their way to the autumn Easton conference and wanted no repeat of the summer's events, ordered a shelter built well away from the fort for Teedyuscung's band and awaited his arrival. Three weeks passed with no sign of Teedyuscung, but plenty of other Delawares soon made themselves comfortable at Fort Allen. More than one hundred Minisinks set up camps near the fort, reportedly planning to seek a separate treaty with the province. Denny was at a loss regarding to deal with them; Sir William Johnson had just been appointed Indian superintendent for the entire Northern District, and the provincial government did not yet know how much of their diplomatic responsibilities he was to assume. The council advised Denny to offer the Minisinks supplies, gifts, and friendship but also to inform them that Pennsylvania could not make a separate peace with Indians who might continue to attack neighboring colonies. News of the Minisinks' arrival came amid new reports of violence in the region:

several settlers had been attacked near Forts Lebanon and Northkill, farther south on the defensive line. Fort Lebanon's commander admitted that the outposts were "too weak to be of any Service to the Frontier" in the face of a large-scale Indian attack or siege. A force of more than one hundred Minisinks could easily overcome tiny Fort Allen and threaten to disrupt the Easton conference if they decided to pursue conflict instead of diplomacy.[26]

It was Teedyuscung's strategy and promises of hospitality, not any nefarious intent, that caused the Minisinks to wait out the Easton conference near Fort Allen. By November 6 Teedyuscung had arrived at Easton, but rumors swirled about a possible Minisink attack on the conference. To combat the rumors, Denny and Teedyuscung sent out Delaware headman Tatamy to meet with the Minisink bands and invite them to the conference. The Minisinks refused politely, saying they preferred the area around Fort Allen and had already arranged with Teedyuscung that they should remain there. As for the treaty talks, they assured Tatamy that they would agree to any terms that Teedyuscung could secure. Back at the conference, Teedyuscung confirmed that the Minisinks had originally agreed to travel "no further than a certain Place" and to allow him to negotiate in their stead. At first glance, the Minisink presence seemed to be a powerful negotiating chip for the Munsee chief. With 140 armed Delawares ready to attack the most vital fort on the frontier line, and with Easton filled to capacity with Delaware and Iroquois delegates, Denny might feel obliged to give Teedyuscung excellent terms. However, Weiser soon began to wonder if the Minisinks' choice of Fort Allen was based more on their preference for the location than on their desire to provide Teedyuscung with negotiating heft.[27]

By this time, Fort Allen had become a principal gateway through the Blue Mountains and into Northampton County for Susquehanna-region Delawares. Rum remained available near the fort, despite orders to limit its sale in the area during the conference. Weiser and his troops could not realistically be expected to enforce liquor regulations; they spent most of their time escorting Indians back and forth between Fort Allen and Easton. To ensure good conduct among the encamped Minisinks, Weiser appointed Teedyuscung to act as a liaison between Fort Allen and the Minisink bands. To Weiser's dismay, his emissary spent most of his time trying to acquire rum so that he might "have a Frolick with his Company" at the fort. Weiser offered liquor to Teedyuscung's party on the condition that they consume it only in the Indian camp outside the fort, warning that if any Indians tried to enter the fort "they must take what follows." That the threat was considered an empty one became clear when one of Teedyuscung's drunken companions tried to climb the palisade one night and shouted curses to the effect of "Damn you all I value you not!" after Weiser made him jump down. Fort Allen's garrison spent a few anxious weeks surrounded by the Minisinks, many of whom spent their time enjoying the availability of liquor in the fort's neighborhood.[28]

To the province's great relief, the autumn Easton conference ended without any serious trouble near Fort Allen. By December, most of the attendees had been escorted back across Blue Mountain and into the Susquehanna country. The province had much work to do: Teedyuscung and other delegates had surprised everyone by claiming that Pennsylvania's fraudulent Walking Purchase land grab of 1737 was the basis for their war. They demanded that the province assuage Delaware chiefs on that matter before they would agree to a final treaty. Events of 1756 had been instructive to visiting Delawares. From a purely social perspective, they had found that Pennsylvanians would protect them while they were in Easton and other towns, rather than kill them, as backcountry rumors continued to assert. They also learned that Fort Allen offered them little in the way of intimidation. Indeed, the small fort tucked on the north side of the Blue Mountains was quickly becoming a favorite Indian place.[29]

Ongoing treaty deliberations throughout 1757 continued to make Fort Allen a desirable stopping point for Delaware and Iroquois delegates and their retinues. Before the winter had passed, more of Teedyuscung's people began to filter into the fort's locale. First came seven women and three children from Tioga, who arrived at the fort in mid-February in advance of Teedyuscung's main company. While Orndt was happy to provision the small party, Parsons suggested they might be better off under the Moravians' care in Bethlehem. Orndt and Parsons probably wished to avoid a replay of the 1756 mutiny and felt that seven unaccompanied Delaware women might provoke too many distractions among the fort's anxious and frequently disgruntled garrison. Parsons also felt that the women and children might be more comfortable with other Indians until their own party arrived, and Bethlehem still seethed with Indian refugees. With a much larger party scheduled to arrive the following month, the province could ill-afford any unpleasantness to befall Teedyuscung's people.[30]

Teedyuscung's main party arrived at Fort Allen at the end of March

1757, though without the "King" himself. The fifty men, women, and children, led by Teedyuscung's two sons and his brother, Captain Harris, proceeded to make themselves at home. "They behave very civil here," reported a relieved Orndt. "They have made Cabbins about 60 perches from the Fort, where they live, and intend to tarry here till the King comes." Even though the visiting Indians maintained their own shelters, Orndt had trouble preventing rum-induced problems. His orders forbade liquor sales at the fort, but visiting Indians still found ways to procure it, especially when visiting Easton on official business. On one occasion, when Orndt sent Indian emissaries to Easton with a military escort the emissaries found and purchased so much rum that some of them "stay'd all Night in the Woods, and the remainder went . . . to Bethlehem," where Orndt feared "there might easily happen any Misbehaviour."[31]

In the middle of April, Teedyuscung sent word from Tioga. He requested that provisions for his journey be sent up to Fort Allen, where his people could then bring them to Tioga on horseback. Denny could not turn him down easily. Fort Allen had become more than a comfortable place for Indian wayfarers. Teedyuscung viewed it as a temporary way station between his country and the English settlements, and keeping a native presence there cemented the fort's position as an Indian-English outpost of importance. Besides, Denny believed it was better that the Munsees await Teedyuscung's arrival at Fort Allen than at Easton, where they were "always in the Way of strong Liquor & in Danger" from intolerant residents. Fort Allen's position as a temporary military outpost had become complicated: in order to protect Indians with whom the province must make peace, the fort must endure the presence of large groups of them before, and probably after, that peace had been achieved. This required the fort to maintain a constant state of alert, at least until Teedyuscung arrived and removed his waiting entourage. Parsons told Horsfield to be ready for Teedyuscung and to have dozens of wagons available to take the King and his baggage to Philadelphia. A few days later the problem took care of itself. The large band encamped near the fort grew tired of waiting for Teedyuscung and left their temporary lodgings, possibly to return home in time to plant corn.[32]

In early July, Teedyuscung arrived at Fort Allen. His large band of delegates and followers strained the provisions of the entire region. Teedyuscung brought along two hundred men, women, and children and expected to stay at the fort for six to seven days. During that time he expected to meet one hundred Senecas at Fort Allen, and then the whole mass of people would have to be shuttled to Easton, where Denny had agreed to meet with them once again. Throughout the month, Orndt and his soldiers continually transferred Indians back and forth between Fort Allen and Easton, a job made less easy by apprehensive settlers and wary Indian emissaries. During the July conference, 285 native travelers went to Easton by way of Fort Allen (112 men, 67 women, and 106 children), though during this period Indians constantly shuttled back and forth between Easton and the fort, and there were always some encamped near the fort. Satisfied by an interim peace arrangement with Denny, Teedyuscung and his party arrived back at Fort Allen on August 13. He and his band took advantage of the fort's hospitality for several more days before departing, "very glad and joyful," on August 17. Several "sick" families stayed on at Fort Allen. September found Teedyuscung still in the region, lingering in overcrowded Bethlehem while awaiting his son's return from a diplomatic trip to the Ohio country. By late 1757 the Fort Allen–Bethlehem corridor had become a familiar, friendly place for Susquehanna natives. Eager to avoid anything that might "give Disgust" to Delawares and threaten the ongoing peace process, Denny tacitly allowed an almost constant native presence at Fort Allen and in the nearby region.[33]

Pennsylvania's settlers unintentionally encouraged this fretful atmosphere of hospitality by demanding the continued presence of forts and garrisons. Settlers in Northampton and Berks Counties petitioned Denny in May 1757 to protect them from reported incursions of Ohio-region Indians. With peace efforts ongoing, settlers feared justifiably that the sparsely garrisoned forts and blockhouses would soon be abandoned entirely. Fort Franklin had never been tenable and was abandoned in November 1756. Forts Norris and Hamilton were still garrisoned, but both would be abandoned within a few months. As violence continued in the Pennsylvania backcountry, petitioners asked that more men be sent to the frontiers and that Fort Allen and other forts be maintained, either not knowing or not caring that the forts' roles as diplomatic posts could encourage a persisting Indian presence in the region. In September, Benjamin Franklin defended the expense of maintaining the several forts and blockhouses and more than eleven hundred men on the frontier, claiming that this policy kept settlers from abandoning their homes altogether.

But with peace negotiations near completion, any forts that remained in the Pennsylvania backcountry would serve mainly to meet Indian needs rather than to allay settlers' fears.[34]

Fort Allen's diplomatic role was prioritized over defense by 1758, and as such only a small military complement was merited. In February, Orndt's garrison consisted of 78 men, though later in the year as few as 50 men occupied the fort. Even the complement of 78 was small compared with that of Fort Augusta (362 men) and smaller Forts Henry (105) and Littleton (110). In addition to being undermanned, the fort was badly in need of repairs that the province was hesitant to fund. Because of Fort Allen's diminished military role and poor condition, rumors of its imminent closing spread in the region throughout 1758, prompting more petitions from fearful local settlers. They need not have worried. Despite the fort's disheveled state and small garrison, Fort Allen would remain necessary as an Indian way station as long as native diplomats and their parties continued to travel through the Blue Mountains. As early as April 1758, Fort Allen had achieved the status of an official diplomatic checkpoint, "the Place where the Susquehannah Indians are by Treaty obliged first to come to, when they arrive on Our Frontiers," according to Denny. With its small garrison and ramshackle condition, Fort Allen remained an important stopover for natives even as threats posed by Delaware hostilities began to subside.[35]

Indians visiting Fort Allen and living nearby often assisted English authorities in ranging the woods for enemies. In doing so, they furthered the peace process while helping to maintain the fort's status as a welcome haven for traveling Delawares. Orndt had always employed Indians, usually Christian converts from Bethlehem, to range the countryside around the fort, but by April 1758 it had become more difficult for him to find reliable native rangers, mainly because of available alcohol. Despite his attempts to limit liquor sales at the fort, Orndt complained that the rangers were "continually drunk," having bought "whole Casks of Rum" in Easton. When Delaware allies could not purchase liquor near the fort, they still expected to be provisioned. "There is dayly Indians Passing and Repassing, and they want Suplys from us," reported a frustrated John Bull, Orndt's successor as Fort Allen's commander, in the summer of 1758. Reduced funding for frontier defenses made such provisioning difficult, but Fort Allen's position as a diplomatic station made it a necessity, at least for the moment.[36]

By 1758, traders near Fort Allen were responding to consumer demand by supplying visiting Indians with liquor. There was little the fort's small complement could do to battle the traders, who openly defied provincial restrictions on alcohol sales. For example, in June 1758 Bull found out that Hans Bowman, a trader who operated five miles from the fort, had "given" five gallons of whiskey to Gabriel Loquus, a visiting Delaware. Outraged, Bull sent a few soldiers to remind Bowman that selling liquor to the Indians was prohibited and could cause civil unrest and violence. The trader replied that the liquor was merely a present for Loquus, that he would give gifts to whomever he pleased, and that not even Fort Allen's troops could stop him. Bull could do little but ignore the incident; arresting Bowman would only offend native visitors and local white settlers. Because of their constant escort responsibilities, the fort's troops could not effectively control consumer affairs in the Northampton County backcountry.[37]

Throughout the summer of 1758, hundreds of Indians moved through the Lehigh water gap, many enjoying lengthy stays at the fort. On June 29, Teedyuscung and fifty Delawares and Iroquois arrived at Fort Allen, hoping to meet with Denny at Germantown a few days later. Bull sent the entire party on to Bethlehem under escort, ordering his men to hand them over to Horsfield and return. With Indians lingering near the fort in search of trade and alcohol, Bull could hardly afford to weaken his force by giving up men for escort duty. Orndt had already lost a detachment of men to General John Forbes's 1758 expedition against Fort Duquesne, and Bull's garrison at Fort Allen had been reduced to thirty men. Pennsylvania had begun to devalue what was left of the defensive chain of forts in favor of more proactive measures against the French and their Indian allies. Teedyuscung returned to the fort in July and settled in for another stay. He sought to position himself strategically to influence British and native diplomatic and military initiatives. He also tried to coerce Denny into sending regular supplies of arms and powder to the fort for his Indian allies. Many could be expected to visit, especially with more treaty talks scheduled at Easton for late 1758. On September 12, Orndt informed Denny that 128 Indians had arrived at Fort Allen "and intended to stay there." From then on, Fort Allen would almost always host more Indians than white Pennsylvanians.[38]

With the date of the new treaty conference fast approaching, Denny moved to limit the hospitable drinking culture near the fort and, even more importantly, at the conference locations. In the summer of 1758 he had already posted an official notice threatening imprisonment for anyone who sold liquor to Teedyuscung and his party during their summer visits. But as more Indians poured into Northampton County in August and September, individual traders and tavern keepers continued to supply Indians with liquor, using their nonofficial status as "private persons" to skirt regulations. Denny knew perfectly well that profit was not always the motive, and that some native and Pennsylvanian parties could gain much by the "Prejudice and Hindrance of the Business" that liquor could provide at important treaty conferences. To prevent such disruptions at Easton, Denny outlawed liquor gifts and sales entirely, "upon any Pretence whatsoever," except by authorized Indian agents. But many Indians came to the conferences expecting entertainment, liquor, and gifts, and Denny could not hope to prohibit them entirely. The province could, however, change Fort Allen's role from a purely defensive outpost and diplomatic transfer point into a place that took better advantage of a steady supply of native consumers.[39]

During the Easton Conference of October 1758, Denny surprised the several Indians present by announcing that Fort Allen would soon become a trading post. In April of that year the province had passed an act enabling a board of Indian commissioners to establish trading posts where they thought most fit. Placed at or near manned forts and overseen by Indian agents, they would prevent "Abuses in the Indian Trade" by traders like Hans Bowman and would supply "Indians, Friends and Allies of Great Britain" with "Goods at more easy Rates." It was hoped that this would help cement the favorable Indian-white relations established at Easton. Fort Augusta, at Shamokin, had already opened a trading post in May 1758, and in October Denny announced to Teedyuscung and many conference attendees that Shamokin was open for business. "The Indians may be Supplied at the most reasonable Rates with any goods they may want," he announced, "And the best Prices will be given to you for such Skins, Furs, and Peltry as you shall bring them." Another trading post would soon be opened at Fort Allen, where Indian consumers could "depend upon it" that Indian agents would ensure the "Strictest Justice" in all dealings there. Robert Tuckness became Fort Allen's first Indian agent on December 11; by December 21 "Quantities of Indian Goods" had arrived at the post, which Denny hoped would please the Susquehanna people and attach them firmly to Britain's interests. It was also hoped that an authorized post at Fort Allen would reduce the influence of unscrupulous traders in the region and transform Indian traffic at the post from a financial drain into a profitable coexistence. Far from its original purpose of providing safety for Blue Mountain settlers and staging invasions against Delawares, the Fort Allen trading post actually became dependent on a regular Indian presence.[40]

During its short tenure as a trading post, Fort Allen enjoyed a relatively robust business. From December 1758 through May 1760 the Pennsylvania Commissioners for Indian Affairs recorded sales amounting to just over £2,333. According to entries in the Fort Allen Daybook for the period of October 1759 through April 1760, the trading post offered a wide variety of goods for settlers and Indians alike. Items sold at Fort Allen were typical of those found at trading posts throughout the Northeast and show the depth to which European trade had infiltrated native material culture. European clothing and textiles are well represented in the Daybook accounts, both utilitarian (shirts and strouds) and fancy ("nonesopretties"). Tools, construction materials, cooking implements, guns, ammunition, decorations, animal tack, locks, and even mousetraps were traded and sold at the post. In return, the traders took cash and every kind of peltry available, mainly deer and beaver, but also mink, martin, and panther. However, despite this fairly robust business, economics dictated that the store's tenure would be short. Trading posts may have contributed to easing tensions between the province and Pennsylvania's Indians and in meeting visiting natives' material needs, but the economic returns never overcame the costs of goods, shipping, and maintaining enough soldiers in the field to protect the trade. At the same time, Fort Allen's diplomatic role began to diminish. Sir William Johnson's Indian Department had taken over most Indian diplomacy by 1758, and Easton would host only one more major Indian conference, in 1761. By January 1760 the province had further reduced Fort Allen's complement to two officers, two sergeants, and twenty-one privates. Fort Allen even proved unable to serve as an effective outpost for equipping Indian diplomatic expeditions. By the summer of 1760, inexperienced leaders, desertions, and mismanagement of stores had made Fort Allen nearly unsustainable.[41]

By late 1760 the province began to consider closing Fort Allen. There was certainly no shortage of Indians near the fort; in fact, one hundred Indians arrived there on August 6 on their way to Philadelphia. The fort's commandant, Lieutenant Andrew Wackerberg, kept native travelers supplied with provisions and rum, despite orders to the contrary. But Fort

Allen had outlived its usefulness, and the Assembly refused to fund it beyond January 1761. Peters ordered Horsfield to pay off and discharge Fort Allen's garrison and take custody of the arms, ammunition, and stores left at the post. On April 27, Horsfield declared the fort closed and returned the land to the Moravian Brethren. In a final ignominy, Indians attending the Easton conference in August 1761 raided Fort Allen, hoping to loot its remaining stores, but found nothing there but a few squatters, one of whom was Lieutenant Wackerberg.[42]

Fort Allen's ignominious end was not unusual. Hundreds of forts, stockades, and blockhouses rose up in the colonial backcountry during the Seven Years' War, only to crumble and return to the earth or be scavenged for materials after their usefulness waned. Nor was it unusual that intercultural contact and negotiation helped redefine the outpost's mission. Colonial militias and the British army built forts for military imperatives, but they almost always saw those imperatives augmented and complicated by Indians, settlers (both men and women), colonial politicians and diplomats, and economic concerns. That native cultures helped determine the identities of remote outposts should surprise no one. Forts were built in Indian country, out of the raw materials found there, and some were bound almost as much by the cultural customs that prevailed among Native Americans as by the colonial imperatives the fort builders brought with them. This often produced surprising and frustrating results. Hospitality and diplomacy defined Fort Allen's ultimate role in Indian-white relations and infused its mission with anxiety and confusion. The fort was designed to stage an invasion against Indians, but instead it became a welcome resting place for them. It never suffered an attack, except by some of its own garrison. Missionaries, not military planners, determined its location. For a brief period, Fort Allen even served as an illegal tavern of sorts. But its use by native visitors made it a link in the chain of Indian-white reciprocal relations. Instead of being a military post intended to keep Indians and Europeans apart, it became a diplomatic post that brought them together. In this respect it was not alone. Throughout North America, military outposts that were meant to introduce European culture, resolve, and domination into Indian country had their identities reshaped by the complexities of Indian-European politics and intercultural contact. Fort Allen became an example of how tiny, short-lived backcountry contact points could, in their own small ways, redefine Indian-European contact and coexistence.

In Franklin's autobiography, the great man seemed embarrassed by the rough little fort he and his men built during the Delaware War. But, of course, he left the region quickly and never enjoyed the post's hospitality. Had Teedyuscung left a memoir, his description of Fort Allen might have been more agreeable.

3

The Greatest Mart of All Trade

Food, Drink, and Interdependence at Michilimackinac, 1761–1796

By the end of the British occupation of the Straits of Mackinac, longtime residents of the region might have been surprised to hear Kegeweskam, a powerful and influential Odawa chief, complain that his people's lives there were nearly finished. He described his settlement of L'Arbre Croche, once a bountiful agricultural center, as a dead place, a sad remnant to be pitied. He professed hope that the subsistence gained from their exhausted cornfields and whatever fish they could catch would be enough to save his people, but he feared that the tide had turned. Once, the French and British occupants of the Straits depended on Odawa and Ojibwa foodways to survive. Now Kegeweskam claimed that his people must have help from the Europeans or die starving in their own land.[1]

Kegeweskam's complaints were almost surely overstated. L'Arbre Croche remained a prominent corn-producing post until well into the nineteenth century. Native American leaders frequently used claims of poverty as diplomatic levers. But the chief's rhetorical flourishes leave the reader with an unmistakable impression of actual environmental and cultural loss. The easy course would be for readers to telescope into a future of perceived native cultural degradation, but that would mistake this turn of fortune as the result of an inevitable process of invasion, dislocation, and oppression. The arrival of the European fur trade and its supplies of manufactured trade goods, quickly adopted and appreciated by Indian consumers, changed the logistics of everyday life at the Straits. By the end of the seventeenth century, peoples of the Great Lakes basin had adapted their lifeways around the European trade. In a teleological view, from the point of view of the survivors, this European alteration of native lives in the Mackinac Straits can appear to have been an unstoppable, inevitable cultural juggernaut. But this was not the reality experienced by the Odawas, Ojibwas, and many others who knew and appreciated the natural gifts of the region centuries before the French and British ever saw the Great Lakes.

Northern Great Lakes Indians were influenced negatively by European expansion in the region, but the story of the British occupation of Fort Michilimackinac is not only one of Indian loss. The fur trade did help bring about the partial dissolution of Indian traditions and power in the region, and the fort maintained by British troops for thirty-five years protected that trade and its tradesmen and voyageurs. But Mackinac's forts were hardly engines of intimidation for native residents at the Straits. Rather, the forts acted as markets, drawing Indians from hundreds of miles around to trade their furs, buy trade goods and provisions, and renew their reciprocal trade agreements with European authorities. Indians valued the fur trade for the advantages that European goods gave them, and demanded trading posts and traders in Indian country. Though most trading took place in the natives' villages, traders kept houses near the post. Fort commandants also gave gifts to Indian visitors to maintain friendship and reciprocity in the Great Lakes economic system. During the French occupation of Michilimackinac, visiting Indians probably made little distinction between the small French fort and palisaded native villages. During the British period, larger garrisons and more impressive edifices were meant to impress and awe Indians, especially during the wars of the late eighteenth century, in which Indians and Europeans allied with and fought against each other. Indian awe proved more difficult to elicit than many Europeans expected. Indians outnumbered Europeans throughout the entire British period at Michilimackinac, reminding the newcomers constantly of their importance in the region.

Efforts to procure food at remote outposts like Michilimackinac displayed this localized Indian-European social and economic parity. European military and diplomatic efforts to manage trade and gain advantages over Indians in the Great Lakes basin certainly loomed large in deciding the outcome of the contest for cultural supremacy in North America. However, local, everyday concerns such as provisioning complicate the picture. Large-scale naval freighting on the lakes became viable during the British occupation of Michilimackinac, making outside provisioning much more efficient than during the earlier French tenure. But despite the best efforts of British quartermasters to provision the lake posts, outside supplies could not fulfill all the dietary needs of Michilimackinac. Unlike Forts Loudoun and Allen, small provincial forts built for temporary wartime expediency, Michilimackinac was an imperial post with long-term military and political significance to Great Britain. The British post at the Straits typically contained more than one hundred soldiers, was almost four hundred miles from Detroit, and greeted thousands of native visitors every summer. Throughout the British occupation, soldiers necessarily depended in part on local foodways and native food suppliers. At the same time, the fur trade changed native material culture significantly. This was especially true regarding alcohol, a trade good that only Europeans could supply, and one that Indians increasingly demanded on their trips to the post. Food and drink defined an interdependent relationship between British newcomers and natives at Michilimackinac that complicates later arguments for economic determinism and inevitable native demise.[2]

Many of the groups that would eventually call the Mackinac region home were Algonquian-speaking peoples displaced by Iroquois expansion west and north during the mid-seventeenth century. Iroquois attacks nearly destroyed Huron culture, and scattered other Iroquoian and Algonquian groups into the Great Lakes basin and further west. In some cases, lifeways and traditions merged in multiethnic refugee villages, creating the ethnic, linguistic, and political divisions later identified and redefined by the earliest European observers. In other cases, Great Lakes Indians maintained traditional lands and kinship networks in the face of these demographic changes. This dramatic profusion of cultures in the mid-seventeenth century makes describing traditional foodways in the region problematic. All descriptions of the ways Odawas, Ojibwas, Potawatomis, Nipissings, and other native peoples of the northern Great Lakes region found, traded, created, and prepared food are based upon the accounts and observations of early French missionaries, traders, and adventurers. But generalizations can still be made about pre-contact Indian foodways from the common practices that survived into the contact period. To one degree or another, almost all Great Lakes natives hunted, fished, and cultivated plants for sustenance. In the ecologically fragile world of the upper Great Lakes, with its six to eight months of freezing temperatures and snowfall measured in yards, Indians worked both with and against nature to provide sustenance, using methods honed and tested over many centuries.[3]

Anthropologists identify prehistoric Indians as horticulturists, agriculturists, and gatherers to describe how they obtained their vegetable food. However, any implications of agricultural lethargy or primitivism are misplaced in describing people who had cultivated plants for thousands of years. Archaeologists have shown that people of the Early Woodland Adena culture cultivated squash well over two thousand years ago. Squash was one of the nutritional "three sisters" crucial to later Eastern Woodland foodways. After about 100 BCE, their Hopewell successors carried on and expanded horticulture, planting larger garden plots and living in more sedentary villages. Mississippian groups expanded even further into the cultivation of large fields of beans and corn, the remaining two "sisters" of the trio.[4]

Maize constituted a vital source of nutrition for contact-era Indians. It could be planted easily in a variety of soil conditions and required little maintenance. Clear-burning fields provided easy fertilization, and as seed the maize kernel was highly reproductive; one kernel could provide up to two hundred kernels for consumption. Combined with squash and beans, maize provided a combination of essential nutrients unsurpassed in any culture or continent. Even so, Indian agriculture was not completely reliable or assuredly bountiful. Untimely frosts, insect infestation, and drought could all affect crop productivity. Ascertaining agricultural success in the early contact period is problematic, since European visitors may have overstated bountiful native crop yields in their exuberant relations to the Old World. Still, maize, beans, and squash proved to be hardy and dependable crops in supporting both sedentary and mobile lifeways in the rugged country north and east of the Great Lakes and in most other parts of eastern North America.[5]

Indians augmented their vegetable crops with wild game and fish. Because Indians did not domesticate food animals, this provided the only available source of animal protein, especially in winter. Animals with thick, warm hides such as bear, beaver, and deer were most desired, as they provided both warmth and nourishment. This would change when the introduction of the European fur trade altered hunting patterns, turning a practical necessity into an economic priority. Great Lakes peoples used assigned hunting grounds to avoid confrontations with other native groups and to keep from overhunting animal populations. Native hunters employed shooting, spearing, and trapping, and the prodigious skills involved made expert hunters highly valued in their societies. Fishing was no less important, and sedentary villages sprang up near especially bountiful rivers and lakes. This was especially true in the fresh waters of the Great Lakes basin, where fish populations had grown and evolved over millennia, providing a diverse source of nutrition. Relatively small human populations prevented excessive fishing and hunting. Archaeological evidence suggests that small villages located near productive hunting and fishing spots had existed in the region for thousands of years, especially on the shores of the Great Lakes themselves. Barring natural factors such as storms and droughts, hunting and fishing worked as part of a well-balanced nutritional ecosystem.[6]

In Great Lakes Indian societies, as in other Eastern Woodland regions, food production and processing were the domain of native women. Women grew vegetables and processed meat and fish for local consumption and for sale to travelers and traders. They also produced craft items and processed skins for the fur trade, making them indispensable to the wide-ranging Indian trade networks that developed long before the arrival of Europeans. This important role in trade and local economics gave women exceptional influence in their societies. After the arrival of Europeans, Great Lakes native women sold provisions to traders, travelers, and soldiers and were important consumers in the emergent European trade.[7]

European travelers, especially those from temperate climatic regions, were often shocked by the physical harshness of the Straits. The weather and topography of the upper Great Lakes region challenged even the hardiest natives and newcomers, especially in winter. Snowstorms buried paths and villages, and driving winds made travel difficult or impossible. Winter travel was always dangerous, especially over frozen lakes and rivers that could break open without warning. In present-day northern Michigan, winter can come as early as September, and snow in April and May is not uncommon. In the seventeenth and eighteenth centuries, during the Little Ice Age, average temperatures might have been even lower than at present, and winters may have lasted longer. The soil was, and still is, sandy and rocky near the lakeshores. Coniferous forests presented challenging obstacles to agriculture while also providing abundant fuel and building materials. People living year-round in this environment

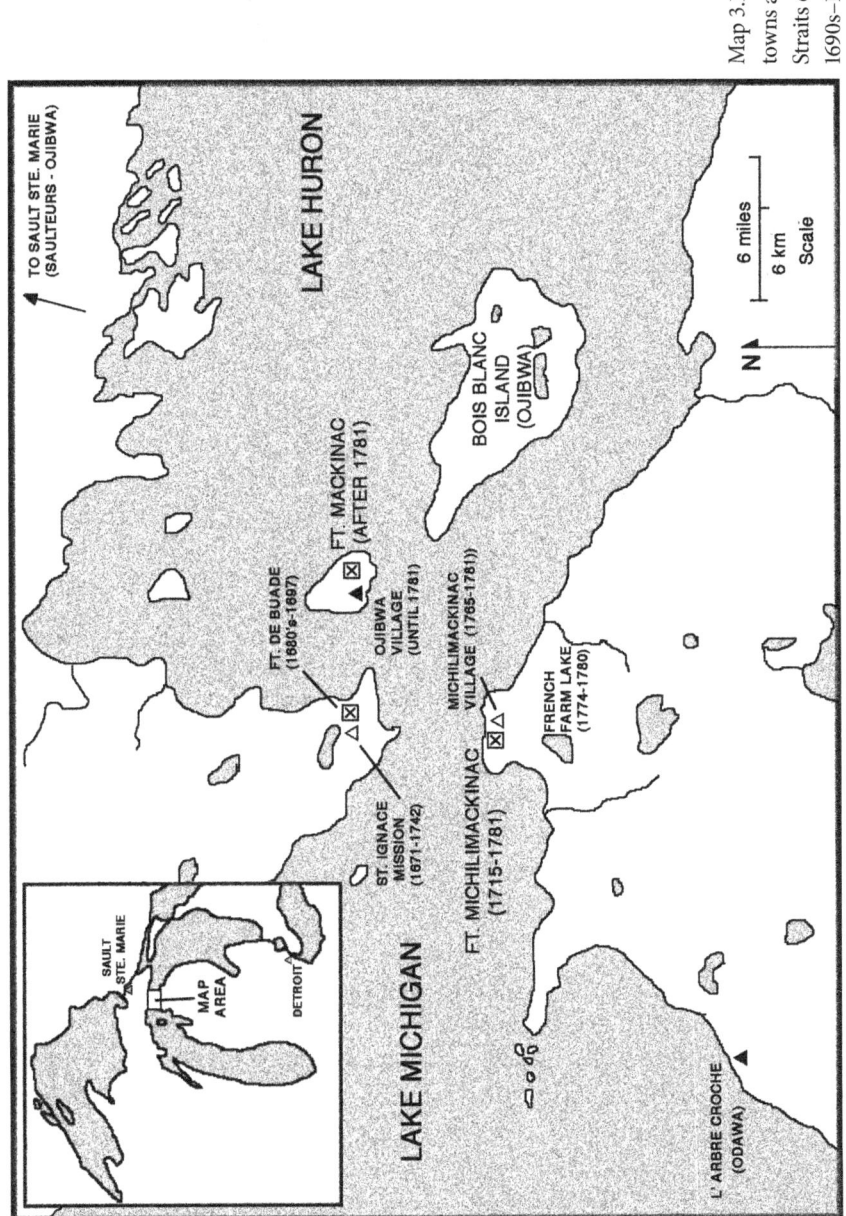

Map 3.1. Forts and towns around the Straits of Mackinac, 1690s–1790s.

required proficiency in a number of vital skills to extract necessities from trees, forests, and lakes. Newcomers to the region depended upon these skilled native women and men, either as suppliers or teachers.[8]

French explorers and missionaries entered the Great Lakes region almost simultaneously in the early seventeenth century. They quickly recognized the strategic importance of the narrow Straits of Mackinac. As Jesuit missionary Claude Dablon explained in 1670, "It is situated exactly in the strait connecting the Lake of the Hurons and that of the Illinois [Lake Michigan], and forms the key and the door, so to speak, for all the peoples of the South, as does the Sault for those of the North; for in these regions there are only those two passages by water for very many Nations." But Dablon also noted that the Indians' fascination with Michilimackinac had more to do with food procurement than with transportation. He described the many different varieties of fish available there, including three kinds of trout, the largest of which was so "monstrous" that native residents had trouble eating them. Local fishermen could spear forty or fifty fish in a few hours, which may have been why the local Odawas, Ojibwas, and Hurons believed that Michilimackinac was the "native country" of all fish.[9]

In addition to fish, Jesuits in the New France missions noted the wondrous availability of corn; in 1639, Jesuit missionary François du Peron described Hurons bringing the French priests gifts of squash, bread, and "more corn than if we had broad lands." Indeed, since Cartier's explorations in the 1530s, French visitors had commented on the amazing proclivity for corn agriculture among many Indian groups along the St. Lawrence River and in the Great Lakes region. In 1710, Jesuit missionary Antoine Silvy reported that "maize grows very well" on the south shore of the Straits and that the Potawatomis of the Lake Michigan islands "sow corn and supply the needs of Michilimackinac," referring to the French habitation there. By the time of Silvy's report, a fort and a mission had already come and gone at the Straits, and the fur trade increasingly determined the nature of both European and Indian existence there.[10]

Excellent fishing, arable land for growing corn, and lake geography were reason enough for Indians to gather at Michilimackinac, but the fur trade and Christian missions provided additional inducements by the end of the seventeenth century. When Jacques Marquette founded the St. Ignace mission on the north shore of the Straits in 1669, he brought his Huron followers with him from Sault Sainte Marie. Aware of the strategic and practical importance of the Straits, he expected that plenty of other potential converts would soon arrive. According to Dablon, "the abundance of fish, and the excellence of the soil for raising Indian corn, have ever proved a very powerful attraction for the tribes of these regions," and Indians would soon be "turning their eyes toward so advantageous a location as this." Of course, frequent and numerous native visitors made Michilimackinac a ripe target for both traders and proselytizers. Establishment of the mission at St. Ignace, and of French Fort de Baude, built there in 1690, was determined less by French missionary, economic, and colonial policies than by the availability of food in the region and the Indian visitors it attracted.[11]

Fort de Baude, the first fort at the Mackinac Straits, was primarily an attempt to hold the area for France as a fur entrepôt before Albany-based British traders tried the same thing. English companies had already established a competitive post on James Bay to handle the northern fur trade, and wished to steer as many beaver skins as possible through the Great Lakes and Iroquoia to Albany. During King William's War in 1694, when Antoine de la Mothe Cadillac took over as commandant of Fort de Baude, he commanded two hundred soldiers, the largest French garrison ever at Michilimackinac. This might have intimidated rival British traders, but it probably did not trouble the hundreds of Odawas, Ojibwas, and Potawatomis who lived nearby or the thousands of other Indians who came to the Straits to trade their beaver pelts for European goods and provisions annually. Indeed, because of the remoteness of the post and the clear superiority of the Indians in numbers, mastery of local transportation and foodways, and other practical advantages, Cadillac never felt safe there. He explained this native advantage in 1700: "With a little Indian corn these people have no difficulty in traversing two hundred leagues to come and take some one's life by stealth, and when we want to get their lands, we are obliged to provide ourselves with stores of all kinds and to make great preparations." Cadillac applied for and received permission to move the post to Detroit, taking as many of his Huron, Odawa, and Ojibwa suppliers/customers with him as would consent to go. Still, the natural geographic and strategic advantages of the Straits and the availability of food there kept voyageurs, traders, and Native Americans flocking to the region.[12]

The primary determinant of native-European coalescence at Michilimackinac was the growing fur trade, the defining economic concern in Canada since the sixteenth century. Recent studies have shown that trading pelts was already an important feature of native social economies even before European contact. After the arrival of Europeans and their manufactured goods, the trade provided arenas for cultural conflict and accommodation into the nineteenth century and beyond. Gender roles, spirituality, demographic change, and consumerism flowed together to create vital new ethnic structures, altering existing kinship, social, and political relationships dramatically. Because so many of the functional mechanics of the fur trade were the domain of native and métis women, including food production for expeditions and dressing peltry, the fur trade altered native gender roles as well. Of course, the trade also changed Great Lakes Indian material culture, introducing new kinds of textiles, tools, weapons, and sundry items into native lifeways and drawing Indians into an intercontinental trade system as spenders and consumers. As with other Eastern Woodlands peoples, European trade goods replaced similar native items, and the trade itself reinforced Indian notions of social reciprocity and mutual obligations. The European trade—often viewed as a gift exchange from the Indians' perspective—and the actual diplomatic gift giving that went with it defined the give-and-take nature of both Indian and European alliances in the seventeenth century.[13]

As in other places throughout eastern North America, Great Lakes peoples traded for alcohol, despite its attendant social and physiological hazards. French missionaries deplored the introduction of liquor into native lifeways and always argued for brandy's restriction among Indians, but once it was in place there was little they could do about it. "How deprive them of it entirely?" wondered French captain Pierre Noyan in 1730. "It has become the basis of their religion! These superstitious men can no longer recover from their diseases, unless they make festivals with brandy . . . they must have it, at whatever cost." Brandy did become an important spiritual and diplomatic feature, but recreation was almost as important. Furthermore, intoxication served as a valid excuse for violence and thievery among some Indian groups, who believed that liquor helped transport them to other worlds or places where the normal restrictions of reciprocity and responsibility did not hold. "When our Savages have received an injury from any one," explained Jesuit priest Jacques Bruyan in 1669, "They get half drunk and do with impunity all that passion suggests to them. All the satisfaction one receives from them is embraced in two words: 'He was drunk; he had lost his reason.'" Indians so desired brandy and other spirituous liquors that its value as a trade commodity made it irresistible to traders both honest and illicit; indeed, in some cases Indians would trade almost anything for it, and intoxicated men were easily cheated.[14]

But some felt that the missionaries overstated their complaints against the liquor trade. Cadillac, whose conflicts with the Jesuits were many, argued that if all the priests' complaints were compiled into a single volume, "a man's life would not suffice to get through the reading of it." He charged Jesuit missionaries with blaming the liquor trade for their own conversion failures. But Indians cared little about the squabbles of French missionaries and soldiers. From the Great Lakes natives' point of view, alcohol was an important new ingestible trade good that served many of their needs despite its attendant social problems. They believed that they had as much right to purchase and consume it as anyone else. Indians could buy their liquor from traders in their villages, but they also expected to find it at the trading posts along with other goods. Traders kept it in good supply. During the French regime at Michilimackinac, alcohol ranked fifth among trade goods kept in inventory when cataloged by use type. Clothing was the premier good, commanding 72 percent of trade expenditures at the post. Hunting implements (including guns, flints, and ammunition) ranked second, adornments ranked third, and cooking and eating implements ranked fourth. Brandy and wine accounted for 3.07 percent of expenditures between 1715 and 1760. These ratios were typical of posts of the Great Lakes region. Through the fur trade, posts like Michilimackinac became a storage place for strong drink as well as useful European goods.[15]

The French occupation of Michilimackinac began in earnest after the conclusion of Queen Anne's War, when the potential returns of the fur trade seemed a sufficient inducement to reestablish a post at the Straits. This time the fort was built on the south shore of the Straits, opposite the decaying ruins of Fort de Baude at St. Ignace, probably in 1715. Fort Michilimackinac enjoyed four decades of relative peace, despite supplying French and Indian attackers during the Fox War of 1716 and King George's War in the 1740s. Only a small garrison served the post—never more than twenty or thirty soldiers and officers—and the fort itself was a small, lightly stockaded complex. Living nearby were small native groups that had been settling in the area since the 1650s. Odawas had lived at the Straits since at least 1650. Some had followed Cadillac to Detroit in

1701, but many stayed in Michilimackinac and the islands of northern Lakes Michigan and Huron. As many as 1,500 Odawas lived near Michilimackinac in 1720, and about 750 more lived farther south near Detroit and Saginaw Bay. Odawas founded the village of L'Arbre Croche thirty miles down the Lake Michigan coast in 1742, which became a major corn supplier.[16]

Thirty miles to the north, small Ojibwa groups that the French called Saulteurs or Saulteaux had long maintained fishing villages along the St. Mary's River. Primarily hunters and fishers from the country north of Lake Superior, Ojibwas moved into the upper Great Lakes area after 1650 and moved south and east during the early eighteenth century, living alongside Odawas at Saginaw, L'Arbre Croche, and Detroit by the 1740s. By the end of the French occupation of the Straits, they also maintained a village of one hundred men on Mackinac Island. Potawatomis, Nipissings, and many other groups visited the narrow strait to trade and fish. Exact censuses of Indians near Michilimackinac during the French regime are difficult to assess, not only because of the lack of dependable records but also because most Indians resorting there did not make the Straits a permanent or even semi-permanent home. By the end of the French period of occupation, about 250 Odawa and 400 Ojibwa men lived close to Michilimackinac; adding in women and children probably would bring this total to more than two thousand overall. Of course, this figure does not take into account the many French traders and their métis and Indian wives who visited and worked near the post. Working within the structure of this dynamic cultural mix challenged fort commandants and garrisons during both French and British regimes at Michilimackinac.[17]

The transition to a British regime at the Straits after French capitulation in 1761 was destined to be a rough one. Most of the region's inhabitants had supported the French in the Seven Years' War. Odawa and Ojibwa men from the region had accompanied the French forces that defeated British general Edward Braddock in 1755 and were among French general Louis-Joseph de Montcalm's native allies in the siege of Fort William Henry in 1757. British superintendent of Indian affairs Sir William Johnson knew that Indians in the Great Lakes region would not welcome British troops or an expanded military presence. They had tolerated the small French garrisons because they brought traders and their goods into Indian country, but they viewed any expansion of the fort system as a "great cause of Suspicion," designed to draw settlers and other unwanted interlopers.

But expanding the European military presence at Michilimackinac was exactly what the British North American commander in chief, Sir Jeffrey Amherst, planned. He also intended to institute a diplomatic policy that would replace the French gift-based system with one that local residents were unlikely to find any better. Under Amherst's regime, Indians would be treated like other British subjects in America. They would be expected to pull their weight in the fur trade for the promise of remuneration alone, without diplomatic gifts or any additional inducements to friendship. Despite warnings from Johnson and other Indian agents that any diminution of gifts would impair British-Indian relations and cause hardship and hunger among native peoples, Amherst determined to end the French practice of gift giving.[18]

In the summer of 1761, Amherst sent a detachment under the command of Captain Henry Balfour to take command of Michilimackinac and the other French posts in the upper lakes. Balfour wasted no time in announcing that the new regime would not coddle the local Indians or dole out gifts as lavishly as the French had. At a Michilimackinac Indian conference in September 1761, in which a Saulteur speaker asked for powder, lead, and other goods for the winter hunting season, Balfour upbraided them for wasting their pelts on rum. "I know well it is not by misfortune you have become miserable," he scolded. "You sold your pelletry for Rum, without even buying powder, Lead, or any other Things; you are continually drunk, and then you behave yourselves not as Men, but as Beasts." He gave them enough goods to hold them over, but exhorted the Saulteurs to "become Wiser for the time to come." Saulteurs and other visitors to Michilimackinac had little experience with, or tolerance for, such lecturing. Their first experience with the new garrison cannot have been a gratifying one. Amherst also sought to license and restrict the activities of traders in the region, who upset British military plans by selling rum and circulating wampum messages without authorization. This further aggravated relations with local Indians. French traders spoke Native American languages and wintered in native villages and camps. Restricting them would not only reduce available consumer goods in the region but also remove people the local Indians considered friends and, in many cases, members of their extended families through marriage or adoption. By the end of 1761 it had become clear to the peoples of the upper Great Lakes that the new regime would be less advantageous and generous than the old one.[19]

As one of the first licensed English traders in the upper lakes had already discovered, regime change at the Straits created an inhospitable atmosphere for commerce. Alexander Henry preceded Balfour in traveling to Michilimackinac, and his reception was not warm. Because of frequent threats that Ojibwas would kill any Englishmen they found, he was forced to disguise himself as a French voyageur on his journey to the Straits. When he and his trading partners arrived they were met by Minavavana, also known as Le Grand Sauteur, a leader of the Ojibwas living on Mackinac Island. Minavavana warned Henry that hostilities would continue unless the new regime met their expectations. Because many of his people had been killed in service to the French, the English who killed them must make amends, either with their own deaths or by "covering the bodies of the dead, and thus allaying the resentment of their relations." According to Minavavana, this could only be accomplished "by making presents." Until the English made such arrangements, the Ojibwas would consider them enemies. Minavavana allowed Henry to stay on the condition that Henry give him a taste of "English milk," or rum. Henry had little choice but to comply. Soon after, two hundred Odawas from L'Arbre Croche descended upon the fort and asked that all the men of their village be given fifty beaver skins' worth of goods on credit until the next year. This would allow them to purchase the bulk of Henry's goods, which had been intended for trade in native villages further west. Henry's first trade mission faced disaster. Either he would lose all of his goods without reliable promise of payment, or he risked angering the Odawas and losing his life. The arrival of Balfour's three hundred British troops saved Henry's skin and livelihood. Still, the local Odawa and Ojibwa men had asserted their importance in the region. Most of Balfour's men would soon move on to other posts on the Great Lakes, leaving Fort Michilimackinac to continue to rely in part upon the hundreds of native inhabitants and their control of food and warfare in the region.[20]

Henry soon discovered that there was no living in the upper Great Lakes without adopting native foodways to some degree. Corn was the nutritional lifeline in the region, especially for canoe voyages, and that made the great corn post of L'Arbre Croche essential. Corn was boiled, mashed, and mixed with animal fat for consumption by voyageurs; on a journey, "a bushel with two pounds of prepared fat" could nourish a man for a month of hard labor. This method was the only way to provision canoes for long trips into the Canadian wilderness, because any other type of food would take up too much space. Production of this corn porridge, known as sagamité, was done by Indian and métis women and was only one of their many tasks in the fur trade. Women grew and processed all kinds of food, including pemmican, maple sugar, and dried berries. If corn was a lifeline in northern fur-trade societies, then Native American and métis women were the anchors. People cannot live on corn alone, however; both Indians and Canadians preferred whitefish and trout, which were easily caught in both winter and summer. But when fishing failed and no beef or pork could be had, British and French inhabitants of Michilimackinac were forced to purchase corn from local producers at sometimes exorbitant prices. Henry paid forty livres' worth of pelts per bushel for corn, and had he paid in less-desirable cash, the price would have doubled.[21]

Luckily for Henry, whitefish were plentiful at Sault Sainte Marie, ninety miles away by canoe. Henry visited the small British post there in 1762. A fire at the Sault post in December left Henry, commander/clerk Lieutenant John Jamet, and translator Jean Baptiste Cadotte and his Ojibwa wife living in a small shack, "subsisting only by hunting and fishing," which kept them alive for two freezing winter months. After returning to Michilimackinac briefly in February 1763, Henry returned to the Sault and learned the Ojibwa method of tapping maple trees and making sugar, which was their main sustenance through April. "I have known Indians to live wholly upon the same and become fat," observed Henry, who seems to have spent his first two years at Michilimackinac living almost entirely on locally produced food.[22]

Henry's most famous contribution to the literature of Michilimackinac is his eyewitness account of the "massacre" and takeover of the fort by local Ojibwas on June 2, 1763. The attack was inspired in part by messages sent by Pontiac and others encouraging a pan-Indian uprising throughout the Great Lakes and Ohio Valley. Using the pretense of a ball game outside the fort, Ojibwa men launched the ball toward the post's gate and raced after it. They then retrieved weapons from Ojibwa women pretending to watch the game, ran into the fort and quickly killed sixteen soldiers, taking the rest of the English occupants prisoner. Most of the garrison and traders were later rescued and taken to Montreal by Odawas from L'Arbre Croche, who were angry at the Ojibwa for attacking the fort without seeking their permission (or perhaps for not requesting their participation). A captive of the Ojibwa victors, Henry was first taken on a boat bound for Beaver Island in Lake Michigan. He might have ended up part of the Ojibwa food chain himself had not the Odawas rescued him. But they soon returned Henry into Ojibwa hands, where the trader and his fellow prisoners were offered bread cut with a knife still covered with the blood of British soldiers as their only sustenance, and were told to "eat the blood of their countrymen." This vivid episode suggested gruesomely what should have been evident to all: Indians influenced the backwoods through control of foodways and, if necessary, violence. Local Indians occupied Fort Michilimackinac until British troops arrived the following year. In the meantime, British authorities worked to rebuild Indian-British relations throughout the Great Lakes region, which had deteriorated during the destructive war named for Pontiac, the Odawa leader and besieger of Detroit.[23]

Sir William Johnson knew that the trade must be continued, but he had his doubts about posts situated deep in Indian country like Michilimackinac. In January 1764, Lieutenant Colonel William Eyre of the King's Engineers encouraged Johnson not to reoccupy the outposts, as there was no way to make such posts defensible against Indians. This was the basic problem for Johnson and the new commander in chief, General Thomas Gage, who needed to continue the trade and resume amicable Indian relations. Johnson recommended that trade be confined to the large forts at Detroit, Niagara, and Oswego, because even enhanced garrisons could not protect smaller posts, except by the "French Maxim" of buying the Indians' protection with presents. Limiting trade to a few posts would likely enrage traders, who eschewed caution and would "run any Risque" in pursuing their occupation, but to Johnson it seemed worth the trouble.[24]

Meanwhile, Gage had already begun the retaking of the Straits. In April 1764 he ordered Colonel John Bradstreet to send a detachment of one hundred men to Michilimackinac with provisions for fifteen to eighteen months. With local Ojibwas still resistant to British occupation of Michilimackinac, chances of procuring food locally would be slim. Gage also instructed Bradstreet to be wary of Indian remonstrances, especially from L'Arbre Croche and their leader, La Fourche, who were likely to demand reciprocal beneficence for their service in rescuing the Michilimackinac garrison. From "their Cunning Old Speaker, who is a very great Rascal," Gage warned, "You will hear of nothing but Poverty and Distress & the Great Services they did Us: they are however the Richest tribe in that whole Country." But such protestations were a commonly used ploy to manage British-Indian relations on native terms. Often the claims of poverty and nakedness were based on reality; indeed, the 1763 uprising restricted trade throughout the Great Lakes region and stressed inhabitants economically. But claims of hardship and pleas for pity were also a tactic for obtaining provisions and goods, and were used alongside threats of violence and promises of aid to pressure British authorities into rewarding native residents as the French had done earlier. These seemingly conflicting tactics merged comfortably in the diplomatic modes of peoples who had faced dislocation and deception repeatedly in the previous century. Faced with a new regime that clearly intended to stay, Mackinac residents used violence, diplomacy, and pleas for help to draw British traders and soldiers into their culture. If Odawas and Ojibwas were to live with a British presence at the Straits, they would do so on their own terms.[25]

Throughout 1764, Bradstreet and his successor as commandant of Detroit, John Campbell, made arrangements to send the requested detachment to Michilimackinac. The attempt was fraught with problems that revealed the difficulties of provisioning remote outposts. Captain William Howard and his two companies reached Michilimackinac on September 22, 1764—too late in the year to purchase local food even if it had been available. Campbell had his doubts about the enterprise, reporting to Gage that if the schooner carrying supplies did not arrive by October 20, Howard and his men may have to return to Detroit "for want of Provision." No supplies arrived, and Howard started to depart when the local priest and inhabitants offered to lend him all the corn they had if he would consent to stay through the winter. With the provisions they had brought with them, Howard reckoned that his men could stay until spring. He wrote to Bradstreet, "I found that I could support 60 Men till the 15 of May every body Included, at 8 Ounces of Pork, half a Pound of Bread and a Pint of Corn (per) Day." However, if no supplies arrived by May 20 he would have to leave, and the inhabitants might starve if he could not replace the borrowed corn. He had already sent some men back to Detroit after he discovered that some of his barrels of flour and pork had not been completely filled.[26]

Food worries continued for Howard at the Straits. All of their flour went bad, and in May he reported that his garrison had been living unhappily on rotten pork and whatever fish they could catch. When provisions did arrive by schooner, Howard found that all of the food had spoiled, especially the barrels of pork, which were deemed "unfit to be issued to the Troops." Campbell sent an emergency relief convoy of an officer and twenty-five voyageurs in canoes to supply the post (a dangerous gambit in late October), because Howard claimed the garrison would run out of provisions by mid-January otherwise. By November 1765, Howard had reached his physical limits. Disease, bad food, and "bodily infirmities contracted in the Service" caused him to request retirement after thirty-two years of military service. But the aging officer stayed on at Michilimackinac until August 1766, when he was relieved by Robert Rogers. With local food supplies strained after the Indian uprising, and the necessity of keeping a large garrison to protect the fur trade, Britain would have a hard time maintaining the post.[27]

The British Michilimackinac of 1766 was quite a different operation from the earlier French endeavor. While the French seldom maintained a garrison of more than twenty soldiers, the British garrison was at least five times larger. Explorer Jonathan Carver described the fort in 1766 as having a "strong stockade" and about thirty houses for its garrison of one hundred men and resident traders. Archaeological evidence of native material culture has been found in the fort, though the greater abundance of this has been isolated to the French period and the early British occupation. Indian slaves or servants may have worked in the fort, or soldiers and traders may have used native manufactures. The British post was more military in character than its French predecessor, and although the fur trade was still the primary justification for maintaining the post, the army and Johnson's Indian Department oversaw all operations.[28]

Archaeology reveals another difference between the French and British occupations. Animal remains in sample refuse pits from both occupations show that the French used locally available sources of food much more than did the British, who tried to rely on outside provisioning. Canoe travel defined the French supply system, and their posts were isolated and largely self-sufficient. Their diet was based on foraging, hunting, fishing, and corn purchased from women at L'Arbre Croche and other Indian corn posts. With sloops and schooners at their disposal, the British were theoretically able to transport enough provisions to last many months, including cows and swine. The hierarchical, socially differentiated military social order under the British regime is displayed in the faunal remains as well. Officers, enlisted men, and traders ate different kinds and qualities of meat. In at least one private soldier's house the diet seems to have been

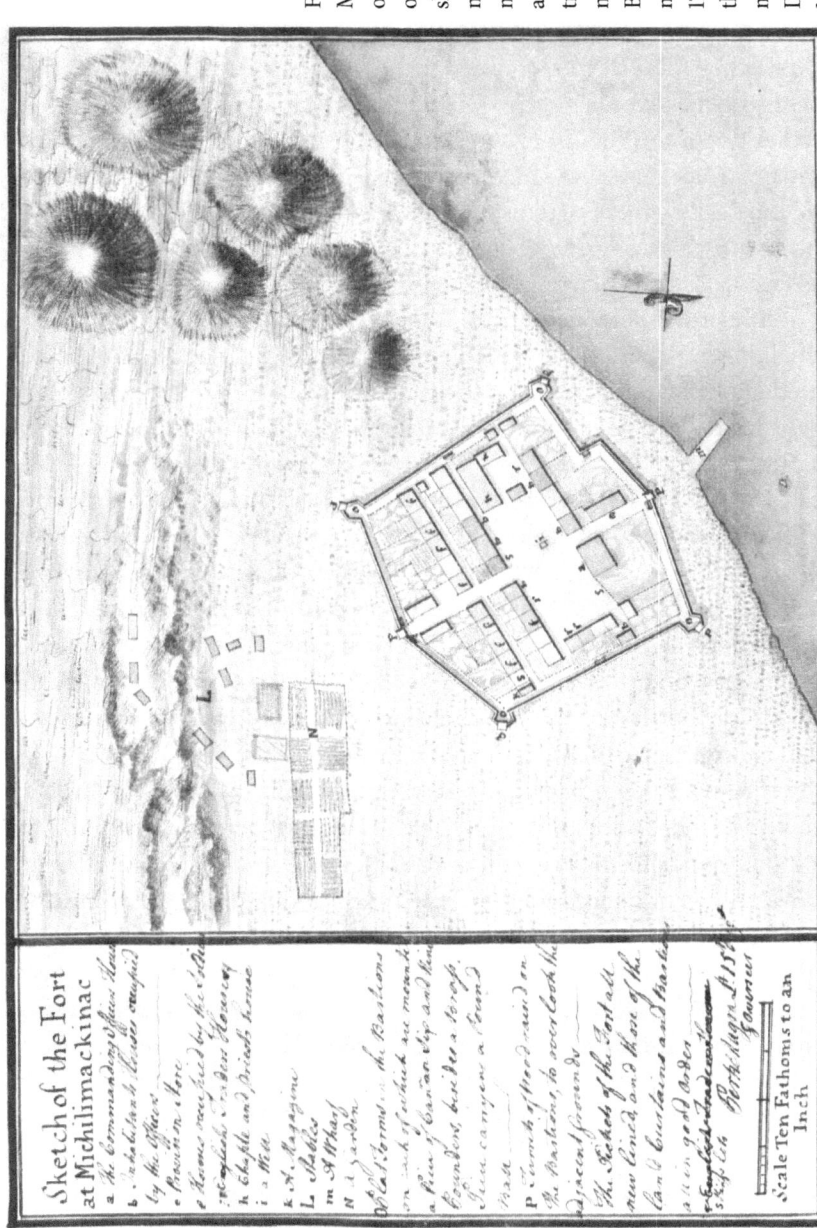

Fig. 3.1. Perkins Magra's 1765 sketch of Michilimackinac, on the southern shore of the Mackinac Straits. Michilimackinac was both a military fort and a trader's town, where native, French, and British cultures merged in the mid-1760s. Courtesy of the William L. Clements Library, Map Division, Ann Arbor, Michigan.

very close to that of the earlier French period, with local game, fish, fowl, and Indian corn supplying much of the nutrition.[29]

Even though the British may have depended more on provisioning from outside sources, Howard's experiences show that the supply chain was hazardous and prone to failure. Supplies could be packed poorly prior to shipping or could be contaminated in transit. Unscrupulous traders could pilfer food from the crates and barrels at many points, and shipments often arrived deficient. Outside supplying worked better for posts farther down the Great Lakes, such as Detroit, though local French and British farmers also provided much-needed food there. At Michilimackinac the local farmers were primarily Odawa women, and despite the best efforts of British quartermasters, Indians and Indian corn were very important to British occupiers of the post.

While British soldiers at the Straits were beginning to show their partial dependence on maize, the Indians still desired English rum and manufactured goods and depended on the traders who supplied it. Gage thought these "Canada-Traders" to be "A terrible Set of People" who would "stick to Nothing true or false," but his opinions bore no relevance within the reality of native consumerist demand. Hundreds and perhaps thousands of Indians visited Michilimackinac in 1765, seeking trade and encouraging the resumption of licensed traders wintering with the Indians in their hunting grounds. Johnson apologized to Michilimackinac traders for the delay in resuming the trade, but he worried that storing goods at the fort would prove too tempting to the Indians who controlled the region. Furthermore, renewed licensing of French traders to winter with Indians would give them too much influence and control in the Canadian wild. French traders had much to gain by wintering with the Indians. They were more accustomed to it than British traders, who would often sell their goods to the French rather than risk life among unfamiliar Indians. French traders could then resell those goods at higher prices. Gage rejected traders' claims that Indians would starve if the traders did not go among them, and thought that simply restricting trade to the larger posts would be preferable to licensing French traders or sending English traders into an environment where they would be at a clear disadvantage.[30]

Gage finally ordered that, under a plan formulated in 1764, only the large trading posts of Michilimackinac, Detroit, Niagara, Erie, Oswego, and Stanwix would remain open. A commissary from the Indian Department would regulate each post, and all who wished to trade must travel to the posts themselves. Gage thought this would probably satisfy the Indians, who were used to traveling long distances in their hunts, and it would allow British authorities to maintain a close watch on the frontiers. But his plan would only put more pressure on the delicate food chain in the Great Lakes. Indians would have to carry even more provisions for the longer journeys to the posts, and then consume more food while waiting for trade goods to arrive. In the end it did not matter much: Gage's plan was never enforced effectively at Michilimackinac, where both French and British traders continued to trade in Indian villages throughout the 1760s, despite the presence of an Indian Department commissary. Gage and Johnson did not count on the kinship-based structure of the fur trade and on the inability of British post commandants and commissaries to restrict French traders and their native wives from trading in Indians' winter villages. The plan was a failure for Johnson and Gage, and it ended officially in 1768.[31]

Gage had further problems with the man who replaced William Howard as commandant of Michilimackinac, Major Robert Rogers. A hero of the Seven Years' War, Rogers had purchased his Michilimackinac appointment while in England. Gage worried that the young officer would be interested only in enriching himself and his friends at Michilimackinac, which the general described as "the greatest Mart of Trade" in the Great Lakes. Gage's biggest fear was the rum trade. He ordered commandants of all the Great Lakes posts not to allow liquor to be sold at the forts themselves. Instead, they were to secure the rum in storage and have the traders deliver it to their Indian buyers at least two leagues from the forts. As far as Michilimackinac was concerned, Gage and Johnson agreed that the Indian Department commissary, Benjamin Roberts, would have ultimate authority over the trade there, allowing Rogers to focus his attention on military matters instead of economic self-interest.[32]

That hope would be short-lived. Upon his arrival Roberts was shocked at the amount of rum sold at the post. He worried that the hundreds of idle Indians waiting for trade goods to arrive might instead exchange all their furs for rum, and that the ensuing drunkenness would fuel native frustrations with the new trade system and lead to attacks on traders and settlers. Subsequent letters to Johnson and other Indian agents reveal Roberts's fear that rum was being sold out of his sight and against Gage's orders. He found the proof he needed when he discovered a cache of "40 Kags" of rum stored on an island in Lake Michigan. Roberts seized the rum, whereupon Rogers demanded it back. Roberts accused Rogers of treason, and over the ensuing months the two engaged in a struggle for control of Michilimackinac that eventually saw Rogers carried in irons to Niagara to await trial for disobedience and insubordination.[33]

The personalities of the individuals involved in this drama certainly played a role in the Rogers-Roberts dispute. But at the center lay the question of the rum trade, which would continue to constitute a controversy in Indian-British relations because furs spent on alcohol could not be traded for guns, ammunition, manufactured goods, and provisions. In a region increasingly defined by British military concerns, where native consumers sometimes found it necessary to travel hundreds of miles to conduct trade and treat with British trade authorities, the availability of critical goods was more important than ever.

Talk of rum haunted the communications from Michilimackinac in the years before the American Revolution, which was not surprising given the great amount of liquor sold on the lakes. A report of trade covering April to November 1768 shows that 68,312 gallons of rum passed down the St. Lawrence for trade at the Great Lakes posts. Roberts admitted that there was little he could do to control it. He despaired to his superior, William Johnson, "The Indians will Visit me, beg so hard in your name for rum, & wheedle so much they have already 10 Eight Gallen Kegs of me." Local Ojibwas and Odawas knew they could buy all the rum Roberts allowed, and in the name of diplomacy and hospitality they could ask for gifts of liquor to acquire even more. This increased costs to the Crown and sapped the profitability of the Mackinac mart; unprofitability represented the ultimate failure of the Indian Department in the far west posts. "I am at a loss what way of life to try," sulked Roberts near the end of his tenure as commissary, frustrated at his inability to advance British interests at the Straits. Even local Ojibwa and Odawa leaders were unsuccessful in their attempts to control liquor usage and its attendant social problems. Johnson had little confidence in native efforts to control the sale of rum. He knew well the power liquor held, both as a trade good and as a new fixture of Native American life. "The Temptation is too great for them," Johnson wrote to Gage, "And altho' at a public Congress the Chiefs, Sensible of it fatal Effects make heavy Complaints against it, I believe very few of them have virtue enough to resist what they Condemn."[34]

Luckily for Michilimackinac, the Odawas of L'Arbre Croche and their most powerful chief, La Fourche, were proving to be good friends to the

British operation as long as a steady supply of gifts maintained reciprocal friendship. "As long as you remain here you and your Garrison Shall always Sleep in Safety," La Fourche promised the post's new commandant, Beamsley Glasier, in 1768. La Fourche made it clear, though, that as the English king's "Obedient Children," when the Odawas visited the fort "Out of pure Affection to See our father," they "must not go away dry." For the cost of periodic gifts of rum, food, tobacco, and ammunition, the allegiance of the important L'Arbre Croche band was a good bargain for the British command.[35]

Glasier liked and respected La Fourche and the other local Odawas, and he recounted to Johnson that despite the ample presence of liquor during their visit to Michilimackinac in August 1768, "there was not one of them drunk." Traveler Peter Pond was a bit more equivocal in 1773, calling the L'Arbre Croche Odawas "the most Sivilised in these Parts," except when they "Drink to Exses." Of course, measuring the diplomatic and cultural value of neighbors by their level of alcohol abuse and comparative degrees of "civilization" displays rampant Eurocentric prejudices, but the emphasis on rum pointed out a problem inherent in occupying Michilimackinac or any other outpost. Profitability in the fur trade necessitated both the existence of outposts and the encouragement of personal industry among native trappers. As troubling as the rum trade was for British interests in the Great Lakes country, liquor had come to be expected by Indians either as a consumer good or as a gift. If Great Lakes natives were to support the British fur economy, they would demand consumerism on their terms. The best Michilimackinac commanders could hope for was that this important commodity be used responsibly if near the fort, or consumed far enough away that it would not matter.[36]

The American Revolution further stressed supply lines and profitable trading in the Great Lakes, though little actual fighting took place in the region. As the "greatest mart of trade" in the lakes, Michilimackinac seemed an obvious target, but its remoteness proved to be its salvation. American combatants, most auspiciously Virginians and Kentuckians led by George Rogers Clark, avoided Detroit and the northern Great Lakes completely, preferring to assail more accessible and more lightly defended British posts further south in Illinois country. During the early years of the Revolution, Michilimackinac's role was to organize and supply native forces from the immediate vicinity of the Straits and points north and west for major engagements in eastern theaters. For example, Michilimackinac

Ojibwas, Odawas, and Menominees from across Lake Michigan followed Charles de Langlade, now a translator in the British Indian Department, in joining General John Burgoyne's failed 1777 offensive in New York. Outfitting and provisioning such large expeditions put increased pressure on the Mackinac food system.

Throughout the war, Michilimackinac's main military role would be as a staging area for engagements elsewhere. Aside from that ancillary wartime role, the post commandant's job was to maintain Indian allegiances and to protect the fur trade, which managed to hum along solidly if not spectacularly during the war. Arent Schuyler de Peyster, commandant of the post after July 1774, spent much of his wartime tenure arranging and provisioning native forays into the Illinois and Wabash regions and fortifying the crumbling ramparts of the fort against the seemingly inevitable rebel assault from the south that would never come. Rising war costs, which included increases in allowances for Indian gifts, stagnation of fur-trade revenues, and disruption of supply lines, all contributed to tense and troubling times at Michilimackinac.[37]

De Peyster tried his best to provision the garrison and the hundreds of Indians moving through the fort headed for distant battles while still maintaining the trade. Rum availability was a problem, forcing De Peyster to purchase liquor for Indian gifts from traders, as well as dipping into his "private stock." Outside provisioning, though greatly increased during the war, proved insufficient to feed the increased number of men moving through the fort, and much of the food arrived spoiled; provisions of poorer quality were given to Indians. More troubling were reports that local supplies of wild meat were becoming strained, either through pressures brought by the war or simply through population changes or environmental stress. Local game populations, once described as amazing by seventeenth-century Europeans, had fallen since the end of the Seven Years' War. "There are not five carcases of any kind brought to this Post in the course of a year," De Peyster complained. "There are fewer animals, and Indians since the beginning of the War are become very idle, even in the hunting Season. I am obliged to help maintain all who live within fifty or sixty miles of this place, were it not for the sugar in the spring many would starve." This meant trouble for De Peyster, because the new British commander in chief, Frederick Haldimand, had been encouraging him to reduce supply costs by moving toward local provisioning sources, especially dried deer meat and fish, using "all such means as the Indians use."[38]

De Peyster had other concerns by 1779, with George Rogers Clark topping the list. Clark successfully defeated Detroit governor William Hamilton at Vincennes in February 1779 and won temporary control of the Illinois country. De Peyster was certain that Clark's forces would soon make their way up the lakes, but he retained confidence in his Indian diplomatic efforts and the loyalty of the Lake Michigan groups. "I don't care how soon Mr. Clarke appears provided he come by Lake Michigan & the Indians prove staunch," he bragged to Haldimand. Preparedness was one of De Peyster's virtues, and he made sure to reinforce the dilapidated fort. This might not help against Clark's militiamen, who would probably bring along artillery and blow the log stockade to pieces. However, it could stave off Indian attacks, which De Peyster believed were more likely than a military assault. Pressures brought by a weakened fur trade and economic hardship might make the fort and its stores an attractive target for its Native American neighbors. In fact, the commandant believed a strong fort was not enough. De Peyster wanted an armed sloop, which he thought would "awe" the Indians more than the fort's guns. He found himself in a difficult and doubly ironic position: his commanding officer wanted him to use more locally produced provisions at a time when the region's food was running out, and he depended on Lake Michigan Indians as his main source of protection at a time when he feared that local Indians were his most likely enemies. De Peyster reminded Haldimand that British strength at the Straits was invested in "the good understanding kept up with the Indians," who could change allegiances with little or no notice. Michilimackinac's Indian neighbors were De Peyster's biggest fear and his best source of protection.[39]

The situation did not change under De Peyster's successor, Patrick Sinclair, who took command in October 1779. Almost immediately he notified Haldimand that the fort's situation was untenable. For one thing, the arable soil and lake conditions around the fort would not serve Haldimand's "scheme" of using local provisions produced through agriculture or fishing. Decades of increased corn production had stressed the area's soil, and fishing on the lakes in fall and winter was so dangerous that three soldiers had almost drowned the previous year (one later died) because of high lake winds. Sinclair recommended that the fort be moved to Mackinac Island, where the soil was much better for agriculture and a small sheltered bay would provide safer fishing and lake travel. On the island, farmers and fishermen could supply the garrison and greatly reduce the Crown's expenses. Also, the fort could be built upon elevated ground overseeing the harbor and land for miles around. The post would be much better protected on the island against any rebel attack by way of Lake Michigan, unlike the "defenceless" old mainland fort, where the garrison depended partially on the availability of fish, Indian-supplied corn, and the scant protection of log palings. Maintaining De Peyster's Indian fears, Sinclair may have been even more afraid of the local native population than he was of Clark's small army far away in the Illinois country, and he was sure that "the Influence it would retain & command with the Indians of this Extended country" would justify construction of a strong new fort on the small island in the Straits.[40]

Until he could carry out his scheme to move the fort, Sinclair still needed to provision the post sufficiently to maintain a war footing. In October 1779, Sinclair ordered Samuel Robertson to take the armed sloop *Felicity* on a loop around Lake Michigan to gather intelligence and look for corn. Sailing the lakes in late autumn was always risky, but with winter approaching, Sinclair felt he must have control of all the provisions he and his men could muster, especially corn.

The mission was both diplomatic and practical. Sinclair worried that the "Dispositions of the Indians in Lake Michigan [were] very wavering" to the British cause. He had heard also that "several Depots of Corn in the rivers there" might be obtainable. The illogic of taking native corn stores at a time when Indian allegiances were unsure did not seem to bother Sinclair. Large supplies of corn in the Indian villages of southern Michigan were not unusual. Native women maintained sizable agricultural operations in the area and produced substantial surpluses of corn and other crops for sale to fur traders. Robertson brought Canadian interpreters and diplomatic gifts for allied Indians on the lake, but provisioning seemed to be the more important function of the trip. He was ordered to purchase "all the grain Grease & Provisions in that Country on the credit of the Merchants and Traders here & to use that of the Government if necessary." If any "refractory disaffected persons" were found, Robertson was to seize as much of their corn as the *Felicity* could hold, give them a receipt, and "destroy the rest" of the food to keep it out of enemy hands. His efforts met with little success; all of the French and Indian inhabitants he met expressed or feigned loyalty to Britain, without providing much military or logistical help. Robertson was unable to find much corn either, despite many rumors of substantial stores. Without capturing any useful intelligence or provisions, the *Felicity*'s trip around the lake did little to help Michilimackinac through the winter.[41]

While Robertson hunted for corn and allies, Sinclair continued with his plan to move the fort to Mackinac Island. Haldimand gave his permission to negotiate with the Ojibwas living on Mackinac Island for the island's purchase. In February, Sinclair hired local Indians to begin cutting planks for the new post, and by the middle of the month they had produced sixteen thousand feet of lumber. Haldimand, a botany enthusiast, seemed delighted with Sinclair's reports of good farmland on the island and offered to send various kinds of seeds with which to carry out his "favorite scheme" of agricultural experimentation. By July, Sinclair had negotiated the Ojibwas' surrender of the island "without any Present[s]," and the Ojibwas had begun moving to the mainland. "I have explained His Excellency's intentions to them, to make Corn Fields of the whole Island—no more of their Country is required for that purpose," reported Sinclair, revealing one of his inducements for gaining the Indians' favor. He added a detail he may have failed to mention to the Ojibwa leaders: "The Fort will be on the upper ground where no Indians will be allowed to enter." Mackinac Island was to be a segregated settlement, with rigid divisions between the military regime in the fort and the economic activities in the traders' town below. Sinclair finalized the official deed delivering Mackinac Island to Great Britain on May 12, 1781. Four Ojibwa chiefs gave up all future claims to the island for a payment of £5,000 New York currency. Despite the hardship that the move to Mackinac Island imposed on Michilimackinac traders, who were forced to transport their houses to the island at their own expense, Sinclair's move was a bold step toward British self-sufficiency at a time when the availability of local provisions seemed to be diminishing.[42]

Other operations aimed at British self-sufficiency had also been tried during the Revolutionary War. By 1774, trader John Askin operated small farms in L'Arbre Croche and at French Farm Lake, about three miles southeast of the fort. Askin continued to produce vegetables there for the garrison, traders, and merchants of the post until 1780, when he moved to Detroit and the post moved to Mackinac Island. The farms undoubtedly supplied much necessary food for the post and were an important part of the local food chain. But with Askin gone and native food production under wartime stress, Sinclair would have to rely on new sources of local production to meet the needs of his garrison.[43]

Sinclair had ambitious plans for producing food in the short term and even to offer provisions to native allies at other posts later on. "I have a Sergeant and six men employed in fishing & perhaps I may be able over & above Indian consumption, to send some thousand weight of fine trout to Niagara for the use of our brown allies there," he promised Haldimand's aide-de-camp, Dederick Brehm. Sinclair also hired three professional Canadian fishermen to supply all the Indian provisions needed at the Straits. But Sinclair's food woes continued. Captain John Mompesson, the new garrison commander, reported in September 1780 that corn supplies were becoming harder to elicit from increasingly hostile Lake Michigan Indians. This hostility may simply reflect wartime food shortages and trade disruptions throughout the Great Lakes. Mompesson held out hope that he might buy corn at L'Arbre Croche and Saginaw.[44]

In July, Sinclair noted the arrival of Indians in "greater numbers than usual" looking for provisions. He optimistically reported satisfying them with "the supply of Indian Corn which the last favourable season furnished us with," but a few weeks later he complained that "the Indians are more expensive when inactive," staying closer to the fort and consuming more and more food. By September 1781 his reports showed increasing levels of frustration, especially after Haldimand began complaining about the enormous expenses of building the new fort, provisioning the men involved, and supplying Indians with gifts. Native men waiting at the post to be sent out against the American rebels or to trade for goods, food, and rum were the biggest problem. Along with draining the post of its short supplies, their inactivity led to increased alcohol abuse. "The Indians cannot be deprived of their usual quantity of Rum, however destructive it is, without creating much discontent, nor can they be detained at the Post to await the arrival of Presents without dissatisfaction, and a waste of Provisions greater in value than the presents they Receive," Sinclair argued. The situation only became worse after hostilities ended in 1781. Haldimand ordered Sinclair and other post commanders to reduce the number of Indian gifts and discourage native visitors. Sinclair knew that this was untenable and troubling for Indian relations. That "Five Hundred families naked & without provisions after coming a great distance" could not enter a post in which they had been welcomed as allies during the war seemed unfair to Sinclair. He argued that to "deprive them of Provisions or Presents necessary for their subsistence would be the same thing as to destroy them." Sinclair was almost surely exaggerating, but he was faced with maintaining friendship and reciprocal relations among local residents and visitors who greatly outnumbered his garrison. As hard as it had been to encourage Indians to fight during the Revolution, Sinclair warned, it might be just as difficult to keep them quiet during peacetime. Unconvinced, Haldimand was determined to forbid excessive Indian gifts and to prevent western native groups from resorting to the post. By September 1782, following accusations of excessive spending on presents and maintaining an improper and inefficient method of provisioning Indians, Sinclair had been relieved of his command.[45]

After the war the primary business of the fort turned again to furs and food, and locally obtained corn proved increasingly to be a Michilimackinac staple. Monthly returns over the following year showed the amount of corn issued out of the king's stores to support Canadian employees, Indians, and the post's cattle: 180 bushels in September, 192 in October, 191 in November, 201 in December, 247 in January 1783, 241 in February, and so on. While the demand for provisions remained steady, the old problems associated with outside provisioning still troubled the supply chain on the Great Lakes. The new commandant, Captain Daniel Robertson, surveyed the post's provisions in December 1782 and found that 1,112 pounds of flour, 506 pounds of oatmeal, and 200 gallons of peas were "unfit for human use." Also, 512 pounds of pork were spoiled, and while they were "unfit for the use of His Majesty's Troops," he thought they "may be apply'd to the use of Savages." Robertson also found that seven barrels of pork had been packed short. Such problems were common sources of complaints throughout the lakes, but they hurt most at remote outposts like Michilimackinac.[46]

To add to the post's food troubles, fur trader George McBeath warned Robertson that the corn crop had failed around Detroit. This forced the post to rely on Saginaw, "the greatest Corn Post in this Country," where the Ojibwas would certainly raise their prices to meet the increased demand. Robertson had already ordered a post buyer to go to L'Arbre Croche to buy two thousand bags of corn for the king's stores before the traders were allowed to purchase any and, subsequently, to inflate the price. After finalizing peace terms with the Americans, British policy turned to reducing the demand for food and presents at Michilimackinac by sending deputations to discourage Siouan and other western groups from traveling to the posts. One such mission prevented a thousand Indians from traveling to the post, saving the cost of "two Bushels Corn with some Grease, a little Bread & Pork... with Rum and other Presents" for each man provisioned, according to Robertson. Such large-scale provisioning was simply no longer feasible at Michilimackinac. Game animal populations had decreased, corn availability had become more prone to failure through soil exhaustion, and demand was up with the peacetime expansion of the fur trade. If local native farmers could not supply the post with needed provisions, and if they were no longer needed for protection, then they would be more hindrance than help to British interests. As British-American negotiations for the transfer of Great Lakes posts to the new United States wore on into the 1780s, the slowly declining role of local Indian groups as food providers would stress the interdependent trade relationship at the Straits.[47]

Talk of Indian discontent pervaded the upper Great Lakes during the postwar period as the British garrison focused on the fur business, not knowing when treaty negotiations would force them to give up their new fort on Mackinac Island to the Americans. Indian agent Alexander McKee credited the rumblings to people "disaffected to us," meaning Canadians and Americans, but changing British policies restricting Indian gifts and increased stress on the local food system helped fan the flames of Indian animosities. Through 1784, Robertson kept the fort on alert amid rumors that Odawas would soon attack the post. Despite being poorly provisioned, he promised Haldimand, "they must give me a hearty Beating before they succeed." But this was mostly bravado on Robertson's part, and he later admitted that his small garrison was "by no means adequate to a Post in those Parts," especially with the fur trade in full swing and local traders with "not less than four Thousand Packs" of furs and goods on hand and ready to be pillaged.[48]

Robertson's frustrations must have reached a peak during a confrontation with a local Indian legend. Matchekewis, a respected local Ojibwa war chief who had participated in and probably helped plan the 1763 assault on Fort Michilimackinac, had been a British ally ever since, and even owned a house near the old mainland fort. In September 1784 he confronted Robertson angrily and, "altho' sober," accused the British of being "all Lyers, Impostures, &c." for talking Matchekewis's people into fighting and dying during the American Revolution, only to "now despise them, and let them starve." Matchekewis suggested, "The Indians ought to chasse [the British] and [their] connections out of the country," and promised to go to Quebec and make a more formal complaint. The Ojibwa chief, who had fought with Burgoyne at Saratoga and expected consideration for it, was clearly upset with Haldimand's limits on Indian gifts. But his berating of Robertson might also have been inspired by a general degradation of local Indian-white relations, in which Indians held less control of the practical necessities of life in the region.[49]

A vivid depiction of changes in Odawa lifeways by 1787 is suggested by an account of an Indian council held that year. John Dease, the Indian agent at Mackinac Island, answered an urgent request from Odawa leaders for a council at L'Arbre Croche. Since the end of the Seven Years' War, the Michilimackinac post had depended on the L'Arbre Croche Odawa band as important allies in both war and peace. The fort depended on the thousands of bushels of corn produced there annually. Unfortunately for the British, and even more so for the Odawas, things had not gone well at L'Arbre Croche since the end of the Revolution. In 1783 the entire corn crop had failed, leaving both Indians and English scurrying to find a replacement for the lost bushels and depriving the Odawas of seed corn for the following year. With no corn to be had at any price in the area, Robertson requested four hundred bushels from Detroit to supply the Indians with seed, but it is unclear if he ever received them. Apparently, the intervening years had provided little sustenance to L'Arbre Croche.[50]

At the council on August 3, 1787, Kegeweskam, the L'Arbre Croche headman whom De Peyster later described as "the most subtile of all the chiefs," spoke unsubtly about the conditions in his village, which he described as "no more than a Village of dead people." Kegeweskam mourned, "Our lands are exhausted, our hunts are ruined, no more Animals remain to call us out to the Woods, the only resource left to us is the cultivation of these sandy plains, and what we can procure from the water." Kegeweskam probably exaggerated his people's condition, and his speech was clearly an attempt to adjust perceived inequalities emerging in the Odawa-British mutual economic relationship. Still, his complaints contained an untypical note of desperation. He upheld his reputation for subtlety by reminding Dease that his village was "not lately the most peaceably inclined among the nations" and that it had taken some effort on his part to prevent his young men from participating in revenge wars. Kegeweskam also complained that with all trade goods in the region confined to a single Indian general store on Mackinac Island, which was frequently closed and inadequately stocked when open, his people often returned from visits to the post empty-handed. Dease promised that the trade situation would change soon and gave the Odawas gifts to hold them over, but Kegeweskam's speech made clear the environmental pressures that were helping to cause old amities to break down at the Straits.[51]

By 1790, British interest in Michilimackinac was clearly waning, despite their continued occupation of the lake posts well after the conclusion of peace in 1783. Sinclair's grand plans for a mighty fort on Mackinac Island surrounded by a prosperous trading town and unlimited supplies of corn had not materialized. The trade prospered, but the unfinished fort fell into near ruin. With the fort indefensible against anything but a small Indian attack, the commander in chief, Lord Dorchester, began to look for other places from which Britain might administer its operations in the upper lakes. Local Indians were increasingly drawn away to better hunting and planting grounds, often selling lands to speculators after the 1795 Treaty of Greenville, the first major land cession by Indians of the Great Lakes region to the new American government in the Old Northwest. Although Indians near the Mackinac Straits had lost some of their old grip on the stressed food supply, they still engaged in provisioning throughout the remainder of the British tenure at Mackinac. Odawas and Ojibwas brought in corn and maple sugar for the use of the garrison, and their contributions were noted in official certificates signed by the post commandant. But the coexistence maintained for thirty-five years between Indians and British at the Straits could not last much longer. British authorities planned to build a new post on St. Joseph Island, a remote but strategic location at the mouth of the St. Mary's River, and any Indians who wished to retain their old allegiance with the Crown were encouraged to move there. With the removal of the British garrison on September 1, 1796, Indian neighbors who chose to stay at Michilimackinac prepared for the changes and challenges of life under the new American regime.[52]

During the American era, Odawas and Ojibwas in the northern Great Lakes continued to operate in an economy that was familiar to them, but without as much influence. Through their roles as trading partners and consumers in the fur trade and as warriors in the various European disputes that occasionally roiled British North America, Great Lakes Indians had managed to maintain power and influence in the cultural and political contests of the eighteenth century. Indians' diplomatic and military power is often cited in the histories of this era and region, but their importance as suppliers of food and provisions is often overlooked. Throughout the British period of occupation at the Straits of Mackinac and during the French regime that preceded it, Europeans throughout the trans-Appalachian backcountry depended on local Indians who taught them centuries-old methods of growing, catching, and killing food, and regularly provided it to the newcomers for a price. In return, Indians received trade goods and alcohol, which had become valued commodities and fixtures of life, however damaging and troubling they might have been to native lifeways. The relationship between British garrisons, Canadian and British traders, and native men and women at the forts of Michilimackinac was one of limited interdependence, but Indians' role as food providers decreased during periods of environmental stresses on game and agriculture and when enough settlers and ships could ply the lakes and supply provisions. When farmers and loggers arrived to strip away Michigan's forests and plow the land, Indians who had spent generations as masters of the local food chain saw their economic importance and cultural influence challenged amid the realities of nineteenth-century America.

In 1835, Father Francis Pierz, a Leopoldine missionary, began his work among the Michigan Indians. His assignment was the new L'Arbre Croche mission, built at Harbor Springs about twenty miles from Cross Village, the site of the old Odawa village of L'Arbre Croche. In 1847 Pierz described the Odawas of Cross Village and his mission:

> There are among them good carpenters, joiners and coopers—they build neat and substantial houses. They are assiduous in cultivating their farms, which they bought from the government and sell much fruit and vegetables. The women are also very industrious and have great proficiency in household economy, making all the clothes for their families, and mats, baskets and other fancy work with porcupine quills, which display great taste and skill. In fine, I can truly assert, of the Indians of these missions, that they make such progress in their schools and in civilization as fully to satisfy their superiors; that they have gained the esteem of the whites, and deserve all the favor of our government.[53]

For all his intended benevolence, Father Pierz lacked historical perspective and missed the point. The Odawas of L'Arbre Croche were not progressing; instead, they were simply displaying the mastery of local crafts and foodways that they had long maintained. Their society remained as dynamic as it had ever been, as was true of native peoples throughout the upper Great Lakes well into the nineteenth century and beyond. They are still there today, as any casual visitor to modern-day Cross Village can attest. Descriptions such as Pierz's belie the ongoing influence that Mackinac-area natives held in the region; indeed, his list of Odawa attributes unintentionally shows how much continuity of tradition they had retained. But such paternalism was part of the price that the old provisioners of the Mackinac forts paid for their lives in the new American Republic. Left to themselves in the rugged environment and economy of northern Michigan and unwilling to leave their homeland, the L'Arbre Croche Odawas used their valuable skills to adapt to changing circumstances and find places for themselves in American society. Subsequent generations of whites measured them not by their long tradition of agricultural effectiveness or their skillful adaptations, but by the apparent success of their assimilation into Euro-American ways. This misconception was long lasting. In a supreme and unfair irony, L'Arbre Croche's twentieth-century ethnographer Mary Belle Shurtleff even credited Father Pierz with teaching the Odawas how to farm.

4

A Year at Niagara

Violence, Diplomacy, and Coexistence in the Eastern Great Lakes, 1763–1764

In early September 1763, the British garrison of Fort Niagara felt lucky. They had been spared the fates of Fort Michilimackinac and the many smaller western forts that had been overtaken or destroyed in the Indian rebellion that would soon be named after the Odawa leader Pontiac. Niagara lay within the nominal country of the Senecas, and some of them had become disaffected with the British backcountry military regime. Many of the westernmost Senecas living in the Genesee River area, often called Chenussios by their contemporaries, had joined in the rebellion and may have played a role in fomenting the uprising in the first place. They had long been friendlier to the old French regime in Canada than most of their English-allied Iroquois kin, and they saw the uprising as a way to assert their influence in regional affairs. However, except for a few small skirmishes mainly in Pennsylvania, the rebellious Chenussios had not yet subjected the Niagara River corridor to the kind of violence that had roiled through the Great Lakes region earlier that summer. This was vital to British plans for quelling the uprising, because Niagara was the main supply point for all the western posts. Any chance of relieving besieged Fort Detroit and stopping the rebellion would begin there. In the meantime, British representatives continued to parley for peace with western Indian groups. To that end, the sloop *Michigan* had sailed into Lake Erie on August 26 carrying provisions for Detroit's besieged garrison and an Iroquois delegation to meet with Pontiac. The small delegation included a Mohawk friend of Sir William Johnson, and their mission was a routine peace negotiation. But soon after the ship entered Lake Erie it was cast ashore about fourteen miles from the southern end of the Niagara River. The effort to reclaim its wreckage from the lakefront initiated a series of events that brought the full force of the Indian uprising to the Niagara region.[1]

With the help of British army engineer John Montresor, a passenger on the *Michigan*, the shipwrecked crew erected a small defensive log breastwork and waited for help to arrive from Fort Niagara. Two companies of Major John Wilkins's regiment, encamped at Fort Niagara, arrived at the wreck site on September 2 in time to fight off a small Seneca attack. Mohawk diplomat Daniel Oughnour's presence prevented further Seneca assaults, giving Wilkins and his regiment time to organize a salvage operation. This was done with some trepidation, because on September 7 Colonel Henry Bouquet reported rumors from Fort Pitt that a force of "800 Western Indians in 80 Canoes were gone towards Niagara to take Post at the carrying Place and cut off all communication with ye Detroit." For days wagons and oxen rolled back and forth across the portage with no sign of trouble. Fort Niagara's interpreter, Jean Baptiste de Couagne, wrote that from the time of the attack on the wreck through September 13, the Senecas who had attacked the shipwreck allowed the wagon trains to "pass, and repass under an escort of 20, or 30 at most, with an Officer." But British luck was about to run out.[2]

On September 14 a large native band of at least three hundred men attacked one of the convoys and its military guard on the six-mile land portage around Niagara Falls. Two companies of British troops waiting at the Lower Landing fort, at the northern end of the portage, raced up the steep Niagara Escarpment and hurried to aid the convoy. They stumbled into a well-laid ambuscade. Several soldiers were killed on the portage; others were forced over the steep cliff, where they plunged into the raging Niagara River whirlpool called Devil's Hole. By the time relief arrived from Fort Niagara the following day, eighty men were dead. The native attackers escaped without serious casualties. To make matters worse for the British, the assailants had slaughtered or stolen all the convoy's draft animals and hurled wagons and harnesses into the swirling rapids. Without the draft teams and wagons the portage was cut off, as were all of the posts on the Great Lakes, including besieged Fort Detroit. The Devil's Hole attack, along with the year of violence, tension, military posturing, and diplomatic negotiation that followed, displayed the uneasy status of intercultural relations in the eastern Great Lakes. Senecas and others in western Iroquoia who wished to broker the terms of their coexistence with British newcomers would need all of their customary tools and techniques, including violence and statecraft.³

Niagara's role in the Indian uprising of 1763 has figured less prominently in studies of the rebellion than more familiar events at Detroit, Michilimackinac, and Pittsburgh. Pontiac and his allies in the Great Lakes region, the Ohio Valley, and Illinois have garnered more attention than the western Seneca group, despite the Chenussios' role as early instigators and supporters of the rebellion and their success in overthrowing the small Pennsylvania forts Venango, Le Boeuf, and Presque Isle in 1763. The Seneca attack on the Niagara portage is usually noted as an important British defeat but it is seen as less important and interesting than the battles of Bushy Run near Fort Pitt, Bloody Run near Detroit, or the successful Ojibwa assault on Michilimackinac. Johnson's 1764 Niagara peace conference is usually depicted as a smashing diplomatic success because it resulted in the supposedly desperate Senecas ceding control of the Niagara corridor to the British. From the British military's point of view and with the benefit of hindsight, these interpretations seem well founded.⁴

However, studying these events from the Senecas' perspective complicates the picture. The Anglocentric vantage emphasizes Iroquoian social and military decline and economic dependency during the eighteenth century. This view locates Seneca actions within a context of desperation over British colonial encroachment that would lead to their eventual dispossession and loss, which has been explored deftly by Anthony F. C. Wallace, Daniel K. Richter, and others. Senecas, using the past as their guide, would have understood the events of the 1760s differently. For most of the previous six decades, Senecas and their Iroquoian kin had worked to establish favorable economic and political relations with both the British and French governments in North America while avoiding participation in European military conflicts. As vital consumers in the Atlantic fur trade, the Six Nations desired fair trade, political neutrality in European affairs, and, like nearly all Eastern Woodland peoples of the eighteenth century, restrictions on white settlement in their country. But the Iroquois Confederacy was not a monolith; the Mohawk, Oneida, Onondaga, Cayuga, Seneca, and Tuscarora nations that made up the Confederacy, and indeed each town within those nations, exercised significant autonomy in managing their own affairs. Chenussio actions should be interpreted partially as a local strategy, connected through strands of diplomacy and kinship with other Iroquoians, but particular to the unique history and geography of the Niagara frontier.

Chenussios held long-established relations with French traders at Niagara, and they viewed French defeat in the Seven Years' War and the new British military hegemony in the Great Lakes with trepidation. Restrictions on trade and gifts, rising prices of English goods, and the threat of English civilian settlement near Niagara gave the Chenussios common cause with Odawa, Shawnee, Ojibwa, and other groups in open rebellion against the British Great Lakes military regime of the early 1760s. There is little evidence of desperation or decline in this initiative; indeed, the Chenussios used time-tested military and diplomatic techniques to strengthen their position. The Seneca attack on soldiers and teamsters traversing the Niagara portage displayed no indications of impulsiveness. It was well executed and made perfect strategic sense, given the ever-increasing British presence at the vital Niagara strait and the portage's importance for supplying Great Lakes outposts. However, the Senecas' subsequent negotiated cession of the Niagara corridor to the British in 1764 should not be seen as a tactic born out of defeat or a reversal of Iroquoian fortunes. The cession continued a lossless diplomatic strategy employed by the Iroquois twice before in the eighteenth century, and the Chenussios had no reason to think that the cession would exclude them from the region or eventually reduce their influence over Niagara's affairs. From the summer of 1763 to the autumn of 1764, Senecas and their allies operating near the Niagara fort system used the best methods available to them, both violent and diplomatic, to maintain the use of their territory and as much of their traditional lifeways as possible in the face of British economic and military expansion. They understood from long practice that maintaining cooperative relationships often involved both intimidation and acquiescence. Therefore, they sought a negotiated coexistence with British military neighbors who had clearly come to stay.

Much of what happened among the forts of Niagara in 1763 and 1764 was influenced by the postwar exigencies of those years. However, interpreting Seneca and British actions of the 1760s also demands an understanding of the century of warfare, peace, and social interaction that preceded that decade. Before returning to the events of the Indian uprising, we must investigate the history of Senecas and their dealings with

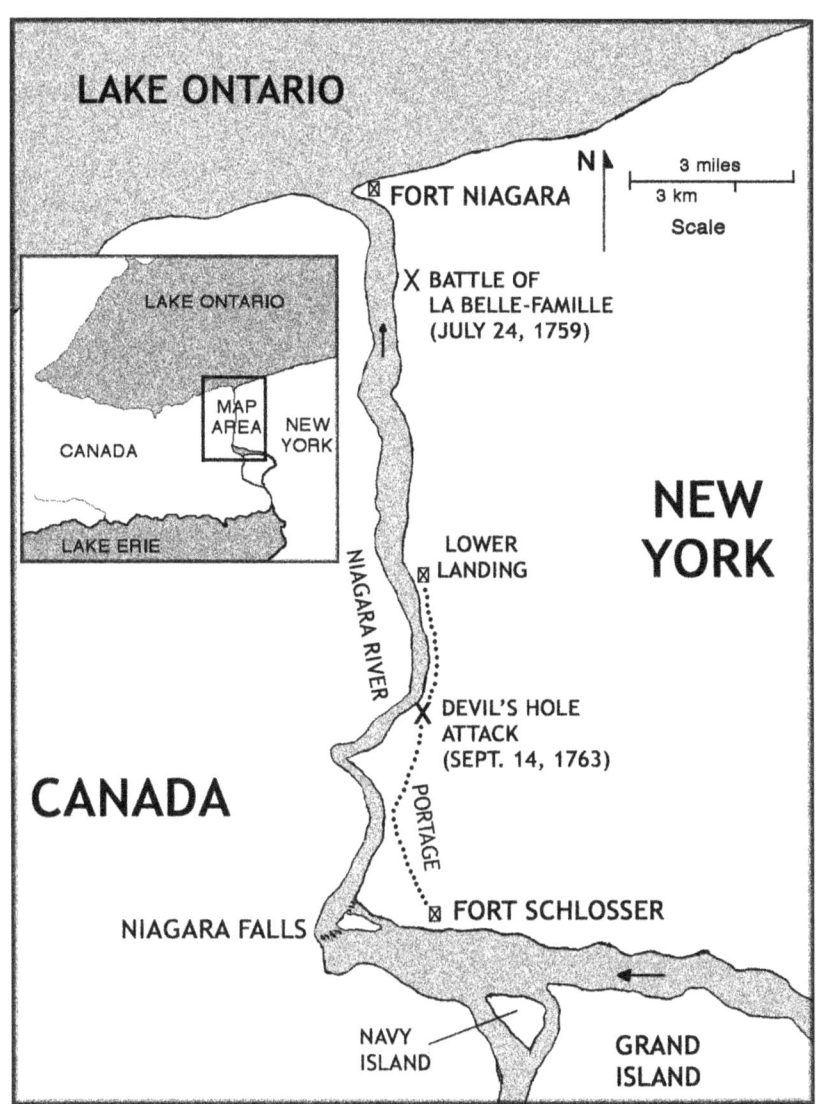

Map 4.1. Niagara River corridor, 1763.

both French and British colonial powers in the Niagara region during the seventeenth and eighteenth centuries.[5]

Millions of visitors flock to the Niagara region annually for many reasons, but the unique topography of the river valley and waterfalls are the vital components that make the location one of America's top tourism spots. Any study of events at Niagara must begin with these natural features and the man-made landscape of the region. To establish an image of Niagara as an eighteenth-century place, one must remove impressions of freeway drives across the plains of southern Ontario or Buffalo's urban landscape. Picture instead Lakes Erie and Ontario, the enormous bodies of fresh water that the Niagara River connects. A traveler returning from the American interior in the 1760s would ply these waterways rather than the rough forest paths used primarily by Native American, French, and British fur traders and hunters. It is from this vantage that the uniqueness and importance of the river corridor becomes apparent. Lake Erie ends abruptly at the Niagara River, transitioning through several islands into a narrow channel less than a mile across. Navigating past Grand Island, the traveler would hear the rumbling of rapids and the huge series of waterfalls tumbling over the Niagara Escarpment, a topographical cleft in the region that parallels the northern Great Lakes for hundreds of miles. Just south of the falls the traveler would disembark from his craft and begin the six-mile land portage around the falls and rapids. As French explorers realized by the 1670s, this portage was the only land carriage in a continuous waterway stretching between Lake Ontario and the Gulf of Mexico. At the northern end of the portage, the traveler might board another craft on the river or take the river road to Fort Niagara, a French-built post resting on a promontory above the spot where the river empties suddenly into western Lake Ontario. From that point many destinations were open, from the British post of Oswego to the large Canadian towns of Montreal and Quebec on the St. Lawrence. The Niagara River was a channel between inland seas; the portage was a transition between open-water navigation and the use of carts and oxen. Even casual travelers could interpret the strategic and functional importance of the waterway and portage easily, though most literate visitors chose to wax eloquently about the crashing cascades of Niagara Falls rather than ruminate on the waterway's influence on human landscapes and activities.

Fort Niagara is a perfect illustration of the environmental nature of military outposts. The fort itself had undergone many alterations before

1763, but it cannot be understood in isolation from its immediate landscape and dependent forts. Niagara was really a fort system, comprising four forts by 1764, plus a fortified naval yard and several small redoubts and checkpoints stretching the length of the Niagara River corridor. Technically, the western Great Lakes forts were dependents of Fort Niagara, which had been reinforced by the French during the Seven Years' War, besieged by British forces, and reinforced again as a major British command post. But the sturdy stone bastions belied the Niagara system's weak point: the land portage around Niagara Falls several miles to the south. The portage was guarded at its northern and southern ends by small forts and garrisons, but until it was fortified with redoubts after the 1763 attack, the short Niagara land carriage represented the breaking point of a system of forts and waterways stretching throughout eastern North America.

European travelers, traders, and soldiers were glassy-eyed newcomers to a region Indians knew and used well. For centuries Native American groups had traveled through the Niagara strait, following the well-defined portage around Niagara Falls. Archaeologists studying the Lower Landing site, near the Niagara River's eastern bank below present-day Lewiston, New York, have found evidence of native use from the Archaic stage (at least thirty-three hundred years ago) through the French and British occupations of the region in the seventeenth and eighteenth centuries. The portage site, located at the top of the steep escarpment above Lower Landing, has produced artifacts that reveal continuous portage activities for at least a millennium. Long before French explorers realized the portage path's strategic importance to European priorities, Indian travelers from throughout the Great Lakes recognized the "carrying place" as a main regional artery for travel and trade.[6]

The seventeenth century was a period of upheaval for the peoples of the Niagara region. By the 1630s and 1640s, the peoples of the Iroquois Five (later Six) Nations had become enmeshed as suppliers and consumers in the growing Atlantic fur trade.[7] Each of the five nations that comprised the Iroquois League played a vital role in supplying furs for European markets. The easternmost nation, the Mohawks, lived closest to Dutch traders in Fort Orange (later Albany) and French traders in Montreal and Quebec, and thus became involved deeply in the trade. The Oneidas, Onondagas, and Cayugas, who occupied the middle territories of Iroquoia in the Finger Lakes region of what is now upstate New York, hunted and hauled furs to Dutch or French traders, sometimes using the Mohawks as middlemen. The most populous nation of the League, the Senecas, occupied the western end of Iroquoia. Their territory extended from the Finger Lakes to just west of the Genesee River. When overhunting reduced the populations of beaver and other fur-bearing animals by the 1630s, Iroquoians sought new hunting grounds to their west, north, and east. Mohawks began this expansion in the 1630s by attacking and dispersing Algonquian groups in the Great Lakes region. Senecas followed by expanding into the Niagara region. From 1638 through the 1640s, the inhabitants of this region, the Iroquoian-speaking Eries, Neutrals, and Wenros, evacuated their territories in western New York and southern Ontario. An Iroquois invasion of the lower Great Lakes followed. Senecas and other Iroquois attacked Eries, Neutrals, Petuns, Hurons, Odawas, Ojibwas, and Susquehannocks from the late 1640s through the 1670s, dispersing several towns throughout the Great Lakes region and devastating Huronia. By at least 1669, when French priest René de Bréhant de Galinée described the existence of a Seneca hunting village near the western end of Lake Ontario, the Niagara region had fallen under nominal Seneca control. However, Senecas and other Indians used the Niagara corridor as a highway and a place for hunting and fishing, not for permanent settlement; there is no record of a Seneca village or post on the Niagara River itself until 1707. Niagara's strategic importance and lack of a large permanent native population made it a natural target for French expansion by the end of the seventeenth century.[8]

Seneca relations with New France had been a mixture of tension and opportunity. As the keepers of Iroquoia's "western door," the Senecas found it difficult to guard against incursions by French traders and their native allies. They also found the proximity of French traders tempting and economically useful. But conflict, rather than cooperation, determined regional events in the seventeenth century. The long series of "beaver wars" fought between the Iroquois and other groups to establish hunting rights and exact reciprocal restitution for dead kin took their toll on Iroquois numbers. Iroquois attempts to establish peace with the French in the 1650s and 1660s never lasted long, and the decades of near-constant war were beginning to stress Iroquois families and villages. In the 1670s the Iroquois lost their Dutch trading partners when New Netherlands passed to England, so they endeavored to keep moderately amicable relations with French traders while establishing new ties with the British regime at Albany. Keeping peace with both European powers would be difficult, especially when unwelcome French missionaries began incursions into Seneca towns. By the 1680s the Iroquois were confident enough in their relations with the British to begin actively resisting French trading in the West. French troops responded by invading the Finger Lakes region in 1687 and burning Seneca corn crops. The French invasion force also built a small fort at the northern end of the Niagara River, in the hopes of gaining a foothold in New York and intimidating the Senecas. The fort did not last; New York's governor, Thomas Dongan, threatened a full-scale Iroquois attack on French posts if they did not remove it. However, the French retreat represented only a temporary respite in their plans to fortify the Niagara River.[9]

By the end of the seventeenth century, warfare and disease had depleted Iroquois ranks, and they began disentangling themselves from deadly European conflicts. In 1700, Iroquois delegations visited Montreal and Albany to conduct peace negotiations that established the Five Nations as neutral middlemen in the economic and political struggles between New France and New York. British-allied Iroquois, led by Onondaga speaker and diplomat Sadekanaktie, knew that the French retained their designs to fortify the Niagara strait and had already begun establishing a western post at Detroit, in what most Iroquois considered part of their territory. In July 1701, Sadekanaktie and other leaders representing all of the five Iroquois nations met with New York's lieutenant governor, John Nanfan, in Albany to establish Iroquoian neutrality and to ensure a peaceful continuance of Iroquois-English trade. To counter French expansion, twenty Iroquois village leaders and chiefs granted the king of England a deed to their professed beaver-hunting grounds, which encompassed most of Michigan and upper Canada between Lakes Michigan and Erie. The land cession included "the great falls Oakinagaro," or Niagara, and gave the British "power to erect Forts and castles" in any part of the ceded territory. In return, the British were required to honor Iroquois rights to hunt in the region forever, "free of all disturbances expecting to be protected therein by the Crown of England."[10]

Of course, this "deed" was not a genuine land cession in either a legal or practical sense. Western native groups, many of them French allies, dominated much of the ceded territory. The government in Montreal did not recognize the deed at all. Any British forts built in the ceded territory would still cause conflict between the European powers with or without Iroquois permission. From the Iroquois viewpoint, however, the treaty was a bond of friendship and mutual protection with powerful allies that could be used to prevent destructive wars with both European and Indian enemies and to continue a steady trade lifeline. Unlike the neutrality provisions of the 1701 settlement treaties, carefully negotiated and signed by representatives of the Five Nations, French-allied western Indian groups, and the colonial governments in Albany and Montreal, the "Beaver Hunting Ground" deed was a marginal factor in subsequent French-Anglo diplomacy. However, it demonstrated the Iroquois' hopes that maintaining amity with the British in Albany would give them leverage in their dealings with French authorities. As for the Niagara strait, the Iroquois diplomats' insistence upon retaining perpetual hunting rights in the ceded region made it clear that Iroquois hunters and travelers intended to continue using the passage as they always had.[11]

Iroquois leaders did not undertake diplomacy of this kind lightly. The Iroquois League (separate from the Five Nations Iroquois Confederacy, the political-diplomatic body that formed in the late seventeenth century) existed specifically to ensure that peaceful relations and friendship could exist between its member nations. The League was not an authoritative body; rather, Iroquois townsfolk, chiefs, elite men and women, and any men old enough to gain respect made the most fundamental decisions in Iroquois life. The fifty sacred sachems of the Grand Council of the League met at Onondaga once per year to renew their friendship, condole each other for deaths, settle minor disputes, and seek continued peace. Because Iroquoians configured formal interpersonal relationships as extended forms of kinship, diplomatic alliances were truly friendships based on love and mutual responsibility. Reciprocity formed the fabric of these friendships; hospitality, gift giving, and condolence rituals were more than exercises in expedient pragmatism. Reciprocal exchange, especially of material goods, represented the love and mutual kinship obligations that ensured peace and prosperity in the face of changing sociopolitical conditions and the constant pressures of the natural world. However, friendships, either between Iroquois kin or between Indians and Europeans, needed constant maintenance to ensure fidelity. Council fires, whether in individual Iroquois and colonial towns or at the Grand Council in Onondaga, provided occasions where friendships, treaties, and authority could be renewed, moderated, or rejected. By the beginning of the eighteenth century the work of Iroquois-European diplomacy had been taken over by the Five Nations Confederacy, a more political body in which the authority of powerful village leaders took precedence over war chiefs, peace chiefs, and other sachems. Even with Europeans, the Iroquois configured relationships as fictive kinships, referring to European equals as "brothers" or "cousins" and to European kings as "fathers." The texture of diplomacy remained the same in Indian-European relationships: the constant and careful maintenance of friendship through reciprocal exchanges. During the period of Iroquois neutrality, from 1701 to 1759, diplomacy would continually define and refine friendships among Iroquois nations and individuals and between Indians and Europeans. In such a diplomatic atmosphere, where local autonomy was retained within the loose framework of the larger Iroquois Confederacy, it is not surprising that regional groups like the Chenussios might diverge in some ways from their Iroquois, and even their Seneca, kin.[12]

Over the next twenty years, hundreds of French traders, settlers, and soldiers traveled over the Niagara portage, and Indian carriers, now wage earners, helped move the baggage. Exactly when Senecas began to work for wages on the portage is unknown. By 1707 Senecas had established a fortified post on the river, encouraged by Chabert de Joncaire the Elder, a French interpreter and adopted Seneca whose family would later establish a permanent trading post at the Lower Landing. It was largely through the efforts of Joncaire and his son Daniel that pro-French sentiment increased among the western Senecas during the early eighteenth century. By 1715 Senecas worked regularly with Joncaire as carriers on the passage, and may have begun much earlier. A 1718 memoir by an unknown writer includes a description of the portagers' town: "Above the first hill [south of the Lower Landing] there is a Seneca village of about ten cabins, where Indian corn, beans, peas, water-melons, and pumpkins are raised, all of which are very fine. These Senecas are employed by the French, from whom they earn money by carrying the goods of those who are going to the Upper Country." When French coureurs de bois returned from the beaver grounds, the Senecas would accept peltry in lieu of currency for carrying their huge packs of furs around the falls. Some native carriers were also said to "pilfer" from French packs to augment their pay. Of course, Indian wage laborers were also consumers. Seneca porters used their pay to buy "mitasses" (leggings), shirts, guns, ammunition, and other manufactured trade goods, including liquor. Sedentary wage-labor jobs near a constant supply of liquor may have exacerbated the social maladies commonly associated with alcohol sales. Seneca sachems oversaw the portage operation, possibly at the behest of the French portage operators, to prevent alcohol-fueled problems.[13]

Wage labor presented both pitfalls and benefits for eastern Great Lakes natives. Permanent Indian wage labor at Niagara and other locations demonstrates the extent to which Iroquoian groups had become dependent on European trade goods and economic culture. It also shows how some Indians living near Europeans found ways to coexist with the newcomers while retaining as much of their independence and way of life as possible in the face of these changes. By the early eighteenth century, hunting had long since moved from a subsistence activity to a way to procure consumer goods. Wage labor served the same purpose, and there is no evidence that Indian laborers gave up their cultural lifeways or identities any more than did hunters.[14]

While some Senecas and Onondagas began migrating to portage locations to find paid employment in the early eighteenth century, France and England worked to position their eastern Great Lakes military and trading posts advantageously in the increasingly competitive fur trade. French posts erected at Detroit (1701) and Michilimackinac (1715) helped capture and protect a good deal of the Great Lakes business. By 1720, Joncaire's diplomatic efforts among the Senecas paid off when some of the Chenussios allowed him to establish a small trading house at the Lower Landing site, about eight miles north of the falls. This post did not meet with general Seneca approval. Iroquois plans emphasized neutrality, and French incursions like this angered the British regime in Albany and complicated their strategy. New York traders responded with a post at Irondequoit (near present-day Rochester) in 1721, adding more fuel to the fire. Further trouble came in 1726 when Joncaire circumvented the Senecas completely and elicited permission from a group of neutrality-minded Onondagas to build a new post at the northern end of the Niagara River, near the ruins of the old French fort built in 1687. Joncaire promised that this new post would be conceptualized as a "house" rather than a fort to avoid violating Iroquois-British treaties. This post, still extant today as the central "castle" of Fort Niagara, formed the center of French and British occupation of the Niagara River for the next seventy years. During those years, some Senecas would establish an even closer relationship with French traders and soldiers at the Niagara fort. Though Senecas generally resented the building of an armed French post in their territory, they determined to make the best of the situation by learning to coexist with its occupants. The building of Fort Niagara and the advent of Indian wage labor opened a new era of tense Seneca-French cooperation near the strategic river corridor. However, though this socioeconomic coexistence worked reasonably well for Senecas, it angered New York officials and tested the Iroquois' ability to retain their neutrality.[15]

Senecas and other Iroquois groups eagerly aimed to minimize the diplomatic damage caused by this new French incursion. At an Albany council in September 1726, New York governor William Burnet suggested to a small delegation of Onondaga, Cayuga, and Seneca sachems that they might show their friendship by reinforcing the little-enforced 1701 Niagara deed. This suited the Iroquois representatives, who hoped that the British king "would be pleased to defend them from the Incroachments of the French." Such renegotiations of alliances were common and required in Iroquois diplomacy. For the Iroquois, alliances and friendship, not the transference of property or land, were the fundamental bases of treaties. Always tenuous, alliances needed to be maintained frequently to reinforce the reciprocal friendship between treaty signatories. English-Iroquois cultural differences enabled agreements like this new treaty, which seemed to give both sides what they desired without altering significantly the friendly balance of French-English-Iroquois relations. This new deed of "Surrender and Submission," signed by seven Iroquois sachems from three nations, once again promised Britain military mastery "all along the river of Oniagara." But, as with the earlier deed, the British role would be that of protectors rather than landlords, defending the ceded territory for the perpetual use of both Iroquoians and the English military.[16]

This new deed would have no greater impact on diplomatic efforts between Indians and Europeans than the 1701 cession. The French completed their fortified post at Niagara, and Albany traders built a new British post at Oswego in 1727 to counter the French expansion and grab some of the Lake Ontario commerce. Furthermore, most Iroquois groups did not recognize the authority of the small negotiating team to represent the entire Iroquois Confederacy in ceding so much of their hunting land to the British. But, the deed exemplified the willingness of some Iroquois to play European diplomatic games for their own benefit. For example, a Seneca speaker, Kanakarighton, insisted that the Senecas had never given permission for the building of Fort Niagara. He promised to rebuke the Onondagas for allowing it, to resist further French encroachment, and to desist from listening to anti-British rumors (though he reminded Burnet that the English also spread rumors of "the Evil of the French, that they have from time to time deceived us"). But Kanakarighton made it clear that the Iroquois also had interests that needed to be maintained. He asked Burnet to restrict alcohol sales in Iroquois towns, to keep other colonial governors from breaching the peace (specifically the lieutenant governor of Virginia, Robert Carter), and, most importantly, to keep trade plentiful and prices low. "We must aquaint you how our fraternity came anciently, it came by the Trade," reminded Kanakarighton. "We received the Goods in former times cheap, and we were convinced of Your goodness, but now the goods are sold to us dearer and dearer." He requested that prices be dropped, especially on gunpowder. "But do not lay powder on one side of the scale and Beavers on the other, that is too little powder," he stipulated. Finally, Kanakarighton asked for the return of a smith and armorer to service the Senecas, reminding Burnet to have these tradesmen "bring all their tools with them."[17]

Burnet may have been angry about Onondagas allowing the construction of Fort Niagara, but the 1726 deed was not an Iroquois capitulation. Iroquois interests were at the heart of the negotiations. They could still use the Niagara corridor, and their powerful British allies would supply protection. Iroquois diplomats understood that transference of land titles held great significance in Europeans affairs, and they hoped that British negotiators might enforce the deed by discouraging further French incursions into Iroquois territory. In ceding these lands, Iroquois representatives gave away nothing, and expected to accrue diplomatic and material advantages they would need to negotiate their way through the complex economic and political climate of the eighteenth century.

Even with French Fort Niagara guarding the northern end of the strait and Little Niagara, a new fort commanding the portage's southern landing after 1751, France required the consent and cooperation of the Iroquois to maintain its control of the Lake Ontario trade. This was especially true regarding the Chenussios, who maintained significant power in the Niagara region. To maintain the Chenussios' approbation and contentment, French authorities at Niagara kept Seneca and Onondaga carriers employed at the waterfall portage and other land carriages in the region. By 1750 this had become an extensive operation. That year, Swedish traveler Peter Kalm reported seeing "above 200 Indians, most of them belonging to the Six Nations, busy in carrying packs of furs, chiefly of deer and bear, over the carrying-place." He also noted that they received twenty pence for each pack they carried around the falls. By midcentury, wage labor had seemingly become a viable alternative to hunting for Chenussios and other Iroquois living near portages.[18]

In 1757, French officer Louis-Antoine de Bougainville confirmed the scope and importance of Indian carriers at Niagara and Fort Presque Isle (near modern-day Erie, Pennsylvania) and encouraged their increase. He noted that at Presque Isle Indian carriers earned six francs per sack. This was twice the rate paid to French porters, but the Indians' superior abilities were worth the expense. Furthermore, Bougainville insisted that using native carriers was both functionally and strategically necessary. "Policy demands that they be employed, especially in times of war," he reported. "When they are employed in portaging they hinder the tribes that might be badly intentioned from troubling our transportation." In addition, the wages they made allowed them to purchase necessities. "Without this resource they would turn to the English who deal with them much better than we do, and it is essential that they should not perceive this difference." Bougainville noted that it was just as "essential" to employ Indians at Niagara, where 250 to 300 trips traversed the portage each year.[19]

Despite their profitable relationship with Niagara traders, the Chenussios maintained some of their old antagonisms against the French portage operators. Their main complaint with French conduct of the portage was with increased use of horses and wagons, a military necessity for the French after the onset of the Seven Years' War. Onondaga chief Chinoniata spoke for the Iroquois Confederacy when he complained about the threat to native livelihoods in a 1756 congress with New France's governor-general, the Marquis de Vaudreuil: "Formerly when we were coming from war we had the Niagara portage; twas promised us that we would always possess it." These complaints may indicate a change in French policy at Niagara during the middle of the Seven Years' War, which Senecas would interpret as a breach of friendship and a threat to their livelihoods. A Seneca delegation visited Montreal in April 1757 and complained directly to Vaudreuil about the increased used of carts on the portage, arguing that Senecas had "formerly" handled all the portaging themselves. This implies that Indian porters may have been excluded from the Niagara carrying trade two years before the British took over Fort Niagara.[20]

Iroquoian anxieties may have been exacerbated by the expanded French military presence at Niagara during the Seven Years' War. The fort's garrison increased from about thirty soldiers and officers in 1754 to a defensive force of over six hundred in 1756. The fort itself was renovated and enlarged in 1756 to include expanded earthen breastworks and several new buildings. Throughout this period, western Indians continued to throng to the fort to trade, as many as two thousand at a time during the summer seasons. By 1759, Fort Niagara and the Niagara portage had become crowded with French soldiers and Great Lakes–based Indians, a situation that was sure to affect Iroquoian neutrality. Chenussios and other Iroquois living close to Fort Niagara would be forced to take sides if the war spread to the Niagara region. Many Senecas became open allies of France during the war. Others adhered to Iroquois neutrality provisions. Niagara-based Indians looked to their old French employers for protection. In the late 1750s, Fort Niagara played host to dozens of French-allied Indians at any given time. When the fort was finally attacked by the British in 1759, around one hundred Niagara Senecas were among its inhabitants.[21]

On July 6, 1759, the Niagara-based Senecas' lives changed abruptly.[22] A few miles from Fort Niagara, a British force of fifteen hundred regular soldiers and a thousand Indians from all six Iroquois nations, including some Chenussios, landed on the Lake Ontario shore to begin the siege and eventual conquest of the fort. Sir William Johnson, the Indian superintendent, had convinced several Iroquois groups to suspend their long-held neutrality and assist in the British conquest of Niagara and Montreal. The presence of so many hitherto neutral Iroquois fighting men allied with the British created a dilemma for the roughly one hundred Niagara Senecas who had joined five hundred French soldiers within Fort Niagara. Working at the portage had helped them maintain friendly relations with the fort's garrison and its commandant, Captain Pierre Pouchot. However, this new military alliance between the British and the rest of the Six Nations Confederacy placed Niagara-based Senecas in the middle of a conflict between their French friends and their Iroquoian confederates. Pouchot's Seneca ally Kaendaé left the fort and negotiated a general Iroquoian withdrawal from the siege, a dubious achievement since siege work was largely the domain of engineers and artillerymen. Kaendaé then turned to Pouchot and negotiated an exit from the fort for his people. On July 26, Johnson's British-Iroquois force defeated a relief army of more than fifteen hundred French soldiers and Ohio-based Indians two miles south of the fort at La Belle-Famille.[23] Without hope of relief, Pouchot surrendered. Fort Niagara and the portage passed into British control,

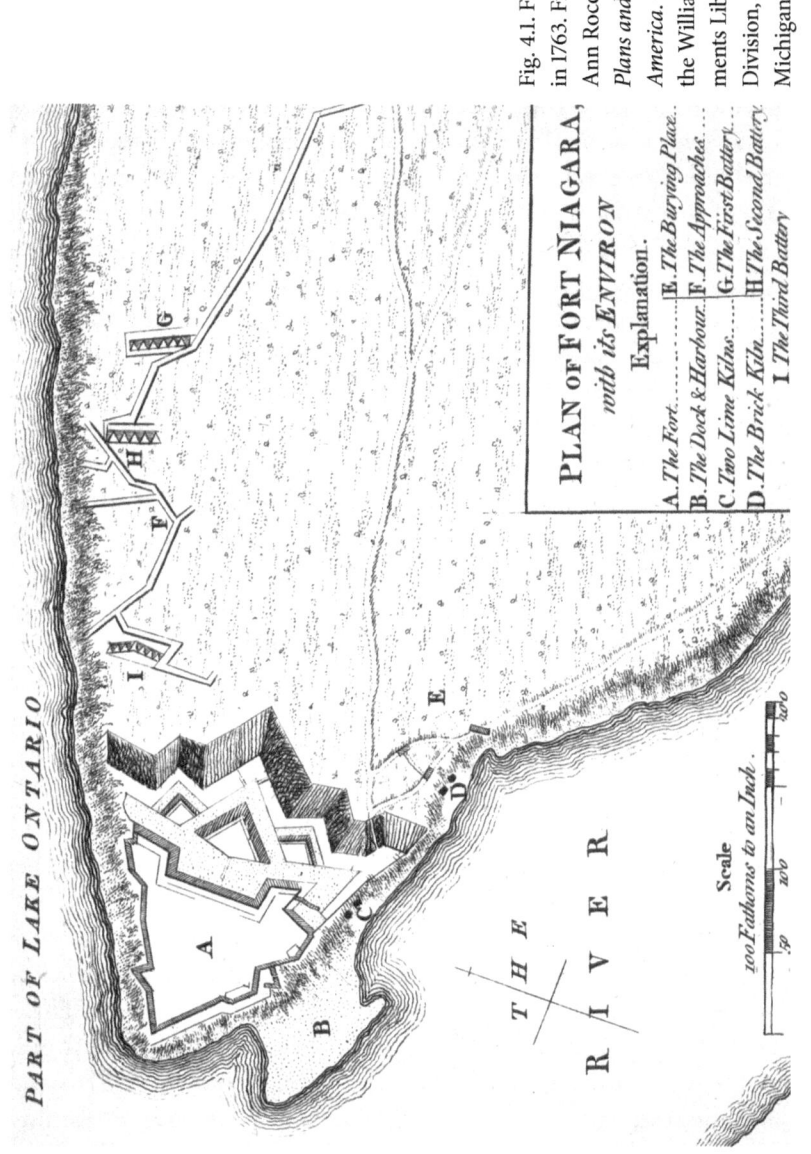

Fig. 4.1. Fort Niagara in 1763. From Mary Ann Rocque, *Set of Plans and Forts in America*. Courtesy of the William L. Clements Library, Map Division, Ann Arbor, Michigan.

and local natives had to discover how to negotiate coexistence under a new regime.[24]

After conquering Fort Niagara, Johnson was left with a problem concerning Senecas living nearby. Though their first allegiance was clearly with Pouchot and his garrison, they had remained neutral during the siege and could hardly be barred from the Niagara region when they had not joined the French in arms against British forces. Johnson chose conciliation. He informed Fort Niagara's new commandant, Hugh Farquhar, that local Senecas would be friendly "at least in appearance" and that Farquhar should "receive them with civility; give them provisions, and assure them that traders will soon arrive to buy their skins more to their advantage than ever the French did." But Johnson also warned Farquhar not to admit more than twenty Senecas into the fort at a time, even if they arrived in large groups. Having given his orders to the fort garrison, Johnson turned to regional diplomacy. He made it clear to Chenussio leaders that he expected them to protect Fort Niagara and its new British garrison. To ensure their cooperation, Johnson sought to drive a wedge between the Chenussios and other Iroquoian groups. For example, he heaped profuse thanks upon most of his Iroquois allies for their assistance at Niagara, giving them wampum belts and other gifts. However, he rebuked the Chenussios for their French sympathies, giving them only a thin black string of wampum and warning them to ensure the safety of the Niagara garrison lest the North American commander in chief, Jeffrey Amherst, "be obliged to take proper measures" to punish them. The initial returns of Johnson's diplomacy were not encouraging. Several Iroquois leaders promised that they would encourage the Chenussios to watch over Niagara, but they made no guarantees for the garrison's safety. They then made it clear that they expected more smiths, traders, and goods at posts throughout Iroquoia. The Iroquois Confederacy would help keep the Chenussios in line, but not for free.[25]

During the first year of British occupation, Fort Niagara's garrison helped prepare the portage trail for resumption of trade and, of more immediate importance during wartime, military traffic. Amherst planned to attack Montreal and rebuild Fort Presque Isle on Lake Erie, destroyed during the war; thus, constant traffic rolled through the portage. Years of war and the siege left much damage at the strait. Fort Niagara required extensive renovation. Joncaire's trading post had been abandoned, and Fort Little Niagara had been burned down by a group of Indians from

Johnson's detachment soon after the end of the siege. By the end of 1760, Fort Niagara's garrison had restored Little Niagara and improved the portage road enough to allow wagons, oxen, and carts to transport goods once carried by Indian porters. Whether local Senecas disapproved of the increased employment of wagons and animals is unclear. Neither Johnson nor Amherst mentioned any Indian complaints about lost portage jobs. But, as revealed by Amherst's subsequent activities, the Chenussios still recognized the Niagara region as part of their country and hunting grounds, with or without Indians working at the portage.[26]

Amherst felt that the best way to secure the portage would be to populate the area with British traders and civilian families. In May 1761 he licensed a group of former army officers to monopolize trade at Fort Little Niagara and to operate the portage. The traders began building a settlement and raising corn, which Johnson feared would confirm the Chenussios's long-held suspicions that the British planned "rooting them out of their Country." Johnson warned Amherst that such settlements would definitely violate the 1726 agreement with the Iroquois, which restricted civilian settlement and reserved the Niagara portage area solely for the Crown's military use. The commander in chief refused initially to remove the traders, despite Johnson's urgent pleas that the Senecas would see the settlement as an attempted land grab. "It was never my design to take an inch from them," Amherst insisted, and he assured Johnson that the settlements were military necessities and not permanent. But Amherst received pressure from unexpected sources. His settlement plans upset Albany merchants based at Fort Niagara, who worried that traders at Little Niagara would scoop up all the Great Lakes profits for themselves. Under emphatic pressure from traders, Senecas, and Johnson, Amherst withdrew his permit, though he maintained his belief that civilian settlement was the best way to secure the Niagara region for Britain.[27]

Amherst's attempt to populate the Niagara region with settlers exacerbated already raw British-Seneca tensions, and over the next two years the relationship deteriorated rapidly. In July 1761, Johnson heard rumors that some Chenussios disapproved of British efforts to garrison former French posts in the West and had sent two Seneca agents to Detroit to foment a general rebellion against British occupation of the Great Lakes posts. When Johnson stopped at Niagara on his way to a Detroit conference, local Senecas stonewalled his attempts to ascertain the depth of imminent danger. Johnson's Mohawk friends warned that Senecas must give up their troublemaking or face the wrath of their Iroquoian kin. Two years into the British tenure at Niagara, soldiers at Niagara found themselves in the middle of a growing internecine Iroquois conflict and on the edge of a possible general uprising.[28]

Over the next two years Amherst did little to encourage peace in the Niagara region. Answering complaints from post commandants and native leaders, he ordered alcohol sales suspended at all the western posts, including Niagara. He also ordered a general retrenchment of Indian gift giving, the fundamental proof of reciprocal friendship in Great Lakes. Amherst had long criticized the Indian gift exchange, which he thought made Indians "Slothfull and Indolent" rather than industrious and responsible. These new restrictions on alcohol sales and gift giving in general only made a bad situation worse, even though they were loosely enforced. Despite the inclinations of Amherst, Johnson, and some native leaders, alcohol was an important and much-desired trade commodity that many expected to find in trading posts and at forts, along with customary gifts of clothing, ammunition, and other goods. Consequently, by 1763, Fort Niagara's garrison found itself frequently beset upon by Senecas increasingly dissatisfied with the new British regime. The situation worsened with the onset of the 1763 Indian uprising. Among the posts to fall that summer were Venango, Le Boeuf, and Presque Isle, a chain of forts between Lake Erie and Fort Pitt, and most of the attackers were Senecas.[29]

Senecas' reasons for rebelling against British hegemony differed from others involved in the uprising. Odawa war chief Pontiac and some of his followers desired a return to traditional lifeways and less dependence upon European trade. He and his fellow rebels, such as the Shawnee leader Charlot Kaské, cared about fair prices and honest trade practices, but they also interpreted British victory in the Seven Years' War as a social and cultural calamity for all Eastern Woodlands peoples. French traders had certainly disrupted native lives with their goods, diseases, and conflicts with other Europeans. However, they had restricted their garrisons' sizes and in most parts of New France kept white farming to moderate levels. Settlers in British colonies sought to extend their agriculture-based economies into Indian country, which would wreak havoc on hunting, fishing, and other staples of traditional native life. Pontiac used the theme of cultural renewal to attract participants to his cause. Only by rejecting European culture and returning to their old lifeways, argued Pontiac, could Native Americans maintain their independence. This message played upon pervasive pan-Indian fears of losing their spiritual and cultural power in the face of endless British expansion. Though Pontiac's direct influence was mainly felt in the southeastern Michigan region, where he and his followers laid siege to Fort Detroit, he sent his message of cultural revitalization, along with wampum belts, throughout the Great Lakes basin and attracted many sympathetic allies.[30]

Senecas probably cared more about preventing British settlement and preserving fair and plentiful trade than about Pontiac and his message of cultural renewal. For example, Senecas stated specifically that they attacked Fort Venango because they were being charged inflated costs for powder and goods and lacked sufficient means to redress unfair trade practices. These factors, along with the establishment and maintenance of new British posts, convinced them that the British intended "to possess all their Country."[31] Johnson blamed the Senecas' disaffection on their proximity to Niagara and feared that their exposure to "assiduous Missionaries" and "zealous Partizans" in Canada would ensure their continued loyalty to France. By late July, small attacks near the Niagara portage threatened the safety of that vital British supply line, and Johnson feared for Detroit and the other upcountry posts if provisions could not be brought over the land carriage.[32]

Unlike other major Great Lakes forts, Fort Niagara did not face attack or siege during the Indian uprising, probably because an easier and more valuable target lay only six miles to the south. As local Senecas knew well, Niagara constituted an integrated fort system. Fort Niagara guarded the outlet of the Niagara River at its northern end, and small forts secured each end of the carrying place. Within the year a new outpost, Fort Erie, would be built at the inlet from Lake Erie, and a shipyard would be established on Navy Island, just upriver from the falls. Fort Niagara was the administrative center of the system, but it had proven to be a poor guard over commerce traveling between Lakes Erie and Ontario. Indians could easily bypass the fort by land or water at night, trading their goods at Little Niagara or other posts on the lakes. Fort Niagara was in a strategic position for defense and to provide refuge for soldiers and local British-allied Indians. However, the crux of the region's defense was not Fort Niagara but the portage itself. Most European goods moving into America's interior passed over the six-mile land carriage. Though the strategic importance of the portage was well known, the British conquerors of Fort Niagara had never fortified the portage path; only Little Niagara, which had been strengthened in June 1763 and renamed Fort Schlosser, and the small fort at the Lower Landing protected the carrying place. With Chenussios now in open rebellion in Pennsylvania, traversing the Niagara portage through the Seneca rebels' own territory must have been terrifying for the civilian teamsters, with their slow oxcarts and small military escorts. But, only small skirmishes troubled the land carriage until September 1763, when the attack on the British convoy above Devil's Hole plunged the Niagara region into warfare and tension as thick as in any other theater of the 1763 Indian uprising. A year of violence and negotiation that would constitute a new Seneca coexistence strategy had begun.

Amherst and Johnson immediately set about repairing the damage and placing blame for the attack, and both found the latter easier than the former. Initially, they supposed that the attacking force was the same one Bouquet had reported the previous month, meaning that some of the Indians had come from western Great Lakes communities. However, all reports of the ambush identified Senecas among the attackers, and this was confirmed by the discovery of tracks leading toward Chenussio. With the onset of Seneca attacks on the portage, fear set in at Niagara and throughout the West. Amherst warned Bouquet to watch out for deception because the attackers had taken uniforms off dead soldiers. Wilkins's Detroit-bound relief expedition was delayed for the year by devastating storms on Lake Erie, which wrecked several boats and killed even more British soldiers than the portage attackers. Provisions for Wilkins's winter camp at Fort Erie had to cross the portage on foot until fresh oxen and wagons arrived on September 25. Johnson warned of worse tidings to come. Knowing that the Chenussios were involved, he feared that "The Success which they met with, may perhaps Encourage all the Senecas to Joyn them, and . . . that Nation consists in the Whole of near *1000* Fighting Men." Continued attacks on the portage, Fort Schlosser, and the Lower Landing throughout the fall of 1763 only exacerbated fears of greater violence in the Niagara corridor. Without the ability to cross the portage safely, venture out for food or fuel, or even make hay to feed cattle on the portage, the entire British military presence in the Niagara River corridor was held in a virtual state of siege.[33]

Amherst believed that dealing quickly and harshly with the Chenussios was the answer to Niagara's problems. In November he ordered Niagara's commandant, William Browning, to plan the destruction of Chenussio itself. "It will Ensure an Uninterrupted Communication from Oswego to

Niagara," he promised; "And probably hinder any further Attacks on the Carrying Place." Despite arguments from Johnson and his Indian Department agents that genocidal attacks and restrictions on gifts would likely make the situation worse rather than better, Amherst was adamant. He remained convinced that his plan to reduce the number of gifts given to Indians at the posts was sensible and just, despite growing suspicions that his restrictions were a major source of animosity among rebel Indians and a primary cause of the uprising. Fortunately for the Chenussios, and probably for British soldiers, Wilkins, Browning, and others convinced Amherst that such an attack would be impossible during the winter.[34]

In November, Amherst's Indian policies, inability to suppress the uprising, and general unpopularity caught up with him. He was recalled to London, and the new British commander in chief, Thomas Gage, took over resolving the Indian uprising. Gage gave Johnson greater latitude to formulate Indian policy than the superintendent had enjoyed under Amherst. Johnson sought to convince the new commander to deal leniently with the Chenussios, arguing that the Senecas were probably not instigators but had been "drawn in as Auxilliaries" by other rebellious groups. He disregarded the reasons for rebellion stated by the attackers of Fort Venango and guessed that the Senecas' disaffection stemmed from the difference between "the present & former possessors of Niagara" and "the loss [the Senecas] sustained at the carrying place where they used to earn a good deal by transporting the Traders & Western Inds goods." A divide-and-rule policy seemed an appropriate way to drive a wedge between the Chenussios and Britain's more dependable Iroquoian allies. Johnson asked Gage for permission to negotiate separately with the Chenussios and the rest of the Six Nations. He suggested that the threat of British vengeance for the Devil's Hole deaths might be enough to induce the Senecas to make a clearer cession of the portage to Britain for military use. Renewing the Niagara land cession might allow the army to solidify Britain's hold on the river corridor and reduce or remove the inconvenience of Seneca sovereignty over the vital passage. Gage deferred to Johnson's deeper understanding of Indian affairs and allowed him to begin parleying with the Chenussios.[35]

Johnson's case for leniency was helped when Chenussio representatives took it upon themselves to begin peace overtures. The rebellion was slowing in the Great Lakes and Ohio country, and France showed no signs of reentering the conflict. On December 15, three Chenussio deputies and more than two hundred delegates from other Iroquois nations met with Johnson at his new home in the Mohawk Valley. The Chenussios agreed to end hostilities against the British, blaming their involvement in the uprising on Delaware and Odawa instigation. Johnson dismissed their arguments as "insignificant & dissatisfactory" and warned that Gage would be unlikely to accept their offers of peace. He left it to the Senecas' Iroquois brethren to remind them that if Gage sent a punitive force against Chenussio, the Iroquois Confederacy would not defend rabble-rousers who had endangered Iroquois-British amity. Conoquieson, an Oneida leader, scolded the Chenussios for endangering the Covenant Chain of peace between the Iroquois and the British. "Take Pity of your Children, and Families—consider also your Country, if you have any Regard for the same, and leave of[f] your silly Pride," he urged. "I speak only to you of *Chenussio*, as the rest of the Confederacy have nothing else in View but to keep up that Friendship with the English which has so long subsisted—do you the same, and perhaps you may live to have *white Heads*." The Chenussio deputies thanked the Oneida speaker for the advice. "You have really *shook* us by the *Head* so often, that we have not a Hair left on it," a Chenussio speaker joked. With most of the Iroquois Confederacy eager for peace and Gage ready to send a punitive force against them in the spring, the Chenussios knew they had played out violence as a negotiating tactic. At the end of the conference, Johnson rewarded all the participants with currency except the Chenussio deputies, telling them that their returning home empty-handed "was owing to their own Folly, and Wickedness." But despite Johnson's threats and Iroquoian warnings, the Chenussios' strategy seemed to be on track. They had made their point at Devil's Hole, and diplomacy would now ensure that they would face no violent reprisals for inflicting the Indian uprising's worst loss to British arms.[36]

In March 1764, Chenussio leaders traveled to Johnson Hall, Johnson's manor house in the Mohawk River Valley, and gave the superintendent exactly what he wanted, much to his surprise and delight. A delegation of British-allied Senecas from Kanadasego had subsequently visited the Chenussios and elicited their agreement to cease hostilities and to reaffirm their adherence to the Covenant Chain. The Seneca Nation agreed to deliver up two Indians accused of killing a trading party in 1762, along with all "Prisoners, Deserters, French men, and Negroes" who had taken refuge among them. They agreed to give free passage and assistance through their country to any British traders or military personnel, and promised not to communicate with any Indians warring against the British. As for the portage, the Senecas ceded to the king full rights to a strip of land fourteen miles long and four miles wide on both sides of the river, from Fort Niagara south to Fort Schlosser. Senecas agreed "never to obstruct the passage of the carrying place, or the free use of any part of the said tract," on the conditions that the ceded tract "be always appropriated to H. M's sole use" and that boundary lines would be drawn with Seneca witnesses present to avoid disputes. In return, Chenussios who had participated in the uprising would receive full pardons and be restored to membership in the Iroquois-British Covenant Chain alliance. "The Chenussios & Enemy Senecas have been here several days," Johnson reported to Gage, "And after due consideration on the Articles of peace, have at length agreed to them beyond my Expectations." But the Senecas had given up very little; they would still be able to use the Niagara corridor, and had established their ability to use violence, if necessary, to push their diplomatic and sociocultural agenda. After dealing the British a horrific loss at Devil's Hole, the Chenussios remained unpunished and in control of their diplomatic direction. However, the culmination of these dealings would not take place until the summer of 1764, at a planned Niagara peace conference. Until then, occasional small attacks near Niagara would remind porters and soldiers that the river corridor was still Seneca country.[37]

Johnson felt that he was on the right path toward pacifying the Chenussios, but as he prepared for his June peace conference, rumors and doubts still plagued the Niagara garrisons. In April a soldier was killed near the Lower Landing, and unidentified Indians continued to harass express riders and convoys on the portage path. Rumors flew through the region that a two-thousand-man "western" Indian force had assembled and intended to attack either Detroit or Niagara. Though neither Johnson nor Gage believed the rumors, Johnson thought it prudent to send a body of Senecas and "a few Whites" to guard the portage. Meanwhile, Colonel John Bradstreet began organizing a large expedition at Niagara to relieve the upcountry posts and to punish warring Indians, for which fortifying the portage became a vital priority.[38]

Engineer John Montresor and a detachment of 550 men arrived at Fort Niagara on May 19 to begin building a series of redoubts along the portage road and to improve the defenses of smaller posts along the Niagara River. The engineer surveyed the entire route of the portage and inspected the system of "cradles," rope-drawn winches and platforms installed to haul goods and bateaux up the escarpment above the Lower Landing. Reinforced by 110 soldiers from the Forty-sixth Regiment, Montresor's total command consisted of 656 men, comprising "Regulars, Canadians, Provincials, Indian Teamsters & Artificers." Their task was to guard the portage, build the redoubts along the portage road, and keep the wagon trains moving. With this large force in place, traffic on the portage began to increase; by June 4 provisions moved through the passage without armed escorts. A few days later, Montresor's men had finished their ten redoubts and began palisading and arming the small posts, improving the portage road, and cutting back the woods 150 yards on both sides of the path. By the end of the month, oxen and wagons carried hundred of barrels of goods per day across the route.[39]

Indians sent to guard the portage maintained a constant presence there during Montresor's efforts, though not always to the engineer's benefit or satisfaction. Indians' disinterest in their mission or outright hostility to the fortification effort diminished their effectiveness as protectors. On June 8, Seneca guards pursued three "enemy Indians" sighted near the portage but were unable or unwilling to catch them. The nervous Fort Schlosser garrison mistakenly fired at thirty friendly Indians the following day, wounding three and angering the entire native force encamped near the portage. The Seneca guards' subsequent efforts to chase down unfriendly Indians were halfhearted at best. Even after the redoubts were finished the Indian guards hesitated to disperse, remaining "as indolent and inactive as ever," according to Montresor. Johnson's Seneca protectors probably provided an important deterrent to attacks by virtue of their presence alone, but they cannot have been happy to see the portage fortified. The new redoubts made the carrying place a vital, armed British stronghold in the heart of Indian country and represented a step backward for Seneca coexistence efforts.[40]

While Montresor and his men labored to secure and improve the portage and Bradstreet planned his expedition to retake and relieve the Great Lakes posts, Johnson prepared for his summer Niagara peace conference. He chose Niagara because it was centrally located for Iroquois, Huron, Odawa, Ojibwa, and other groups participating in the rebellion and because it lay well outside the territory of the most belligerent groups in Illinois and the western Great Lakes. Of course, Niagara sat within the

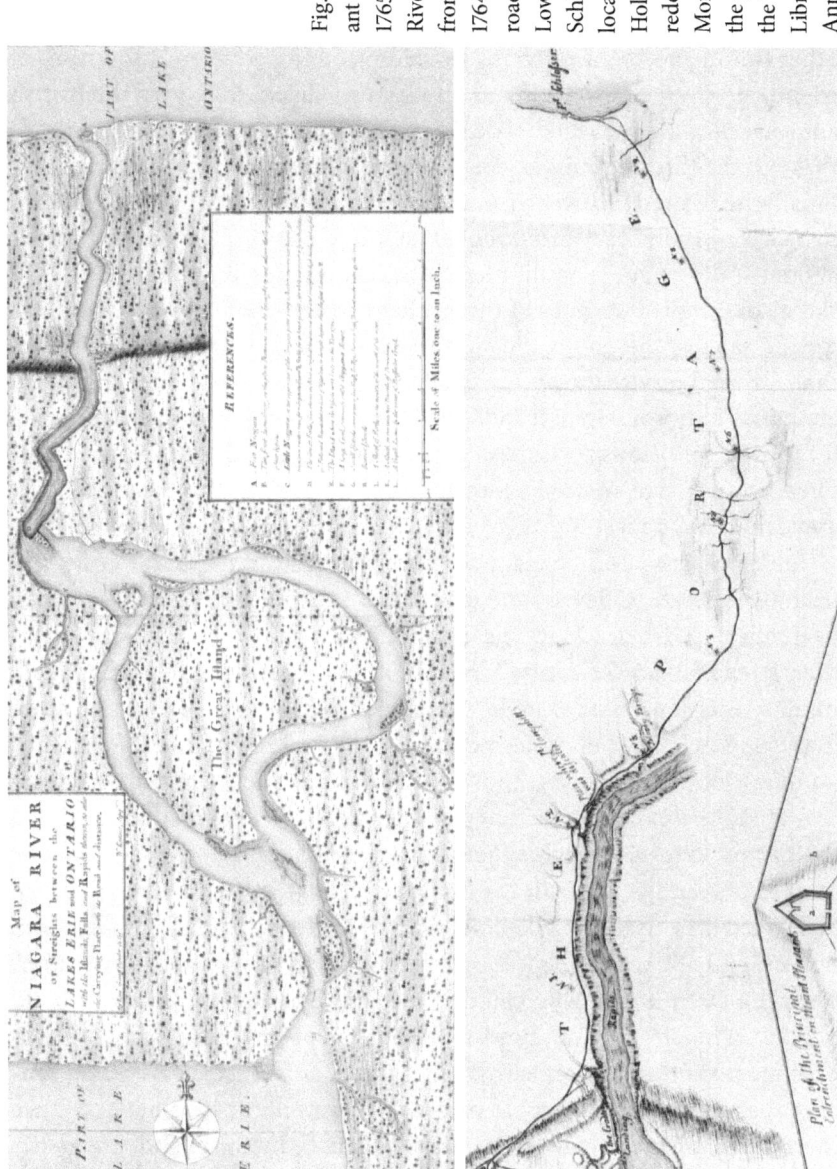

Fig. 4.2. *Top*: Lieutenant George Demler's 1765 map of the Niagara River. *Bottom*: Detail from Bernard Ratzer's 1764 drawing of the road between the Lower Landing and Fort Schlosser, showing the location of the Devil's Hole attack and the redoubts erected by John Montresor to protect the portage. Courtesy of the William L. Clements Library, Map Division, Ann Arbor, Michigan.

country of the Crown's other enemies in the uprising, the Chenussios, but this also served Johnson's plan to treat with the Senecas and the Great Lakes groups separately in order to drive a wedge between them and to prevent further collusion between belligerents of the two regions.[41]

Indians throughout the Great Lakes had suffered for want of essential trade goods after the siege of Detroit and the fall of Michilimackinac and other trading posts the previous year. Johnson hoped to elicit promises of friendship from western Indians already well disposed toward the British and eager for a renewal of trade. He planned also to quell hostile groups through the threat of military force and the inducement of trade renewal. Finally, he desired Indian assistance for the punitive and relief expeditions to be led by Bradstreet and Bouquet later in 1764. Johnson was optimistic about the diplomatic possibilities for the conference, but others remained skeptical. Bradstreet thought that Indians would come to Niagara "more for the sake of the goods they are to receive and to watch our Motions than any real service they intend us." Indeed, Johnson intended to reward attendees handsomely; £25,000 New York currency had been budgeted for Indian provisions and gifts at the conference. News of the general conference must have seemed a blessing to Indians eager for trade and gifts and exhausted by war.[42]

Johnson arrived at Niagara on June 9 to find that several groups of friendly Ojibwas, Odawas, and others from the western Great Lakes had been filtering in since May. These delegates quickly reminded Johnson of their friendship and promised the aid of their young men in Bradstreet's military mission. Most attendees denied any knowledge or participation in the uprising. Several professed great poverty and requested provisions, ammunition, trade goods, and especially rum, either through trade or as gifts. Johnson had expected to reward rebels who agreed to lay down their arms, and was even happier to supply staunch friends who could be used to encourage peace in the embattled Great Lakes region. However, he elicited little useful intelligence and met with few combatants early on; not until July 17 would he meet with actual belligerents, a group of Hurons from the Detroit area who claimed that the Odawas forced them to aid Pontiac in his siege. So far, Bradstreet's suspicions had been partially justified: most visiting natives saw the Niagara Conference as a trading rendezvous and an opportunity to receive gifts and reinforce alliances. Once there they affirmed their attachment to British interests and friendship to Johnson and, either through actual ignorance or willful dissemblance, gave the superintendent little useful war intelligence.[43]

Indians at the conference took full advantage of opportunities for trade and recreation, and an abundant supply of rum helped lubricate the latter. Johnson had hesitated to allow rum sales at the conference, but after conferring with Gage he conceded to the inescapable reality of native consumerist demand. Conference visitors could purchase a gallon of rum for one beaver skin, half the price of a stroud blanket or a calico-lined bed gown. Montresor complained of several episodes of Indian drunkenness during his term at the portage, from his arrival in May, when a group of Ojibwas and Mohawks left Fort Niagara for the portage "almost all Drunk," to June 13, when intoxicated Indians in the portage encampment threatened to kill Métis officer and interpreter Andrew Montour. On July 17, Montresor groused that the twelve hundred Indians attending the conference were being given "Rum and Oxen" to "regale with." Trader Alexander Henry also ran into problems with frolicking delegates. He arrived on July 10 in command of a ninety-six-man "Indian battalion" from the Lake Erie region, which he ordered to Fort Schlosser to join Bradstreet's expedition. After visiting Fort Niagara and receiving provisions and gifts, most of them left immediately for home. The fourteen who stayed went on to Fort Erie and drank until Bradstreet cut off their liquor. Then they too went home, leaving an embarrassed Henry without his battalion. In addition to any serious diplomatic motives and to the occasional detriment of British military expectations, war-weary Indians intended to enjoy themselves at Niagara.[44]

Although most attendees were already friendly to the British and treated the conference as a trade jamboree, Johnson was still determined to convey his main diplomatic message: that resumption of trade in the Great Lakes region depended on the cessation of violence. "What you suffer by this prohibition," Johnson told a group of friendly Odawas from Michilimackinac, "Should convince you of the ill consequences of Quarreling with the English who Command all the Doors into your Country & without whose Consent you can receive no Supplys." Johnson made it clear that those loyal to Britain must make every effort to curtail other Indians' belligerence. "Soon as that is done," he told the Odawa leader Bildanowan, "Trade will immediately flourish, & not before." Native attendees seemed amenable to Johnson's argument, professing their noninvolvement, blaming the uprising on "those Indians who became drunk," and asking Johnson to "Indulge them with a fair Trade." Johnson interpreted his efforts to marshal friendly Indians as a success. Rebellious Indians were another matter. Pontiac and other leaders of the uprising did not show up at Johnson's conference, and as of July 23 neither had any Chenussios. A peace arrangement with at least one of the major hostile groups would be needed for the conference to be called a success.[45]

Amid the general commotion caused by a major Indian conference and the muster and organization of Bradstreet's large invasion force, the absence of the region's masters, the Chenussios, must have added great tension for soldiers and Indians alike. They had not yet complied with their treaty obligations, nor had they delivered all the prisoners, British deserters, and slaves demanded by Johnson. To make matters worse for the British, a band of rebellious Delawares had taken refuge near Chenussio, despite Seneca promises to steer clear of belligerent Indians. Johnson began to spread dire warnings among conference attendees about the violent consequences that would ensue if the Chenussios did not arrive and fulfill their treaty requirements. Chenussios had a perfectly good reason to delay their arrival, though Johnson did not know it at the time: a rumor had spread in the Genesee region that the British had no intention of forgiving the Devil's Hole attack and that Johnson would order the Chenussios' destruction as soon as he had the chance. Unexpectedly, the Chenussios' participation had become the vital focus of the conference. Without a conclusion to the Seneca peace treaty, the portage would not be secure and Bradstreet's military expedition would leave behind a threatened Niagara.[46]

Much to Johnson's (and everyone's) relief, Chenussio messengers arrived on July 23 and agreed to hold a general meeting the next day. Johnson rebuked them for breaching their treaty obligations and for keeping him waiting so long at the conference. At the meeting the following day, Johnson lost no time in bringing up his latest sore point. "I little expected you would have been capable of Acting so bad a Part," he scolded the Seneca delegation, "As to give shelter to the Enemy Delawares, after the Promises made by your People last Spring." Noting that they brought only four prisoners from Chenussio, Johnson told them that they must deliver up the Delaware ringleaders within thirty days and leave two of their chiefs as hostages or Gage would cut off their trade indefinitely. A Chenussio chief, Tohaditkarawa, answered that their whole party had not yet arrived with the rest of the prisoners and that they were prepared to comply fully with the April treaty. "We Chenussios acknowledge our selves to be great Transgressors," the chief admitted. He promised to provide young men to fight in the West and to finalize their cession of the land around the Niagara portage. However, they regretted not being able to supply the two "murderers" of the trading party as stipulated in the treaty; one of the assailants had died recently, and the other fled upon hearing he was to be given up. The Chenussios hoped their failure to deliver the suspects would not be considered a breach of the treaty. "We are not Masters over the Lives of our People," the Seneca chief glumly reminded Johnson, who knew well how Iroquois community politics worked.[47]

On August 5 the Chenussio delegates agreed to deliver the Delaware leaders Squash Cutter and Attyatawitsera to Johnson, and they handed over a total of thirteen prisoners and one British deserter. They also provided Bradstreet with twenty-three young men for his expedition. "The most of our People being drunk ever since they came here, we are not yet able to collect any more," the Chenussio speaker apologized, but promised to supply more fighting men as soon as his people finished celebrating. Johnson's only alteration of the original deal, aside from the requirement to deliver the Delaware leaders, was an augmentation to the land cession. "I would further recommend it to you to give a higher Proof of your friendship," Johnson suggested, "that you should cede to his Majesty the Lands from above your late Gift, to the *Rapids* at Lake Erie on both sides of the Straights, in Breadth as the former, and to include all the Islands." With this new cession, England would have the entire Niagara strait from Fort Niagara to Fort Erie, four miles in breadth on both sides, "for (the King's) sole use, and that of his Garrisons, but not as private property." The Senecas agreed to the augmentation of the land cession, though they insisted on designating the islands in the Niagara River as a present for Johnson. "We have for some time had it in view to give them to you as a small Reward for your great trouble, and Care of us," they told Johnson, eager to prevent further British-Seneca hostilities. The final treaty, signed by seven Chenussio sachems, gave Johnson assurance of a safe British portage protected by Seneca neighbors. In turn, Johnson's stipulation that the ceded land would be for military use and not for civilian settlement gave the Chenussios assurance that the sociopolitical status quo would be protected, albeit at the cost of an increased British military presence. Chenussios had escaped punishment, and they remained free to use the

Niagara River region as they had for generations. From their point of view, coexistence had been maintained.[48]

Despite his lofty goals of western pacification, Johnson's main accomplishment at the 1764 Niagara conference was in laying groundwork for the British subjugation of Niagara itself. He did not know the Chenussios' intentions toward the British until the very end, and Bradstreet's expedition to the western Great Lakes was held hostage to this uncertainty. For their part, most of the more than two thousand Indians who attended the conference did well for themselves. They were rewarded for their past friendship, allowed to trade at Fort Niagara, and charged only with encouraging warring Indians to put down the hatchet. In the end, the conference was more about the security of the Niagara passage and resumption of trade in the West than it was a harsh subjugation of Indians participating in the Indian uprising of 1763. Pressured by Johnson's economic coaxing and the warnings of other Six Nations groups, the Chenussios appeared to have given up control of the most strategically important land carriage on the Great Lakes to the sole remaining European power in eastern North America. However, they suffered no punishment and paid little for their attack on the portage and other posts, and maintained the right to hunt, fish, and travel through the Niagara corridor. But, at the end of this turbulent year at Niagara, much remained unresolved.[49]

Johnson was optimistic about the future of the portage when he wrote to the Lords of Trade on August 30 to boast of his success at Niagara. "The cession made by the Senecas is very considerable, and will, I hope, put a stop to all future disputes about the carrying place," he crowed, noting that the Senecas "have been great losers by us concerning it." Johnson still suspected that the loss of the old French carrying concession on the Niagara portage was a possible cause of Seneca disaffection. Gage and Johnson briefly discussed returning this concession to the Chenussios to retain their cooperation. As long as goods kept moving through the Niagara corridor to support the fur trade and provision the forts, it would not matter to the king or the Lords of Trade who carried them; however, it might mean much to the Senecas because of their former employment there. However, keeping local Senecas happy was not the only rationale for renewing their carrying concession. British carriers had been a source of frustration for the army and traders throughout 1765. John Stedman, the civilian portage master who had survived the Devil's Hole attack, was not in the army's good graces that year; in fact, Bradstreet caught him overcharging the Crown and replaced him briefly. Gage did not trust any of the "waggon men," insisting that they would leave the military's stores to rot if a fur trader paid them extra to bring his trade goods across. At the end of 1765, Gage still considered the possibility of a Seneca carrying concession at Niagara, but economic and military necessity had come to dictate events at the portage, and keeping wagons and goods moving edged out Indian diplomacy.[50]

Senecas would never work at the portage again. While Gage and Johnson considered restoring Indian carriers, Stedman and his military partner, Lieutenant Francis Pfister, had already established themselves among traders as portage masters. Rather than shake up the system, Gage awarded Pfister and Stedman the sole rights to the concession in March 1766 and allowed Pfister to set up shop at Fort Schlosser. This would entail Pfister's planting corn and keeping cattle at the fort, which worried Johnson just as much as when Amherst had proposed the same arrangement four years earlier. Indians always objected to "the Establishment of familys, which they know will encrease (when once a beginning is made)," he wrote to Gage, and he agreed to talk to the Senecas before they interpreted the expanded settlement as an insult. But the portage trade had become lucrative for Gage's British contractors, and their successful enterprise at the portage ensured that Senecas would never again work as carriers at Niagara, and that ever more Europeans would begin to move into the region to stay.[51]

With their role as masters of the Niagara region diminishing each year, Senecas began to act out their frustrations. Local Senecas began stealing animals, harassing porters, and making incessant demands on Fort Niagara's garrison for gifts. In coexistence as in diplomacy, Senecas based their relationships on reciprocity. If their roles were to be diminished at Niagara, they would take whatever compensation they could find.[52]

As British-Seneca animosities increased over the ensuing years, Indian agents such as Daniel Claus blamed the frustrations solely on the Chenussios' loss of the portage carrying trade, which he claimed had greatly "enriched" the Seneca nation. This began a persistent tradition of overstating the importance of the Chenussio carrying trade at Niagara. The myth that the Devil's Hole attack was a native labor uprising and that wage labor at the portage constituted a major source of overall Seneca revenue endures to the present day. But there is scant evidence of any Indians working as carriers at Niagara under the British regime, except during Montresor's fortifying mission from May to August 1764, and every reason to think that native portaging ended during the French tenure. Neither is there any evidence that the Devil's Hole attackers had any connection with native portage workers, though it seems likely that some were involved. Johnson himself noted that the Chenussios never stipulated any interest in the carrying concession during their 1764 talks. Wage labor at the portage was undoubtedly important to the livelihoods of those Indians who performed the work under the French regime, and it established visibly the Seneca's influence at Niagara while it lasted, but it was not the cause of the Senecas' rebelliousness toward the British.[53]

From the summer of 1763 to the fall of 1764, Chenussios used familiar methods to preserve a solid cultural and political footing in the face of increasing European expansion. They had always occupied a middle position between the French in Canada and the English in New York. After the British triumph in the Seven Years' War, they foresaw a new economic and political climate where the price of goods could rise without possibility of redress and their hunting lands might be subject to white settlement. Some of them took action immediately after the British victory in 1761 by unsuccessfully trying to stir up rebellion in the West. More actually turned to violence to achieve their ends during the Indian uprising of 1763. The Devil's Hole attack provided a conspicuous display of Seneca power at a time when native hegemony seemed to be under attack. The attack eventually worsened their negotiating position by ensuring the fortification of the important Niagara portage, but by then the Chenussios had already turned away from violence and returned to the diplomatic tactics of the early eighteenth century. They gave away a strip of land that had already been given away in 1701 and 1726, and with almost the same terms as before. As long as they could pass freely through the lands and hold off British civilian settlement, they risked nothing. Agreeing to Johnson's terms ensured that none of their people would be punished for the Devil's Hole attack, the worst loss to British arms in the entire Indian uprising. But much had changed in the thirty-eight years since the last Iroquois cession of the Niagara corridor. In 1764, British military authorities and traders had the economic and demographic means to begin settling the Niagara region in earnest. Contrary to Seneca expectations, and unlike the two earlier deeds, the treaty of 1764 would eventually turn out to be a true land cession. By the time of the American Revolution, Niagara had become a vital British military outpost and an unhappy place for Senecas.

This would become clear during the Revolutionary War. Ravaged by fighting and disease, their towns destroyed by Washington's troops, thousands of Iroquoian refugees flocked to Niagara for protection. Hundreds, and perhaps thousands, died of disease and starvation in the shadow of Niagara's House of Peace. European-Seneca coexistence took increasingly ugly turns thereafter.[54]

Fort Niagara, the carrying place, and Indian wage labor were all manifestations of the European fur trade, and they all worked toward the same ultimate, if sometimes unconscious, goal: remaking Indian country for the Europeans' benefit. Indians operating as suppliers and consumers in the fur-trade economy made the best of it, and that sometimes included performing manual labor for wages, a livelihood that has seldom "enriched" anyone despite what Daniel Claus and others may have thought. But, Chenussios and other native participants in the rebellion of 1763–64 did not fight against European encroachment and change to preserve wage labor. They fought to protect their customary use of Indian country, where they had hunted, lit council fires, and buried ancestors for generations. The events of 1763 and 1764 showed Chenussios attempting to maintain something more substantial than carrying packs around a waterfall. They joined the rebellion and attacked at Niagara to establish their power and defend their territory. When the rebellion ceased they agreed to a treaty that they thought would preserve their rights to live and hunt on their traditional lands at the cost of a negotiated coexistence with familiar British military personnel. In the autumn of 1764, neither the Chenussios nor their new British landlord-tenants understood the full extent to which events were already moving out of their control.

5

Like Stars That Fall

Keeping Up Appearances at Fort Chartres, 1765–1772

In June 1772, a small company of British regular soldiers, newly arrived in the Illinois country, ascertained the depth of British authority in Kaskaskia. Fifteen miles away, Fort Chartres, the seat of British operations in Illinois for seven years, crumbled into the encroaching Mississippi.[1] Sir Thomas Gage had ordered the post's commandant, Major Isaac Hamilton, to abandon and destroy the fort. He also instructed Hamilton to send fifty men to guard Kaskaskia, the largest trading town in the area. Soon after the soldiers' arrival, a small band of visiting Chickasaws entered William Murray's trading house and ransacked it. According to Hugh Lord, the British detachment's captain, the fifteen Chickasaws entered the house, beat Murray's servants, and broke everything in the shop. They seemed bent more on intimidation or revenge than theft. Lord sent an officer and some men to turn out the invaders and guard the house until the Indians left town. The soldiers took one prisoner, a man Lord described as a renegade Chickasaw living in Illinois who had "always used his utmost endeavours to breach the peace that has so long subsisted between the English and the Chickesaws." When the soldiers reached their guardhouse, they heard gunfire. The remaining Chickasaws had begun firing on the trader's house, killing one of Murray's servants. When Lord sent his men back to drive off the attackers, the Indians fired at the soldiers and fled, losing two of their number in the exchange. Lord and his soldiers might have expected more respect and cooperation, but this violent display of social enforcement suggested that seven years of British occupation had done little to impress or intimidate Indians in the Illinois country.[2]

At the conclusion of the Seven Years' War, Britain needed badly to make good impressions in their newly won territories. This would be especially difficult in Illinois, where supply and communication lines stretched for hundreds, even thousands, of miles. The quickest way *out* of Illinois was down the Mississippi River and then by ship back to the eastern colonies. The fastest way *in* for British travelers was down the Ohio River. Both ways were time-consuming and dangerous. But Britain had won control of Illinois by treaty and sought to establish its sovereignty. France had operated a colony in Illinois for decades, and Britain needed to show the region's French and native inhabitants that they could perform as well as their erstwhile enemies. This would entail finding a way to garrison Fort Chartres, the seat of French power in the region and the westernmost of all posts ceded to the British.

British occupation of Fort Chartres was intended to constitute a physical manifestation of British ambitions in the American interior. Unfortunately for Britain's architects of empire, Indians in the Great Lakes area were not cooperative. The Indian uprising of 1763–64 delayed plans for the occupation of Illinois. Even after the uprising ended, belligerent activities continued in Illinois, ensuring that British garrisons would encounter resentful, confrontational Native American populations during their occupation attempt. British personnel at Fort Chartres would need to appear fully capable of meeting the region's Indians on British terms. To accomplish this goal, it was imperative that the British occupiers of Illinois appear as strong and sound as the fort itself. For the unfortunate men destined to carry out this mission, this appearance of strength would prove elusive. Forts and military initiatives may have been effective in some other parts of America, but in Illinois during the 1760s and early 1770s, Indians remained dominant and unimpressed by the British attempt to master Illinois.

Despite the confrontational aspect conveyed by operating forts and garrisons deep within Indian country, few British military leaders thought that the presence of manned posts alone could intimidate or overawe natives. Dependence on European trade could bind Indians to British interests better than force of arms. At any rate, military intimidation was impractical in remote regions like Illinois, where British units could not be relieved or provisioned easily in the event of an attack. Indians in Illinois knew that relatively small British garrisons manning regional outposts were susceptible to general native offensives, especially after so many frontier forts fell during the Indian uprising of 1763–64. But military units still needed to show Indians that they could punish renegade bands of attackers, maintain law and order, and protect settlers and traders from small-scale attacks. Fort commandants met with local and visiting Indians almost daily, and every meeting was a new test of strength. From the Indians' perspective, these meetings were negotiations of friendship, alliance, and promises of future aid. Commandants needed, at least, to manifest the appearance of power and potential violence in order to negotiate from a position of strength.

Even if the appearance of strength could not be maintained, garrisons and their commanders could never afford to look foolish or incompetent. They had to show that they could live, work, and accomplish their goals in Indian country as well as natives could. Susceptibility to disease or other environmental hazards would make newcomers appear weak to better-acclimated Indians. Forts themselves needed to seem sturdy enough to withstand at least a small attack. Eastern Woodland and Plains Indians infused their war cultures with rituals and dress that would bring them spiritual power and human respect, and they would be quick to notice if British soldiers did not maintain their own regalia. And basic proofs of manliness mattered to Native Americans as well. Soldiers were expected to be able to fight and operate on rivers and in forests and fields. If men could not hunt, fish, and gather fuel well enough to survive in an environment that provided all these things in abundance, then Indians were unlikely to take them very seriously. Penalties for appearing unprepared or foolish varied but were always serious. After the bloody examples of the Seven Years' War and the following uprising, Indians in the Illinois and Great Lakes regions knew that all but the largest forts could be attacked and reduced easily.[3]

Illinois natives also knew that a demolished or besieged outpost was of little use to anyone. A functioning outpost, on the other hand, could maintain the flow of European goods and provisions by protecting trade and supplying presents. The latter was preferable to Indians, who saw gift giving as a cementing of reciprocal Indian-European friendship. Gifts were the physical component of friendship between individuals, groups, and even nations. As was the case at the other forts in this study, Indians expected gifts when performing the rites and responsibilities of friendship, and felt abused and slighted when gifts were not forthcoming. Presents of food, weapons, ammunition, and clothing were also necessities

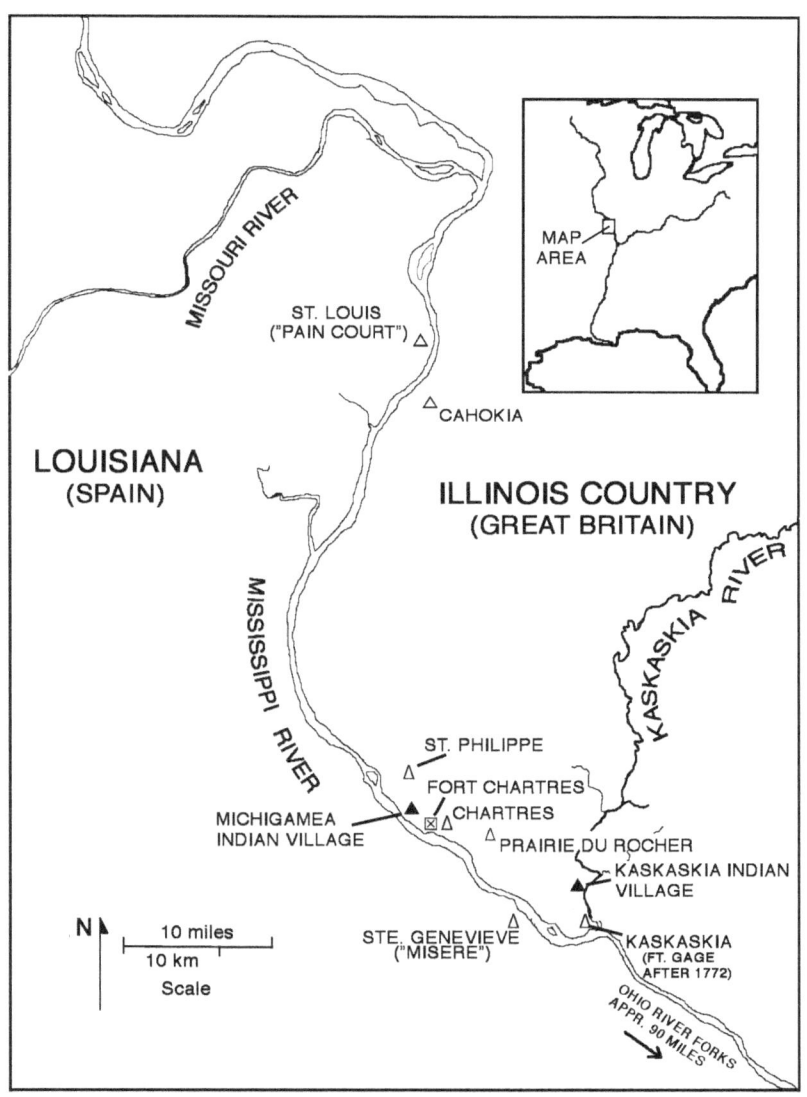

Map 5.1. Fort Chartres and the western Illinois country, 1765–1771.

that Indians came to depend upon. In regions such as Illinois, where Europeans lived outnumbered by native inhabitants and at the mercy of an uncompromising environment, gifts were even more important. A particularly feeble European presence mandated a greater need to placate Indian allies. Soldiers and forts that failed to impress Indians would have to pay well to maintain their love and friendship.[4]

Keeping up appearances cannot have topped the list of concerns for Britons contemplating the occupation of Fort Chartres in 1764. Chartres was the remotest of all French outposts won in the Seven Years' War, but it was also one of the strongest and most impressive. Built during the 1750s to counter the growing British threat to New Orleans and the Mississippi interior, Fort Chartres was a limestone giant that would have looked impressive anywhere in North America. Earlier forts at this site, near the Mississippi River about a hundred miles above the confluence of the Ohio, were substantial wooden structures that failed to withstand the wet environment of the Mississippi sloughs. In 1751, French authorities began construction of a new stone fort, designed by noted engineer François Saucier in the popular European Vauban style. Compared to other French posts in the Illinois country, such as those at Kaskaskia and St. Louis, Fort Chartres was huge. Its sides measured 490 feet each, with walls eighteen feet tall and more than two feet thick. The interior encompassed almost four acres and several buildings, most two stories high and built of stone. Fort Chartres usually held garrisons of 150 men or more and was defended by at least twenty cannon. As a defensive outpost, it must have seemed nearly impenetrable to the region's Indians, who probably had little or no familiarity with stone forts.[5]

But for all its impressiveness, Fort Chartres was not built with intimidation in mind. The fort's stone construction was a response to the environmental hazards of the Mississippi Valley region, where wooden forts could not expect to last more than a couple of decades in the humid, frequently flooded lowlands. Its effectiveness as a defensive outpost was never tested by British or Indian attack during the Seven Years' War; indeed, its main function was not military. Fort Chartres acted as the administrative center of the French Illinois colony and as the seat of the colony's governors. Though protecting the fur trade remained an important consideration at Fort Chartres, most trading took place in the area's trading towns, especially Kaskaskia to the south and Cahokia to the north, or deep within Indian country itself. Fort Chartres's garrison was more concerned with administering the sale and distribution of farmland and maintaining order among thousands of nearby settlers and hundreds of slaves. Almost all them were engaged in agricultural activities rather than the fur business. With a civilian population employed almost entirely in farming, Illinois resembled Britain's Atlantic coast colonies more than it did France's Canadian colonies, where fishing and fur-trading dominated economic activity. This familiarity should have provided an advantage to incoming English administrators.[6]

Thousands of permanent Indian residents lived alongside the French settlers and African and Creole slaves inhabiting the villages around Fort Chartres. Michigameas occupied two villages only a couple of miles from the fort. Fifteen miles to the south, Kaskaskias maintained a permanent village about a mile from the French village of that name. Even at those nearby towns, Indian residents disappeared for months at a time on hunting trips. Other Illinois groups, including Peorias and Cahokias from farther north, made frequent visits to the French posts up and down the Mississippi.

Local Indians looked to the French for protection as well as economic opportunities and presents. Through the early and mid-eighteenth century, Illinois groups suffered attacks by Fox and Sauk groups from the north, Kickapoos and Potawatomis from the Wabash region, and Chickasaws, Creeks, and Cherokees from the southeast. Equally powerful Osage, Missouri, and Sioux groups pressured the Illinois region from west of the Mississippi. Illinois Indians fought and negotiated with surrounding groups of Indians and maintained modest livings through the fur trade. By 1757, Illinois Indians reportedly sent several hundred packs of furs down the Mississippi each year. Because of Fort Chartres's strategic geographic location beside the Mississippi between the mouths of the Ohio and the Missouri, its garrison would encounter diverse Indian groups from throughout the American interior.[7]

Not surprisingly, Indians whom British newcomers met at Fort Chartres were sometimes belligerent. Many Illinois groups participated in the 1763 Indian uprising, and long after the main hostilities ceased they maintained their animus. Much of the credit for preparing such a harsh reception for the new British masters of Illinois must go to Pontiac himself, who concentrated on fomenting rebellion in the Illinois heartland after his siege of Detroit failed. Charlot Kaské, a Shawnee resistance leader, may have accomplished even more in turning the region's residents against

British rule. Both of these insurgents lobbied Illinois's French administrators forcefully for aid in their rebellion. When rebuffed, they and other leaders organized Illinois Indians and French habitants into anti-British cadres who they hoped would prevent British takeover of the Illinois country. But opposition to British rule also sprang from local grassroots sources and was remarkably heartfelt. Local natives feared that the new regime would attract English settlers and expansionist Indian groups from the East. They also worried that British commandants would be less generous with gifts than their French forebears. Up and down the Mississippi, Indians took up arms against English traders and dismissed official French pleas to accept the inevitability of British rule. Rumors warned that French habitants and traders were inciting Indians and preparing to resist British occupiers. This spirit of resistance manifested itself during the first futile British attempts to occupy Fort Chartres.[8]

On February 27, 1764, twelve boats carrying 324 soldiers and 47 women and children, under the command of Major Arthur Loftus, attempted to ascend the Mississippi from New Orleans. Ascents against the river's current were always arduous, time-consuming, and dangerous. Three weeks into the expedition, about two hundred miles upriver from New Orleans, a small party of Tunica Indians attacked the convoy. Already terrified by French warnings of Indian depredations on the Mississippi and lacking knowledge of local Indian ways, Loftus ordered a full retreat to New Orleans. He blamed Louisiana governor Jean-Jacques D'Abbadie for encouraging the attacks, despite the governor's many warnings against attempting the ascent. But the attack was a warning to Britain and served as a harsh welcome to the region for the new masters of Illinois. Gage seemed unsurprised and somewhat relieved that more people were not lost in the attack; he had been warned by his Indian Department agents that lavish presents would be necessary to possess the Illinois country. "We have been obliged to do the same with many States in Africa we despise," he wrote glumly to William Johnson. The commander in chief began planning for an expensive occupation.[9]

It is unlikely that even lavish gifts would have made much of a difference in 1764, especially in the region between New Orleans and Fort Chartres. The area's native inhabitants retained long-standing alliances with the French regime in New Orleans and Fort Chartres, and their hatred of British soldiers, traders, and settlers had only increased during wartime. Two Tunicas, Perruquier and Bride le Boeuf, explained their motives for attacking Loftus's convoy and described their solidarity with Illinois Indians to a regional French commandant:

> The red men of that territory will never let them pass. The French, our brothers, have never given us any disease, but the English have scarcely arrived, and they have caused nearly all our children to die by the smallpox they have brought. Notice, father, if we were to let them settle on the river, they would build forts and forts; and as soon as they were established, they would kill our brothers, the French, and poison us. Father, become angry if you will; our plan is to go and await them on the Point aux Ecors; and if they wish to return, we shall have the glory of driving them away again.[10]

With Illinois still in native and French hands at the close of 1764, occupying the region began to seem impractical. Reports from the few British intelligence sources in Illinois (mostly British traders) confirmed the enormity of the undertaking. John Bradstreet, fresh from squandering his chance to negotiate a meaningful denouement to the Indian uprising in Ohio country, informed his superiors of his views on the Illinois problem. He had been assured by "persons lately from the Illinois" that six hundred French habitants and a thousand black slaves, all armed and ready to fight, would never allow British troops to take possession of the region. Furthermore, French residents had so incited the western Indians with tales of imminent British depredations that no convoys would ever be allowed up the Mississippi. "The only way to establish ourselves amongst the Savages," he opined, "is to begin, by coming upon them by ways unfrequented, undiscovered, and with such Force, as shall make such an impression as shall be lasting." Bradstreet may have lacked political acumen, but he understood the value of overawing Indians with a strong first impression. He suggested sending at least three thousand British regulars down the Ohio River quickly and quietly. With such a strong and sudden occupation, and with the purchased aid of other native groups in the region, Illinois and Wabash-area Indians and habitants would put aside their dreams of a French return and accept British authority.[11]

If Bradstreet suspected that only a large, rapid invasion could quickly implant British rule on the Mississippi, then the terrible thought must have crossed the minds of Indian resistance leaders as well. They continued to lobby and plan for French military help, but as time went on it became clear that the long-rumored awakening of the French father in America would never happen. After D'Abbadie's death on February 4, 1765, Charlot Kaské lost no time in meeting with the new governor of Louisiana, Charles Aubry. Accompanied by Illinois chief Levancher, he was surprised and unhappy to find Aubry accompanied by three English officers, including the Indian superintendent for the Southern Department, John Stuart, and his agent, Pierce Sinnot. Kaské was polite to the British visitors but warned them to stay out of his own village of Scioto. Shawnees there feared losing their lands to settlers, and Kaské could not answer for the safety of any British interloper. Levancher was more direct. "I came from the Illinois to see if it were true that the country had been ceded to the English and having learned it I am surprised that the emperor has ceded it," he groused to Aubry and his visitors. "Since he rejects us, we are masters of our bodies and our lands." Turning to the British officers, he warned them that it would take some time to earn the Illinois Indians' trust: "You English only ask to kill; you have caused the red men to die; do not be surprised if I speak to you likewise; if I scold you, my heart is still sore because I have seen so many French and Indians die together. When the English conduct themselves well toward the red men, we shall look upon them with pleasure." With the French governor's influence fading among resistant Illinois natives, the British would be on their own in finding a solution to the impasse.[12]

Through the winter and spring of 1765, individual British emissaries made their way to Fort Chartres, with varying degrees of success. Alexander Maisonville and Jacques Godfroi, two trader-interpreters with wide and deep connections in Indian country, visited Chartres in early February and elicited guarded suggestions from several Illinois chiefs that they might agree to live under a British regime. The next effort, by Lieutenant John Ross and trader Hugh Crawford, did not end as well. When the two arrived at Fort Chartres later that month, a group of Kaskaskia, Cahokia, Peoria, Michigamea, Osage, and Missouri headmen declared angrily that they would never live under British rule. Only the intervention of Louis St. Ange de Bellerive, the fort's commandant, saved Ross from being killed by an outraged Osage chief. Tomeroy, a local Kaskaskia chief, threatened to make sure any future British interlopers would "fall in the water" upon their arrival. Ross and Crawford fled for their lives down the Mississippi upon hearing that Ojibwas and Potawatomis were on their way to Fort Chartres to capture them. Initial attempts at establishing British possession of the fort had failed to impress the region's Indians. So far, native

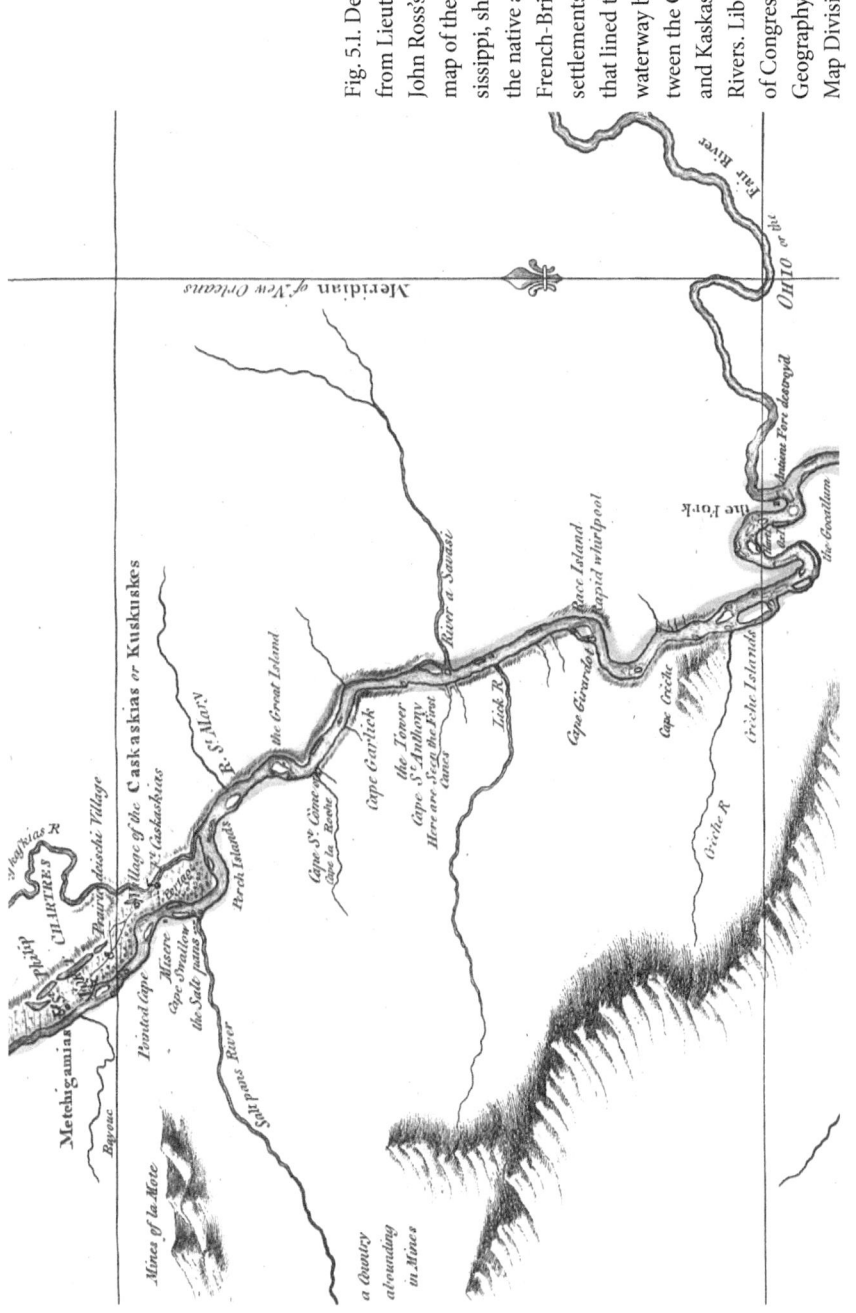

Fig. 5.1. Detail from Lieutenant John Ross's 1765 map of the Mississippi, showing the native and French-British settlements that lined the waterway between the Ohio and Kaskaskia Rivers. Library of Congress, Geography and Map Division.

leaders had done all the intimidating, and more diplomacy would be needed.[13]

Gage hoped that veteran Indian agent and trader George Croghan would have better luck. Croghan and Lieutenant Alexander Fraser were to travel down the Ohio from Fort Pitt to Fort Chartres to size up the situation. They would take several respected Shawnee and Delaware chiefs with them to avoid trouble with angry Indians and to prove that those nations had made their peace with Britain. Gage suggested that Croghan remind Indians in Illinois that Cherokees and Chickasaws could be induced to ravage the region on Britain's behalf and that Sauk, Fox, and western Plains groups were eager to help as well. Above all, Illinois Indians were to be told that the English would not attempt the kind of invasion suggested by Bradstreet, unless the Indians "by their own folly and Obstinancy" forced them to do so. While Croghan and company plied the Ohio River, another Mississippi convoy, commanded by Major Robert Farmar, would proceed upriver and occupy Fort Chartres and its surrounding towns.[14]

Croghan's expedition did not go as planned, but it did secure a diplomatic opportunity for the British to occupy Fort Chartres. A violent encounter with the anti-Indian "Black Boys"—white Pennsylvania settlers operating in the "Paxton Boys" mode—delayed his departure. Croghan was carrying trade goods to Illinois (illegally, as it turned out), and the rebel settlers had determined to restrict any goods moving into Indian country. Croghan had also scheduled a conference with Shawnee and Delaware chiefs at Fort Pitt, causing a further delay. Fraser grew tired of waiting for Croghan and set out for Illinois with Maisonville and ten other men. When they arrived at Kaskaskia in April, the small party fell immediately into the hands of Pontiac and his followers and were taken to Fort Chartres. After many threats, Fraser and his men fled down the Mississippi, but their bravery made a better impression on the Indians at Fort Chartres than John Ross had done a few months earlier. Croghan's party never made it as far as Fort Chartres. A large party of Kickapoos and Mascoutins attacked his company near the confluence of the Wabash and Ohio Rivers, killing five people, three of whom were Shawnee chiefs. Even as a prisoner, Croghan realized that the deaths of the chiefs could start a violent blood feud in the region that Illinois Indians would prefer to avoid. At Fort Ouiatenon he met with Pontiac, just arrived from his meeting with Fraser at Fort Chartres. Pontiac had heard about the mishap and was willing to negotiate. He guaranteed that British forces would have safe passage into Illinois. British troops would be allowed to garrison French posts but would not be permitted to expand civilian settlements without Indians' permission. Croghan later admitted to Johnson, "The Killing of the Shawanese Deputies, & Plundering me hath been of more Service to his Majesty's Indian Interest, than a considerable Sum Expended in presents." The door to Illinois was finally open, owing more to an excess of Indian exuberance than to any appearance of British strength. To accomplish their goals in Illinois, the new British occupants of Fort Chartres would still need to prove their mettle.[15]

British authorities at Fort Pitt took advantage of the unexpected peace made at Ouiatenon, as well as unseasonably high water levels in the Ohio River, and immediately sent a company of the Forty-second Infantry under the command of Captain Thomas Sterling to hold Fort Chartres. Sterling's detail made rapid progress through the Ohio country, reaching Chartres on October 10. Local Indians were caught by surprise; usually they received intelligence from their Shawnee and Potawatomi allies about any large convoy traveling down the Ohio. When Sterling's men appeared suddenly, Indians "came running with pipes and belts." When they discovered that Sterling brought only a small detachment and a dozen Indians, they began to act insolently and threaten the soldiers, but by then Sterling and his men were safely ensconced in the fort. This was a lucky break for Sterling. None of the local chiefs had been at Ouiatenon or knew about the peace made there, and they might have felt free to attack the British company.[16]

Sterling raised the British colors over Fort Chartres and took official possession of what his lieutenant described as "one of the prettiest stone forts" he had ever seen. Unfortunately, the fort was almost completely devoid of ammunition and stores, and the French had removed most of the functioning artillery. Sterling took note of the fort's deficiencies and counted the local Indians living near the fort. He reported 150 warriors living in the Kaskaskia Indian village, and 40 Michigameas and 250 Peorias living in the closest village, about a mile upriver from the fort. He then proceeded to read Gage's proclamation announcing the new regime to any French habitants that remained in the nearby villages of Chartres and Kaskaskia. Sterling reported that only a few French troops had garrisoned the fort since the end of the Seven Years' War and that the Indians had been "quite Masters" of the region, treating the habitants "as they thought proper." This, thought Sterling, accounted for the flight of so many French residents to the western side of the river. It is more likely that the French settlers simply did not wish to remain under British rule and expected violence to erupt during the takeover. This remained a possibility for the new garrison. Farmar's occupying force had not yet arrived from Mobile, and winter was closing in. Surrounded by hostile native groups and lacking sufficient stores, ammunition, working cannon, or even an interpreter, Sterling and his small band faced tense times in the great limestone fort.[17]

Croghan was not going to let Sterling's inconveniences interrupt the diplomatic momentum he had started at Ouiatenon and Detroit. He wrote optimistically to Johnson, "All doubts are removed respecting our obtaining Possession of the Illinois Country; Captain Sterling being Arrived and received, at Fort Chartres, with open Arms by the Natives & without meeting, with the least Interruption, on his Passage thither." Although the region was surrounded by "four very Powerful Indian Confederacys," Croghan was happy to note that their possession of Illinois was brought about "with the Natives Consent, which however, we could not do by Force, Tho' attempted, at a very Considerable expence, for two years past." Of course, a garrison of any size was vulnerable to a native siege, especially with long, fragile supply lines leading up the Ohio that could be cut off at any time. Croghan recommended making a colony out of the Illinois and establishing civil government, as the French had done. With an influx of British settlers, the European population would soon exceed that of the Indians and allow Illinois to become a profitable agricultural colony instead of a drain on the Crown's assets.[18]

Sterling's stay at Fort Chartres was short. On December 2, 1765, Farmar and the Thirty-fourth Regiment arrived to relieve Sterling's men and begin the occupation of Illinois in earnest. It had taken five arduous months for Farmar's convoy to pole their barges upstream from Mobile, partly because his river pilot had deserted along the way. The situation he found offered little compensation for his troubles. Farmar immediately realized that Fort Chartres was "likely to be carried away by the River" in a matter of months, despite its size and stone construction. Furthermore, local farmers could supply no more than 50,000 pounds of flour and 1,250 pounds of cornmeal, which would supply the men of the garrison only until July and leave none for the roughly four thousand regional native visitors that could be expected in the summer. Presents would be needed to placate Indian visitors, but most of Farmar's had been ruined in the journey, and the rest had been given to friendly Indians they met along the way. Finally, Farmar found the remaining habitants to be just as hostile to his presence as many of the Indians. But the biggest problem might have been Farmar himself, who saw French intrigue everywhere and, according to Gage, was "not very knowing in the Treating or Management of Indians." Britain had occupied Illinois, but creating an appearance of strength would take more time.[19]

Provisioning problems would remain a constant detriment to the British occupation of Fort Chartres. Planted amid what Croghan had once called the "granary of Louisiana," the British garrison lacked sufficient numbers to police the fur trade, placate local Indians, and still provide agricultural labor. French residents had always faced a labor shortage in the region, necessitating the use of more than a thousand imported slaves. The French had provisioned Fort Chartres twice a year with huge convoys sent from New Orleans. With that city under Spanish control, most provisions would have to come down the Ohio from Fort Pitt or through the Wabash region from Detroit. In March 1766, Farmar reported that he would need 50,000 more pounds of flour from local sources before he could hope to be provisioned again. In April only 2,000 pounds of wheat flour and 7,000 pounds of cornmeal were available from the area's farmers. Buffalo meat could suffice when grain supplies ran low, but armed hunting parties roaming the heavily contested native hunting grounds of Illinois could easily provoke violence. Even when buffalo meat could be provided, supplies of cured or salted meat spoiled easily in the Illinois heat. In one unimpressive incident, a group of western Indians arrived at Fort Chartres and asked for some meat; the French had always given it to them, they claimed. Farmar was reduced to telling them that the British had no meat even for themselves. This actually incurred some sympathy from the visiting Indians, who offered the garrison some of their own meager supplies. However, such a lack of provisions probably did not engender much respect.[20]

Part of this supply problem stemmed from the French habitants' lack of affection for the new British regime. Labor shortages remained throughout the British occupation, even after some French farmers returned to their lands east of the Mississippi. But with the threat of Indian attacks always present, French farmers could not be relied upon to help the garrison in times of trouble. Croghan suggested that sufficient provisions might be purchased at Vincennes, the largest settlement between Fort Chartres and Detroit, but the farmers there would not take currency as payment. He argued that, as dangerous as it might be to ship caches of silver through Indian country, buying from Vincennes would still be easier and more convenient than provisioning Fort Chartres from Fort Pitt or New Orleans. But Chartres was such a large operation that provisions from all possible sources would be needed throughout British tenure. Fort Chartres and the smaller posts at Cahokia and Kaskaskia had to maintain huge, expensive stockpiles of consumable (and perishable) goods in store in case of Indian attacks, Spanish incursions, or any number of other troubles.[21]

Suspicious local Indians fled the region during the early years of the British regime, adding to the new garrison's troubles. This may have been caused by rumors of French or British threats against Indians in the region. Farmer and one of his officers, Captain James Campbell, both reported rumors supposedly spread by French traders that the English were poisoning food and liquor given to Indians. A group of Missouris made a long trip to Fort Chartres in April 1766 specifically to ascertain the veracity of this report, and to warn Farmar that if any of their people died from poisoned English food or drink, other nations would avenge them. These Missouris believed the rumor to such an extent that they refused to drink any English liquor until they saw Farmar and his men drink it first. Many Indians who fled across the Mississippi thought the British would assail them for their role in the Indian uprising. Others feared that the English would kill them to steal their land, or out of pure hatred. Though some natives returned as soon as they saw that the garrison had no interest in harming them, dislocation of local populations made stabilizing the region a hard task for the fort's beleaguered garrison.[22]

English attitudes and prejudices toward the French and Indian inhabitants of Illinois cannot have made the situation any easier to handle. French colonists were a rough and hardy lot, as were many English backcountry settlers, but the vitriol evident in some British communications shows the nationalistic and racial hatred that complicated British-French-Indian relations. Croghan, for example, hated the French of Illinois and the Wabash country passionately. He described the residents of Vincennes as "an idle, lazy people, a parcel of renegadoes from Canada" who were "much worse than the Indians." He thought that French settlers living near St. Joseph and Detroit were similarly lazy and indolent, "fond of breeding mischief, and spiriting up the Indians against the English." Fraser held much the same attitude. Of the Illinois Indians, he wrote: "Nothing can equal their passion for drunkenness, but that of the French Inhabitants, who are for the greatest part drunk every day while they can get Drink to buy in the Colony." Fraser derided French settlers for their dependence on black slaves, who were "obliged to Labour very hard to Support their Masters in their extravagant Debaucheries." He suspected that the French of Illinois were descendants of convicts and described them as cruel, deceitful, and incapable of honest labor. And these two men were British diplomats; one can only imagine what the garrison's rank and file might have thought of Britain's new French subjects. This French-British cultural conflict only served to empower local Indians, who could always play Europeans against one another for their own purposes.[23]

In August 1766, Croghan arrived in Illinois with a contingent of Six Nations and Delaware delegates to settle local Indians' complaints and negotiate a working peace. More than one thousand Indians attended his conference, from eight nations on both sides of the Mississippi. Colonel John Reed had replaced Farmar as commandant that summer; Farmar had been unable to negotiate a solution to local Indian claims to vacated French lands in Cahokia. Croghan was more successful, eliciting promises of support and protection for the new garrison from several visiting groups. "With a little good Usage, they will soon become a very quiet & Peacable People," Croghan wrote optimistically to Johnson. "At present Indian Affairs [wear] a different Face in this Country." But Croghan's diplomatic success came at a premium price: it was generosity with gifts that turned the tide. Having already given away most of his £3,000 worth of Indian presents to Shawnees and others at Scioto, Croghan was forced to purchase expensive trade goods and provisions for the conference from local traders. Given the large numbers of attendees, he felt that "there was an absolute necessity of Convincing them at this time that the English were as able to Support them as the French." Croghan's lavishness satisfied the conference delegates for the moment. However, if shortages in goods and high local prices continued, the diplomatic gains would be short-lived, and would require more gifts. In any case, it appeared in 1766 that amicable British-Indian relations in Illinois would be expensive.[24]

If lack of provisions threatened to challenge the garrison's thin veneer of competence, deadly epidemics must have made local Indians wonder if the newcomers could function at all in the Mississippi Valley. During the British occupation, hundreds of English residents fell victim to a feverish "disorder of the country" that disabled and killed dozens of people every year. Fort Chartres had been constructed, over many objections, in a low-lying region that flooded every spring, leaving sloughs and pools of rancid standing water that served as remarkably efficient breeding grounds for disease. Trader George Morgan, who arrived at Kaskaskia in 1766 to represent the Philadelphia trading firm of Baynton, Wharton, and Morgan, noted that between June and October 1766 few inhabitants of Fort Chartres or Kaskaskia escaped the ague and fever that accompanied the disease. The sickness was "not in itself Mortal," according to Morgan, but the frequency and severity of its onsets made victims susceptible to other, more dangerous diseases. Morgan claimed that no Europeans born in Illinois, English or French, lived beyond the age of fifty, and few made it past forty. During Croghan's 1766 conference at Fort Chartres, only three officers and fifty men remained well enough to perform their duties. Croghan himself became so sick that he was forced to return down the Mississippi and take ship at New Orleans rather than face the more arduous upstream journey to Fort Pitt. The disorder hit most newcomers to the region almost upon arrival and could incapacitate victims for months at a time until they became acclimated, which usually took at least two years.[25]

Ensign George Butricke, who accompanied Colonel John Wilkins to Fort Chartres in 1768, described the worst outbreak of the disease. Butricke observed that the five companies of his Royal American regiment appeared perfectly healthy upon their arrival at Kaskaskia in early September. Within three weeks, most of the regiment had contracted the disease. Wilkins, all of his officers, and almost every soldier fell victim to the alternating bouts of chills, shakes, and fever at a rate of twenty men per day. After a week of this epidemiological onslaught, only nineteen men remained healthy enough to guard the post. By late October, twenty-eight men, twelve women, and fifteen children lay dead. Winter exacerbated the problem, and by February 1769 fifteen more men had died, along with "almost all the Women and thirty-Seven Children that arrived here with the five companys in perfect health," according to Butricke. Many of these later deaths were attributed to an outbreak of dysentery that roiled the garrison after the initial fevers had abated. This "Bluddy flux" continued to strike the garrison throughout 1769, leaving one of the largest forts in North America virtually unprotected.[26]

To the outnumbered and sickly men of Fort Chartres's garrison, the Illinois mission must have seemed perplexing. They could not hope to withstand a general Indian uprising without the help of their eastern and southern Indian allies. Captain Henry Gordon, who escorted English traders to Illinois in the summer of 1766, could hardly believe the conditions and situation he found at Fort Chartres. The garrison was sickly, the Mississippi had moved to within twenty-six yards of one of the fort's bastions, and provisions and ammunition were low. The deer and beaver skin trade, England's main economic purpose in the region, had not lived up to expectations because of persistent French competition. To Gordon, English occupation of Illinois served only one purpose: to impress British mastery upon the Indians. Given the deplorable state of the British occupation, the show was unlikely to impress anyone. "Coop'd up at Fort Chartres only, we make a foolish figure," he complained. Britain could not influence either Indians or habitants with a post that lacked sufficient funding and provisions. Local French residents refused even to extend financial credit to the garrison. Still, Gage defended the Fort Chartres operation in 1767, suggesting to the skeptical Earl of Shelburne that, despite the obvious problems and expenses of the Illinois occupation, the post maintained "a kind of Superiority over the Indians" and a check against duplicitous French habitants.[27]

Gage's optimism soon began to sour, mainly because of the Illinois occupation's high costs and meager economic returns. Trader George Morgan bemoaned the shrinking fur trade in late 1767, arguing that the corruption of the fort's commandant, danger to traders from unfriendly Indians, and a persistent shortage of Indian customers made his mission to the Illinois country an unprofitable waste of time. He made up the difference by selling goods and slaves to French and British inhabitants. In addition, the fort itself was close to crumbling into the Mississippi, and Gage had trouble justifying the expense of repairs. By the middle of 1768, with the trade "entirely Ruined" according to James Campbell, traders and soldiers alike argued for a reallocation of military assets closer to healthier and better-established trading posts like Vincennes. Many called for civilian colonization of the region instead of military control, as Croghan had done earlier. Fort Chartres was rapidly becoming an elaborate post without a mission.[28]

Prospects for bringing the region under control were frustrated from the start by the garrison's inability to control even the local habitants who looked to the fort for protection. Major John Forbes, who succeeded Reed in April 1768, wished to "strike a terror" into local Indian groups by convincing them that the French residents of Kaskaskia and the English soldiers were bound together as one people. To this end, he sent the Kaskaskia habitants a proclamation ordering them to form a militia and to muster under arms immediately. The French settlers refused, claiming that their recent oath of allegiance to Britain contained no such requirement. They sensibly feared inciting the local Indians with a public show of arms. French residents had no quarrel with the nearby Kaskaskia Indians and were determined to remain neutral in any conflict Britain might find itself in, whether against Indians or Europeans. They accused Forbes of acting high-handedly and dismissed his threats. Frustrated, Forbes told the French Kaskaskians that he had no intention of sending their militia into the field, but he insisted that they muster to show their allegiance to Britain. When he arrived in Kaskaskia, the residents again refused to turn out, threatening to move across the Mississippi if he pressed the point, "which indeed they threaten to do whenever any thing happens that displeases them," complained Forbes. He eventually convinced them to muster, but the episode reveals the complete disdain shown for British government in Illinois. Forbes's successor, Colonel John Wilkins, was similarly ineffective in encouraging French cooperation, admitting in 1770 that the locals looked upon him "nearly as a Cypher." Inability to control the eight hundred European and enslaved residents of Kaskaskia bode poorly for a garrison hoping to impress thousands of Indian visitors annually.[29]

Rumors of imminent violence forced Reed, Forbes, and Wilkins to keep seeking local French aid. Throughout the British tenure at Fort Chartres, rumors of imminent Indian uprisings raced through the region, necessitating a condition of nearly constant alert. Reports of circulating war belts and angry native and French agents, though ubiquitous and usually groundless, could not be dismissed out of hand. "Intelligence of this kind is frequently sent," Gage wrote to the Earl of Hillsborough, "And tho' very often without Foundation is not to be Neglected; for we never can be certain of the Designs of the Indians, who are dextrous in Striking a Severe and Sudden Blow when they are least expected." Indians stood to gain much by spreading these rumors. Specious intelligence of Indian threats kept the British penned up in their forts and out of Indian country. Intelligence of any quality also sustained a constant hunger for more intelligence, which Indians gladly provided, expecting presents and friendship in return. "The Truth is We are much in the Dark with Respect to all those Nations Notwithstanding the great Sums which have been laid out here," Morgan fretted to his business partners, having just heard (untrue) reports that a new uprising had begun among the Shawnees and Delawares and that Fort Detroit had fallen. Communication between Fort Chartres and Fort Pitt took months, making rumors and backcountry gossip the information standard in British Illinois.[30]

Rumors were especially efficacious when directed at Morgan and other traders because of increasingly violent attacks on their personnel. Morgan's company maintained trading houses in Vincennes, Kaskaskia, and Cahokia, and the small military blockhouses and garrisons in each town offered little protection for traders in the case of Indian attack. Through 1768 and 1769, native attackers plundered blockhouses and killed several of Morgan's employees at Kaskaskia and Cahokia. Indians even pillaged Morgan's store at Fort Chartres twice in late 1769, right beneath the sickly garrison's guns. But the worst attack happened far from Fort Chartres. In April 1768 a party of Indians from the Vincennes area attacked one of Morgan's buffalo-hunting parties on the Cumberland River, killing twenty men and plundering the party's provisions and pelts. The attackers felt they had every right to defend their hunting grounds and livelihoods; a Cherokee chief told Wilkins that the victims should have restricted their activities to hunting for food instead of peltry. The incident inflamed local English-Indian animosities to such a degree that Gage ordered Wilkins to placate the Ohio and Wabash region's Indians immediately. It would be August 1769 before Wilkins could arrange a conference, and throughout the intervening year violence continued in the central Illinois country.[31]

Almost a year after his arrival in Illinois, Wilkins called a meeting with disgruntled Potawatomis, Shawnees, and others from the Wabash and Ohio country. He decided to confront the unhappy Indians angrily, suspecting that they might interpret friendship overtures as weakness. At the conference, he listed several depredations committed by Indians from the Vincennes area, including the attack on traders' boats and men, plundering stores, and threatening to kill Indians allied to the British. Wilkins warned that even though the British soldiers at Fort Chartres might appear outnumbered and weak, the empire could be counted on to avenge Indian insults. "We are a Nation not easily made Angry," Wilkins told the delegates, "But when once we are determined on Striking an Enemy, they soon feel the weight of our resentment. Our Numbers are as the Stars in the firmament, and it is not in the power of all the Nations in the World to destroy us." Without subtlety or equivocation, Wilkins warned that if they did not stop threatening the peace, he would take it as an open declaration of war. British soldiers and their native allies would descend upon the troublesome Indians of the Wabash and Ohio region and destroy them.[32]

To Wilkins's surprise, the delegates met his threats with open defiance. Maringouin, an old chief from the Wabash region, rejected Wilkins's hard-line tactics and threats. "Since you entered this country you alone have caused the misfortunes which have come upon us," he scolded Wilkins. Cadenette, a war chief, refused to meet with Wilkins at all; he feared that he would be unable to control his temper. Hananaa, another war chief and village headman, warned Wilkins that English guns and trade held no power over his people. Using the revitalist language that had been popular and effective during the Indian uprising of 1763, he told Wilkins that depriving the Indians of English trade goods would make no difference:

> You must know that I know how to use wood to make my weapons and that with this same wood I would kill men. You must be convinced that my father the French will not let me die and that he will satisfy my wants. I shall die holding his hand if you make war on me. You take me for a beast that is destitute of reason, Think you that, having neither powder nor ball, I shall die of hunger? No, and in the belt which you send us there is a man who shuts up the road between us? Do you think that we do not understand this, though I have not as much wit as you?

Hananaa even ridiculed Wilkins's metaphor and turned it against him. "You talk to me of stars and say that you are as numerous as they are in the sky," he chided Wilkins. "The stars that fall hurt nothing. As for me I am as the trees in the forest; and, when a tree falls, it does harm and kills a man." Wilkins knew that Hananaa's comment about shutting the road meant that these Indians would never support British interests and that anti-British hostility would dominate Illinois and the Wabash country despite his threats. But the beleaguered commandant must have paled before the Wabash Indians' withering verbal pummeling, so different from the protestations of poverty and subjection common at Indian conferences farther east. Having just arrived in Illinois, Wilkins found out quickly how insubstantial the British presence appeared to some of the region's powerful indigenous populations.[33]

In addition to attacking Morgan's economic enterprises, Indians of the Wabash and St. Joseph area made it clear to the British military government at Fort Chartres that their substantial fort could not protect everyone. Many soldiers lived in Chartres Village, especially those with families. Other soldiers frequently left the fort to hunt and forage, despite orders to be careful and to travel in companies. British-allied Illinois lived in their own villages and could not depend on the garrison to protect them. Throughout 1768 and 1769, Potawatomis, Kickapoos, Sauks, Foxes, and others from the central and northern Illinois country attacked both fort personnel and allied Indians. Some of these attacks happened within shouting distance of the fort, causing almost perpetual states of alert for the sick, unhappy garrison. By late December 1769, according to Butricke, the garrison was in a "melancholy situation," with no word from Fort Pitt in over six months, and rumors circulating that the Spanish had closed off New Orleans to the British.[34]

Fears of Indian attacks only increased after Pontiac's death at the hands of a Peoria chief in Cahokia in April 1769. Several of Pontiac's western allies vowed to sweep into Illinois and avenge the revolutionary's ignominious murder. But it is difficult to ascertain whether the constant Indian threats and small-scale raids by Potawatomis and Kickapoos that did occur were intended as revenge or to provide simple, everyday intimidation. Indeed, Fort Chartres's commissary, Edward Cole, warned against worrying too much about Pontiac's avengers. Better to worry about the Illinois Indians themselves, he urged, who were pretty discontented to begin with and did not need outside help to make trouble. Gage agreed that the real trouble would likely come from unruly Illinois Indians rather than rumored Shawnee and Odawa insurgents. Indeed, by 1769 Pontiac had pledged allegiance to Britain, and it was an Illinois chief that had breached the peace. "It seems very Necessary that Something Should be done to keep those Nations [the Illinois] in order," Gage told Johnson. "They seem more and more inclined to raise Commotions as well with the Indians and the White People." But with native tempers flaring and British military threats unable to enforce security, expensive gifts remained the only sure way to gain Indian cooperation.[35]

Such gifts continued to be the price the British paid for failing to impress Fort Chartres's Indian visitors. Croghan spent lavishly on presents during his important conference in 1766, but even after the amicable conclusion of those negotiations the cost of conducting Indian affairs at Fort Chartres remained high. For example, from July 1 through September 25, 1766, Indian Department expenditures at the fort ran to £1,568. This included the cost of provisions and presents for Indians, transportation costs, interpreters and smiths, and construction and repairs. The next six months were almost as expensive. Compared to the cost of normal military operations at the fort, these sums were immense. For example, the cost of augmenting the provisions of the personnel of the Royal Regiment of Artillery and the Civil Branch of Ordinance at Fort Chartres (from local sources) for the period from January 1767 to June 1769 amounted to just over £44. Part of the Indian Department's enormous cost derived from the remoteness of the region and the high cost of transporting goods. A calculation made in January 1767 estimated that it would cost £5,217 sterling for a convoy of forty-five bateaux to carry goods down the Ohio River from Fort Pitt, not counting the value of the goods themselves. But the high cost of Indian diplomacy in Illinois had more to do with how frequently gifts were given than the expense of transporting them. Fort Chartres's precarious social and political position among the Illinois natives made gift giving an all-too-common necessity.[36]

All of Fort Chartres's commandants lavished presents upon visiting Indians, though the problem was worse at the beginning of the British occupation when memories of the Indian uprising were still fresh. Gage, whose responsibility it was to justify Indian Department expenses to skeptical financial auditors at Whitehall, became impatient very quickly. Unlike his predecessor Amherst, who cringed at the very idea of rewarding Indians for good behavior, Gage knew perfectly well that presents were needed to maintain Indian-British amities. But all things had their limits, and Gage told his remote commanders to give Indians "only what is absolutely Necessary . . . and to deal out Presents with a Sparing hand." He told John Reed that presents "must not be lavished any longer" in March 1767 and ordered Cole to have his commandant certify all Indian Department bills before remitting them. Cole's early drafts for Indian expenses shocked Gage and Johnson. The commander in chief once warned Cole that if another exorbitant account should cross his desk, he would be "under Necessity of refusing Payment to it." He ordered Reed to keep an eye on Cole, who met with Indians more regularly than anyone else at the fort and was liable to be the most easily intimidated. "The Commissarys at the Posts are not Sent there, to lavish away Presents to every Strolling Indian that comes to a Fort," Gage chided Reed. "Presents are only to be given to the Heads of Nations, & then frugally and on particular & necessary Occasions."[37]

Although Cole agreed to have his accounts certified by the fort commandant, he wondered how he could manage Indian affairs without giving out extravagant gifts to visitors. Indians living very near the fort were well enough disposed, though they visited quite often and always asked for gifts. But it was the droves of Indians coming in from the Missouri country that made matters difficult. The French had always supplied them in the past, they told Cole, and they expected the same from the British. In the summer of 1767 so many arrived that they monopolized all of Cole's time and greatly overtaxed his budget. Cole had already sent Gage a six-month draft for over £5,000 in March, and the summer season would be even more expensive. To make matters worse, the western Indians did not bring any trade to the fort; they wanted gifts, but they sold their furs to French traders operating on the Spanish side of the Mississippi. They knew that the British must give presents to them as the only way to secure their friendship and prevent them from conspiring with the French and Spanish. At the end of that summer, Reed agreed to try keeping costs in check but worried that it would be impossible with the region under constant Indian domination. "There must be expenses attending the Indians, and very considerable ones," he warned Gage, "Or the Military and Inhabitants must Starve, nothing but Presents prevents them from Destroying the Stock in the Country." With four thousand Indians visiting Fort Chartres that summer, and with goods costing twice as much as in "any other part of America," Reed worried that subsequent bills would be just as enormous.[38]

Indian expenses continued to vex Gage and the Indian Department through 1768. Cole's expenses amounted to £10,742 for a single year of activity at Fort Chartres. "This is really so monstrous an Account that I hardly know what can be done with it," Gage despaired to Johnson. He could not understand why "Missilimakinak and the Detroit together . . . did not cost more hundreds than the Illinois has cost Thousands," though he suspected it was because of native intimidation at Fort Chartres. This was not a sufficient justification for the commander in chief. After all, Detroit was just as vulnerable to attack and siege as Fort Chartres, if not more so, and Michilimackinac had fallen to an Ojibwa attack in 1763. Johnson felt even worse about the situation. His own man, Cole, was apparently being intimidated into doling out the most lavish gifts in North America. Gage agreed to let Johnson handle the problem, even if it meant replacing

Cole. "After first taking Possession of Posts extraordinary Expences may be necessary," Gage admitted, "but there is no Reason to continue them."[39]

Indian demands for presents stoked all of the old prejudices and mistrusts that had preceded the 1763 Indian uprising. For some local natives, gifts had become an important part of their livelihood. Illinois Indians offered friendship and protection in return, but they contributed few pelts to the local economy. This must have irked the men of the garrison, even if the deal seemed reasonable enough to the natives themselves. After all, given the weak position of the British presence at the fort, Indians might have felt that there was little the British could offer them *except* gifts. But the growing importance and profusion of this wholly gift-based system of alliance had begun to strain nerves. A letter to Gage from Forbes or one of his officers painted a harsh picture of the British hostilities forming at Fort Chartres:

> The immense Expence attending the Indian Department must be a considerable Burthn to the Crown if all the other Nations, on the Continent are so plentifully Supplyed as those in this Neighbourhood.... I have for some time observed that the more Presents they receive, the oftner they Return, and are less contented; and that their chief dependence rests more upon his Majesty's Bounty, than their own industry; for while they never move from their Village, but beging and hanging upon the Inhabitants, which gives them such a habit of Idleness (particularly the four Tribes in this District) that they are by the constant use of Spiritous Liquors become Effeminate and Debilitated: so much that nothing can be apprehended, from such a Dastardly Race of Cowards, who impute, the bounty they Receive, [proceeds] from fear not of Love.[40]

British occupation of Illinois had become, by late 1768, a cause célèbre for British politicians opposed to military governance of the trans-Appalachian west. The costs attending the operation of Fort Chartres threatened the entire fort system. In August 1768, Gage told Johnson that the Board of Trade was considering closing both Forts Pitt and Chartres because of the "great and constant Drains of Cash for Indian Presents. The two ... equal the Expences of half your whole Department." Johnson could not provide a reason why Reed and Forbes had not been able to retrench expenses. He told Gage that Reed, Forbes, and Cole (who kept his job until 1769) could not be entirely blamed and that their tendency toward lavishness seemed to go with the job. "Gentlemen, whatever their sentiments of Indians are previous to their going to the Outposts, seem to alter them when there," Johnson admitted to Gage, "And to Consider all Expences incurred as Extremely necessary to Publick Service." Cole finally began to bring costs under control in late 1768. But even with a retrenchment in cost, the gift-based system had become deeply ingrained in British-Indian relations to a degree that was probably not surmountable. Indian Department provisioning had become part of the native food system, and it could not be easily reduced without introducing hardship to native populations. From April 1766 to September 1768, Fort Chartres issued more than 65,000 pounds of flour, 8,000 pounds of cornmeal, 24,000 pounds of beef, 8,000 pounds of pork, and large quantities of other necessities to local and visiting Indians. Local Indians could not reasonably turn away from a relationship that offered them amounts of food and trade goods in proportion to the amount of influence they held in the region. Threats of trade restrictions could not be used against them, because French and Spanish competition offered better prices just across the Mississippi. Sick and disgruntled, often penned up inside their crumbling fort out of fear, and at the mercy of both friendly and unfriendly Indian nations on both sides of the Mississippi, the garrison could do little to compel their Indian neighbors to support themselves through the fur trade. If the British wished to stay in the region, presents would be the primary currency of friendship.[41]

Wilkins made reducing the number of presents dispensed at Illinois his top priority when he took command in September 1768. Upon arriving with his seven companies of the Royal Irish Regiment, he informed George Morgan that his policies would revive the moribund Illinois trade and keep local Indians busy and productive. "The Chief design of my Talk with the Indians has hitherto been and will in the future to encourage them to an Active Life," he told the trader optimistically, "And not to encourage Dranes who will stroll from Post to Post as Beggars only . . . we want to bring the Trade to this place and I will act as a Father to the Industrious." Wilkins took over the management of Indian affairs from Cole in the spring of 1769, after the Board of Trade forced the Indian Departments to cease their direct involvement in trade and to dismiss all commissaries, interpreters, and smiths in the outposts. Wilkins did reduce expenses, though it is unclear whether his retrenchments were substantial enough to please his superiors. Of more interest to modern ethnohistorians is the documentation he prepared to demonstrate his thrift. Upon his arrival he immediately began a detailed journal of his dealings with local Indians, and he continued to make entries throughout his tenure as commandant. The journal reveals that, even if the amount of gifts diminished, Fort Chartres still hosted frequent and insistent native demands for British favors.[42]

Most entries in Wilkins's journal describe visits by Illinois Indian neighbors, but parties of Osages, Missouris, Kickapoos, Potawatomis, and others also arrived in great numbers. Groups of Michigameas and Kaskaskias, who lived a few miles from the fort, were the most frequent visitors. Kaskaskias visited the forts at least thirteen times during Wilkins's tenure, often accompanied by their influential chief, Tomeroy. Michigameas, whose village was only a mile away, were practically residents of the fort, visiting at least thirty-five separate times and sometimes staying for several days. Peorias and Cahokias were also frequent visitors. Local Indians would always stop by the fort en route to their hunting grounds or returning from them, to be greeted and rewarded by the British commander. Wilkins almost always gave visitors rum and ammunition, and usually clothing as well. Visiting Kaskaskias took away a typical complement of gifts on December 23, 1768: four pounds of powder, two pounds of lead, a large plug of tobacco, a half-gallon of rum, one breechclout, and one pair of leggings. But Wilkins was just as generous to Indians from far away, even those from the troublesome Wabash region. For example, when Kickapoos visited the post in January 1769, Wilkins gave them the usual complement of goods, plus such extras as a "squaw's lace gown" and a "tincel laced hat."[43]

Wilkins's journal also shows which local native elites visited the fort most frequently. Tomeroy tops the list, visiting the fort at least thirteen times during the three years of Wilkins's command. Tomeroy forged a personal relationship with Wilkins, based on their mutual fear of enemy interlopers and their need to maintain security in the immediate locale. He asked for gifts when going to hunt, just as others did, but many of Wilkins's entries reveal that the Kaskaskia chief was one of the garrison's main sources of reconnaissance and information. Men from the Kaskaskia village ranged the locale regularly, though Wilkins always suspected that their alarming reports of rumored interlopers and the extent of their scouting efforts were exaggerated to obtain more presents. Still, Wilkins placed an enormous amount of trust in Tomeroy, despite his personal dislike of the chief. In return, Tomeroy made the fort commandant an important functionary in Kaskaskia ritual life, as when he asked Wilkins to hold a ceremony appointing a new chief. Of course, Tomeroy expected Wilkins to pay the bill for the ceremony; this was no mean amount, since it entailed hosting the entire Kaskaskia nation. Because of the Kaskaskias' proximity and numbers and Tomeroy's great influence in the region, Wilkins had no choice but to accede to the local chief's "requests," but he did not trust him. He described Tomeroy as a "great Church going man to the French Church, a great Speaker & I believe like most Savages very deceitful." Deceitful or not, Tomeroy held the upper hand among Indians of the region. Wilkins had no choice but to share his regional authority with the influential chief.[44]

Peoria chief Black Dog also visited the post regularly, as did the Michigameas' Young Chief and One-Eyed Chief. Unlike Tomeroy, who tried to insert himself into the local authority structure and influence British decisions, Black Dog seemed mainly interested in extracting presents from the beleaguered commandant. He would visit on his way to hunt and would usually tell Wilkins that he had encountered native or Spanish troublemakers who wished to turn his people against the British. Like all recipients of Fort Chartres's largesse, Black Dog knew how to influence Wilkins into rewarding his people. During one unusual visit he told Wilkins a tear-jerking story about an Indian woman who was to be put to death for marrying against her people's customs. Somehow, six gallons of rum would remedy the problem, which Wilkins dolefully handed over. But Black Dog usually told routine tales of imminent depredations by Kickapoos, Potawatomis, Shawnees, or whichever enemy was rumored to threaten the region at the time. His "thundering reports," were effective at keeping his people well supplied with provisions and presents, without providing much in return apart from promises of friendship and alliance. Nearby Michigamea headmen enjoyed a similar relationship with Wilkins. Since Young Chief and One-Eyed Chief lived almost within sight of the fort, they offered some scouting and information in return for their presents. But local Indians did not see this as a quid pro quo relationship; they expected presents because of their status as British friends, and received them every time they visited the post.[45]

Fort Chartres was a news outlet as well as a goods store and provisioning center, and local chiefs resorted to Wilkins for information about activities in the Wabash and Ohio country and further east. For example,

Black Dog visited in February 1769 to discover whether Indians from the Wabash would harass his people. Tomeroy and two other Kaskaskia chiefs, Baptiste and Laudeviet, arrived a month later to ask if Chickasaws would invade the area soon. But news traveled both ways, and all local Indians knew that they would be rewarded for intelligence gained while hunting. On March 22, Indians from all four Illinois nations arrived at the fort, bringing rumors of imminent trouble and wishing to know if the Chickasaws would attack. Wilkins reassured them that the Chickasaws were British allies and would not bother the Illinois, and he gave them all presents. The visitors grumbled about the diminished quantities of rum, food, and clothing and "talk'd of former times, & of going to War & much such Stuff," according to the commandant.[46]

Wilkins even helped Michigameas perform death rituals for two of their chiefs killed by Osages. Most of the Michigamea nation came to the fort for condolence rites, and Wilkins gave them shelter and provisions. Soon, Peorias and Kaskaskias arrived to add their condolences and be provisioned. Such congresses of Indian neighbors were common events, intended to display power and dominance as well as friendship. For example, in May 1769 all the Michigamea and Peoria warriors held a congress at the fort. They told Wilkins that unnamed Indians had tried to recruit all four Illinois nations to join a general uprising but that they had refused. On that instance, so many armed Indians arrived that Wilkins allowed only fifty into the post at a time and put the garrison on parade, just in case. But he still gave the warriors presents and allowed them to have their guns repaired.[47]

Indians also brought offers of help and expected to be rewarded for them. Sometimes these were small favors, such as when twenty-two men brought back a boat that had drifted away in the Mississippi. Indians also offered their expertise as scouts, always accompanied by extra requests for presents. On July 17, 1769, several chiefs of the four Illinois nations descended on the fort with rumors that the Senecas and Potawatomis would soon join in a major war against them. They asked Wilkins to visit the Michigamea village to help them prepare for an assault. Wilkins agreed to do so and gave the Michigameas five gallons of rum, "As there is no seeing them without a present." He asked that the Michigameas scout the area for signs of enemies, but by the July 26 they had not yet sent out any scouts. They told Wilkins that they could not find anyone willing to reconnoiter the area unless the commandant promised them a feast. Wilkins agreed, and forty men scouted the area immediately. They found no Wabash interlopers and hurried back for Wilkins's party on July 31. Though rumors persisted of Potawatomis and Kickapoos hiding behind every shrub, the Michigameas and Kaskaskias insisted that the danger had passed and "in very pressing terms desir'd they might be indulg'd to drink & feast on the occasion." Wilkins gave them ten gallons of rum for their revels because their nations were too "numerous" to refuse it, though he admitted that he was suspicious of their rumors and intelligence.[48]

Indians displayed great confidence in visiting the fort, frequently demanding presents. The common use of "demand" in Wilkins's journal need not suggest coercion; it may only have signified requests or needs. It is, however, a choice of words that implies Indian social parity, at least, in their meetings with British personnel. For example, Wilkins noted that Kaskaskias demanded powder and lead to defend their nation against Pontiac in March 1769. In May of that year, Peoria chiefs and warriors demanded a meeting with Wilkins to discuss how the Indians and British would protect each other. In August, Peorias leaving on a hunting trip "demanded assistance." And in March 1770, Black Dog and other Peorias "demanded Strongly" that they be allowed to move their village next to Fort Chartres. Indian demands for British resources continued throughout Wilkins's tenure, and he noted few examples where Indians returned the favors. Whether Wilkins intended it or not, his language throughout the journal implies that native visitors and neighbors held a strong hand in negotiations. They used the fort as a repository of free goods, demanding them as friends, but demanding them still. With much of his garrison perennially stricken with disease and with military relief hundreds of miles and at least two months away, Wilkins could only agree to such friendly demands.[49]

Indian demands for presents increased with new imperial diplomatic efforts. The days when Cole and Croghan could dole out almost £1,000 in presents in a single day were long gone by 1771, but Wilkins was still willing to be generous with the Crown's money in the interests of a profitable Indian policy. In April a party of thirty Chickasaws, "ornamented and well-appointed," arrived unexpectedly at Fort Chartres. This sent shock waves throughout the immediate region; Kaskaskias raised an alarm in their village, expecting that the long-awaited Chickasaw incursion had finally come. But the delegation wanted only to meet with Illinois chiefs and discuss peaceful relations, though they admitted that they carried no diplomatic mandate to speak for their nation. Wilkins was delighted that the Chickasaws might offer their help to defend the Illinois country against attacks by angry Wabash-region Kickapoos and Potawatomis. He hoped that the Chickasaws might even be induced to live near Fort Chartres as a permanent deterrent to attack. The delegation stayed for a week, meeting with all local Indians and many of the French habitants. Of course, Wilkins gave them many gifts, and even a draft for £20 that they could cash in for rum with British traders in their own country. After a week of dancing and feasting, Wilkins had no desire to introduce even more alcohol into the local social mix.[50]

Wilkins had plenty to worry about by 1771, and the prospect of Chickasaw aid would solve some of his problems. New rumors of imminent Indian uprisings dominated the early part of the year, and Wilkins once again put the garrison on alert and confined them to the fort. In March a party of Potawatomis from St. Joseph killed a soldier who had left the fort to hunt ducks in defiance of Wilkins's restrictions. Fear spread rapidly, and Wilkins worried (in a panicky letter to Gage) that there might be as many as six hundred hostile Indians surrounding the fort, though only a dozen had been seen. Wilkins kept his men penned up in the fort, which did not inspire the garrison's Illinois neighbors.[51]

In May, Tomeroy visited Wilkins to warn him that all of the area's Indians were preparing to fend off an imminent invasion, and he asked how the English could help his Kaskaskias. Wilkins told the chief not to be afraid and boasted that the Potawatomis would pay dearly for the soldier they had killed. By then, Wilkins had learned a little about the proper use of metaphors. Mirroring Hananaa, he told Tomeroy that the British "were as numerous as the Trees in the Woods." Even if the British could not come in time, their new Chickasaw friends would happily help them destroy the Wabash Indians. This pleased Tomeroy, but not Gage when he was told about Wilkins's Chickasaw threat. He knew that such threats of southern Indian incursions, if spread as rumors, would only confirm the Potawatomis' and Kickapoos' worst fears and make the situation even more dangerous. Gage's criticism seemed to imply excessive reticence on Wilkins's part, if not outright cowardice. He thought that Wilkins should have used his own men to chastise the Indians who killed the soldier, rather than negotiating with the Chickasaws to do it for him. "You talk of the Party (of Potawatomis) being 5 or 600 Strong. All the Indians of St. Joseph would scarcely amount to Sixty Warriors," Gage admonished

Wilkins. But this episode makes clear the difference between establishing imperial military policy from a distance and executing it on the ground. After three years there, Wilkins understood the balance of power in the Illinois country. Foolish appearances or not, he chose to keep his men in the fort.[52]

Wilkins also continued to defend his record in reducing Indian expenditures. As is well documented in his journal, native visitors made it perfectly clear that friendship depended upon the giving of gifts. "Every Art is used to Influence me to be more liberal or lavish of the publick money in presents to Indians," he complained to Gage. He also fretted that his "schemes of Oeconomy" were not being taken seriously; local residents had a gift-based system that provided many of their necessities, and they had no reason to dive any further into the fur trade. Still, Wilkins argued that his measures had reduced Indian expenses to one-twentieth of those at another (unnamed) post, and he promised to reduce expenditures even more. "Savages are easily Satisfied if properly managed," he wrote to Gage in June. Wilkins beamed with confidence and felt that he alone had succeeded where other commandants had failed.[53]

By September, Wilkins's tune had changed. "Several Scalping parties of the Kickapous & Potawatomis being about us, my Garrison very Sickly & hardly a relief for the Guard, hands wanted to face the Bank & the Necessary Escort in our present Scattar Situation," he complained, had pushed the Illinois mission to the limit. At the same time, he was fending off complaints from British and French traders of Indian attacks and intimidation and was unable to send any troops into the interior to protect the trade. Gage's patience with the Illinois mission was almost at an end. With new reports that Kickapoos had attacked George Morgan's plantation, killing two people and kidnapping a trader, the region was practically in a state of uprising. Gage ordered Wilkins to instruct his men in "scouting and wood Fighting" and to muster friendly Indians to chastise the Potawatomis and Kickapoos. But the garrison's sick and downtrodden men seemed barely able to help themselves; carrying a war deep into the Illinois interior was beyond them.[54]

By late 1771, Wilkins's position had worsened significantly. He spent much of his time fending off complaints and lawsuits by local traders and farmers. Morgan, by this time a staunch enemy of Wilkins, fought with the commandant over a plan to set up a distillery and brewery at Kaskaskia. More and cheaper liquor was the last thing the British garrison needed in the region, but Gage overruled Wilkins's initial refusal to allow it; Morgan's trade operations were among the only profitable British operations in the area. Threats against the British regime from the Illinois interior increased with time, compounded by the near outbreak of war with Spain in 1770 and 1771. Disease continued to shake the military foundations of the Illinois government. Finally, the fort itself was again susceptible to damage. Though Wilkins kept the garrison busy shoring up the riverbank almost constantly during his three years there, the river could not be kept at bay forever. In May, Fort Chartres seemed sure to be damaged by the next Mississippi flood. Gage wrote to inquire, sarcastically, if Wilkins might find a new location where disease would not decimate the troops.[55]

As a final humiliation for the garrison, the troops' regalia looked comical. Soldiers were either threadbare or out of uniform completely by the end of 1771. When Wilkins first came to Fort Chartres, in 1768, he and his regiment had brought along only one year's worth of clothing. Unfortunately, their replacement clothing ended up under water in May 1770 when an inexperienced lieutenant commanding a convoy had to dump his cargo near the falls of the Ohio River. In September 1771, Wilkins finally requested more replacement uniforms, complaining that many of his men still wore the same clothing they brought with them three years earlier. Others had resorted to buying civilian clothing from local traders, at high Illinois prices. Gage was unsympathetic. He scolded Wilkins for not bringing replacement clothing with him in the first place and for not requesting more from Fort Pitt after the cargo was lost. Sick, disheveled soldiers in worn-out uniforms or civilian clothing must have been quite a sight to local and visiting Indians. As for Gage, he had already joined the anti-Illinois chorus. Fort Chartres's future was nearly sealed.[56]

Wilkins tried one last gambit to save the Illinois mission. In May 1771 he formulated a new Illinois plan that would involve destroying Fort Chartres, establishing a civil provincial government, attracting thousands of industrious British settlers to the new province, and reducing Indian expenses to only £500 per annum. Gage had heard such plans before. He rejected everything except the proposal to reduce Indian expenses, which he thought needed no new form of government to put into action. As for the rest of the plan, Gage thought that increasing the western flow of settlers would be the worst possible development. "I would be happy for Britain, that there was neither Settler nor Soldier in any part

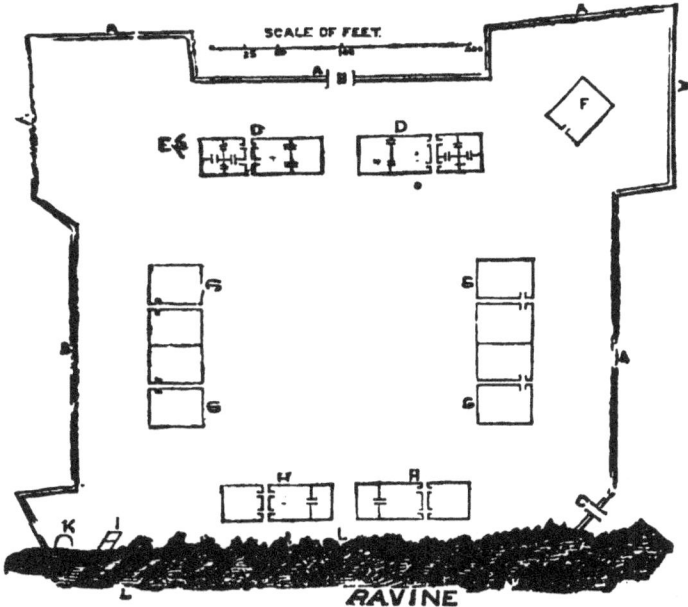

PLAN OF FORT CHARTRES
ON THE MISSISSIPPI.

Drawn from a survey made in 1820 by Nicholas Hansen of Illinois, and Lewis C. Beck.

A A A The exterior wall—1447 feet.
B The gate or entrance to the fort.
C A small gate.
D D The two houses formerly occupied by the commandant and commissary, each 96 feet in length and 30 in breadth.
E The well.
F The magazine.
G G G G Houses formerly occupied as barracks, 135 feet in length, 36 in breadth.
H H Formerly occupied as a storehouse and guard-house, 90 feet by 24.
I The remains of small magazine.
K The remains of a furnace.
L L L A ravine, which in the spring is filled with water. Between this and the river, which is about half-a-mile, is a thick growth of cotton-wood.

The area of the fort is about four square acres.

Fig. 5.2. Plan of the ruins of Fort Chartres, 1820. This geographical survey shows the damage caused by the Mississippi, which obliterated the south curtain and bastions. From John Moses, *Illinois: Historical and Statistical* (1889). Courtesy of Bracken Library, Ball State University, Muncie, Indiana.

of the Indian Country," he had written to Wilkins earlier. "Indians alone render this Country of the least Benefit to England, who will decrease as White People increase, and then there will be an end to Commerce." The enormous cost of presents made Gage wish the French had never left them any forts or settlements. With the revolutionary spirit of "leveling" growing throughout the eastern colonies, Britain might need every available troop and shilling to maintain its North American holdings. Illinois had not enriched Britain, and resentment against the British occupation had only caused the effects of the 1763 Indian uprising to linger on in Illinois and the Wabash River country. With new reports at the end of 1771 that Miamis and Potawatomis would fall on Fort Chartres in the spring and cut off the Ohio River supply line, Gage finally reached the breaking point. Only a massive punitive expedition could possibly reduce hostilities and chastise belligerent Indians, and a costly Indian war was exactly what Gage and Johnson could not have.[57]

In September 1771, Gage ordered Major Isaac Hamilton to take over command of the Illinois from Wilkins and to form a force to chastise the Wabash Indians. Hamilton and his men arrived at Fort Pitt too late in the year to set out on the freezing Ohio. When they finally embarked in February 1772, Fort Chartres's fate had already been sealed in London. Weary of the ridiculously high expenses at the fort, "which has proved to be of so little Use or Benefit to the Publick," according to Gage, Whitehall had pulled its support for the entire mission. The fort's regular soldiers were needed in the East to garrison Boston and manage increasingly unruly colonists. Fort Chartres was to be razed as cheaply as possible, preferably by ceasing to reinforce the river banks and letting "the Torrents of the River" demolish the limestone giant. British settlers were to be evacuated from Vincennes and all interior posts. All interpreters, smiths, surgeons, and artillerymen were ordered to leave Illinois. A small, temporary post would be established at Kaskaskia to guard British trade interests there. And Indian presents would be provided only as needed; no more bills from traders would be approved. Johnson worried about how the Illinois Indians would interpret such a precipitous withdrawal of troops, but he hoped that he could handle it with more diplomacy, and a few well-placed gifts.[58]

Many factors contributed to Fort Chartres's failure to establish British mastery over the Illinois country. Its commandants were often corrupt and combative. The region was simply too far from supply centers to be affordably supported. The mission always faced opposition, both from imperial officials, who grated at its expense, and from colonialist supporters of a civil government and province in Illinois. But the impression left by the sources is that the British occupation foundered even during the rare times when it was adequately supported. Gage frequently noted his disapproval of the post's inability to manage the local Indians except through lavish use of presents. But this inability came honestly to the post's beleaguered garrison. Undermanned, insufficiently funded, laid low by disease, and surrounded by unimpressed Indians and resentful habitants, the post could never hope to impress Indians enough to make the Illinois country into a profitable operation for Britain, or even to establish the fort as an intimidating "mark of possession." It could have been worse for everyone involved. Had Gage not aborted the British mission and abandoned Fort Chartres, the long-rumored prospect of a new Indian uprising might have become a reality. Instead, the status quo of small-scale British-Indian conflict continued into the Revolutionary period, when George Rogers Clark and the American independence movement imposed a new, destructive identity on the contest for political and cultural control of Illinois and the Wabash River region.[59]

Indian impressions and British appearances figured prominently in the story of Fort Chartres. The British attempt to garrison the fort was an abject failure by any measure. But more important than its failure to survive and establish physical and political control was its inability to impose the *idea* of British mastery on the Illinois Indian population. Without proper resources, the fort's personnel could never hope to project images of strength, competence, manliness, and mastery upon their native audience. From the earliest British attempts to send agents into Illinois, the region's Indians proved that they could easily confront British representatives in ways that native groups in other locales could not. When they wished, they could attack convoys, harass traders, plunder storehouses, and kill livestock. In essence, they could carry on a de facto uprising against British rule without worrying about the consequences. Indians, both friendly and hostile, would wait in vain for the British garrison in Illinois to avenge these affronts with violent chastisement. Fort Chartres's men could not hope to carry out a punitive war. They could only respond to threats of violence with harsh words and threats, accompanied by counteractive presents.

Even Illinois Indian allies, who had thrown their lots in with the new

British regime, understood their dominant position and demanded frequent and extravagant presents in return for their friendship. Sick, threadbare, and exhausted, Fort Chartres's garrison finally left Illinois to its indigenous residents, at least for a while. No sense of inevitability, no invisible, deterministic historical or economic forces could have convinced that region's Indian populations that Britons and their descendants would someday be capable of overcoming native hegemony in the region or mastering the entire continent. In this western theater of the long confrontation of cultures in North America, natives had overcome newcomers in the cultural battle of Fort Chartres. As predicted by Hananaa, British stars had fallen from the firmament, and hurt nobody.

Conclusion

The Mohawks' New World

Poulous could not understand why a man he barely knew had taken his rum. The Mohawk had lived for a while in and around Fort Hendrick, the small British fort adjacent to his village of Canajoharie, and kept a "Cagg of Rum" there for his own use. In March 1756 his peaceful life took an unexpected turn. A British officer and twenty-five regular soldiers arrived to garrison the fort, named for the renowned Mohawk leader "King" Hendrick. After months of insulting the Canajoharie Mohawks, the garrison went even further. In September the new men proceeded to bar Poulous from his own home, not to mention his rum. Ironically, Fort Hendrick had been built at the Mohawks' request several years earlier and recently renovated. The newly arrived regulars had come at the Mohawks' bidding to protect their homes and families from the French and their native allies. Now the fort and its soldiers were demonstrating the extent to which some Mohawks had left behind the in-between world of forts and villages and joined the new colonial world of their longtime British allies.

Canajoharie, the Mohawk River "Upper Castle," had been a Mohawk population center since early in the eighteenth century. The village was surrounded by a light stockade and probably contained twenty to thirty houses and some two hundred inhabitants by the 1740s. Canajoharie's residents enjoyed convenient river access to Fort Oswego on Lake Ontario and William Johnson's home at Fort Johnson. They also maintained a long-standing and firm alliance to British interests. Since early in the century, Mohawks at Canajoharie had received British missionaries and teachers in their village, and by the 1740s almost all of them had converted to Christianity. They considered Johnson their kinsman; indeed, he would later take Molly Brant, an influential Canajoharie Mohawk of the Wolf clan, as his common-law wife. So when the British and French brought warfare into the Mohawks' country, the natives felt it was only fair that the British build them a protective fort at Canajoharie.[1]

The first requests for a fort at the Upper Castle came during King George's War in 1747. New York governor George Clinton ordered Johnson to build a small fort "without blockhouses" at the Mohawk village, which cost the province £49. As was often the case with wartime outposts, the fort was a transitory structure that was built to stand only a short time. When the Seven Years' War broke out six years later, the Mohawks again requested forts at their castles for their families' protection. Clinton agreed again to this reasonable request; £500 was a small price to pay for the allegiance of the Mohawks and their powerful Six Nations Confederacy. But this time a fort was not enough. The Canajoharie Mohawks wanted a substantial garrison at the fort to protect their town and their families. They probably desired status equal to the Mohawks of the Lower Castle of Tiononderoge, who already possessed a fort (Fort Hunter, built in 1710) and a significant garrison. Johnson sent an officer and twenty-five men to the Canajoharie fort in March 1756.[2]

Then the complaints began. Mohawk headmen began to fret that the British regulars were not treating the Mohawks' fort as a welcome place for Indians. British affronts and clashes commenced almost immediately. A delegation of Canajoharie headmen complained to Johnson that they were not satisfied with the "Red Coats" and wanted them replaced with local men who understood their ways. Johnson knew that the Mohawks' friendship with Britain was staunch, and immediately wrote to Commander in Chief William Shirley for reinforcements. But Johnson was suspicious of some of the local settlers, especially Palatine German immigrants with whom he had a long history of legal disputes and other problems. Johnson recommended that the men be hired from Albany or Schenectady rather than the immediate area near Canajoharie. He also asked Loudoun to bar them from selling rum to the Mohawks and to have them avoid the Indians whenever they could. Loudoun issued those orders, but the garrison took them too far.[3]

When Poulous left his house one day in the late summer of 1756, the new commandant confiscated his keg of rum and took it to his own apartment. He posted sentries and ordered them to shoot any Indian who came into the fort looking for the rum. When Poulous returned and found his keg missing, he walked right past those same sentries, who sensibly did not shoot the annoyed Mohawk. Poulous simply entered the officer's house and took back his property. The commandant was livid upon returning and finding the rum gone. "Did I Nott order you to Shute any Indian that should Come of itt?" he railed at a sentry. "I see No Indian you have Shott." He confined the sentries and whipped one of them severely. Four Mohawk headmen soon arrived at the fort to complain about Poulous's treatment. Though very angry (they did not like the way the sentry had been whipped either), they acted diplomatically and provided the officer with a way to compensate for the insult. The Mohawks noted that the officer's "fatt Catle" had been foraging in their gardens and that Warroghioggy (Johnson) would surely want the garrison to compensate them for the loss. This compensation would smooth over the incident. But the officer was unaccustomed to Iroquois diplomacy. He told them to complain all they wished to Johnson. The fort belonged to the king, the officer told the shocked Mohawks, and British officers answered to their monarch, not to an Indian agent. Annoyed and frustrated, the Mohawk leaders took the dispute to the next level. When they complained to Johnson, they were polite but firm. They made it very clear that the Canajoharie residents wanted a dependable garrison made up of local "Country People" who understood Iroquois ways and would respect them. The "Red Coats" and their officer must be sent away before conflict ensued. "He has Slept hear as we May Say butt One Night and we are Afread if he Sleeps hear a Second Night we Shall all be Distroyd," warned the sachems.[4]

Intercultural relations were not a top British-American military priority in 1756, and the regulars stayed in Fort Hendrick. Mohawk complaints continued into the following year. Influential Mohawk sachem Nickas claimed that the soldiers had ceased to let his people into the fort at all, saying it was the king's property and the Mohawks had "nothing to do with it." Soldiers also warned that if the French attacked, the Indians would still not be allowed inside, although the fort had been built for their protection. This confused and enraged Nickas. "It is on our Land & built with our Timber," he protested to Johnson. "Therefore we have a right to it, at least to protection in time of danger, but they tell us not." Nickas issued an ultimatum: either Johnson withdraw the garrison or the Mohawks would never suspend their neutrality and send fighting men to help the British war effort, as Johnson had requested. Johnson denied that the king had designs on their land. He offered to withdraw the men if the Mohawks insisted, but he advised against it. Johnson then berated them for issuing such an unfriendly ultimatum and warned that such tactics could endanger the Covenant Chain of friendship and alliance. The men remained at Fort Hendrick. Johnson wrote off the complaints to Mohawk drunkenness and the rabble-rousing of local Dutch and German settlers who possessed long ties to the Mohawks and resented the presence of British troops in the region. Nickas later complained that Fort Hendrick's soldiers were cutting trees on Indian land instead of asking the Canajoharie people to supply the firewood; this deprived them of a small source of wages. Instead of answering the complaint, Johnson once again blamed the local settlers, and posted an advertisement offering a £20 reward for information about any "evil low designing People among the Inhabitants" who might be stirring up the Mohawks against the garrison.[5]

Fort Hendrick had started out as a temporary measure designed to protect Iroquois lives and property. By the 1760s it reflected the new Indian-British world that Canajoharie had become. In 1761 the fort lapsed into disuse, and the Canajoharie Mohawks moved toward a more Anglicized existence. Johnson sent them a new schoolteacher in March. Mohawk headmen asked if Johnson might let them use one of the fort's dilapidated blockhouses as a school, but they were disappointed to discover that local settlers were already using it as a stable. Fort Hendrick finally disappeared in 1768 when local farmers pulled it down to reuse the materials. Its last mention in Johnson's published papers is in a Mohawk request that the land be cleared so that they could build a new church.[6]

This small episode in Canajoharie's evolution as an Indian-British place reveals many of the themes and problems that occupied the lives of Indians who lived near forts. The fort was built at the behest of the Mohawks, but outside considerations created a confusing and frustrating situation for the Indians who occupied the liminal world of Canajoharie-Hendrick. As in other places, Indian leaders sought to mediate the authority of the commanders of such posts, but with less success than at the five forts examined in this study.

Trade, presents, and respect for native customs mattered just as much to the Canajoharie Mohawks as it did to other Native Americans throughout eastern North America. But the Mohawks faced a problem that those other groups did not: Britain took them for granted. Britain needed the Mohawks' military help during the Seven Years' War (they received it only at the very end) and again during the Revolutionary War. During times of peace the British needed only their docility. Mohawks no longer commanded their country the way Illinois and Cherokees controlled their regions. They could not use their knowledge of foodways to display and augment their power the way Odawas and Ojibwas did at Michilimackinac. As long-standing allies of Britain whose numbers decreased every year, they could not wield violence and diplomacy with the same vigor that their Seneca kin used at Niagara. And without much to offer their British allies except their friendship, they could do little to address the dearth of hospitality shown them at Fort Hendrick. Canajoharie Mohawks evinced as much diplomatic importance as other native groups who had requested British forts to protect their homes. But instead of revealing the unsettled nature of the contest for cultural domination of Indian country, as had happened in many places throughout North America, Canajoharie's experience with fort building only laid bare the extent to which they had already moved into an incipient stage of European social and cultural domination. By attaching themselves firmly to British culture, Mohawks had joined the European club. The dynamic social and cultural interplay that dominated other fort-Indian sites in the continent no longer provided the advantages to the Mohawks that Indians enjoyed near those other forts.

Canajoharie is a reminder that native cultural and demographic loss is a common end to stories of Indians and British forts. While Indians may have employed substantial adeptness in affecting and reordering British military imperatives in Indian country, their futures held depressingly consistent scenarios of dispossession and poverty. The Canajoharie Mohawks actually did better than most Indian groups that interacted with forts and soldiers. As New York residents and landlords, on par socially with New York's English citizens, they were able to live with relative economic success. But even as they sought to assimilate themselves into the British colonial world, the Mohawks continued unsuccessfully to search for coexistence strategies to help them maintain their lands and ways in the midst of ever-increasing numbers of European settlers. It was not poverty or disease that caused them to leave Canajoharie; rather, it was their strong and effective roles as British loyalists during the Revolution that caused many of them to migrate eventually to Canada.[7]

Indians' experiences with British forts do not reveal a historical landscape where America's first peoples ended up as winners. But neither did forts necessarily introduce devastation to Indian country or greatly contribute to native loss. Instead, they frequently implanted opportunities for new coexistence and resistance strategies that Indians used effectively to maintain as much of their traditional ways as possible for as long as they could. In this sense, most Indians who interacted with British fort communities resisted the European invasion, using mixtures of accommodation, intimidation, cooperation, and occasional violence. Such efforts may lack the drama of more confrontational resistance movements, such as those led by Pontiac and Tecumseh, but Indians should not be criticized for trying to find reasonable methods of coexistence and cooperation simply because their efforts do not satisfy modern desires for heroic narratives. If Indians were eventually dispossessed of their lands and cultures, it was the fault of the invaders, not the invaded.

Examining the American backcountry of the middle and late eighteenth century becomes necessarily a study of empires and colonialism. In so many subsequent novels, poems, paintings, plays, and films, forts have provided the apparent exposed face of European expansion. Their military nature leads toward an inevitable perception that armed garrisons and martial force supplied the heavy lifting and violent confrontation required to replace a native landscape with a European-American nation. Historians, too, have viewed the roles played by forts, soldiers, and Indians within an organizational matrix defined by European empires. Even when local cultural accommodations are emphasized, in perceptive studies like Richard White's *The Middle Ground*, the final story appears as a pageant of continental and imperial maneuvering. That framework rightly positions localism as vital to the European spread of empire and native resistance to expansion, but it may lead to a distorted view of the smaller local stories themselves. Forts were often lightly defended and underfunded at any rate. Even without the substantial influence that Indians exercised in and around backcountry forts, their missions might have remained only side stories in the narrative of British America's creation.

But Native Americans did affect the creation, operation, and definition of Britain's outposts of empire. Fort commandants, usually unused to direct interaction with Indian cultures, responded to these local challenges as best they could, which was often not very well at all. Imperial objectives, originating either in London or in provincial capitals, often fell flat against the hard walls of localism. Costs could not be reduced, local officials claimed, because local elites would not cooperate without presents and other considerations. Trade could not be regulated, commandants groused, because its intercultural structure defied the power of small garrisons to control it. This was true even in outposts close to heavy British settlement, such as Fort Allen. In places where the empire builders were hopelessly out of their depth, like Fort Chartres, the constant flood of complaints and demands from superiors in the East must have seemed surreal to local commandants. In the big picture, forts penetrated the backcountry and blazed the way for settlers, who would eventually break the back of Indian country with their plows. In the small picture, forts become small intercultural worlds that perform according to the demands of both Indian and white worlds; they simply tried to stay in place and mark a region, sometimes futilely, in the name of Britain. If the future of empire was on the minds of the thousands of soldiers and officers who endured life in their tiny enclaves, then they balanced that consideration with the numerous daily concerns that defined life and death in their imperial posts. Those concerns were often intercultural—in many cases, much more so than the settler outposts that would eventually transform the continent.

At the beginning of this book I insisted that this is not a study of Native American lifeways and that I cannot provide a view from a Native American perspective. The sources do not permit it, and even if they did, I doubt that I would be capable of capturing the feelings of peoples from cultures fundamentally different than my own, and forced to interact with unwelcome, armed visitors to their neighborhoods. Perhaps nobody can anymore; Native American oral historians would come closer to that goal than I ever can. However, it is still native cultural influence, different in every small contact point but similar in some respects, that is most useful in redirecting the study of forts from strictly military worlds to dynamic social arenas. Native cultures affected both economic and social exchanges profoundly. Soldiers and Indians took part in each other's rituals. Indians infused the forts' missions with their notions of consumerism, hospitality, kinship, and reciprocal fairness. Native individuals, too, imposed their desires to obtain personal status and protect their villages and families upon forts that came and went in Indian country. In some cases, interchanges between a commandant like John Wilkins and a local headman like the Peoria Black Dog defined the nature of empire for a single day. With all their edicts and proclamations, the planners of empire could never hope to alter political and social priorities in those localities as much as the men and women who could see each other's eyes.

Finally, the Canajoharie episode stands out because of Nickas's bold statement of Mohawk proprietorship. He pointed out to Johnson directly what other Indians must have thought and said to fort commandants throughout the continent. Whether constructed by Dutch, French, Spanish, or British newcomers, forts were built on Indian land with the natural materials natives had used for generations. Forts were familiar objects in that respect, just as if they were canoes or shelters. But by the mid-1700s, Indians in eastern North America understood European notions of reciprocal exchange and merged them with their own traditions. If forts were to occupy their country, then some consideration must be made for the social and cultural changes they brought with them. So, the back-and-forth process of diplomacy, presents, intimidation, and politeness emerged whenever and wherever forts sprang up in the backcountry, reducing the invasion of America to small, local exchanges in remote forests and plains. The closer one looks at the experiences of people living in these remote arenas, the more it becomes clear that British military outposts and fort personnel were not usually the agents of continental change imagined in subsequent American fiction and mythology. In retrospect, it might be more fruitful to reflect on the many ways in which experiences with Native Americans changed the occupiers, some of whom later became traders, married native women, and produced métis offspring.

Forts implanted new worlds in Indian country. In these worlds, where fort personnel and Indians made creative social negotiations an everyday activity, both Indians and Europeans could separate themselves partially from their cultural imperatives and sometimes find new paths to cooperation. But forts were not isolated from outside demands and responsibilities, either for Europeans or Indians. Competing meanings and levels of social power dominated these negotiations. Each side sought advantages as much as it did cooperation and safety. This made the worlds of backcountry forts dangerous as well as complex. In every case, Indians acted as full participants in ordering life and deciding outcomes in these contact points.

The traditional view of British outposts bristling with bayonets as places of military refuge is deserved; both settlers and Indians sought their protection in times of trouble. But *cultural* refuge was harder to come by for British fort personnel. To live in Indian country, Europeans had to meet native inhabitants on native terms, at least to some degree. For Old Hop, Matchekewis, Teedyuscung, Black Dog, and thousands of others who chose to absorb forts into their cultural orbits, officers and garrisons were their best chance at affecting or controlling the terms of the invasion of their countries. That the British-American culture that stood behind the forts eventually came to dominate the continent should never diminish the efforts of Native Americans to decide their own fates in the shadows of the newcomers' bulwarks and palisades.

Notes

Abbreviations

BWMP John Baynton, Samuel Wharton, and George Morgan Papers. Pennsylvania State Archives. Microfilm.

CRP Samuel Hazard, ed. *Colonial Records of Pennsylvania*. 16 vols. Harrisburg: T. Fenn, 1851.

DRIA William L. McDowell Jr., ed. *Documents Relating to Indian Affairs*. Colonial Records of South Carolina. [Ser. 2: The Indian Books.] 2 vols. Columbia: South Carolina Archives Department, 1958–70.

FP Leonard W. Labaree et al., eds. *The Papers of Benjamin Franklin*. 38 vols. New Haven: Yale University Press, 1959.

GPAS Thomas Gage Papers, American Series. William C. Clements Library, University of Michigan, Ann Arbor.

GPES Thomas Gage Papers, English Series. William C. Clements Library, University of Michigan, Ann Arbor.

IHC Illinois State Historical Library. *Collections of the Illinois State Historical Library*. 37 vols. Springfield: The Library, 1903–75.

JCHA J. H. Easterby et al., eds. *Journal of the Commons House of Assembly*. 14 vols. Colonial Records of South Carolina. Columbia: Historical Commission of South Carolina, 1951.

MPHC Michigan Pioneer and Historical Society. *Collections and Researches Made by the Michigan Pioneer and Historical Society*. 40 vols. Lansing: The Society, 1877–1929.

NYCD E. B. O'Callaghan and Berthold Fernow, eds. *Documents Relative to the Colonial History of the State of New York*. 15 vols. Albany, N.Y.: Weed, Parsons, 1853–87.

ORRD Brock, R. A., ed. *The Official Records of Robert Dinwiddie, Lieutenant-Governor of the Colony of Virginia, 1751–1758*. 2 vols. Richmond: Virginia Historical Society, 1971.

PA   Samuel Hazard, ed. *Pennsylvania Archives*. 1st series. 12 vols. Philadelphia and Harrisburg, 1852–56.
THP   Timothy Horsfeld Papers. American Philosophical Society, Philadelphia.
WHLP   William Henry Lyttelton Papers. William C. Clements Library, University of Michigan, Ann Arbor.
WJP   James Sullivan et al., eds. *The Papers of Sir William Johnson*. 14 vols. Albany: University of the State of New York, 1921–65.

Introduction: British Forts and Indian Neighbors

1. For a study of the literary and historical treatment of the siege and fall of Fort William Henry that explains the event's impact on subsequent French, British, and American nationalist mythologies, see Steele, *Betrayals*, 149–85.

2. For an overview of Parkman's views on Indians and their place in the heroic historical tradition, see Trigger, *Natives and Newcomers*, 9–19. The foundational essay on the frontier and its relation to American democratic values is Frederick Jackson Turner, "The Significance of the Frontier in American History." For discussions of Turner's thesis of frontier-based democratic rejuvenation and of frontier-oriented mythology in general, see Smith, *The Virgin Land*, 250–60, and Cronon, Miles, and Gitlin, "Becoming West: Toward a New Meaning for Western History," in *Under an Open Sky*, 3–27. For the changing uses of Indians in American society, mythology, and popular culture, see Berkhofer, *The White Man's Indian*.

3. Notable early attempts to correct such ethnocentric distortions are Nash, "The Image of the Indian" and *Red, White, and Black*, 1–6, and Berkhofer, *The White Man's Indian*, 1–31. For the problems of colonialist rhetorical baggage in literature, see Jennings, *The Invasion of America*, 10–14. For the merits and promise of the ethnohistorical approach, see Axtell, *The European and the Indian*, 1–15. For some of the problems encountered by historians using this method, see Merrell, "Some Thoughts on Colonial Historians and American Indians," and Richter, "Whose Indian History?" Richard White's study of the Choctaws in *The Roots of Dependency*, 1–146, shows an application of dependency and world system theory to Native American history; there are many others. For the origins of this core-periphery model of global economic domination and exploitation, see Wallerstein, *The Modern World-System II*. For critiques of the world system model, see van Hoak, "Untangling the Roots of Dependency." For an example of American Indian activist scholarship, which seeks to unchain Indian history from the structures of European scholarship that some Native Americans see as a form of colonialist oppression, see Vine Deloria's work, especially his influential manifesto *Custer Died for Your Sins*. For an excellent introduction to the historiography of Native America, see Philip J. Deloria, "Historiography," in Deloria and Salisbury, *A Companion to American Indian History*, 6–24. The 1992 film version of *Last of the Mohicans* used an adaptation of the 1936 script, which makes comparison of the two especially rewarding.

4. Richard White's *The Middle Ground* has become paradigmatic in ethnohistorical studies, though not without significant critiques of some of his methods and assumptions. See the articles in the *William and Mary Quarterly*'s January 2006 forum on *The Middle Ground*, especially Bohaker, "'Nindoodemag': The Significance of Algonquian

Kinship Networks," and Rushforth, "Slavery, the Fox Wars, and the Limits of Alliance." For a study of the historiographical impact of White's study, see Desbarats, "Following *The Middle Ground*," in the same volume. For evidence of common ground and friendship between Europeans and Indians at the local level, see David L. Preston, *The Texture of Contact*, and Philip Levy, *Fellow Travelers*. For the roles of cultural brokers, see Richter, "Cultural Brokers and Intercultural Politics," and Merrell, *Into the American Woods*, esp. 28–34; see also the essays in Szasz, *Between Indian and White Worlds*. For the importance of localized contact points in redefining frontiers and empires, see Cayton and Teute, "Introduction: On the Connection of Frontiers," in *Contact Points*, 1–15.

5. A good example of this archaeological paucity is David R. Starbuck's survey of British military sites in upstate New York, where thousands of Indians joined British soldiers in staging military operations during the colonial wars of the eighteenth century. The material culture found or reported at these sites displays much useful information about army life but little about native activities. Fort archaeology is often limited by the goals or preconceptions of historical societies, donors, or the archaeologists themselves. If archaeologists look for military evidence instead of native culture, then that is what they are more likely to find. But in the case of Crown Point, Fort Edwards, and other New York sites, it is more likely that Indian presence was too ephemeral for archaeological detection and that Indians used European goods and materials that might not be interpretable as native activity in the archaeological record. Starbuck, *The Great Warpath*. A recent exception to the problems of studying fort-based Indian-white interactions is James H. Merrell's study of the multiethnic Indian village of Shamokin, whose residents experienced significant change when Pennsylvanians erected Fort Augusta there. Merrell, "Shamokin, 'The Very Seat of the Prince of Darkness.'"

6. For a succinct social history of British military experience in the American backcountry see McConnell, *Army and Empire*, esp. 32–52, for an overview of the various kinds of forts used west of the Appalachians. For the roles of backcountry forts and soldiers in Virginia and Pennsylvania during the Seven Years' War, see Ward, *Breaking the Backcountry*, and Stephenson, "Pennsylvania Provincial Soldiers in the Seven Years' War." Establishing larger European backcountry forts in the second half of the eighteenth century transformed Indian-European combat. Guerrilla-style fighting, which dominated North American warfare throughout the previous century, gave way to siege warfare as French, and later British, military contingencies demanded more substantial forts to guard larger regional troop units and naval operations. Steele, *Warpaths*, 221–22.

7. For the problems encountered at forts or trading posts transitioning from French to British control, see Sleeper-Smith, *Indian Women and French Men*, 54–72.

8. Johnson to Shirley, Apr. 9, 1756, *WJP*, 9:424–25; "An Indian Conference," *WJP*, 9:378–79. For other instances of Iroquois requests for forts, see *WJP* 2:488–90, 768–69, 9:334, 370, 414–16, 457–58, 498, 568–69.

9. For British attempts, often unsuccessful, to understand how kinship controlled the fur trade, see Sleeper-Smith, *Indian Women and French Men*, 54–72. For the importance of intercultural kinship and the resulting Creole communities in the western Great Lakes, see Murphy, *A Gathering of Rivers*, 32, 46–56. For intermarriage between Cherokee women and English traders and soldiers, see Perdue, *Cherokee Women*, 81–84.

10. For Cherokee examples of women's control of agriculture and its role in intercultural relations, see Perdue, *Cherokee Women*, 74–76. For Great Lakes examples, see Sleeper-Smith, *Indian Women and French Men*, 73–85, and Murphy, *A Gathering of Rivers*, 23–24, 29–30.

11. For examples of changing gender roles emerging from the wars of the eighteenth century, see Perdue, *Cherokee Women*, 99–108. For changes in gender roles emanating from the proliferation of the fur trade among the Creeks, see Saunt, *A New Order of Things*, 143–51.

12. For Iroquoians' dislike of garrisons, see Johnson to Clinton, Mar. 18, 1746, *WJP*, 1:80–82. For the social backgrounds of provincial soldiers, see Ward, *Breaking the Backcountry*, 107–21. For warnings about "young men," see "Journal of Indian Affairs," *WJP*, 13:104–7; Johnson to James Abercromby, Jan. 14, 1758, *WJP*, 2:771–73.

13. "An Indian Conference," *WJP*, 10:505–8. For a Pennsylvania example of Indian complaints against garrisons, see Croghan to Johnson, Sept. 4, 1762, *WJP*, 3:873–75.

14. For Indians' fears of encroaching white settlers, see Johnson to Gage, Sept. 22, 1767, GPAS. Indian-settler relations were not always, or even usually, contentious. Indians and settlers often found much common ground, and their mutual animosities are accentuated here only because it was a common source for native fears of forts. Studying relations between European settlers and Indians in the backcountry demands a nuanced approach that takes into account the religious, racial, cultural, national, and economic issues involved. See Preston, *The Texture of Contact*, for a recent study that emphasizes Iroquois-European cooperation and friendship rather than conflict and violence. For a concise discussion and synthesis of these issues, see Nobles, "Breaking into the Backcountry." For lower Mississippi examples of Indian-settler-slave interactions, see Usner, *Indians, Settlers, and Slaves in a Frontier Exchange Economy*, 149–218. For a post-Revolution look at New York Indian-settler issues, see Taylor, *The Divided Ground*, 128–41. For a full-length study of Indian-settler violence and how it affected notions of frontiers and nationalism, see Griffin, *American Leviathan*.

15. For Onondaga distrust of English forts, see "Extracts of Indian Papers," *WJP*, 9:517. For Cherokee descriptions, see "Preliminary Articles of Peace between Kerlerac and the Cherokees," *WJP*, 9:574–81. For demands to remove forts during peacetime, see *WJP*, 3:707, 870–72, 4:125, 196–203, 8:644–47.

16. After many years in which Parkman's *The Conspiracy of Pontiac* and Howard H. Peckham's *Pontiac and the Indian Uprising* remained the most familiar and substantial studies of the conflict, recent writers have contributed a wave of scholarship on this important period. Richard White asserts the reemergence of Indian diplomatic potential because of the rebellion in *The Middle Ground*, 269–314. Michael N. McConnell sees the uprising as a collection of local conflicts woven together, including a "Western Indian Defensive War" against further British encroachment in the Ohio Valley. *A Country Between*, 182–206. William R. Nester revisits an older model, blaming the uprising on British commander in chief Jeffrey Amherst's incompetent and intolerant Indian policies in *"Haughty Conquerors."* In *War under Heaven*, Gregory Evans Dowd reinterprets the war as an imperial conflict between the increasingly polarizing qualities of both British and Indian combatants; each side's notions of leadership, autonomy, and spirituality led

to a breakdown in efforts to interact amicably. See also Dixon, *Never Come to Peace Again*, and Middleton, *Pontiac's War*. For sources describing the fall of forts during the Indian uprising of 1763, see *WJP* 10:690–746. See also Dowd, *War under Heaven*, 124–28.

17. Gage to Hillsborough, Nov. 10, 1770, GPES, vol. 19.

18. Johnson to the Earl of Egremont, May 1762, *WJP*, 460–65; Johnson to the Lords of Trade, Aug. 20, 1762, *WJP*, 3:865–69; Johnson to Cadwallader Colden, June 9, 1764, *WJP*, 4:442–44.

19. A classic study of Indian gifts is Jacobs, *Diplomacy and Indian Gifts*. For a more recent exploration of the ways Indians understood and used gifts, see Murray, *Indian Giving*, 27–38. On the social and cultural meanings of Indian presents, see R. White, *The Middle Ground*, 112–15, 403–4. For a concise study showing the importance of gift giving in maintaining Indian-European reciprocal relations, and how native pleas for pity and claims of poverty often represented more ritual than reality, see B. M. White, "'Give Us a Little Milk.'"

20. Amherst to Johnson, Sept. 30, 1763, *NYCD*, 7:568–69. Generations of historians have placed most of the blame for the uprising on Amherst's unfortunate Indian policies. Parkman, *The Conspiracy of Pontiac*, 1:181, 195; Peckham, *Pontiac and the Indian Uprising*, 70–72; Nester, *"Haughty Conquerors."* Dowd sees Amherst's gift policy not as the cause of the uprising, but as the trigger for a cultural, political, and spiritual conflict already embedded deeply in English-Indian relations. *War under Heaven*, 72–78.

21. Gage to Hillsborough, Sept. 9, 1769, *WJP*, 6:356.

22. For a recent study that covers the topic in detail, including alcohol's importance in native rituals and social practices, see Mancall, *Deadly Medicine*. See also Dowd, *War under Heaven*, 103–4, and Axtell, *The Invasion Within*, 64–67.

23. William Dunbar to Gage, Aug. 31, 1763, GPAS, vol. 9; Johnson to Gage, Mar. 1759, GPAS, vol. 2; "An Indian Conference," Aug. 11, 1762, *WJP*, 10:480–83; Gage to Hillsborough, Sept. 8, 1770, GPES, vol. 18; "Indian Proceedings," Apr. 26–27, 1757, *WJP*, 9:693–94.

Chapter 1. The Key to Carolina: Old Hop, Little Carpenter, and the Making of Fort Loudoun, 1756–1759

1. English documents use the names "Little Carpenter" and "Old Hop" to refer to the Cherokees Attakullakulla and Connecorte, respectively. This study uses the English names to avoid confusion with material quoted from the original documents. Titles of entries in the South Carolina Indian Books use many variations of the two leaders' names. In these citations the English names are used instead,to avoid further confusion. For a biography of Little Carpenter, see Kelley, "Notable Persons in Cherokee History: Attakullakulla."

2. "Proceedings of the Council Concerning Indian Affairs," July 4, 1753, *DRIA*, 2:433–34.

3. Jacobs, *Appalachian Indian Frontier*, 40. Previous studies of the fort have taken into account the prodigious effort expended by Cherokee leaders to influence the construction of Fort Loudoun but still maintain the prominence of perceived British motives to "control" the Cherokees. See Kelley, "Fort Loudoun: British Stronghold in the Tennessee Country."

4. Hatley, *Dividing Paths*, 67–71; Glen to the Board of Trade, Mar. 1751, WHLP; Glen to the Commons House of Assembly [hereafter CHA], Mar. 7, 1755, *JCHA*, 12:157–59.

5. Jacobs, *Appalachian Indian Frontier*, 51; Atkin to Thomas Robinson, Aug. 29, 1755, WHLP; Ludovic Grant to Glen, Aug. 20, 1755, *DRIA*, 1:74–75. For an overview of the British-Cherokee alliance and its attendant problems, see Dowd, "'Insidious Friends.'"

6. Talk of Old Hop et al., Apr. 22, 1752, *DRIA*, 1:253–54; Paul Demere to Lyttelton, Jan. 1, 1759, WHLP; Raymond Demere to William Henry Lyttelton, July 30, 1757, *DRIA*, 2:392. For the importance of status in village politics, see Hatley, *Dividing Paths*, 10–12.

7. Talk of Old Hop to Glen, Apr. 29, 1752, *DRIA*, 1:258–59; Ludovic Grant and Joseph Axson to Glen, Mar. 23, 1759, *DRIA*, 2:47–48; "Proceedings of the Council Concerning Indian Affairs," *DRIA*, 1:439; Little Carpenter to Lyttelton, Aug. 15, 1756, *DRIA*, 2:166; Speech of Little Carpenter to Raymond Demere," July 13, 1756, *DRIA*, 2:137–38. The visit of the 1730 Cherokee embassy to London is described in Crane, *The Southern Frontier*, 295–302. For a full study of Indian experiences in Britain, see Vaughan, *Transatlantic Encounters*, esp. 137–50, for a more recent description of the Cherokees' London visit. Hatley emphasizes the persistence of the memory of the Yamasee War of 1715 in English-Cherokee relations and views the London treaty as a solidification of the uncertain alliance promised after that conflict. Hatley, *Dividing Paths*, 67–68.

8. For Cherokees and traders, see Hatley, *Dividing Paths*, 43–44, 47–48. On Native American consumerism in general, see Axtell, *Beyond 1492*, 125–51.

9. James Beamer to Glen, Feb. 21, 1756, *DRIA*, 2:104–6; Old Hop to Raymond Demere, and Raymond Demere to Lyttelton, Aug. 3, 1756, *DRIA*, 2:157–61; Glen to Old Hop, and Old Hop to Glen, Oct. 14, 1755, *DRIA*, 2:77–79.

10. "Proceedings of the Council Concerning Indian Affairs," *DRIA*, 1:442; Grant to Glen, Mar. 27, 1755, *DRIA*, 2:41–42; Talk of the Mankiller of Great Tellico to Raymond Demere, Jan. 15, 1757, *DRIA*, 2:320.

11. Jacobs, *Appalachian Indian Frontier*, 51. My emphasis.

12. Little Carpenter to Glen, *DRIA*, 2:77–78; Glen to Little Carpenter, Oct. 14, 1755, *DRIA*, 2:75–76. For the Saluda conference, see Corkran, *Cherokee Frontier*, 58–61; Hatley, *Dividing Paths*, 75–77. Glen took the Cherokee land cession at face value and disregarded the largely symbolic Indian perception of the exchange at Saluda.

13. Dinwiddie to Glen, Oct. 25, 1754, *ORRD*, 1:379; "Committee on Indian Affairs Report," Mar. 12–13, 1755, Upper House of Assembly [hereafter UHA] to CHA, CHA to Glen, and CHA to UHA, Mar. 14, 1755, all in *JCHA*, 12:168–69, 181, 182–83, 183, 188; Dinwiddie to Glen, *ORRD*, 2:26.

14. Glen to CHA, and CHA to Glen, Jan. 23, 1756, *JCHA*, 13:46–47, 48.

15. CHA Record, Feb. 3, 1756, *JCHA*, 13:78–79, 91–92; Old Hop to Glen, Mar. 20, 1756, *DRIA*, 2:108–9; Glen to CHA, Apr. 8–9, 1756, *JCHA*, 13:206–7, 210–11; Lyttelton to CHA, and CHA to Lyttelton, June 30, 1756, *JCHA*, 13:263, 266; *JCHA*, 13:xxviii, 247, 251. For an overview of Glen's prominent role in negotiating the building of the fort, see Stumpf, "James Glen, Cherokee Diplomacy, and the Construction of an Overhill Fort."

16. "Minutes of a Council with the Cherokees," Sept. 5, 1755, *ORRD*, 2:187–88; Dinwiddie to Glen, Sept. 25, 1755, *ORRD*, 2:215.

17. Dinwiddie to Arthur Dobbs, Apr. 13, 1756, *ORRD*, 2:382; Dinwiddie to Washington,

Apr. 23, 1756, *ORRD*, 2:388; Dinwiddie to Lewis, Apr. 24, 1756, 2:389–90; Dinwiddie to William Shirley, Apr. 28, 1756, *ORRD*, 2:395–96; Dinwiddie to Lewis, Apr. 28, 1756, *ORRD*, 2:395–96.

18. Lyttelton to Old Hop, June 3, 1756, *DRIA*, 2:115–16; Talk of Raymond Demere to Old Hop and Little Carpenter, June 30, 1756, *DRIA*, 2:128–29; Raymond Demere to Lyttelton, July 2, 1756, *DRIA*, 2:129–34; Old Hop to Lyttelton, July 2, 1756, *DRIA*, 2:141–42; Old Hop and Little Carpenter to Raymond Demere, July 12, 1756, *DRIA*, 2:134; Dinwiddie to Lyttelton, Sept. 18, 1756, *ORRD*, 2:510; Dinwiddie to Dobbs, Sept. 18, 1756, *ORRD*, 2:511–12.

19. Lewis to Raymond Demere, July 7, 1756, Raymond Demere to Lewis, July 17, 1756, and Raymond Demere to Lewis, Aug. 7, 1756, all in WHLP; Raymond Demere to Lyttelton, July 19, 1756, *DRIA*, 2:143–45; Old Hop and Little Carpenter to Dinwiddie, Aug. 23, 1756, WHLP.

20. Harrison to Shrubshoal, June 2, 1756, *DRIA*, 2:116–17. Gregory Evans Dowd has shown how rumors of Indian activities affected Indian-English policy in Cherokee country, and how they must be accounted for in writing those histories today. Separated by hundreds of miles controlled by Indians whose loyalties were always a matter of speculation for the South Carolinians in Charlestown, communication between the Overhill region and the colonial capital was frequently infused with uncorroborated claims of intended Indian depredations that were often exaggerated or spun of whole cloth. However, the effects of the rumors on those who listened to them were real enough and usually played a role in the mutual distrust and cautiousness that colored the Cherokee-British alliance in the late 1750s. See Dowd, "The Panic of 1751."

21. Harrison to Shrubshoal, June 6, 1756, *DRIA*, 2:117–18.

22. Raymond Demere to Lyttelton, June 23 and 24, 1756, *DRIA*, 2:125–27. On Cherokee women and vegetable production, including their views on trade and hospitality, see Perdue, *Cherokee Women*, 72–74.

23. Answer of the Cherokee Chiefs to Raymond Demere, June 20, 1756, *DRIA*, 2:124; Raymond Demere to Lyttelton, July 13, 1756, *DRIA*, 2:136; Speech of Little Carpenter to Raymond Demere, July 13, 1756, *DRIA*, 2:137.

24. Raymond Demere to Lyttelton, July 20 and 21, 1756, *DRIA*, 2:145–47.

25. Raymond Demere to Lyttelton, July 25, 1756, *DRIA*, 2:147–48; "Paper Signed by Captain Raymond Demere," Aug. 3, 1756, *DRIA*, 2:158. Demere consulted the report's bearer, Tiftoa, who told him that the large body of Indians were in actuality French-allied Nottowagoes and that Old Hop always received the Savannahs as friends.

26. Gibbs to Raymond Demere, Aug. 6, 1756, *DRIA*, 2:163; Raymond Demere to Lyttelton, Aug. 11, 1756, *DRIA*, 2:161–62; Old Hop to Dinwiddie, Aug. 15, 1756, *DRIA*, 2:167–68; Cherokee Headmen to Raymond Demere, Aug. 28, 1756, *DRIA*, 2:182.

27. De Brahm to Lyttelton, Sept. 7, 1756, WHLP.

28. Raymond Demere to Lyttelton, Sept. 9, 1756, *DRIA*, 2:197–98; Lewis to Raymond Demere, Sept. 11, 1756, *DRIA*, 2:203–4; Lewis to Lyttelton, Sept. 14, 1756, *DRIA*, 2:205.

29. Raymond Demere to Lyttelton, Oct. 13, 1756, *DRIA*, 2:216; Reply of Old Hop to Raymond Demere, Oct. 3, 1756, *DRIA*, 2:224; Raymond Demere to Lyttelton, Oct. 13 and 16, 1756, *DRIA*, 2:214–20, 225. Descriptions of Indian poverty by both European

and native observers frequently feature descriptions of "nakedness" and starvation, and while this was often a figurative conception of the Indians' condition, stressing their desires for comparative levels of status and authority, the descriptions must have been at least partially true given the verifiable Indian hardships evident throughout Eastern North America in the eighteenth century. In English sources such as Demere's the descriptions of poverty seem real enough, and this is not surprising considering the extent to which Cherokees had begun to rely on trade, interruptions in commerce brought on by the conflict with France, and the remoteness of the Overhill region. On Cherokee descriptions of nakedness and poverty as reflections of status anxiety, see Hatley, *Dividing Paths*, 10.

30. Glen had sent a surveyor to Tomotley in February 1756 to check out available conditions for a fort and to confer with Little Carpenter to decide upon a good site. Glen to Little Carpenter, Feb. 17, 1756, *DRIA*, 2:99–100. For the fort site argument, see Raymond Demere to Lyttelton, Oct. 13, 1756, *DRIA*, 2:217–18. De Brahm's description of the argument over the fort's location is somewhat different and makes it seem as though the Indians bowed to his better judgment. De Brahm, *De Brahm's Report of the General Survey*, 101–2.

31. Raymond Demere to De Brahm, Oct. 14, 1756, and Raymond Demere to Lyttelton, Oct. 26, 1756, WHLP; Raymond Demere to Lyttelton, Nov. 18, 1756, *DRIA*, 2:248–51.

32. Raymond Demere to Lyttelton, Oct. 28 and Nov. 7, 1756, *DRIA*, 2:232–34, 241; Old Hop to Raymond Demere, Oct. 28, 1756, *DRIA*, 2:234–37.

33. Raymond Demere to Lyttelton, Dec. 16, 1756, and "Council of War," *DRIA*, 2:274–75; Demere and Other Officers to De Brahm, Dec. 23, 1756, and Demere to Lyttelton, Dec. 24, 1756, *DRIA*, 2:287–90.

34. "Dinwiddie's Message to the Cherokee Indians," Nov. 14, 1756, *ORRD*, 2:548–49; Dinwiddie to Lyttelton, Nov. 20, 1756, *ORRD*, 2:555–56.

35. Glen to Little Carpenter, Feb. 17, 1756, *DRIA*, 2:99–100; Lyttelton to Old Hop, June 3, 1756, *DRIA*, 2:116; Raymond Demere to Lyttelton, Jan. 2 and 6, 1757, *DRIA*, 2:303, 310; Talk of the Mankiller of Great Tellico to Raymond Demere, Feb. 6, 1757, *DRIA*, 2:333. Cherokee women also made baskets of renowned quality, though by the mid-eighteenth century this commodity had decreased in importance and Indian women usually sold them through intermediary traders. Perdue, *Cherokee Women*, 74–75. Cherokee women were shrewd consumers, and they pressured their men to maintain peaceful relations with the provinces and ensure a healthy trade. "Their Women are so much used to our Commodities, Ribbands, Paint, etc. that they soon feel the want of it," an officer at Fort Prince George wrote to Gage in 1764. "That contributed by all Accounts as much at least to the last Peace with the Cherokees as the Burning of their Towns." Augustine Prevost to Gage, May 20, 1764, GPAS, vol. 15.

36. Perdue, *Cherokee Women*, 82–84, 100–101.

37. "Intelligence from Captain Demere," *DRIA*, 2:243–44; Old Warrior of Tomotley to Raymond Demere, Nov. 13, 1756, *DRIA*, 2:244–45; Raymond Demere to Lyttelton, Dec. 11, 1756, *DRIA*, 2:267–68.

38. Raymond Demere to Lyttelton, Jan. 2, 1756, *DRIA*, 301–5; Talk of Wall to the Tellico Indians, Jan. 11, 1757, *DRIA*, 2:317–19; Raymond Demere to Lyttelton, Jan. 12,

1757, *DRIA,* 2:311–13; Wall to Raymond Demere, Jan. 13, 1757, *DRIA,* 2:321–24; Talk of Mankiller of Great Tellico to Demere, Jan. 15, 1757, *DRIA,* 2:319–20.

39. Talk of Raymond Demere to Old Hop and the Upper Cherokee Headmen, Jan. 25, 1757, *DRIA,* 2:331–33. On the prevalence and uses of scalp bounties for colonial purposes, see Axtell, *The European and the Indian,* 215–23.

40. Lyttelton to CHA, Feb. 3, 1757, *JCHA,* 13:321, 325–26; Raymond Demere to Lyttelton, Aug. 26, 1757, *DRIA,* 2:404–5; Summary of Talks of Old Hop, Little Carpenter, and Paul Demere, Aug. 30, 1757, WHLP.

41. Raymond Demere to Lyttelton, June 10 and 13, 1757, *DRIA,* 2:381–86; John Stuart to Lyttelton, June 12, 1757, WHLP.

42. Raymond Demere to Lyttelton, Feb. 5 and 15, 1757, *DRIA,* 2:333–35, 338–40.

43. John Chevillette [Fort Loudoun's commissary] to Lyttelton, Mar. 1, 1757, *DRIA,* 2:344; Raymond Demere to Lyttelton, Apr. 1, 1757, *DRIA,* 2:357–59; Lyttelton to CHA, Apr. 1, 1757, *DRIA,* 2:402; CHA Proceedings, *DRIA,* 2:413, 422.

44. Raymond Demere to Lyttelton, July 11 and 23, 1757, WHLP.

45. Atkin to Lyttelton, Apr. 30, 1757, and Stuart to Lyttelton, May 29, 1757, WHLP; Daniel Pepper to Raymond Demere, June 27, 1757, *DRIA,* 2:390; Paul Demere to Lyttelton, Aug. 18, 1757, *DRIA,* 2:401–4.

46. Raymond Demere to Lyttelton, July 11, 1757, WHLP.

47. Raymond Demere to Lyttelton, July 9, 1757, WHLP; Raymond Demere to Lyttelton, July 30 and Aug. 10, 1757, *DRIA,* 2:391–401; Talk of Wallanawa, Oct. 9, 1757, WHLP.

48. Talk of Paul Demere to the Indians at Fort Loudoun, Aug. 25, 1757, and Paul Demere to Lyttelton, Feb. 20 and Sept. 30, 1758, WHLP.

49. Paul Demere to Lyttelton, Oct. 11, 1757, WHLP; Lyttelton to Paul Demere, Dec. 15, 1757, Lyttelton Letterbook, 57–58, WHLP.

50. Little Carpenter to Paul Demere, Jan. 4, 1758, *DRIA,* 2:434–35; Paul Demere to Lyttelton, Mar. 2 and Apr. 2, 1758, *DRIA,* 2:434–35, 455–56.

51. Paul Demere to Lyttelton, Mar. 7 and Apr. 2, *DRIA,* 2:439–40, 455–56; Paul Demere to Lyttelton, June 24, 1758, WHLP; Lyttelton to Paul Demere, July 5, 1757, Lyttelton Letterbook, 148–50, WHLP; Paul Demere to Lyttelton, July 30, 1758, WHLP; Lyttelton to Old Hop, Little Carpenter, Standing Turkey, and Woolinawa, Aug. 28, 1758, Lyttelton Letterbook, 207–8, WHLP.

52. Lyttelton to Paul Demere, Feb. 2, Mar. 20, and May 2, 1759, Lyttelton Letterbook, 206–7, 315, 341, WHLP; Corkran, *Cherokee Frontier,* 168; Hatley, *Dividing Paths,* 102. Settlers had killed Settico Cherokees as they passed through the backcountry on their way home from fighting as British allies in the Forbes campaign. Hatley, *Dividing Paths,* 100–101.

53. Corkran, *Cherokee Frontier,* 168–90; Hatley, *Dividing Paths,* 107–15. Lyttelton's warnings of the onset of hostilities are in the Lyttelton Letterbook, WHLP.

54. Corkran, *Cherokee Frontier,* 216–21; Hatley, *Dividing Paths,* 133; Perdue, *Cherokee Women,* 100. For a detailed account of the surrender of Fort Loudoun and the fate of its garrison, see R. G. Stone, "Captain Paul Demere at Fort Loudoun," 30–32. A large British force invaded the Middle and Overhills regions in 1762, destroying several towns. Initiatives led by Oconostota, Little Carpenter, and others led to a beneficial state of neutrality

over the following years. This was broken during the American Revolution, when status, trade, and loyalties led to a new round of destructive alliances and reprisals from both Indians and American forces. See Calloway, *The American Revolution in Indian Country*, 182–212, for ensuing events of Overhill Cherokees in the 1760s–1780s.

Chapter 2. Anxious Hospitality: Loitering at Fort Allen, 1756–1761

1. Fort Allen has received scant historical attention as a cultural contact point. The most complete description of the fort's history is Hunter, *Forts on the Pennsylvania Frontier*, 233–59. For an older and more antiquarian account, see Richards, "The Indian Forts of the Blue Mountains." See also Charles Morse Stolz's valuable illustrations and description in *Outposts of the War for Empire*, 106–7. For descriptions of the political and social contexts in which Fort Allen was built, see Mayer, "From Forts to Families," 5–43; Schutt, *Peoples of the River Valleys*, 94–123; A. F. C. Wallace, *King of the Delawares*; Ward, *Breaking the Backcountry*, 92–122; Ketcham, "Conscience, War, and Politics in Pennsylvania"; Waddell, "Defending the Long Perimeter"; Stephenson, "Pennsylvania Provincial Soldiers in the Seven Years' War."

2. For the urbanization of Northampton and surrounding counties after 1730, see Lemon, *The Best Poor Man's Country*, 130–35. For the organization of Bethlehem's communal "General Economy," see Smaby, *The Transformation of Moravian Bethlehem*. See also *History of Northampton County*, 48, for county population figures in 1752.

3. A. F. C. Wallace, *King of the Delawares*, 41. For a description of Gnadenhütten's founding and organization, see Loskiel, *History of the Mission*, 2:82–87, 97–105.

4. Merritt, *At the Crossroads*, 169–78.

5. Weslager, *Delaware Indians*, 223. For an example of Delawares requesting British protection for their families during Braddock's failed expedition, see Croghan to Morris, July 21, 1755, *CRP*, 6:494–95. For requests from Reading leaders for help, see Conrad Weiser et al. to Morris, Oct. 31, 1755, THP. For Moravian reports of imminent trouble, see Horsfield to Morris, Nov. 2 and Nov. 10, 1755, THP; Horsfield to Morris, Nov. 15, 1755, Timothy Horsfield Letterbook, Historical Society of Pennsylvania, Philadelphia [hereafter Horsfield Letterbook]. For more descriptions of the spread of panic following Braddock's defeat and subsequent English problems maintaining Delaware alliances, see A. F. C. Wallace, *King of the Delawares*, 67–72; Weslager, *Delaware Indians*, 226–32.

6. "Examination of David Zeisberger," Nov. 22, 1755, Morris to Horsfield, Dec. 4, 1755, Horsfield to Morris, Dec. 8, 1755, and Spangenberg to Morris, Dec. 17, 1755, all in THP; Hunter, *Forts on the Pennsylvania Frontier*, 234–35. For a description of the Gnadenhütten attack, its causes, and its significance, see Merritt, *At the Crossroads*, 184–86. See also Horsfield to Morris, Nov. 26, 1755, *PA*, 2:520–23, and Horsfield to Morris, Nov. 29, 1755, Horsfield Letterbook, for Horsfield's frantic call for assistance and fears that the Indian attacks might endanger the province's western settlement ambitions. For the attack on Hays's company, see William Hays to Morris and the Provincial Commissioners, Jan. 3, 1756, *FP*, 6:341–42. The settlers fleeing from Allemangel soon met a party of seventeen men led by trader Jacob Levan, and they regrouped and fought off the pursuing Indians. Franklin to David Hall, *FP*, 6:348–49.

7. Address of Gnadenhütten Indians to Morris, Nov. 30, 1755, and Morris to the

Gnadenhütten Indians, Dec. 4, 1755, THP; Answer of Gnadenhütten Indians to Morris, Horsfield Letterbook; Sipe, *The Indian Wars of Pennsylvania*, 252; Morris to Horsfield, Dec. 4, 1755, Horsfield to Morris, Dec. 8, 1755, and Spangenberg to Morris, Dec. 17, 1755, THP; Hunter, *Forts on the Pennsylvania Frontier*, 234–35. The plan for a defensive fort line and increased troop presence in the Blue Mountain frontier came amid new reports of French-allied Indian attacks on settlers and incidents of settler mayhem and vigilantism. Address of Horsfield et al., Nov. 24, 1755, THP; Horsfield to Morris, Dec. 1, 1755, Horsfield Letterbook; Horsfield to the Constables of Northampton County, and Horsfield to Morris, Dec. 12, 1755, Horsfield Letterbook.

8. Franklin to John Vanetta (Van Etten), Jan. 12, 1756, *PA*, 2:546–47; Franklin to Morris, Jan. 14, 1756, *PA*, 2:548–50; Franklin to Deborah Franklin, Jan. 15, 1756, *FP*, 6:360–61; Ensign Thomas Lloyd to [Unknown], Jan. 30, 1756, *FP*, 6:380–82.

9. Franklin, *The Autobiography and Other Writings*, 123–24. Franklin's later self-deprecation was probably an effort to downplay the importance of a fort that ended up being manned for a short period. For his quote and some of his letters describing Fort Allen's construction, see *FP*, 6:365–71. For a general account of the fort's construction, see also Hunter, *Forts on the Pennsylvania Frontier*, 259.

10. Morris to George Washington, Feb. 2, 1756, *PA*, 2:564–65; Morris to William Shirley, Feb. 9, 1756, *PA*, 2:569–70; "Position of Troops in Northampton County," Feb. 23, 1756, *FP*, 6:408. For a typical example of settlers' requests for protection while performing their routine chores, see Petition of John Hughes to Morris, Apr. 21, 1756, *PA*, 2:638. For militias preferring to guard settlements and the use of scalp bounties, see Pennsylvania Commissioners to Morris, June 14, 1756, *CRP*, 7:153–54.

11. "A Journal from Reading to the Sundry Forts and Garrisons Along the Northern Frontiers of the Province," June 21, 1756, *PA*, 2:677–78; Reynolds to Parsons, July 10, 1756, and William Franklin to Horsfield, June 21, 1756, THP.

12. Horsfield to Morris, June 21, 1756, THP; "Memorandum Regarding Unfriendly Indians," June 30, 1756, THP; Letter from Unnamed Bethlehem Resident, Apr. 1756, THP. British officials often referred to Kanuksusy as Captain Newcastle, and he is so called in reports surrounding these events. "Captain Newcastle's Instructions," June 28, 1756, THP; Newcastle to the Captain of Fort Allen, July 1, 1756, *CRP*, 7:189; Newcastle to Spangenberg, July 1, 1756, THP.

13. Some of the earliest European visitors to North America commented on native hospitality. Jesuit missionaries noted that Indians in New France would sometimes extend hospitality to friendly guests even at the cost of their own health and comfort. Father Superior Francesco Bressani claimed that this hospitable attitude was not even considered a virtue among the Hurons, just a standard feature of reciprocal native relations. For some seventeenth-century descriptions of Indian hospitality, see Thwaites, *Jesuit Relations*, 35:207–9, 38:267, 58:79.

14. Merrell, *Into the American Woods*, 137–43; Weslager, *Delaware Indians*, 51; P. A. W. Wallace, *Indians in Pennsylvania*, 129. For Zeisberger, see his *History of Northern American Indians*, 116, 120, 129. For Heckewelder, see his *Account*, 148–49. For hospitable attitudes toward native ambassadors, see Zeisberger, *History*, 93; and Heckewelder, *Account*, 181–82.

15. For gift giving, see Murray, *Indian Giving*, especially 31–38, for Indian generosity and the ambiguities of native notions of reciprocity. See also Axtell, *The European and the Indian*, 136, 348 n. 8. For the "redistributive" reciprocal nature of Indian exchange, especially among the Iroquois, see Richter, *The Ordeal of the Longhouse*, 21–22, 47.

16. For settler complaints about the location of the fort line, see Hunter, *Forts on the Pennsylvania Frontier*, 214–15. The forts on the Blue Mountain ranging line must have had social cultures that were very different from those of the larger forts in western Pennsylvania, which featured garrison communities, responsibilities for civil authority, and, especially, numerous women, whose presence brought eastern social customs that both meshed with and complicated the forts' military cultures. Mayer, "From Forts to Families." White women may have lived at or near the fort during its post-1758 tenure as a trading post; the Fort Allen Daybook lists many English female given names as customers, though these could be Christian Indians or women from settlements south of Blue Mountain.

17. Morris to Parsons, July 11, 1756, and Morris to Horsfield, July 14, 1756, THP. For the belligerent "Jersey Men," see Merrell, *Into the American Woods*, 269–70, 420 n. 60.

18. Reynolds to William Edwards, July 14, 1756, and Parsons to Horsfield, July 18, 1756, THP. After fifty years, A. F. C. Wallace's *King of the Delawares* remains the most rewarding study of Teedyuscung, certainly one of the most colorful, complicated, and intriguing figures in eighteenth-century North America. See pages 83–86 for details of his participation in the uprising. For an explanation of Teedyuscung's approach to diplomacy, which involved positioning the Delawares in rewarding alliances with the English and native groups, see Schutt, *Peoples of the River Valleys*, 115–16. For an amusing and informative description of how treaty conference organizers worried about attendees' revels, see Merrell, *Into the American Woods*, 262–64. For Teedyuscung's insistence on determining the direction of Pennsylvania-Delaware diplomacy, see Merrell, "'I Desire All That I Have Said.'" Weiser spent prodigious energy keeping visiting diplomats from engaging in liquor-fueled violence. For example, in one instance he mediated a dispute between Teedyuscung and Kanuksusy, who feared that the Munsee chief meant to kill him with witchcraft. Parsons's Diary of a Council Held at Easton, July 24–27, 1756, in Hirsch, *Pennsylvania Treaties*, 106–9. Indians' recreational use of alcohol is stressed in this article because of the focus on hospitality, but it should not be overemphasized; Indians had many uses for liquor. For native uses of alcohol in rituals, diplomatic encounters, and as a consumer commodity, see Mancall, *Deadly Medicine*. An influential article establishing the importance of alcohol and gift giving in establishing intercultural relationships between whites and Indians, especially in the western fur trade, is B. M. White, "'Give Us a Little Milk.'"

19. Reply of Teedyuscung to Morris, *PA*, 2:721–22.

20. Horsfield to Parsons, Aug. 9, 1756, Teedyuscung to Horsfield and Parsons, Aug. 9, 1756, Peters to Parsons, Aug. 11, 1756, Horsfield to Teedyuscung, Aug. 12, 1756, and Morris to Horsfield, Aug. 13, 1756, all in THP. For Teedyuscung's earlier history as an unhappy Christian convert in Gnadenhütten, see A. F. C. Wallace, *King of the Delawares*, 39–53.

21. Parsons to Morris, Aug. 8, 1756, *PA*, 2:745–46; Reynolds to Parsons, Aug. 12, 1756,

THP. Discipline was a major problem among provincial forces during the Seven Years' War for a variety of reasons, including a lack of capable officers, inability or unwillingness of officers to inflict the full brunt of military punishment, and the socioeconomic backgrounds of the troops themselves. This was especially true in Pennsylvania, where most troops were day laborers or artisans and were unused to harsh discipline and unwilling to easily change their ways. Ward, *Breaking the Backcountry*, 107–21.

22. Reynolds to Weiser, Aug. 11, 1756, in Hunter, *Forts on the Pennsylvania Frontier*, 241; Parsons to Wetterhold and Wetterhold to Parsons, Aug. 12, 1756, *PA*, 2:741, 754–55. See A. F. C. Wallace, *King of the Delawares*, 116–18, for a full description of the mutiny and its causes. Wallace claims that Teedyuscung "struck the match" that sparked the mutiny by bringing women into the fort, but that seems an unfair burden to place upon Teedyuscung, and especially upon the women, who were possibly raped by drunken soldiers.

23. Parsons to Richard Peters, Aug. 15, 1756, *PA* 2:747; Parsons to Morris, Aug. 15, 1756, and Horsfield to Parsons, Aug. 15, 1756, THP; Parsons to Morris, *PA*, 2:749; Horsfield to Parsons, Aug. 19, 1756, THP.

24. Pennsylvania Council, Aug. 21, 1756, *CRP*, 7:222–23; Denny to Sir Charles Hardy, Aug. 21, 1756, *CRP*, 7:223–25; Denny to Weiser, Aug. 21, 1756, THP. On Teedyuscung's sedition: earlier in August, rumors spread that he had been encouraging English-allied Indians to leave the region or be killed along with their white friends. Horsfield to Parsons, Aug. 19, 1756, THP.

25. Parsons to Morris, Aug. 21, 1756, and Jacob Orndt to Weiser, Aug. 24, 1756, THP. Reynolds and Miller did face charges for turning Fort Allen into a virtual pub and allowing a mutiny to occur, but they defended themselves successfully and avoided a court-martial. Reynolds to Weiser, Aug. 26, 1756, THP.

26. Orndt and Reynolds to Parsons, Oct. 9, 1756, *PA*, 3:5–6; Horsfield to Denny, Oct. 27, 1756, THP; Council to Denny, Oct. 29, 1756, *FP*, 7:6–7; Jacob Morgan to Denny, Nov. 4, 1756, *PA*, 3:30–31. Even worse rumors soon emerged; the band of Minisinks was larger than previously supposed (140 or more) and intended to fall upon either Easton or Bethlehem, making themselves "Masters of the whole Country." Weiser remained skeptical; such rumors were common currency in the Pennsylvania backcountry. "Extract of Conrad Weiser's Journal," Nov. 5, 1756, *PA*, 3:32–33.

27. Weiser and Parsons to Denny, Nov. 6, 1756, *PA*, 3:35; "Council Held at Easton," Hirsch, *Pennsylvania Treaties*, 144–45.

28. "Journal of the Proceedings of Conrad Weiser with the Indians, to Fort Allen, by his Honour the Governours Order," Nov. 18, 1756, *PA*, 3:66–68.

29. The Walking Purchase was a colonial land acquisition in which Pennsylvania's proprietors intentionally used ambiguities between Delaware and English notions of land tenure and measurement to acquire much more property than the Delawares had intended to sell. The area of this acquisition contained much of Northampton County south of Blue Mountain. With the support of influential Quakers who were political opponents of the proprietors and Pennsylvania government, Teedyuscung demanded that the province revisit and rectify the specious land deal. This surprise tactic pushed the proprietors into a defensive posture and delayed hopes for an immediate peace treaty indefinitely. A. F. C. Wallace, *King of the Delawares*, 130–36; Merritt, *At the Crossroads*,

225–26. For Delaware-Pennsylvania land issues and disputes, see Harper, "Delawares and Pennsylvanians after the Walking Purchase," and Preston, "Squatters, Indians, Proprietary Government, and Land in the Susquehanna Valley." For a recent overview of the Walking Purchase, including an excellent new map of the land cession, see Harper, *Promised Land*.

30. Orndt to Parsons, Feb. 18, 1757, *CRP,* 7:429; Parsons to Horsfield, Feb. 20, 1757, THP.

31. Orndt to Parsons, Mar. 31, 1757, *CRP,* 7:474; Parsons to Richard Peters, Apr. 3, 1757, *PA,* 3:104; Orndt to Parsons, Apr. 5, 1757, *CRP,* 7:474–75.

32. Denny to Parsons, Apr. 12, 1757, *CRP,* 7:476–77; Teedyuscung to Parsons, Apr. 13, 1757, *CRP,* 7:477–78; Denny to Horsfield and Denny to [unknown], Apr. 26, 1757, and Parsons to Horsfield, Apr. 28, 1757, THP; William Trent to Denny, May 2, 1757, *PA,* 3:149–50.

33. Orndt to Weiser, July 5, 1757, *PA,* 3:207; Orndt to Denny, July 8, 1757, *PA,* 3:209–10; "Report of Indians that Came to Easton by Way of Fort Allen," Aug. 1, 1757, *PA,* 3:210; Orndt to Denny, Aug. 19, 1757, *CRP,* 7:723–24; Denny to Horsfield, Sept. 5, 1757, THP. The worst threat posed to peace during this period came when a fifteen-year-old "foolish white boy" shot and wounded William Dattamy, an unaccompanied Indian on his way to Bethlehem. Orndt was forced to remain in Easton with some of his men to prevent Indian-white animosities from flaring over the incident, despite the fact that fifty or more Indians remained encamped around Fort Allen.

34. Horsfield to Parsons, Apr. 27, 1757, *PA,* 3:142–43; "Petition from Northampton County," *PA,* 3:151–52; "Petition from the Frontiers," *PA,* 3:153–54; Franklin to the Printer of *The Citizen, FP,* 7:261–62; Wetterhold to Parsons, July 7, 1757, *PA,* 3:211; Weiser to Denny, July 7, 1757, *PA,* 3:218. Weiser had reported the untenable state of Fort Franklin in November 1756 and ordered Wetterhold and his men to evacuate the fort and proceed to Lynn Township, Northampton County, where they remained in May 1757. "Journal of the Proceedings of Conrad Weiser with the Indians, to Fort Allen, by His Honour the Governour's Order," *PA,* 3:66–68. Morale continued to be a problem at the outposts. In March 1757 another near-mutiny took place at Fort Norris when a soldier, Hieronymous Faxtor, was discharged for insubordination. He fired his gun at the fort upon leaving and then attacked a passing settler. Ensign Jacob Snider to Parsons, Mar. 3, 1757, THP. By April 1757, Denny had decided that only three forts—Allen, Henry, and Hamilton—would be maintained on the frontier, each to be garrisoned with one hundred men. Denny to Proprietors, Apr. 10, 1757, *PA,* 3:119–20.

35. "Position of Troops in Northampton County, 1758," *PA,* 3:325; "Return of the Stations of Nine Companies of the Pennsylvania Regiment," *PA,* 3:339; "Number of Forces," *PA* 3:341; "Exact State of the Forces between Susquehanna and the Delaware" and "Number of Forces in the Pay of the Province," *PA,* 3:340–41; Journal of James Burd, 1758," *PA,* 3:355; "Petition from Northampton County," *PA,* 3:359–60; Burd to Orndt, Mar. 7, 1758, *PA,* 3:351; Orndt to Burd, Mar. 29, 1758, *PA,* 3:367; Denny to James Abercrombie, Apr. 7, 1758, *WJP,* 2:814.

36. Robert Strettell to Horsfield, Apr. 14, 1758, THP; John Edwin to [unknown], Apr.

23, 1758, *CRP,* 8:98–99. Orndt had been promoted to major and given command of the Blue Mountain region. Bull to Peters, June 14, 1758, *PA,* 3:423.

37. "Report of Charles Thomson and F. Post, of a Journey in 1758," *PA,* 3:412–22.

38. Orndt to Denny, Sept. 12, 1758, *CRP,* 8:167; Lt. Samuel Price to Denny, June 29, 1758, *PA,* 3:429; Horsfield to Denny, July 4, 1758, *PA,* 3:436; Hunter, *Forts on the Pennsylvania Frontier,* 252–53; Journal of Frederick Post, 1758," *PA,* 3:521; Orndt to Denny, July 24, 1758, *PA,* 3:490–91; Orndt to Denny, Sept. 12, 1758, *CRP,* 8:167.

39. "Advertisement against Selling Rum to Indians," *PA,* 3:437; "Proclamation against Selling Rum to the Indians," *PA,* 3:519.

40. Hunter, *Forts on the Pennsylvania Frontier,* 254–55; "Conference with the Indians Held at Easton," Hirsch, *Pennsylvania Treaties,* 451; Denny to Assembly, Dec. 21, 1758, *CRP,* 8:238.

41. The figure of £2,333 exceeded the £2,313 brought in at Fort Augusta for the same period, though both of the smaller forts paled in comparison with the center of western Pennsylvania trade, the new post at Fort Pitt. From December 1758 through May 1760, Fort Pitt recorded returns of more than £10,166. Commissioners for Indian Affairs, Indian Trade at Fort Augusta, Pitsberg, and Fort Allen, Cash Book, Apr. 28, 1758–Apr. 19, 1763. For the lack of profitability of Pennsylvania trading posts, see Merritt, *At the Crossroads,* 241–42. For some of the problems besetting Fort Allen near the end of its tenure, see Hunter, *Forts on the Pennsylvania Frontier,* 255–56.

42. Hunter, *Forts on the Pennsylvania Frontier,* 257; *CRP,* 8:514; Hoban and MacKinney, *Pennsylvania Archives,* 6:586–87; Peters to Horsfield, Jan. 17, 1761, THP. Not much was left to salvage from Fort Allen after the garrison had plundered the stores in 1760. Some of the few remaining guns were broken, as were several of the tools. Horsfield sold the utilitarian goods for just over £9 and sent the guns and ammunition to Philadelphia. "Account of Ammunition Stores &ca in Fort Allen, Taken the 21st Sept. 1761," and Horsfield to James Hamilton, Sept. 3, 1761, THP. For an account of the fort's final days, see Levering, *History of Bethlehem,* 370.

Chapter 3. The Greatest Mart of All Trade: Food, Drink, and Interdependence at Michilimackinac, 1761–1796

1. "Indian Council," *MPHC,* 11:493–94.

2. For a concise overview of the diets and foodways of soldiers manning forts throughout the trans-Appalachian west, including the problems encountered in transporting, storing, and procuring provisions, see McConnell, *Army and Empire,* 101–13.

3. On Indian refugees in the seventeenth century, see R. White, *The Middle Ground,* 1–49. White's description of most post-1650 Great Lakes Indian societies as fragmented refugee groups has been challenged by Heidi Bohaker. She argues that Anishinaabe expressive symbols imply kinship networks and traditions in some locations that predate and postdate 1650, revealing a much more stable native social landscape in the region than proposed by White. Cultural creativity and change may have existed hand in hand with long-held traditions in some multiethnic towns. Bohaker, "'Nindoodemag': The Significance of Algonquian Kinship Networks."

4. Hurt, *Indian Agriculture in America*, 11–15.

5. Richter, *Facing East from Indian Country*, 54–56; Cronon, *Changes in the Land*, 41–46. On the unreliability of European corn crop descriptions, see Schroeder, "Maize Productivity," 502.

6. Richter, *Facing East from Indian Country*, 57; Kinietz, *Indians of the Western Great Lakes*, 236–39; 322. For prehistoric and protohistoric villages on the lakes and other information on prehistoric Great Lakes culture, see Brose, "Late Prehistory," 577–79.

7. Murphy, *A Gathering of Rivers*, 29–30.

8. For an overview of this period of global climate change, see Fagan, *The Little Ice Age*, esp. 129–47, for the seventeenth and eighteenth centuries. For the problems involved in determining historical climate change and conditions, see Bryson and Padoch, "On the Climates of History." In the absence of documentation, historical climate change can be determined through archaeological means, especially through the analysis of tree rings, forest fire ash stratigraphy, pollen and lichen analysis, ice cores, etc. For a Great Lakes region example, see Clark, "Fire and Climate Change," 135–59.

9. Thwaites, *Jesuit Relations*, 55:155–57.

10. Thwaites, *Jesuit Relations*, 15:157; Silvy et al., *Letters from North America*, 161–63; Hurt, *Indian Agriculture in America*, 33.

11. Thwaites, *Jesuit Relations*, 55:159–61; R. White, *The Middle Ground*, 23, 42–49.

12. Cadillac to Comte de Ponchartrain [secretary of state for the provinces], Oct. 18, 1700, *MPHC*, 33:97.

13. Recent research has transformed our understanding of the social nature of fur-trade relationships, revealing especially the fundamental domestic and public roles played by women. Some groundbreaking works in this new understanding of the trade are Brown, *Strangers in Blood*; Van Kirk, *Many Tender Ties*; Sleeper-Smith, *Indian Women and French Men*; and B. M. White, "The Woman Who Married a Beaver." Bruce White has argued for a nuanced view of trade that emphasizes native spiritual views about goods. He shows that Indians of the western Great Lakes thought French trade goods, especially metal goods and guns, were imbued with powerful spirits and possessed greater-than-human powers. Ojibwas desired goods for both ritual and practical reasons and made little distinction between those values. B. M. White, "Encounters with Spirits," 369–405. For classic studies of the fur trade, see Ray, *Indians in the Fur Trade*, and Innis, *The Fur Trade in Canada*.

14. Noyan, "State of Canada in 1730," *MPHC*, 34:75; Thwaites, *Jesuit Relations*, 53:257; Mancall, *Deadly Medicine*, 63–84; Axtell, *The Invasion Within*, 64–67; Eccles, *France in America*, 55–56.

15. Cadillac, "Description of Detroit," *MPHC*, 33:142–43. For Michilimackinac trade inventories, see D. L. Anderson, "The Flow of European Trade Goods," 107.

16. L. M. Stone, *Fort Michilimackinac*, 8; Kinietz, *Indians of the Western Great Lakes*, 228–32; Feest and Feest, "Ottawa," 772–74.

17. Rogers, "Southeastern Ojibwa," 760–62. Descriptions of native populations often included only men, or "warriors," as they were usually called. In sedentary villages it is assumed that women and children were present, and those population estimates can

be increased conservatively by a factor of four, bringing the population of Mackinac Island to at least four hundred if the original report can be believed. Henry, *Travels and Adventures*, 37–38; "A List of the Indian Nations," *WJP,* 10:544–46. Negotiating the kinship-based networks that dominated the fur trade and neighboring villages was vital for French success during their military and trade mission at the Straits. The later British regime would have less success working within this kinship structure at posts throughout the Great Lakes region. Sleeper-Smith, *Indian Women and French Men*, 54–72.

18. Armour, "Who Remembers La Fourche?" 13; Henry, *Travels and Adventures*, 57–58; "Niagara and Detroit Proceedings, July–September 1761," *WJP,* 3:502; R. White, *The Middle Ground*, 256–68; Dowd, *War under Heaven*, 73–75.

19. "Henry Balfour's Conference with the Indians," *WJP,* 3:544; Amherst to Johnson, Nov. 21, 1762, *WJP,* 3:941–43.

20. Henry, *Travels and Adventures*, 34–38, 42–45, 48–50. Minavavana used the term "milk" to denote a gift of rum as a mark of friendship and understanding. Requesting rum in this way denoted the diplomatic sustenance provided by gifts of alcohol. It allowed Indians to transfer their metaphor of kinship to the trade relationship, with the natives like children receiving milk from their parents. This also allowed Indians to impose a familiar and valuable feature from their own lives onto an important foreign product. In this way, Ojibwas and other Great Lakes peoples bridged cultural gaps in trading and were able to come to reciprocal agreements with British newcomers. Without this reciprocity, friendly trade and personal trust were impossible. B. M. White, "'Give Us a Little Milk,'" 191–92.

21. Henry, *Travels and Adventures*, 54–62. On food production and the role of women, see Van Kirk, *Many Tender Ties*, 53–73.

22. Henry, *Travels and Adventures,* 65, 69–70. Cadotte became Henry's trading partner, and his family was among the most important in the Great Lakes fur trade. Schenk, "The Cadottes," 189–98.

23. Henry, *Travels and Adventures*, 78–85; 97–99; Dowd, *War under Heaven*, 126. The Ojibwas' attack on Michilimackinac was not prompted only by their pro-French political leanings. In "The Fear of Pillaging," Bruce White argues that the attack was an example of a trade pillage that resulted from the Britons' lack of establishing proper trade and friendship protocols, especially through gift giving. Threats of pillaging (imagined or real) were an important tactic used by native leaders, diplomats, and consumers in enforcing reciprocity in the Great Lakes trade.

24. William Eyre to Johnson, Jan. 7, 1764, *WJP,* 11:20–23; Johnson to Cadwallader Colden, June 9, 1764, *WJP,* 4:442–44.

25. Gage to Bradstreet, Apr. 2, 1764, GPAS, vol. 16. For the complex metaphorical meanings of Indian pleas for pity, see B. M. White, "'Give Us a Little Milk,'" 187–88. At the 1764 summer peace conference at Niagara, Johnson heard many such protestations of hardship, usually from friendly Indians who had no part in the hostilities and had come to the congress to renew friendships, to trade, or to receive British gifts. For examples see *WJP,* 4:466–83, 11:262–76. See chapter 4 for more information on the Niagara conference of 1764.

26. Campbell to Gage, Oct. 3, 1764, GPAS, vol. 25; Campbell to Bradstreet, Dec. 7, 1764, GPAS, vol. 29. Pilfering from military stores in transit was a common and oft-cited problem in provisioning remote forts.

27. Howard to Bradstreet, Jan. 6, 1765, GPAS, vol. 29; Campbell to Gage, May 31, 1765, GPAS, vol. 37; Campbell to Gage, Oct. 31, 1765, and Campbell to Gage, Nov. 1, 1765, GPAS, vol. 45.

28. Carver, *Travels*, 18; Whitaker, *The Functions of Four Colonial Yards*, 117–19. Archaeologists have confirmed the differences between the British and French tenures in vocational uses of Fort Michilimackinac and its adjacent village. However, despite the increased emphasis on military activity by the British, trading still dominated as the post's primary economic endeavor. Heldman and Grange, *Excavations at Fort Michilimackinac*, 202.

29. Cleland, "Comparison of the Faunal Remains," 7–23. Elizabeth Scott's study of subsistence patterns under the French regime show much differentiation based on profession (clergy and traders) and socioeconomic class. She also bases her arguments on analysis of refuse pits and patterns of dispersal. Scott, *French Subsistence at Fort Michilimackinac*. L. M. Stone makes the same argument for greater differentiation in material culture under the British regime compared with the French occupation of Fort Michilimackinac, but he bases his argument on artifact analysis rather than zooarchaeology. *Fort Michilimackinac*, 348–56. For a concise description of the outside provisioning system at the fort, see Dunnigan, *The Necessity of Regularity in Quartering Soldiers*, 17–21. For evidence of soldiers eating more wild and local food than officers or wealthier townspeople, see Evans, *House D of the Southeast Row House*, 60–73.

30. Gage to Johnson, Nov. 24, 1765, *WJP*, 4:878–79; Daniel Claus to Johnson, July 11, 1765, *WJP*, 4:789–91; Porteous, *Schenectady to Michilimackinac*, 91; Johnson to the Traders at Michilimackinac, July 1, 1765, *WJP*, 4:810; Johnson to Gage, Aug. 28, 1765, *WJP*, 4:833–34; Gage to Johnson, Aug. 28, 1765, *WJP*, 11:915–17.

31. Gage to Johnson, *WJP*, 5:30–31. For the failure of Gage's trade restrictions, see Sleeper-Smith, *Indian Women and French Men*, 62–63.

32. Gage to Johnson, Mar. 23, 1766, *WJP*, 5:94; Johnson to Gage, Jan. 25, 1766, *WJP*, 12:8–10; Gage to Post Commanders, Jan. 16, 1766, Gage Papers Supplementary Account, Box 47, Thomas Gage Papers, William C. Clements Library, University of Michigan, Ann Arbor.

33. Roberts to Daniel Claus, July 23, 1767 *WJP*, 12:342. For a thorough treatment of the Roberts-Rogers conflict, see Marshall, "The Michilimackinac Misfortunes of Commissary Roberts," 285–98.

34. "Report of Indian Trade," Nov. 16, 1768, *WJP*, 12:650; Roberts to Johnson, Aug. 29, 1769, *WJP*, 7:146–47; Johnson to Gage, Dec. 31, 1770, *WJP*, 7:1053–54.

35. "Speech of La Force and Other Ottawas," Aug. 30, 1768, *WJP*, 6:348–49.

36. Ibid., 349; "Journal of Peter Pond," *WHC*, 18:314–54 at 328–29.

37. The most exhaustive treatment of the American Revolution at Michilimackinac is Armour and Widder, *At the Crossroads*. For a brief treatment, see Widder, "Effects of the American Revolution on Fur-Trade Society at Michilimackinac." For the effects of

the Revolution on Great Lakes Indian social interactions with whites and each other, see R. White, *The Middle Ground*, 366–412.

38. De Peyster to Carleton, May 30, 1778, *MPHC*, 9:365–66; De Peyster to Haldimand, June 14, 1779, *MPHC*, 9:385; Haldimand to De Peyster, Dec. 25, 1778, *MPHC*, 9:355–56.

39. De Peyster to Haldimand, May 13, 1779, *MPHC*, 9:381; De Peyster to Brehm, June 20, 1779, *MPHC*, 9:386–87; De Peyster to Carleton, May 30, 1778, *MPHC*, 9:366; De Peyster to Haldimand, Oct. 7, 1778, *MPHC*, 9:373.

40. Sinclair to Brehm, Oct. 7, 1779, *MPHC*, 9:524–25, 528.

41. Sinclair to Brehm, Oct. 29, 1779, *MPHC*, 9:530; "A Voyage on Lake Michigan, 1779," *WHC*, 11:207–12. For an example of southern Michigan natives' agricultural potential, see Sleeper-Smith's study of Potawatomi women who traded food at Fort St. Joseph in *Indian Women and French Men*, 73–85.

42. Sinclair to Brehm, Feb. 15, 1780, *MPHC*, 9:538; Brehm to Sinclair, Apr. 17, 1780, *MPHC*, 9:537; Sinclair to Brehm, July 8, 1780, *MPHC*, 9:579; "Indian Deed for the Island of Mackinac," *MPHC*, 19:633–34.

43. Heldman, *Archaeological Investigations at French Farm Lake*, 7–15, 69.

44. Sinclair to Brehm, Feb. 15, 1780, *MPHC*, 9:540–41; Mompesson to De Peyster, Sept. 20, 1780, *MPHC*, 19:575.

45. Sinclair to [unknown], July 8, 1781, *MPHC*, 10:495; Sinclair to [unknown], July 31, 1781, *MPHC*, 10:504; Sinclair to Haldimand, July 5, 1782, *MPHC*, 10:596–97; Armour and Widder, *At the Crossroads*, 180.

46. "Returns of Corn," Sept. 24, 1781–Mar. 24, 1782, *MPHC*, 10:666, 11:325, 331, 339, 346, 352; "Surveys of Provisions," Dec. 28, 1782, *MPHC*, 11:332; Henry Hope to Haldimand, Oct. 19, 1782, *MPHC*, 10:656–59.

47. McBeath to Robertson, Dec. 29, 1782, *MPHC*, 11:333; Hope et al. to Robertson, Sept. 20, 1782, *MPHC*, 10:638–40; Robertson to Robert Mathews, Aug. 9, 1783, *WHC*, 11:173–74.

48. McKee to John Johnson, June 2, 1784, *MPHC*, 20:229; Robertson to Mathews, May 6, 1784, *MPHC*, 11:414; Robertson to Haldimand, Aug. 5, 1784, *MPHC*, 11:442.

49. Robertson to Mathews, Sept. 7, 1784, *MPHC*, 11:453.

50. Robertson to Mathews, Oct. 29, 1783, *MPHC*, 11:395–96.

51. DePeyster, "Speech to the Western Indians, *WHC*, 18:389 n. 84; "Indian Council," *MPHC*, 11:490–96.

52. Dorchester to W. W. Grenville, Mar. 8, 1790, *MPHC*, 12:22–23; "Report on the State of Fort Lernoult, Michilimackinac, &c.," Mar. 3, 1790, *MPHC*, 12:30–37; Doyle to R. J. England, May 16, 1793, *MPHC*, 12:48–49. For the last year of British-Indian relations and provisioning, see Duggan to Prideaux Selby, Jan. 10, 1796, *MPHC*, 12:192–93, and Selby to Chew, Apr. 19, 1796, *MPHC*, 12:200–201. For certificates describing incoming native provisions right up to the end of the British tenure, see "Certification of Indian Supplies of Sugar," Mar. 26–June 14, 1796, *MPHC*, 12:208, 215–16, 240. For British provisioning of Indians in their last year at Mackinac, see "Corn and Sugar Issued as Indian Presents," July 12, 1796, *MPHC*, 12:207.

53. Shurtleff, *Old Arbre Croche*, 25.

Chapter 4. A Year at Niagara: Violence, Diplomacy, and Coexistence in the Eastern Great Lakes, 1763–1764

1. "Chenussio" is an orthographic variation of "Genesee" or "Geneseo" commonly used in eighteenth-century English and French documents. It refers to the western Seneca group, its people, and their primary town on the Genesee River in northwestern New York. This Seneca group is sometimes called the western Senecas, Genesees, or Geneseos in ethnohistorical studies. I use "Chenussios" to avoid confusion with material quoted from the primary documents.

2. Montresor, "Journal of John Montresor's Expedition to Detroit," 14–18; Couagne to Johnson, Sept. 8, 1763, *WJP,* 10:812; Collin Andrews to Johnson, Sept. 9, 1763, *WJP,* 10:812–13; John Stoughton to Johnson, Sept. 16, 1763, *WJP,* 10:814; Couagne to Johnson, Sept. 16, 1763, *WJP,* 10:815; Bouquet to Amherst, Sept. 7, 1763, *MPHC,* 19:230–31.

3. The size of the attacking force was disputed. Early reports put the Indian party at 400 to 500 men, but later a Seneca chief told Johnson that the attackers numbered 309. Later reports asserted that one Indian attacker was wounded. William Browning to Johnson, Sept. 17, 1763, *WJP,* 10:816; George Etherington to Johnson, Sept. 17, 1763, *WJP,* 10:817–18; Johnson to Lords of Trade, Sept. 25, 1763, *NYCD,* 7:559–62; Johnson to Amherst, Oct. 6, 1763, *WJP,* 10:866–70.

4. Studies of the uprising typically devote only a few pages to events in New York, concentrating instead on the western center of the rebellion. See Parkman, *The Conspiracy of Pontiac*; Peckham, *Pontiac and the Indian Uprising*; Dowd, *War under Heaven*; Dixon, *Never Come to Peace Again*; Middleton, *Pontiac's War*. For the diplomatic motives of Iroquois rebels and nonparticipants, see Parmenter, "Pontiac's War." William R. Nester is especially complimentary of Johnson's diplomatic efforts in forcing Seneca submission. He asserts unconvincingly that in gaining the Iroquois' cooperation in opposing rebel Indians, "the Iroquois had little choice but to accept Johnson's demands. The Six Nations were now surrounded by Union Jacks floating above frontier forts." According to Nester, the Senecas "begged for mercy" at Johnson Hall in March 1764, and at the Niagara conference in August Johnson "was generous with British friends and tough toward foes," which glosses over the overabundance of "friends" and virtual absence of any "foes" there, except for the Senecas and a small band of Hurons. Nester, *"Haughty Conquerors,"* 191, 193, 208. Dixon gives only a brief paragraph about the submission of the "meek" Senecas at Niagara. *Never Come to Peace Again*, 228.

5. For persuasive arguments challenging the notion that eighteenth-century Iroquois change was driven mainly by economic decline, see Brandão and Starna, "The Treaties of 1701," and Jordan, *The Seneca Restoration*, 1–25.

6. For archaeological investigations of native activities in and around the Niagara portage, see S. D. Scott, *An Archaeological Survey of Artpark*, 7–17; and M. E. White, "Late Woodland Archaeology," 115–16. For some early French accounts of Niagara's strategic value and its native visitors, see Frontenac to Colbert, Nov. 14, 1674, *NYCD,* 9:116–21; M. E. White, *Iroquois Culture History*, 50; Severance, *Studies of the Niagara Frontier*, 315, and *An Old Frontier of France*, 1:35.

7. Approximately two thousand Tuscaroras left their homes in North Carolina after

a devastating war with British colonists from 1711 to 1713. The Oneidas sponsored their entry into the Iroquois League as the sixth nation in 1713. After the mid-1720s the Iroquois were referred to as the Six Nations.

8. Iroquoian expansion into the Great Lakes region is described most thoroughly in Richter, *The Ordeal of the Longhouse*, 50–104. For the disturbances caused by this expansion, see R. White, *The Middle Ground*, 1–49. See also Abler and Tooker, "Seneca," and M. E. White, "Neutral and Wenro" and "Erie," in Trigger, *Handbook*, 409–10, 415–16, 506–7. For the first account of a Seneca village in the Niagara frontier region, see Galinée and Casson, *Exploration of the Great Lakes*, 176. For the Seneca village on the Niagara River, see *NYCD*, 9:805.

9. For French-Dutch-British-Iroquois contestation and alliances in the seventeenth century and a rich exploration of the "beaver wars," see Richter, *The Ordeal of the Longhouse*, 1–161. For French conflicts with New York over the fort built on the Niagara, see Denonville to Seignelay, May 8, 1686, *NYCD*, 9:287–92; Leder, *Livingston Indian Records*, 101; "Establishment of the French at Niagara," *NYCD*, 9:335–36; "Examination of Adandidaghko," *NYCD*, 9:435; Dongan to Palmer, *NYCD*, 9:476; "Dongan's First Demand of French Agents," *NYCD*, 9:520–21; "Journal of Denonville and Champigny," *NYCD*, 9:393–98.

10. "Conference of Lieutenant Governor Nanfan with the Indians," *NYCD*, 4:896–908; "Deed from the Five Nations to the King of Their Beaver Hunting Ground," *NYCD*, 4:908–11.

11. The Iroquois "Grand Settlement" of 1700–1701 has been much studied. See A. F. C. Wallace, "The Origins of Iroquois Neutrality," 223–35, for a general study of the treaty's effect on subsequent British-Iroquois relations. For more recent essays that give conflicting treatments of this important subject in Iroquois studies, see Richter, *The Ordeal of the Longhouse*, 206–13, and Brandão and Starna, "The Treaties of 1701." Richter argues that desperation led the Iroquois to seek neutrality, while Brandão and Starna insist that the 1701 treaties were negotiated from a position of Iroquois strength, were advantageous to all parties concerned, and represented a diplomatic victory for the Iroquois.

12. Iroquois diplomacy has been much studied in the past several decades. Scholars have expanded knowledge of the fractious nature of Iroquois interactions, the fragility of their confederacy, the importance of gifts and reciprocity, and the constant maintenance that made diplomacy work in Iroquoia. For a recent synthesis of Iroquois diplomacy studies and an exploration of how this diplomacy played out between the Iroquois, French, and British in North America, see Shannon, *Iroquois Diplomacy*.

13. "Instructions to M. de Clerambaut d'Aigremont," *NYCD*, 9:805–8; Severance, *An Old Frontier of France*, 1:163; Beauharnois to Maurapas, Nov. 7, 1744, *NYCD*, 9:1111–12; "Memoir on the Indians between Lake Erie and the Mississippi, 1718," *NYCD*, 9:885. The Seneca village at the portage is mentioned again in a 1736 census of Indians in Canada. "Enumeration of the Indian Tribes Connected with the Government of Canada, 1736," *NYCD*, 9:1057.

14. Permanent Iroquois portaging was present elsewhere in the early eighteenth century and represented important attempts by native groups to work within the troubling

socioeconomic context of European expansion. For example, an even more robust operation existed at the Great Carrying Place south of Lake Oneida. Leder, *Livingston Indian Records*, 214; Bartram, Evans, and Weiser, *A Journey from Pennsylvania to Onondaga*, 64–65; "Conference between Lieutenant-Governor Clarke and the Six Nations," *NYCD*, 6:172; Richter, *The Ordeal of the Longhouse*, 262.

15. "Proposal to Take Possession of Niagara in Canada, 1706," *NYCD*, 9:773–75; Journal of Schuyler and Livingston," *NYCD*, 5:542–45; "Journal of Lawrence Clawsen's Visit to Niagara," *NYCD*, 5:550–51; Robert Livingston to Peter Schuyler, Aug. 23, 1723, *NYCD*, 5:559–60; Colden, "Colden's Account," 50:128–34; Burnet to Lords of Trade, June 25, 1723, *NYCD*, 5:684–85. For an overview of the French-British fort controversies of the 1720s, see Richter, *The Ordeal of the Longhouse*, 246–54.

16. "A Conference Held at Albany," *NYCD*, 5:799; "Deed in Trust from Three of the Five Nations of Indians to the King," *NYCD*, 5:800–801. Adding to the tenuous nature of Iroquois diplomacy was the looseness of the Confederacy itself. English authorities frequently attributed undue unity to the Confederacy. Iroquois diplomacy, based on kinship ties and village authority, was complex and fragile. Treaties made by small groups were often challenged and countermanded over subsequent council fires. It was within this context that the various treaties and land cessions regarding the Niagara corridor were concluded. For brief explanations of Iroquois treaty fundamentals, see Becker, "Linking Arms," and Haan, "Covenant and Consensus." For the mechanics of Iroquois diplomacy, see Fenton, "Structure, Continuity, and Change," 3–36.

17. "Conference between Governor Burnet and the Indians," *NYCD*, 5:795–97. For more on the 1726 treaty, albeit with more of an emphasis on Iroquois capitulation, see Richter, *The Ordeal of the Longhouse*, 252–53.

18. Severance, *Studies of the Niagara Frontier*, 326.

19. Bougainville, "Memoir of Bougainville," 180–83.

20. "Indian Conference," *NYCD*, 10:503; "Account of the Embassy of the Five Nations," *NYCD*, 10:559.

21. For a brief overview of Fort Niagara's history, including its expansion in the 1750s, see Dunnigan, *A History and Guide to Old Fort Niagara*.

22. It is unknown how many Indian residents of the Niagara region were Chenussios. Since the Chenussio Senecas lived closer to the region than other Iroquoian groups, it is reasonable to assume that they constituted much of the Niagara population. However, it is equally reasonable to speculate that other Indians may have joined them. Therefore, in referring to Niagara-based Indians of the late 1750s I hesitate to call them Chenussios. "Niagara Indians" or "Niagara Senecas" is probably safer.

23. Sources are unclear about the makeup of the attacking Indian forces at La Belle Famille, usually referring to them simply as "Ohio Indians" or "French Indians." The French relief army was organized at Fort Venango in Pennsylvania by its commander, Captain Le Marchand de Lignery, and Charles Phillipe Aubry, an officer in Illinois who gathered hundreds of Indians for the relief army on his way to Venango. It is reasonable to assume that the forces contained French-allied Odawas, Potawatomis, Eries, Shawnees, Ojibwas, Wyandots, Miamis, and other groups known to be allied at one time or

another with Lignery and Aubry. Delawares may have also joined the French column, as they were known to communicate with Lignery at Venango. Severance, *An Old Frontier of France*, 2:313–24.

24. Pouchot, *Memoir*, 1:171–78. Johnson commanded British forces at Niagara after the death of Brigadier General John Prideaux. The full story of the Fort Niagara siege from the French perspective is in Pouchot, *Memoir*, 1:165–206. Johnson's more utilitarian account of the siege is in "The Prideaux and Johnson Orderly Book," *WJP*, 3:48–105. See also Gipson, *The Great War for the Empire*, 348–55, and F. Anderson, *Crucible of War*, 331–39.

25. "Orders for William Farquhar et al.," *WJP*, 13:156–59; "Journal of the Niagara Campaign," *WJP*, 13:120, 149, 156.

26. Dunnigan, "Portaging Niagara," 181–82; Johnson to Amherst, July 31, 1759, *WJP*, 3:115–16. During the two years following the British takeover of Niagara, portaging was the domain of the army, which used many methods to carry goods along the portage road, including horses, soldiers, and finally oxen. For a description of portaging during the early British tenure at Niagara, see McConnell, *Army and Empire*, 16–17.

27. Johnson to Daniel Claus, May 20, 1761, *WJP*, 10:270; Johnson to Amherst, July 29, 1761, *WJP*, 10:322; "Petition of Merchants of Albany to the Lords of Trade," *NYCD*, 7:488–89; Johnson to Amherst, Feb. 6, 1762, *WJP*, 3:620, 623; Amherst to Johnson, Aug. 9, 1761, *WJP*, 3:515; Amherst to Johnson, Feb. 14, 1762, *WJP*, 10:382–83; Amherst to William Sharpe, Oct. 20, 1762, *NYCD*, 7:509.

28. "Journal to Detroit," *WJP*, 13:227; Johnson to George Croghan, July 26, 1761, *WJP*, 10:319–20; Johnson to Daniel Claus, Aug. 9, 1761, *WJP*, 10:323–25; "Niagara and Detroit Proceedings," *WJP*, 3:463–67; "Journal to Detroit," *WJP*, 13:236.

29. "Niagara and Detroit Proceedings," *WJP*, 3:448–50; Bouquet to Amherst, Mar. 7, 1762, *MPHC*, 19:131; "Journal of Indian Affairs," *WJP*, 10:387; Amherst to Johnson, Jan. 16 and Feb. 14, 1762, *WJP*, 10:354, 382–83; "Journal of Indian Affairs," *WJP*, 10:386–88; William Walters to Johnson, Apr. 5 and 27, 1762, *WJP*, 3:721–23, 10:426–28; Couagne to Johnson, June 5, 1763, *WJP*, 4:134–35.

30. For the best primary source revealing Pontiac's message of cultural renewal, see Burton and Burton, *Journal of Pontiac's Conspiracy, 1763*. For literature on the 1763 Indian uprising, see note 16 for the introduction.

31. These Senecas killed most of Fort Venango's garrison and then forced the fort's commandant to write out their reasons for attacking before executing him. Johnson to Amherst, July 11, 1763, *WJP*, 7:533.

32. Johnson to Lords of Trade, July 1 and 26, 1763, *NYCD*, 7:525–27, 559–62.

33. William Dunbar to Gage, Sept. 15, 1763, GPAS, vol. 9; Johnson to Amherst, Sept. 30, 1763, *WJP*, 4:209–11; Amherst to Johnson, Oct. 1, 1763, *WJP*, 10:860–61; Amherst to Bouquet, Oct. 3, 1763, *MPHC* 19:237–38; Thomas Moncrieffe to Johnson, Oct. 4, 1763, *WJP*, 4:212–13; Browning to Johnson, Oct. 22, 1763, *WJP*, 10:906–7; Couagne to Johnson, Oct. 17 and Nov. 11, 1763, *WJP*, 10:884, 921–22; Browning to Amherst, Nov. 10, 1763, Amherst Papers, vol. 7.

34. Amherst to Browning, Nov. 11, 1763, in Haldimand, Unpublished Papers and

Correspondence, reel 8, section 21678, 29 [hereafter cited as Haldimand Papers]; Amherst to Johnson, Sept. 30, 1763, *NYCD*, 7:568–69; Wilkins to Amherst, Nov. 27, 1763 and Browning to Amherst, Nov. 28, 1763, Amherst Papers vol. 7.

35. Johnson to Gage, Jan. 27, 1764, *WJP*, 4:308–10; Gage to Johnson, Jan. 12 and 31, 1764, *WJP*, 4:290–93, 314–15; Johnson to Lords of Trade, Jan. 20, 1764, *NYCD*, 7:599–602.

36. "Journal of Indian Congress," *WJP*, 10:968–71.

37. "An Indian Conference," *WJP*, 11:139–40; "Articles of Peace Concluded with the Seneca Indians," *NYCD*, 7:621–23; Johnson to Gage, Apr. 6, 1764, *WJP*, 4:389.

38. Browning to Johnson, Apr. 10, 1764, *WJP*, 11:124–25; Johnson to Gage, Apr. 27, 1764, *WJP*, 11:162–63; Johnson to Colden, Apr. 28, 1764, in Colden, *Letters and Papers*, 6:304–5; Gage to Johnson, Apr. 25, 1764, *WJP*, 4:408–9. References to "western" or "Ohio" Indians usually signified those groups in rebellion against Britain. These might have included Odawa, Shawnee, Potawatomi, Ojibwa, or any number of other Lower Great Lakes groups.

39. "The Journals of Captain John Montresor," 259–62 [hereafter cited as "Montresor's Journals"]. Montresor is often credited as the cradles' builder, an attribution that is probably incorrect. The apparatus was already in use when Montresor arrived at Niagara, and though his journal entries imply that he had heard about them, he expressed doubt that they would "answer the purpose intended." "Montresor's Journals," 258; Dunnigan, "Portaging Niagara," 217–18; McConnell, *Army and Empire*, 16–17.

40. "Montresor's Journals," 261–62, 265, 268; Johnson to Gage, June 29, 1764, *WJP*, 11:245–46.

41. Johnson to Gage, Jan. 27, 1764, *WJP*, 4:308–10; Johnson to Lords of Trade, May 11, 1764, *NYCD*, 7:624–26.

42. Bradstreet to Gage, June 4, 1764, GPAS, vol. 19; "Montresor's Journals," 275.

43. "Conference with Indians," *WJP*, 11:262–73; "An Indian Congress," *WJP*, 11:273–89.

44. Johnson to Gage, May 11, 1764, *WJP*, 11:189–90; Gage to Johnson, May 28, 1764, *WJP*, 4:432–33; "Equivalents in Barter," *WJP*, 4:490–91; "Montresor's Journals," 259, 263, 272; Henry, *Travels and Adventures*, 182–84.

45. "Conference with Indians," *WJP*, 11:266–69. Indians at the conference frequently referred to rebellious groups as being "drunk," meaning only that they had lost their good sense. "An Indian Congress," *WJP*, 11:284–86.

46. Browning to Johnson, May 23, 1764, *WJP*, 11:196; "Journal of Indian Affairs," *WJP*, 11:236; "An Indian Congress," *WJP*, 11:288; Johnson to Gage, Aug. 5, 1764, *WJP*, 11:325.

47. Johnson to Gage, Aug. 5, 1764, *WJP*, 11:325; "An Indian Congress," *WJP*, 11:290–297.

48. "An Indian Congress," *WJP*, 11:316, 319, 321–22; "Articles of Peace between Sir William Johnson and the Genesee Indians," *NYCD*, 7:652–53. Johnson accepted the islands for diplomatic reasons, but he never intended to keep them for himself. He turned them over to the Crown along with the other ceded territory.

49. Johnson to Gage, Aug. 5, 1764, *WJP*, 11:324–25.

50. Johnson to the Lords of Trade, Aug. 30, 1764, *NYCD*, 7:647–48; Gage to Johnson, Sept. 25, 1764, GPAS, vol. 24; Johnson to Gage, Sept. 30, 1764, *WJP*, 11:365; Bradstreet to Gage, Apr. 7, 1765, GPAS, vol. 33; Gage to Bradstreet, Apr. 15, 1765, and Gage to Vaughan,

Apr. 18, 1765, GPAS, vol. 34; Gage to Johnson, Nov. 24, 1765, *WJP,* 4:878-79; Johnson to Gage, Dec. 21, 1765, *WJP,* 11:983.

51. Gage to Johnson, Mar. 17, 1766, *WJP,* 12:44; Dunnigan, "Portaging Niagara," 219-21.

52. Gage to John Brown, July 28, 1764, Haldimand Papers, reel 8, section 21678, 89; "Journal of Indian Transactions at Niagara in the Year 1767," in O'Callaghan, *Documentary History of the State of New York,* 2:871-80; Brown to Johnson, Oct. 26, 1767, *WJP,* 5:759.

53. Daniel Claus to Alexander Knox, Mar. 1, 1777, *NYCD,* 7:702-3; Johnson to Gage, Dec. 21, 1765, *WJP,* 11:983. There are many examples of this persistent notion in popular literature and on the Internet. A recent popular propagation of the labor-unrest theory of the Devil's Hole ambush is in Strand, *Inventing Niagara.* Appropriately, Strand's excellent and entertaining study portrays Niagara as a place defined by decades of invented tradition and outright falsehoods.

54. For the activities of Senecas and other Iroquois groups in subsequent decades, see Taylor, *The Divided Ground.* For the horrific experiences of native refugees at Niagara during the Revolution, see Calloway, *The American Revolution in Indian Country,* 129-57. For Seneca revitalization efforts in the 1790s and after, see A. F. C. Wallace, *The Death and Rebirth of the Seneca.*

Chapter 5. Like Stars That Fall: Keeping Up Appearances at Fort Chartres, 1765-1772

1. French Fort de Chartres had been officially renamed Fort Cavendish upon its occupation by British forces in 1765, but almost all subsequent documents continued to use the old name.

2. Lord to Gage, June 10, 1772, GPAS, vol. 111; Gage to Johnson, Sept. 7, 1772, *WJP,* 8:593.

3. On Eastern Woodland war rituals and their relationship to power, see Dowd, *A Spirited Resistance,* 9-16. First impressions were particularly important among Indians and played a vital role in determining how well Indian-European endeavors would play out. Axtell, *The Invasion Within,* 72-73. Among Illinois Indians, prowess in war was a fundamental facet of leadership, and the Illinois set the bar for success high. A successful war leader overcame his enemies without any losses to his own party, and two raids with losses could make a war chief lose his status. Callender, "Illinois," 676. Manliness and gender roles permeated native relations with Europeans. This is most noticeable in their use of gender-flavored language and metaphors in formal interactions and diplomacy. See Shoemaker, "An Alliance between Men," especially 246-48, for Indian and European associations of war skills and masculinity. During the eighteenth century, the "masculine" warrior role was elevated in importance in some native societies, to the detriment of traditional Indian gender identifications. This was energized by European needs for Indian aid in war and the fur trade. Saunt, "'Domestick . . . Quiet being Broke.'" For a full discussion of Indian-white competition and interaction between backcountry travelers, and the roles played by manliness and mutual understandings of gender identifications in intercultural contestation, see Levy, *Fellow Travelers,* 105-33.

4. For Indian concepts of reciprocity, gift giving, and Indian-white exchanges as

contests of power, see Murray, *Indian Giving*, 15–47. Presents were not bribery; to Indians, they represented "the visible evidence of love, devotion, and good faith." R. White, *The Middle Ground*, 112–19, 380.

5. For descriptions of the two earlier wooden French forts, also named Chartres, see Babson, "Architecture of Early Illinois Forts," 17–22; Keene, "Fort de Chartres," 30–31; and Jelks, Ekberg, and Martin, *Excavations at the Laurens Site*. Saucier was a draftsman in great demand in Louisiana and Illinois, and at the time of his appointment to design Fort de Chartres he was busy planning improvements to the French fort at Mobile. See Saucier and Seineke, "François Saucier, Engineer of Fort de Chartres, Illinois." The Vauban style of fort was the prevalent plan of the day for substantial forts in America and Europe; it consisted of a polygonal design with bastions at the corners to command the curtains. For a general description of the fort and its surroundings, see Babson, "Architecture of Early Illinois Forts," 23–28.

6. Fort de Chartres's occupation as a mercantile administrative center rather than a fur entrepôt has been established in part through archaeological study of its settlement pattern compared with other French sites. See Keene, "Fort de Chartres," 33–41, for a discussion and summary of archaeological research on the site. Agriculture, social patterns, and village organization made French colonial Illinois resemble English colonial patterns more than prevalent French ones. Illinois agriculture produced exceptional surpluses of grain and provisioned French forts throughout Illinois, as well as sending hundreds of tons of food down the Mississippi for export. An incisive study of agricultural life in French Illinois is Ekberg, *French Roots in the Illinois Country*. For a briefer description and comparison between French Illinois and English colonies, which posits that the shared manorial village experience of English and French farmers dictated colonial settlement patterns to a far greater degree than religious, national, or legal traditions, see Briggs, "Le Pays de Illinois."

7. For numbers of packs in the Illinois fur trade, see Bougainville, "Memoir of Bougainville," 176–77. For an overview of the many Illinois Indian groups living near Fort Chartres during the century preceding the British occupation, see Blasingham, "Depopulation of the Illinois Indians, Part 1." In *The Native Ground*, Kathleen DuVal provides a full study of Osage and Quapaw dominance in the lower and central Mississippi Valley, which presents clues as to why the British would encounter difficulties in impressing and negotiating with powerful Indians in the area.

8. Until recently, historians granted Pontiac most of the credit for inciting anti-British fervor in Illinois. Schlarman, *From Quebec to New Orleans*, 265–87. He was undoubtedly effective at inspiring Illinois Indians, and even better at convincing British authorities of his influence. For much of 1764 and 1765, Gage was convinced that Pontiac was the key to effectively implanting British rule in Illinois and that the Odawa headman must either be brought over to British interests or "knocked in the head." Gage to Johnson, July 2, 1764, *WJP*, 11:249–50. Richard White argues that Pontiac's status was, at least in part, a creation of British Indian policy. By imbuing the Odawa leader with pan-Indian importance, Gage and Johnson made dealing with him the solution to Indian resistance in Illinois. *The Middle Ground*, 295–300. More recently, historians have elevated Kaské's role in

encouraging native and habitant resistance to British rule. Gregory Evans Dowd suggests that Kaské might have been a stauncher advocate of the Delaware Prophet Néolin's message of native cultural rebirth than Pontiac himself. Dowd also emphasizes Kaské's close associations and friendships with French officials in Illinois and New Orleans. *War under Heaven*, 217–19. White emphasizes Kaské's role as a resistance leader after Pontiac decided to moderate his anti-British efforts. *The Middle Ground*, 300–305. In late 1763, at the height of the Indian uprising, French officials could do little to placate Indian belligerents in Illinois, despite many genuine attempts. Pierre Joseph Neyon de Villiers to Jean-Jacques Blaise D'Abbadie, Dec. 1, 1763, *WHC*, 18:259–61.

9. Johnson to Gage, June 9, 1764, *WJP*, 11:223. For the French account of Loftus's failed expedition, see *IHC*, 10:225–32. For Loftus's account of the attack, see Loftus to Gage, Apr. 9, 1764, *IHC*, 10:237–38. French leaders criticized Loftus for disregarding their warnings and retreating in the face of what they considered a small, routine Indian attack. They estimated the number of attackers as about thirty men. Loftus thought two hundred Indians had attacked, and he and his four officers immediately agreed to retreat all the way to New Orleans.

10. D'Esmazellieres to D'Abbadie, Mar. 14, 1764, *IHC*, 10:236.

11. "[John] Bradstreet's Thoughts on Indian Affairs," Dec. 4, 1764, *NYCD*, 7:693.

12. Speeches of Charlot Kaské and Levancher to Aubry et al., Feb. 24, 1765, *IHC*, 10:448–51. Except for the occasional gossip of French traders, there was probably little reason for Indians to believe that the French would try to retake their holdings in North America. Gregory Evans Dowd has argued convincingly that Indians spread such rumors to influence the French and induce them to return. Dowd, "The French King Wakes Up in Detroit," 254–78.

13. Ross to Robert Farmar, Feb. 21, 1765, *IHC*, 10:442–43; Ross to Farmar, May 25, 1765, *IHC*, 10:481–83; "Crawford's Statement," Aug. 10, 1765, *IHC*, 10:481–83; St. Ange to D'Abbadie, April 7, 1765, *IHC*, 10:476–80. St. Ange had not yet heard about D'Abbadie's death; news could take months to travel up the Mississippi. See also Dowd, *War under Heaven*, 219–21.

14. Gage to Fraser, and Gage to Croghan, Dec. 30, 1764, GPAS, vol. 29.

15. For Croghan's unfortunate encounter with the Pennsylvania settler uprising, see Johnson to Croghan, Apr. 4, 1765, *WJP*, 4:706–7; Johnson to John Penn, Apr. 12, 1765, *WJP*, 4:710–11; Gage to Johnson, Apr. 15, 1765, *WJP*, 4:717–19; Johnson to Penn, June 7, 1765, *WJP*, 11:776–77. For the Indian conference at Fort Pitt, see Parmenter, "Pontiac's War," 635–36. For Fraser's exploits, see "Report of Alexander Fraser on Indians in the Illinois Country," GPAS, vol. 137:4; Fraser to Gage, May 15, 1765, *IHC*, 10:491–92; Fraser to Campbell, May 17, 1765, *IHC*, 10:493–94; Fraser to Gage, May 18, 1765, *IHC*, 10:494–95; Fraser to Campbell, May 20, 1765, *IHC*, 10:495–97; Gage to Johnson, July 25, 1765, *WJP*, 4:798–800. Another delegation, consisting of traders Pierce Acton Sinnot and Harpain de la Gauterais, met with a fate similar to Fraser's later that year. Croghan to Johnson, August 17, 1765, *WJP*, 11:900; Gage to Johnson, June 30, 1765, *WJP*, 4:779; Dowd, *War under Heaven*, 223–25. For Croghan's experiences in Illinois and at Ouiatenon, see Croghan, "Croghan's Journal, 1765"; Croghan to Johnson, July 12, 1765, *WJP*, 11:836–41;

Johnson to Gage, Aug. 9, 1765, *WJP,* 11:880; Croghan to Johnson, Aug. 17, 1765, *WJP,* 11:900–901; Johnson to Gage, Oct. 26, 1765, *WJP,* 4:859; Croghan to Johnson, Nov. 1765, *NYCD,* 7:788.

16. The British description of the official surrender of Fort Chartres is in *IHC,* 11:275–76. For the reactions of the Indians, see Gage to Johnson, Dec. 30, 1765, and Feb. 10, 1766, *WJP,* 11:988, 12:16.

17. For the depleted stores, see James Eddingstone to [unknown], Oct. 17, 1765, *IHC,* 11:105–6. For the count of local Indians, see Sterling to Gage, Dec. 15, 1765, *IHC,* 11:124–27. For Sterling's interpretation of the French withdrawal, see Sterling to Gage, Oct. 18, 1765, *IHC,* 11:107–11.

18. Croghan to Johnson, Dec. 27, 1765, *WJP,* 4:886–89.

19. Farmar to Gage, Dec. 16–19, 1765, *IHC,* 11:131–34; Gage to Johnson, Mar. 9, 1766, *WJP,* 12:39–40.

20. Farmar to Gage, Mar. 28 and Apr. 8, 1766, GPAS, vol. 50; Farmar to Gage, May 9, 1766, GPAS, vol. 51.

21. Croghan to Gage, Jan. 12, 1767, *WJP,* 12:253–55; "Return of Provisions in Store at Fort Chartres, Kaskaskia, and Cahokia," May 24, 1770, GPAS, vol. 93; "Return of Provisions in Store at Fort Chartres," May 24, 1771, GPAS, vol. 106. None of the French villages recovered their pre-1763 populations; Cahokia, Kaskaskia, Chartres Village, and others fell into disrepair, and farms went untended for years. Illinois Indians felt they should be able to reoccupy some of those vacated lands, creating legal disputes that the new British administration did not want or need. For Cahokia, see Pittman to Gage, Feb. 24, 1766, GPAS, vol. 48. For Chartres Village, see "Return of Houses" Mar. 19, 1766, GPAS, vol. 50; Jennings, "Journal from Fort Pitt to Fort Chartres," 145–56. For land title disputes, see Farmar to Gage, Apr. 24, 1766, GPAS, vol. 50.

22. Campbell to Gage, Apr. 10, 1766, and Farmar to Gage, Apr. 24, 1766, GPAS, vol. 50; John Reed to Gage, Apr. 3, 1767, GPAS, vol. 63.

23. Croghan, "Croghan's Journal, 1765," 145–46; Fraser to Haldimand, May 4, 1766, *IHC,* 11:228.

24. Farmar to Gage, May 9, 1766, GPAS, vol. 51; Croghan to Johnson, Sept. 10, 1766, *WJP,* 12:176–77; "Report of George Croghan," Jan. 16, 1767, GPAS, vol. 61.

25. George Morgan, "Voyage down the Mississippi," Nov. 21, 1766, *IHC,* 11:439; Croghan to Johnson, Sept. 10, 1766, *WJP,* 12:177.

26. Butricke to Barnsley, Oct. 30, 1768, and Feb. 12, 1769, *IHC,* 16:448–50, 496–500; Morgan to Baynton and Wharton, Oct. 30, 1768, *IHC,* 16:439–40. Disease was a common and deadly problem for soldiers and others at forts throughout North America, but few locations matched Fort Chartres's mortality and infection rates. McConnell, *Army and Empire,* 114–26.

27. Harry Gordon, "Gordon's Journal," Aug. 20, 1766, *IHC,* 11:301; Gage to Shelburne, Feb. 22, 1767, in Carter, *Correspondence,* 122.

28. Gage to Shelburne, June 16, 1768, in Carter, *Correspondence,* 177–78; Reed to Gage, July 21, 1767, GPAS, vol. 67; William Johnson, "Review of the Trade and Affairs of the Indians in the Northern District of America," *NYCD,* 7:974; Croghan to Johnson, Oct.

18, 1767, *WJP,* 5:736; William Franklin, "Advantages of an Illinois Colony," July 10, 1766, *WJP,* 5:320–30; Campbell to Gage, June 22, 1768, GPAS, vol. 78; Morgan to Baynton and Wharton, Dec. 10–22, 1767, and Feb. 1768, *IHC,* 16:128–53, 161–65; George Phyn to Johnson, Apr. 15, 1768, *WJP,* 6:194–95; "Sale of Negroes Kaskaskias," Oct. 29, 1768, BWMP, reel 10, 206–7. Slaves in Illinois were not always African or Creole. See Ekberg, *Stealing Indian Women.*

29. Forbes to Gage, Apr. 15, 1768, and Inhabitants of Kaskaskia to Forbes, Apr. 15, 1768, GPAS, vol. 76; Wilkins to Gage, Nov. 11, 1770, GPAS, vol. 98; "Census of Illinois, 1767," *IHC,* 11:469.

30. Gage to Hillsborough, Oct. 7, 1769, in Carter, *Correspondence,* 239; Cole to Gage, Oct. 28, 1767, GPAS, vol. 71; "Indian Intelligence," *WJP,* 12:601–3; Johnson to Gage, Apr. 6, 1770, *WJP,* 12:813; Wilkins to Gage, Nov. 12, 1770, GPAS, vol. 98.

31. John Finley to James Rumsey, Nov. 1, 1769, BWMP, reel 6, 11–12; James Rumsey to Brown, Nov. 14, 1769, BWMP, reel 6, 127–28; Morgan to Baynton and Wharton, Apr. 24, 1769, *IHC,* 16:526–27; Windsor Brown to Morgan, Sept. 23, 1769, BWMP, reel 5, 824; Wilkins to Gage, Dec. 5, 1769, GPAS, vol. 88; Morgan to Baynton and Wharton, Mar. 14, 1770, BWMP, reel 1, 417; John Hanson to Wilkins, GPAS, Apr. 24, 1770, vol. 92; Forbes to Gage, July 18, 1768, GPAS, vol. 79; Morgan to Baynton and Wharton, July 20, 1768, *IHC,* 16:354–67; Forbes to Gage, July 28, 1768, *WJP,* 6:294; Wilkins to Gage, *WJP,* 6:326; Gage to Hillsborough, Oct. 9, 1768, in Carter, *Correspondence,* 199; Gage to Johnson, Oct. 10, 1768, *IHC,* 16:417; Gage to Wilkins, Oct. 11, 1768, *IHC,* 16:418–19.

32. Speech of Wilkins to Post Vincent, Wabash, and Ohio Indians, August 1769, Native American History Collection.

33. "Indian Speeches," *WJP,* 7:132–39.

34. Campbell to Gage, June 26, 1768, GPAS, vol. 78; Forbes to Gage, June 23 and July 18, 1768, GPAS, vol. 79; Cole to Johnson, June 13, 1769, *WJP,* 7:16; Butricke to Barnsley, June 27, 1769, *IHC,* 16:566–67; Butricke to Barnsley, Dec. 29, 1769, *WHC* 18:299.

35. Cole to Johnson, June 13, 1769, *WJP,* 7:16; Gage to Johnson, Aug. 8, 1769, *WJP,* 7:76–77.

36. "Indian Expenditures," *WJP,* 5:514, 13:396–400; "Account of the Number of Rations of Provisions," June 24, 1769, GPAS, vol. 78; "Cost of Transporting Provisions," *IHC,* 11:476–77.

37. Gage to Reed, Mar. 8, 1767, GPAS, vol. 62; Gage to Reed, Apr. 14, 1767, GPAS, vol. 63.

38. Cole to Croghan, July 3, 1767, *WJP,* 5:578; Gage to Johnson, July 20, 1767, *WJP,* 5:600–601; Cole to Johnson, Oct. 25, 1767, *WJP,* 5:748–52; Cole to Croghan, Oct. 25, 1767, *WJP,* 5:753–55; Reed to Gage, Oct. 5, 1767, GPAS, vol. 70; Reed to Gage, Oct. 28, 1767, GPAS, vol. 71.

39. Gage to Johnson, Apr. 4, 1768, *WJP,* 6:176–77; Johnson to Gage, Apr. 8, 1768, *WJP,* 6:187; Gage to Johnson, Apr. 18, 1768, *WJP,* 6:199.

40. "Presents to Indians," *WJP,* 6:298–99. Another copy of this letter appears in GPAS, vol. 79, which adds that the French had little use for the Illinois Indians and gave them only small, inexpensive presents. For a further account of gift expenses, which lists some

of the small tasks and favors local Indians would proffer the British, see "Account of Baynton, Wharton, and Morgan," *WJP,* 6:366–94.

41. Gage to Johnson, August 7, 1768, *WJP,* 6:313; "General Abstract of Provisions Issued to Indians of Different Nations at Fort Chartres," Sept. 14, 1768, GPAS, vol. 83; Johnson to Gage, *IHC,* 16:384; Cole to Gage, Sept. 13, 1768, GPAS, vol. 80. Gage's complaints were based ostensibly on the limitations of his operating budget and the dim prospect of profits accruing from backcountry operations. However, Catherine M. Desbarats has shown that imperial ambivalence regarding continental operations often fueled official complaints about Indian expenses. Indian gifts, though expensive, were a good bargain for France during their Canadian tenure, when native warriors were the best defense available. But administrative rhetoric, accounting practices, and military pride forced colonial functionaries to constantly defend Indian expenses and repel complaints from Paris. It is reasonable to assume that Gage was under similar pressures from his superiors in Whitehall. Desbarats, "The Costs of Early Canada's Native Alliances," 609–30.

42. Wilkins to Morgan, Oct. 6, 1768, GPAS, vol. 98; Gage to Penn, Mar. 24, 1769, *IHC,* 16:516–17; Wilkins, Journal of Transactions and Presents. Wilkins frequently stressed his promises to reduce Indian presents, but proof that he was successful is difficult to find. See Savelle, *George Morgan,* 51, for unsubstantiated claims that Wilkins significantly retrenched Indian expenses. If he did reduce costs appreciably, it was not enough to satisfy Gage, who was still impatient about expenses in 1772 when he ordered Fort Chartres closed. Gage to Johnson, Mar. 9, 1772, *WJP,* 8:417–18.

43. Wilkins, Journal of Transactions and Presents, 1–2.

44. Ibid., 21–22, 52–53.

45. Ibid., 33–34, 42–43.

46. Ibid., 5–6.

47. Ibid., 4–11.

48. Ibid., 3, 17–21.

49. Ibid., 6–7, 11–12, 26–27.

50. Ibid., 39–42; Wilkins to Gage, May 11, 1771, GPAS, vol. 102. No record is available for how much Wilkins spent on the visiting delegation, but Ensign William Connolly, who commanded the small fort at Kaskaskia, entertained the delegates for a couple of days and recorded Indian expenses for January to June of just over £194. The Chickasaw visit accounted for much of this amount. "Payment Order of William Connolly," June 28, 1771, GPAS, vol. 109.

51. Gage to Hillsborough, Jan. 16 and Mar. 6, 1771, in Carter, *Correspondence,* 289, 292; Croghan to Edmonstone, Feb. 19, 1771, *WJP,* 7:1149; Wilkins to Gage, Mar. 26, 1771, GPAS, vol. 101.

52. Wilkins to Gage, May 11, 1771, GPAS, vol. 102; Gage to Wilkins, Aug. 20, 1771, GPAS, vol. 105.

53. Wilkins to Gage, June 9, 1771, GPAS, vol. 103.

54. Wilkins to Gage, Sept. 5, 1771, GPAS, vol. 106; Gage to Johnson, Sept. 24, 1771, *WJP,* 8:278–79.

55. George Morgan, "Some Reasons Why the Distillation of Spirits from Grain Ought

to be Encouraged at the Illinois," GPAS, vol. 88; Wilkins to Gage, Feb. 20, 1771, GPAS, vol. 100; "Proclamation," Apr. 12, 1771, GPAS, vol. 102; Gage to Wilkins, May 13, 1771, GPAS, vol. 103. For an overview of Wilkins's contentious land and trade dealings in Illinois, which eventually involved litigation and disgrace for the commandant, see Savelle, *George Morgan*, 55-75.

56. Lewis Wynne to Wilkins, May 3, 1771, GPAS, vol. 92; Gage to Wilkins, Sept. 16, 1771, GPAS, vol. 106.

57. Gage to Wilkins, Aug. 21, 1771, GPAS, vol. 105; Gage to Wilkins, Aug. 27, 1770, GPAS, vol. 95; Gage to Wilkins, Dec. 2, 1770, GPAS, vol. 98; Gage to Johnson, Dec. 11, 1771, *WJP*, 8:343; Johnson to Gage, Dec. 23, 1771, *WJP*, 8:348.

58. Gage to Wilkins, Sept. 20, 1771, and Gage to Hamilton, Sept. 20, 1771, GPAS, vol. 106; Hamilton to Gage, Nov. 18, 1771, GPAS, vol. 107; Gage to Hamilton, Feb. 24, 1772, and Edmonstone to Gage, Mar. 1, 1772, GPAS, vol. 109; Gage to Johnson, Mar. 9, 1772, *WJP*, 8:417-18; Gage to Wilkins, Mar. 9, 1771, GPAS, vol. 109; Johnson to Gage, Sept. 2, 1772, *WJP*, 8:588.

59. The exploits of Clark and his band of Kentucky volunteers during the American Revolution, which included their taking of Kaskaskia and Cahokia and victory over Henry Hamilton's forces at Vincennes, have long been the stuff of American heroic myth. As a backcountry "Indian fighter" who overcame a much larger British force with a small band of volunteers, Clark has been seen as an epitome of American republican virtues who "won the West." He stirred up French and Indian anti-British animosities in Illinois more than anyone since Pontiac and Kaské, and he attracted a full-scale British invasion of the Wabash country for the first time. His military achievements were ultimately of little note: he could not control Illinois or challenge Detroit as he had hoped. But his subsequent battles with British-allied Iroquois, Shawnees, and Miamis in the Ohio Valley sparked an American-Indian war that did not abate until the 1790s. Because of his virulent hatred of Indians and his questionable record as a military leader, many recent scholars have avoided him and his operations in treatments of the Revolutionary War. Such biographies that have appeared in recent decades have sought to reify his heroic image, as in Harrison, *George Rogers Clark and the War in the West*. For a more nuanced approach to the violent events in the Illinois and Wabash country in the years after the fall of Fort Chartres, see Griffin, *American Leviathan*, 142-49, 269-77, and R. White, *The Middle Ground*, 368-78. For a traditional "heroic" biography, see Bakeless, *Background to Glory*.

Conclusion: The Mohawks' New World

1. For a description of the village, see Fenton and Tooker, "Mohawk," 474. For a nuanced description and study of intercultural relations at Canajoharie, see Preston, *The Texture of Contact*, 97-112.

2. Clinton to Johnson, July 2, 1747, *WJP*, 1:103-4; Johnson to Clinton, July 28, 1748, *WJP*, 9:30; James De Lancey to Johnson, May 3, 1755, *WJP*, 1:484-85; Johnson to De Lancey, Aug. 1755, *WJP* 1:842; Johnson to Shirley, Apr. 1756, *WJP*, 9:416.

3. Johnson to Shirley, May 26, 1756, *WJP*, 9:461.

4. "Complaint of the Canajoharie Indians," Sept. 27, 1756, *WJP,* 9:546–48.

5. "An Indian Conference," Feb. 7, 1757, *WJP,* 9:600–601; Archibald McAulay to Johnson, Dec. 2, 1758, *WJP* 10:56; "An Advertisement," *WJP,* 10:63.

6. "Journal of Indian Affairs," *WJP,* 10:219, 228; Johnson to Gage, July 20, 1768, *WJP,* 12:555.

7. For the Mohawk experience after the American Revolution, see Calloway, *The American Revolution in Indian Country,* 287.

Bibliography

Primary Sources

Amherst, Jeffrey. Papers. William C. Clements Library. University of Michigan, Ann Arbor.

Bartram, John, Lewis Evans, and Conrad Weiser. *A Journey from Pennsylvania to Onondaga in 1743*. Barre, Mass.: Imprint Society, 1973.

Baynton, John, Samuel Wharton, and George Morgan. Papers in the Pennsylvania State Archives. Microfilm, 10 reels. Ed. George R. Beyer. Harrisburg: Pennsylvania Historical and Museum Commission, 1967.

Bogaert, Harmen Meyndertsz van den. *A Journey into Mohawk and Oneida Country, 1634–1635: the Journal of Harmen Meyndertsz van den Bogaert*. Trans. and ed. Charles T. Gehring and William A. Starna. Syracuse, N.Y.: Syracuse University Press, 1991.

Bougainville, Louis Antoine. "Memoir of Bougainville." In *Collections of the State Historical Society of Wisconsin* 18:167–95.

Brock, R. A., ed. *The Official Records of Robert Dinwiddie, Lieutenant-Governor of the Colony of Virginia, 1751–1758*. 2 vols. Richmond: Virginia Historical Society, 1971.

Burton, Clarence Monroe, and M. Agnes Burton, eds., and R. Clyde Ford, trans. *Journal of Pontiac's Conspiracy, 1763*. Detroit: Speaker-Hines, 1912.

Butricke, George. "Affairs at Fort Chartres, 1768–1781." *The Historical Magazine, and Notes and Queries Concerning the Antiquities* 8, no. 8 (1864): 257–66.

Butterfield, Willshire. *History of Brule's Discoveries and Explorations, 1610–1626*. Cleveland: Helman-Taylor, 1898.

Carter, Clarence Edward, ed. *The Correspondence of General Thomas Gage with the Secretaries of State, 1763–1775*. 2 vols. New Haven: Yale University Press, 1931.

Carver, Jonathan. *Travels through the Interior Parts of North America, in the Years 1766, 1767, and 1768*. 3rd ed. Minneapolis: Ross and Haines, 1956.

Colden, Cadwallader. "Colden's Account of the Conference between Governor Burnet and the Five Nations, 1721." In *New York Historical Society Collections* (1917), 50: 128–34.

———. *The Letters and Papers of Cadwallader Colden.* 9 vols. New York: New York Historical Society, 1918–37.
Commissioners for Indian Affairs (Pennsylvania). Indian Trade at Fort Augusta, Pitsberg, and Fort Allen. Cash Book, April 28, 1758–April 19, 1763. Simon Gratz Collection. Historical Society of Pennsylvania, Philadelphia.
Croghan, George. "Croghan's Journal, 1765." In Thwaites, *Early Western Travels*, 1:126–66.
De Brahm, William Gerard. *De Brahm's Report of the General Survey in the Southern District of North America.* Ed. Louis De Vorsey Jr. Columbia: University of South Carolina Press, 1971.
Easterby, J. H., et al., eds. *Journal of the Commons House of Assembly.* 14 vols. Colonial Records of South Carolina. Columbia: Historical Commission of South Carolina, 1951.
Fort Allen Daybook. Indian Affairs. Simon Gratz Collection. Historical Society of Pennsylvania, Philadelphia.
Franklin, Benjamin. *The Autobiography and Other Writings on Politics, Economics, and Virtue.* Ed. Alan Houston. New York: Cambridge University Press, 2004.
Gage, Thomas. Papers. William C. Clements Library. University of Michigan, Ann Arbor.
Galinée, René Brehan de, and François Dollier de Casson. *Exploration of the Great Lakes, 1669-1670.* Trans. James H. Coyne. Toronto: Ontario Historical Society, 1903.
Haldimand, Frederick. Unpublished Papers and Correspondence, 1758–84. Microfilm, 115 reels. London: World Microfilm Publications, 1977.
Hazard, Samuel, ed. *Colonial Records of Pennsylvania.* 16 vols. Harrisburg: T. Fenn, 1851.
———. *Pennsylvania Archives.* 1st series. 12 vols. Philadelphia and Harrisburg, 1852–56.
Heckewelder, John Gottlieb Ernestus. *Account of the History, Manners, and Customs of the Indian Nations Who Once Inhabited Pennsylvania and the Neighboring States.* 1876. Reprint, New York: Arno Press, 1971.
———. *Thirty Thousand Miles with John Heckewelder.* Ed. Paul A. W. Wallace. Pittsburgh: University of Pittsburgh Press, 1958.
Henry, Alexander. *Travels and Adventures in Canada in the Years 1760–1776.* 1809. Reprint, Chicago: Donnelly, 1921.
Hirsch, Alison Duncan, ed. *Pennsylvania Treaties, 1756–1775.* Vol. 3 of *Early American Indian Documents: Treaties and Laws, 1607–1789.* 20 vols. Ed. Alden T. Vaughan. Washington, D.C.: University Publications of America, 1979.
Hoban, C. F., and Gertrude MacKinney, eds. *Pennsylvania Archives.* 8th series. 8 vols. Philadelphia and Harrisburg, 1931.
Horsfield, Timothy. Papers. American Philosophical Society, Philadelphia.
———. Letterbook, 1754–1755. Historical Society of Pennsylvania, Philadelphia.
Illinois State Historical Library. *Collections of the Illinois State Historical Library.* 37 vols. Springfield: The Library, 1903–75.
Jacobs, Wilbur R., ed. *The Appalachian Indian Frontier: The Edmond Atkin Report and Plan of 1755.* Lincoln: University of Nebraska Press, 1967.
Jefferys, Thomas. *A General Topography of North America and the West Indies, Being a*

collection of all the maps, charts, plans, and particular surveys, that have been published of that part of the world, either in Europe or America. London: R. Sayer, 1768.

Jennings, John. "John Jennings' Journal at Fort Chartres and Trip to New Orleans, 1768." *Pennsylvania Magazine of History and Biography* 31, no. 3 (1907): 304–10.

———. "Journal from Fort Pitt to Fort Chartres in the Illinois Country," March–April 1766. *Pennsylvania Magazine of History and Biography* 31, no. 2 (1907): 145–56.

Labaree, Leonard W., et al., eds. *The Papers of Benjamin Franklin*. 38 vols. New Haven: Yale University Press, 1959.

Leder, Lawrence H., ed. *The Livingston Indian Records*. Gettysburg: Pennsylvania Historical Association, 1956.

Loskiel, George Henry. *History of the Mission of the United Brethren among the Indians in North America*. Trans. Christian Ignatius Latrobe. London: Brethren's Society for the Furtherance of the Gospel, 1794.

Lyttelton, William Henry. Letterbook Commencing in 1757. William Henry Lyttelton Papers. William C. Clements Library. University of Michigan, Ann Arbor.

———. Papers. William C. Clements Library. University of Michigan, Ann Arbor.

McDowell, William L. Jr., ed. *Documents Relating to Indian Affairs*. Colonial Records of South Carolina. [Ser. 2: The Indian Books.] 2 vols. Columbia: South Carolina Archives Department, 1958–70.

Michigan Pioneer and Historical Society. *Collections and Researches Made by the Michigan Pioneer and Historical Society*. 40 vols. Lansing: The Society, 1877–1929.

Montresor, John. "Journal of John Montresor's Expedition to Detroit in 1763." In J. C. Webster, "Life of John Montresor." *Transactions of the Royal Society of Canada* 3, no. 22 (1928): 1–31.

———. "The Journals of Captain John Montresor." Ed. G. D. Scull. Vol. 14 of *Collections of the New York Historical Society* (1881).

Moravian Church (Bethlehem, Penn.). Moravian Mission Records among the North American Indians. Microfilm, 40 reels. New Haven, Conn.: Research Publications, 1970.

Native American History Collection. William C. Clements Library. University of Michigan, Ann Arbor.

New York Historical Society. *Collections of the New York Historical Society*. 85 vols. New York: The Society, 1868–1975.

O'Callaghan, E. B., ed. *Documentary History of the State of New York*. 4 vols. Albany, N.Y.: Weed, Parsons, 1849–51.

O'Callaghan, E. B., and Berthold Fernow, eds. *Documents Relative to the Colonial History of the State of New York*. 15 vols. Albany, N.Y.: Weed, Parsons, 1853–87.

Pond, Peter. "Journal of Peter Pond." In *Collections of the State Historical Society of Wisconsin* 18 (1908): 314–54.

Porteous, John. *Schenectady to Michilimackinac, 1765 and 1766: Journal of John Porteous*. Toronto: Ontario Historical Society, 1939.

Pouchot, M. (Pierre). *Memoir upon the Late War in North America between the French and the English, 1755–60*. Ed. and trans. Franklin B. Hough. 2 vols. Roxbury, Mass.: W. Elliot Woodward, 1866.

Silvy, Antoine, et al. *Letters from North America*. Trans. Ivy Alice Dickson. Belleville, Ont.: Mika Publishing Company, 1980.

Sullivan, James, et al., eds. *Papers of Sir William Johnson*. 14 vols. Albany: University of the State of New York, 1921–65.

Tanner, John. *A Narrative of the Captivity and Adventures of John Tanner (U. S. Interpreter at the Sault de Ste. Marie) during Thirty Years Residence among the Indians in the Interior of North America*. Ed. Edwin James. Minneapolis: Ross and Haines, 1956.

Thwaites, Rueben Gold, ed. *Early Western Travels, 1748–1846*. 32 vols. Cleveland: A. H. Clark, 1904–7.

———. *The Jesuit Relations and Allied Documents: Travels and Explorations of the Jesuit Missionaries in New France, 1610–1791*. 73 vols. Cleveland: Burrows Brothers, 1896, 1901.

Timberlake, Henry. *The Memoirs of Lieutenant Henry Timberlake: The Story of a Soldier, Adventurer, and Emissary to the Cherokees, 1756–1765*. Ed. Duane H. King. Chapel Hill: University of North Carolina Press, 2007.

Wilkins, John. Journal of Transactions and Presents Given to Indians from 23d December 1768. Thomas Gage Papers, American Series, Volume 138, Folder 20. William C. Clements Library. University of Michigan, Ann Arbor.

Wisconsin State Historical Society. *Collections of the State Historical Society of Wisconsin*. 31 vols. Madison: The Society, 1854–1931.

Zeisberger, David. *David Zeisberger's History of Northern American Indians*. Ed. Archer Butler Hulbert and William Nathaniel Schwarze. Columbus: Ohio State Archaeological and Historical Society, 1910.

Secondary Sources

Abler, Thomas S. and Elisabeth Tooker, "Seneca." In Trigger, *Handbook of North American Indians*, 505–17.

Anderson, Dean L. "The Flow of European Trade Goods into the Western Great Lakes Region, 1715–1760." In Brown, Eccles, and Heldman, *The Fur Trade Revisited*, 93–115.

Anderson, Fred. *Crucible of War: The Seven Years War and the Fate of Empire in British North America, 1754–1766*. New York: Knopf, 2000.

———. *A People's Army: Massachusetts Soldiers and Society in the Seven Years' War*. Chapel Hill: University of North Carolina Press, 1984.

Armour, David A. "Who Remembers La Fourche?" *Chronicle: Historical Society of Michigan Newsletter* 16, no. 2 (1980): 12–16.

Armour, David A., and Keith R. Widder. *At the Crossroads: Michilimackinac during the American Revolution*. Mackinac Island, Mich.: Mackinac Island State Park Commission, 1978.

Axtell, James. *After Columbus: Essays in the Ethnohistory of Colonial North America*. New York: Oxford University Press, 1988.

———. *Beyond 1492: Encounters in Colonial North America*. New York: Oxford University Press, 1992.

———. *The European and the Indian: Essays in the Ethnohistory of Colonial North America*. New York: Oxford University Press, 1981.

———. *The Indians' New South: Cultural Change in the Colonial Southeast.* Baton Rouge: Louisiana State University Press, 1997.
———. *The Invasion Within: The Contest of Cultures in Colonial North America.* New York: Oxford University Press, 1985.
Babson, Jane F. "The Architecture of Early Illinois Forts." *Journal of the Illinois State Historical Society* 61 (1968): 9–40.
Bakeless, John Edwin. *Background to Glory: The Life of George Rogers Clark.* Philadelphia: Lippincott, 1957.
Becker, Mary Druke. "Linking Arms: The Structure of Iroquois Intertribal Diplomacy." In Richter and Merrell, *Beyond the Covenant Chain,* 29–40.
Beers, Henry Putney. *The French and British in the Old Northwest: A Bibliographical Guide to Archive and Manuscript Sources.* Detroit: Wayne State University Press, 1964.
Berkhofer, Robert F., Jr. *The White Man's Indian: Images of the American Indian from Columbus to the Present.* New York: Vintage Books, 1978.
Blasingham, Emily J. "The Depopulation of the Illinois Indians, Part 1." *Ethnohistory* 3, no. 3 (1956): 193–211.
———. "The Depopulation of the Illinois Indians, Part 2, Concluded." *Ethnohistory* 3, no. 4 (1956): 361–412.
Bohaker, Heidi. "'Nindoodemag': The Significance of Algonquian Kinship Networks in the Eastern Great Lakes Region, 1600–1701." *William and Mary Quarterly,* 3rd ser., 63, no. 1 (2006): 23–52.
Brandão, J. A., and William A. Starna. "The Treaties of 1701: A Triumph of Iroquois Diplomacy." *Ethnohistory* 43, no. 2 (1996): 209–44.
Briggs, Winstanley. "Le Pays de Illinois." *William and Mary Quarterly,* 3rd ser., 47, no. 1 (1990): 30–56.
Brose, David S. "Late Prehistory of the Upper Great Lakes Area." In Trigger, *Handbook of North American Indians,* 569–82.
Brown, Jennifer S. H. *Strangers in Blood: Fur Trade Company Families in Indian Country.* 1980. Paperback ed. Norman: University of Oklahoma Press, 1996.
Brown, Jennifer S. H., W. J. Eccles, and Donald P. Heldman, eds. *The Fur Trade Revisited: Selected Papers of the Sixth North American Fur Trade Conference, Mackinac Island, Michigan, 1991.* East Lansing: Michigan State University Press, 1994.
Bryson, Reid A., and Christine Padoch. "On the Climates of History." *Journal of Interdisciplinary History* 10, no. 4 (1980): 583–97.
Buckley, Thomas C., ed. *Rendezvous: Selected Papers of the Fourth North American Fur Trade Conference, 1981.* St. Paul, Minn.: The Conference, 1984.
Callender, Charles. "Illinois." In Trigger, *Handbook of North American Indians,* 673–80.
Calloway, Colin G. *The American Revolution in Indian Country: Crisis and Diversity in Native American Communities.* New York: Cambridge University Press, 1995.
———. *New Worlds for All: Indians, Europeans, and the Remaking of Early America.* Baltimore: Johns Hopkins University Press, 1998.
Cayton, Andrew R. L., and Fredrika J. Teute, eds. *Contact Points: American Frontiers from the Mohawk Valley to the Mississippi, 1750–1830.* Chapel Hill: University of North Carolina Press, 1998.

Clark, James S. "Fire and Climate Change during the Last 750 Years in Northwestern Minnesota." *Ecological Monographs* 60, no. 2 (1990): 135–59.

Cleland, Charles. "Comparison of the Faunal Remains from French and British Refuse Pits at Fort Michilimackinac: A Study in Subsistence Patterns." *Canadian Historic Sites: Occasional Papers in Archaeology and History* 3 (1970): 7–23.

Cooper, James Fenimore. *The Last of the Mohicans: A Narrative of 1757.* New York: Scribner, 1919.

Corkran, David H. *The Cherokee Frontier: Conflict and Survival, 1740–62.* Norman: University of Oklahoma Press, 1962.

Countryman, Edward. "Indians, the Colonial Order, and the Social Significance of the American Revolution." *William and Mary Quarterly,* 3rd ser., 53, no. 2 (1996): 342–62.

Crane, Verner W. *The Southern Frontier, 1670–1732.* 1928. Reprint, Tuscaloosa: University of Alabama Press, 2004.

Cronon, William. *Changes in the Land: Indians, Colonists, and the Ecology of New England.* New York: Hill and Wang, 1983.

Cronon, William, George Miles, and Jay Gitlin, eds. *Under an Open Sky: Rethinking America's Western Past.* New York: Norton, 1992.

Daniels, Christine, and Michael V. Kennedy, eds. *Negotiated Empires: Centers and Peripheries in the Americas, 1520–1800.* New York: Routledge, 2002.

Deloria, Philip J., and Neal Salisbury. *A Companion to American Indian History.* Malden, Mass.: Blackwell, 2002.

Deloria, Vine, Jr. *Custer Died for Your Sins: An Indian Manifesto.* New York: MacMillan, 1969.

Desbarats, Catherine M. "The Costs of Early Canada's Native Alliances: Reality and Scarcity's Rhetoric." *William and Mary Quarterly,* 3rd ser., 52, no. 4 (1995): 609–30.

———. "Following *The Middle Ground.*" *William and Mary Quarterly,* 3rd ser., 63, no. 1 (2006): 81–96.

Dixon, David. *Never Come to Peace Again: Pontiac's Uprising and the Fate of the British Empire in North America.* Norman: University of Oklahoma Press, 2005.

Dowd, Gregory Evans. "The French King Wakes Up in Detroit: 'Pontiac's War' in Rumor and History." *Ethnohistory* 37, no. 3 (1990): 254–78.

———. "'Insidious Friends': Gift-Giving and the Cherokee-British Alliance in the Seven Years' War." In Cayton and Teute, *Contact Points,* 114–50.

———. "The Panic of 1751: The Significance of Rumors on the South Carolina-Cherokee Frontier." *William and Mary Quarterly,* 3rd ser., 53, no. 3 (1996): 527–60.

———. *A Spirited Resistance: The North American Indian Struggle for Unity, 1745–1815.* Baltimore: Johns Hopkins University Press, 1992.

———. *War under Heaven: Pontiac, the Indian Nations, and the British Empire.* Baltimore: Johns Hopkins University Press, 2002.

Dunnigan, Brian Leigh. *A History and Guide to Old Fort Niagara.* Youngstown, N.Y.: Old Fort Niagara Association, 1985.

———. *The Necessity of Regularity in Quartering Soldiers: The Organization, Material Culture and Quartering of the British Soldier at Michilimackinac.* Mackinac Island, Mich.: Mackinac State Historic Parks, 1999.

———. "Portaging Niagara." *Inland Seas* 42, no. 3 (1986): 177–223.
DuVal, Kathleen. *The Native Ground: Indians and Colonists in the Heart of the Continent.* Philadelphia: University of Pennsylvania Press, 2006.
Eccles, W. J. *France in America.* New York: Harper & Row, 1972.
Edmonds, Walter. *Drums along the Mohawk.* Boston: Little, Brown, 1936.
Ekberg, Carl J. *French Roots in the Illinois Country: The Mississippi Frontier in Colonial Times.* Urbana: University of Illinois Press, 1998.
———. *Stealing Indian Women: Native Slavery in the Illinois Country.* Urbana: University of Illinois Press, 2007.
Evans, Lynn L. M. *House D of the Southeast Row House: Excavations at Fort Michilimackinac, 1989–1997.* Archaeological Completion Report Series, 17. Mackinac Island, Mich.: Mackinac Island State Park Commission, 2001.
Fagan, Brian M. *The Little Ice Age: How Climate Made History, 1300–1850.* New York: Basic Books, 2000.
Feest, Johanna E., and Christian Feest. "Ottawa." In Trigger, *Handbook of North American Indians*, 772–86.
Fenton, William N. "Structure, Continuity, and Change in the Process of Iroquois Treaty Making." In Jennings et al., *The History and Culture of Iroquois Diplomacy*, 3–36.
Fenton, William N., and Elisabeth Tooker. "Mohawk." In Trigger, *Handbook of North American Indians*, 466–80.
Gipson, Lawrence Henry. *The Great War for the Empire: The Victorious Years, 1758–1760.* Vol. 7 of *The British Empire before the American Revolution.* New York: Knopf, 1949.
———. *Zones of International Friction: The Great Lakes Frontier, Canada, the West Indies, India, 1748–54.* Vol. 5 of *The British Empire before the American Revolution.* New York: Knopf, 1942.
Goodwin, Gary C. *Cherokees in Transition: A Study of Changing Culture and Environment Prior to 1775.* Chicago: University of Chicago, Department of Geography, 1977.
Grange, Roger T. *Excavations at Fort Mackinac, 1980–82: The Provision Storehouse.* Archaeological Completion Report Series, 12. Mackinac Island, Mich.: Mackinac Island State Park Commission, 1987.
Greene, Jack P. *Peripheries and Center: Constitutional Development in the Extended Polities of the British Empire and the United States, 1607–1788.* New York: Norton, 1990.
———. "Transatlantic Colonization and the Redefinition of Empire in the Early Modern Era." In Daniels and Kennedy, *Negotiated Empires*, 267–82.
Griffin, Patrick. *American Leviathan: Empire, Nation, and Revolutionary Frontier.* New York: Hill and Wang, 2007.
Haan, Richard. "Covenant and Consensus: Iroquois and English, 1676–1760." In Richter and Merrell, *Beyond the Covenant Chain*, 41–57.
Halchin, Jill Yvonne. *Excavations at Fort Michilimackinac, 1983–1985: House C of the Southeast Row House, the Solomon-Levy-Parant House.* Archaeological Completion Report Series, 11. Mackinac Island, Mich.: Mackinac Island State Park Commission, 1985.
Harper, Steven C. "Delawares and Pennsylvanians after the Walking Purchase." In Pencak and Richter, *Friends and Enemies in Penn's Woods*, 167–79.

———. *Promised Land: Penn's Holy Experiment, the Walking Purchase, and the Dispossession of Delawares, 1600–1763*. Bethlehem, Pa.: Lehigh University Press, 2006.

Harrison, Lowell H. *George Rogers Clark and the War in the West*. Lexington: University Press of Kentucky, 1976.

Hatley, Tom. *The Dividing Paths: Cherokees and South Carolinians Through the Era of the Revolution*. New York: Oxford University Press, 1993.

Heldman, Donald P. *Archaeological Investigations at French Farm Lake in Northern Michigan, 1981–82: A British Colonial Farm Site*. Archaeological Completion Report Series, 6. Mackinac Island, Mich.: Mackinac Island State Park Commission, 1983.

———. *Excavations at Fort Michilimackinac, 1976: The Southeast and the South-Southeast Row Houses*. Archaeological Completion Report Series, 1. Mackinac Island, Mich.: Mackinac Island State Park Commission, 1977.

———. *Excavations at Fort Michilimackinac, 1977: House 1 of the South-Southeast Row House*. Archaeological Completion Report Series, 2. Mackinac Island, Mich.: Mackinac Island State Park Commission, 1978.

Heldman, Donald P., and Roger T. Grange Jr. *Excavations at Fort Michilimackinac, 1978–1979: The Rue de la Babillarde*. Archaeological Completion Report Series, 3. Mackinac Island, Mich.: Mackinac Island State Park Commission, 1981.

Hinderaker, Eric. *Elusive Empires: Constructing Colonialism in the Ohio Valley, 1673–1800*. New York: Cambridge University Press, 1997.

History of Northampton County, Pennsylvania, with Illustrations Descriptive of Its Scenery. Philadelphia: Peter Fritts, 1877.

Hoffman, John, ed. *A Guide to the History of Illinois*. New York: Greenwood Press, 1991.

Hunter, William A. *Forts on the Pennsylvania Frontier, 1753–1758*. Harrisburg: Pennsylvania Historical and Museum Commission, 1960.

Hurt, R. Douglas. *Indian Agriculture in America: Prehistory to Present*. Lawrence: University of Kansas Press, 1987.

Innis, Harold Adams. *The Fur Trade in Canada: An Introduction to Canadian Economic History*. New edition. Toronto: University of Toronto Press, 1999.

Jacobs, Wilbur R. *Diplomacy and Indian Gifts: Anglo-French Rivalry along the Ohio and Northwest Frontiers, 1748–1763*. Stanford: Stanford University Press, 1950.

Jelks, Edward B., Carl J. Ekberg, and Terrance J. Martin. *Excavations at the Laurens Site: Probable Location of Fort de Chartres I*. Springfield: Illinois Historic Preservation Agency, 1989.

Jennings, Francis. *Empire of Fortune: Crowns, Colonies and Tribes in the Seven Years' War in America*. New York: Norton, 1988.

———. *The Invasion of America: Indians, Colonialism, and the Cant of Conquest*. Chapel Hill: University of North Carolina Press, 1975.

Jennings, Francis, et al., eds. *The History and Culture of Iroquois Diplomacy: An Interdisciplinary Guide to the Treaties of the Six Nations and their League*. Syracuse, N.Y.: Syracuse University Press, 1985.

Johnson, Ida Amanda. *The Michigan Fur Trade*. 1919. Reprint, Grand Rapids, Mich.: Black Letter Press, 1971.

Jordan, Kurt A. *The Seneca Restoration, 1715–1754: An Iroquois Local Political Economy*. Gainesville: University Press of Florida, 2008.
Judd, Carol M., and Arthur J. Ray. *Old Trails and New Directions: Papers of the Third North American Fur Trade Conference*. Toronto: University of Toronto Press, 1980.
Keel, Bennie C. *Cherokee Archaeology: A Study of the Appalachian Summit*. Knoxville: University of Tennessee Press, 1976.
Keene, David. "Fort de Chartres: Archaeology in the Illinois Country." In *French Colonial Archaeology: The Illinois Country and the Western Great Lakes*, ed. John A. Walthall, 29–41. Urbana: University of Illinois Press, 1991.
Kelley, James C. "Fort Loudoun: British Stronghold in the Tennessee Country." *East Tennessee Historical Society Publications* 50 (1978): 72–91.
———. "Notable Persons in Cherokee History: Attakullakulla." *Journal of Cherokee Studies* 3, no. 1 (1978): 2–34.
Ketcham, Ralph M. "Conscience, War and Politics in Pennsylvania, 1755–1757." *William and Mary Quarterly*, 3rd ser., 20, no. 3 (1963): 416–39.
King, Duane H., ed. *The Cherokee Indian Nation: A Troubled History*. Knoxville: University of Tennessee Press, 1979.
Kinietz, W. Vernon. *The Indians of the Western Great Lakes, 1615–1760*. Ann Arbor: University of Michigan Press, 1965.
Lemon, James T. *The Best Poor Man's Country: A Geographical Study of Early Southeastern Pennsylvania*. Baltimore: Johns Hopkins University Press, 1972.
Levering, Joseph Mortimer. *History of Bethlehem, Pennsylvania, 1742–1892*. Bethlehem: Times Publishing, 1903.
Levy, Philip. *Fellow Travelers: Indians and Europeans Contesting the Early American Trail*. Gainesville: University Press of Florida, 2007.
Mahdi, Louise Carus, Steven Foster, and Meredith Little, eds. *Betwixt and Between: Patterns of Masculine and Feminine Initiation*. La Salle, Ill.: Open Court, 1987.
Mancall, Peter C. *Deadly Medicine: Indians and Alcohol in Early America*. Ithaca: Cornell University Press, 1995.
Marshall, Peter. "The Michilimackinac Misfortunes of Commissary Roberts." In Brown, Eccles, and Heldman, *The Fur Trade Revisited*, 285–98.
Mayer, Holly A. *Belonging to the Army: Camp Followers and Community during the American Revolution*. Columbia: University of South Carolina Press, 1996.
———. "From Forts to Families: Following the Army into Western Pennsylvania, 1758–1766." *Pennsylvania Magazine of History and Biography* 130, no. 1 (2006): 5–43.
McConnell, Michael N. *Army and Empire: British Soldiers on the American Frontier, 1758–1775*. Lincoln: University of Nebraska Press, 2005.
———. *A Country Between: The Upper Ohio Valley and Its Peoples, 1724–1774*. Lincoln: University of Nebraska Press, 1992.
McDermott, John Francis, ed. *Frenchmen and French Ways in the Mississippi Valley*. Urbana: University of Illinois Press, 1969.
Merrell, James H. "'I Desire All That I Have Said . . . May Be Taken down Aright': Revisiting Teedyuscung's 1756 Treaty Council Speeches." *William and Mary Quarterly*, 3rd ser., 63, no. 4 (2006): 777–826.

———. *The Indians' New World: Catawbas and Their Neighbors from European Contact through the Era of Removal.* New York: Norton, 1989.

———. *Into the American Woods: Negotiators on the Pennsylvania Frontier.* New York: Norton, 1999.

———. "Shamokin, 'The Very Seat of the Prince of Darkness': Unsettling the Early American Frontier." In Cayton and Teute, *Contact Points*, 16–59.

———. "Some Thoughts on Colonial Historians and American Indians." *William and Mary Quarterly*, 3rd ser., 46, no. 1 (1989): 94–119.

Merritt, Jane T. *At the Crossroads: Indians and Empires on a Mid-Atlantic Frontier, 1700–1763.* Chapel Hill: University of North Carolina Press, 2003.

Middleton, Richard. *Pontiac's War: Its Causes, Course, and Consequences.* New York: Routledge, 2007.

Morand, Lynn L. *Craft Industries at Fort Michilimackinac, 1715–1781.* Archaeological Completion Report Series, no. 15. Mackinac Island, Mich.: Mackinac Island State Park Commission, 1994.

Moses, John. *Illinois, Historical and Statistical: Comprising the Essential Facts of its Planting and Growth as a Province, County, Territory, and State.* Chicago: Fergus Printing Company, 1889.

Murphy, Lucy Eldersveld. *A Gathering of Rivers: Indians, Métis, and Mining in the Western Great Lakes, 1737–1832.* Lincoln: University of Nebraska Press, 1980.

———. "To Live among Us: Accommodation, Gender, and Conflict in the Western Great Lakes Region, 1760–1832." In Cayton and Teute, *Contact Points*, 270–303.

Murray, David. *Indian Giving: Economies of Power in Indian-White Exchanges.* Amherst: University of Massachusetts Press, 2000.

Nash, Gary B. "The Image of the Indian in the Southern Colonial Mind." *William and Mary Quarterly*, 3rd ser., 29, no. 2 (1972): 197–230.

———. *Red, White, and Black: The Peoples of Early America.* Englewood Cliffs, N.J.: Prentice-Hall, 1974.

Nester, William R. *"Haughty Conquerors": Amherst and the Great Indian Uprising of 1763.* Westport, Conn.: Praeger, 2000.

Nobles, Gregory H. "Breaking into the Backcountry: New Approaches to the Early American Frontier, 1750–1800." *William and Mary Quarterly*, 3rd ser., 43, no. 4 (1989): 641–70.

Parkman, Francis. *The Conspiracy of Pontiac and the Indian War after the Conquest of Canada.* 2 vols. Lincoln: University of Nebraska Press, 1994.

Parmenter, Jon William. "Pontiac's War: Forging New Links in the Anglo-Iroquois Covenant Chain." *Ethnohistory* 44, no. 4 (1997): 617–54.

Peckham, Howard H. *The Colonial Wars, 1689–1762.* Chicago: University of Chicago Press, 1964.

———. *Pontiac and the Indian Uprising.* 1947. Reprint, Detroit: Wayne State University Press, 1994.

Pencak, William A., and Daniel K. Richter, eds. *Friends and Enemies in Penn's Woods: Indians, Colonists, and the Racial Construction of Pennsylvania.* University Park: Pennsylvania State University Press, 2004.

Perdue, Theda. *Cherokee Women: Gender and Culture Change, 1700–1835*. Lincoln: University of Nebraska Press, 1998.
Preston, David L. "Squatters, Indians, Proprietary Government, and Land in the Susquehanna Valley." In Pencak and Richter, *Friends and Enemies in Penn's Woods*, 180–200.
——. *The Texture of Contact: European and Indian Settler Communities on the Frontiers of Iroquoia, 1667–1783*. Lincoln: University of Nebraska Press, 2009.
Ray, Arthur J. "Indians as Consumers in the Eighteenth Century." In Judd and Ray, *Old Trails and New Directions*, 255–71.
——. *Indians in the Fur Trade: Their Role as Hunters, Trappers, and Middlemen in the Lands Southwest of Hudson's Bay, 1660–1870*. Toronto: University of Toronto Press, 1974.
Richards, H. M. M. "The Indian Forts of the Blue Mountains." In Richards et al., *Report of the Commission*, 3–347.
Richards, H. M. M., et al. *Report of the Commission to Locate the Site of the Frontier Forts of Pennsylvania*. Harrisburg: C. M. Busch, State Printer, 1896.
Richter, Daniel K. "Cultural Brokers and Intercultural Politics: New York–Iroquois Relations, 1664–1701." *Journal of American History* 75, no. 1 (1988): 40–67.
——. *Facing East from Indian Country: A Native History of Early America*. Cambridge: Harvard University Press, 2001.
——. *The Ordeal of the Longhouse: The Peoples of the Iroquois League in the Era of European Colonization*. Chapel Hill: University of North Carolina Press, 1992.
——. "Whose Indian History?" *William and Mary Quarterly*, 3rd ser., 50, no. 2 (1993): 379–95.
Richter, Daniel K., and James H. Merrell, eds. *Beyond the Covenant Chain: The Iroquois and their Neighbors in Indian North America, 1600–1800*. Syracuse: Syracuse University Press, 1987.
Roberts, Kenneth. *Northwest Passage*. New York: Doubleday, Doran, 1938.
Rogers, E. S. "Southeastern Ojibwa." In Trigger, *Handbook of North American Indians*, 760–71.
Rushforth, Brett. "Slavery, the Fox Wars, and the Limits of Alliance." *William and Mary Quarterly*, 3rd ser., 63, no. 1 (2006): 53–80.
Saucier, Walter J., and Kathrine Wagner Seineke. "François Saucier, Engineer of Fort de Chartres, Illinois." In *Frenchmen and French Ways in the Mississippi Valley*, ed. John Francis McDermott, 199–227. Urbana: University of Illinois Press, 1969.
Saunt, Claudio. "'Domestick . . . Quiet being Broke': Gender Conflict among Creek Indians in the Eighteenth Century." In Cayton and Teute, *Contact Points*, 151–74.
——. *A New Order of Things: Property, Power, and the Transformation of the Creek Indians, 1733–1816*. New York: Cambridge University Press, 1999.
Savelle, Max. *George Morgan: Colony Builder*. New York: Columbia University Press, 1932.
Schenk, Theresa. "The Cadottes: Five Generations of Fur Traders on Lake Superior." In Brown, Eccles, and Heldman, *The Fur Trade Revisited*, 189–98.
Schlarman, J. H. *From Quebec to New Orleans: The Story of the French in America, Illustrated: Fort de Chartres*. Belleville, Ill.: Buechler Publishing Co., 1929.

Schroeder, Sissel. "Maize Productivity in the Eastern Woodlands and Great Plains of North America." *American Antiquity* 64, no. 2 (1999): 499–516.

Schutt, Amy C. *Peoples of the River Valleys: The Odyssey of the Delaware Indians*. Philadelphia: University of Pennsylvania Press, 2007.

Scott, Elizabeth M. *French Subsistence at Fort Michilimackinac, 1715–1781: The Clergy and the Traders*. Archaeological Completion Report Series, 9. Mackinac Island, Mich.: Mackinac Island State Park Commission, 1985.

Scott, Stuart D. *An Archaeological Survey of Artpark and the Lower Landing, Lewiston, New York*. Lewiston: Edwin Mellen Press, 1993.

Severance, Frank H. *An Old Frontier of France: The Niagara Region and Adjacent Lakes under French Control*. 2 vols. New York: Dodd, Mead, 1917.

———. *Studies of the Niagara Frontier*. Buffalo: Buffalo Historical Society, 1911.

Shannon, Timothy J. *Iroquois Diplomacy on the Early American Frontier*. New York: Viking, 2008.

Shoemaker, Nancy. "An Alliance between Men: Gender Metaphors in Eighteenth-Century American Indian Diplomacy East of the Mississippi." *Ethnohistory* 46, no. 2 (1999): 239–63.

———. *Negotiators of Change: Historical Perspectives on Native American Women*. New York: Routledge, 1995.

Shurtleff, Mary Belle. *Old Arbre Croche*. n.p., 1945.

Sipe, C. Hale. *The Indian Wars of Pennsylvania*. Harrisburg: The Telegraph Press, 1929.

Sleeper-Smith, Susan. *Indian Women and French Men: Rethinking Cultural Encounter in the Western Great Lakes*. Amherst: University of Massachusetts Press, 2001.

Smaby, Beverly Prior. *The Transformation of Moravian Bethlehem: From Communal Mission to Family Economy*. Philadelphia: University of Pennsylvania Press, 1988.

Smith, Henry Nash. *The Virgin Land: The American West as Symbol and Myth*. Cambridge: Harvard University Press, 1950.

Starbuck, David R. *The Great Warpath: British Military Sites from Albany to Crown Point*. Hanover, N.H.: University Press of New England, 1999.

Steele, Ian K. *Betrayals: Fort William Henry and the Massacre*. New York: Oxford University Press, 1990.

———. *Warpaths: Invasions of North America*. New York: Oxford University Press, 1994.

Stephenson, R. S. "Pennsylvania Provincial Soldiers in the Seven Years' War." *Pennsylvania History* 62, no. 2 (1995): 196–213.

Stolz, Charles Morse. *Outposts of the War for Empire*. Pittsburgh: University of Pittsburgh Press, 2005.

Stone, Lyle M. *Fort Michilimackinac, 1715–1781: An Archaeological Perspective on the Revolutionary Frontier*. East Lansing: The Museum, Michigan State University, 1974.

Stone, Richard G., Jr. "Captain Paul Demere at Fort Loudoun, 1757–1760." *East Tennessee Historical Society Publications* 41 (1969): 17–32.

Strand, Ginger. *Inventing Niagara: Beauty, Power, and Lies*. New York: Simon and Schuster, 2009.

Stumpf, Stuart. "James Glen, Cherokee Diplomacy, and the Construction of an Overhill Fort." *East Tennessee Historical Society Publications* 50 (1978): 21–30.

Szasz, Margaret, ed. *Between Indian and White Worlds: The Cultural Broker*. Norman: University of Oklahoma Press, 2001.
Taylor, Alan B. *The Divided Ground: Indians, Settlers, and the Northern Borderland of the America Revolution*. New York: Knopf, 2006.
Trigger, Bruce G., ed. *Handbook of North American Indians: Northeast*. Vol. 15 of *Handbook of North American Indians*. Ed. William C. Sturtevant. Washington, D.C.: Smithsonian Institution, 1978.
———. *Natives and Newcomers: Canada's "Heroic Age" Reconsidered*. Kingston, Ont.: McGill-Queen's University Press, 1985.
Turner, Frederick Jackson. "The Significance of the Frontier in American History." *Annual Report of the American Historical Association* (1893): 197–227.
Usner, Daniel H., Jr. *Indians, Settlers, and Slaves in a Frontier Exchange Economy: The Lower Mississippi Valley before 1783*. Chapel Hill: University of North Carolina Press, 1992.
Van Hoak, Stephen P. "Untangling the Roots of Dependency: Choctaw Economics, 1700–1860." *American Indian Quarterly* 23, nos. 3–4 (1999): 113–28.
Van Kirk, Sylvia. *Many Tender Ties: Women in Fur Trade Society, 1670–1870*. Norman: University of Oklahoma Press, 1983.
Vaughan, Alden T. *Transatlantic Encounters: American Indians in Britain, 1500–1776*. New York: Cambridge University Press, 2006.
Waddell, Louis M. "Defending the Long Perimeter: Forts on the Pennsylvania, Maryland, and Virginia Frontier, 1755–1765." *Pennsylvania History* 62, no. 2 (1995): 171–95.
Wallace, Anthony F. C. *The Death and Rebirth of the Seneca*. New York: Vintage Books, 1972.
———. *King of the Delawares: Teedyuscung, 1700–1763*. 2nd ed. Syracuse, N.Y.: Syracuse University Press, 1990.
———. "The Origins of Iroquois Neutrality: The Grand Settlement of 1701." *Pennsylvania History* 24, no. 3 (1957): 223–35.
Wallace, Paul A. W. *Indians in Pennsylvania*. Harrisburg: Pennsylvania Historical and Museum Commission, 1964.
Wallerstein, Immanuel. *The Modern World-System II: Mercantilism and the Consolidation of the European World-Economy, 1600–1750*. New York: Academic Press, 1980.
Ward, Matthew C. *Breaking the Backcountry: The Seven Years' War in Virginia and Pennsylvania, 1754–1765*. Pittsburgh: University of Pittsburgh Press, 2003.
Weslager, C. A. *The Delaware Indians: A History*. New Brunswick: Rutgers University Press, 1972.
Whitaker, John Martin Francis. *The Functions of Four Colonial Yards of the Southeast Row House, Fort Michilimackinac, Michigan*. Archaeological Completion Report Series, 16. Mackinac Island, Mich.: Mackinac Island State Park Commission, 1998.
White, Bruce M. "Encounters with Spirits: Ojibwa and Dakota Theories about the French and Their Merchandise." *Ethnohistory* 41, no. 3 (1994): 369–405.
———. "The Fear of Pillaging: Folktales of the Great Lakes Fur Trade." In Brown, Eccles, and Heldman, *The Fur Trade Revisited*, 199–213.
———. "'Give Us a Little Milk': The Social and Cultural Meaning of Gift Giving in the

Lake Superior Fur Trade." In *Rendezvous: Selected Papers of the Fourth North American Fur Trade Conference, 1981*, ed. Thomas C. Buckley, 185–97. St. Paul, Minn.: The Conference, 1984.

———. "The Woman Who Married a Beaver: Trade Patterns and Gender Roles in the Ojibwa Fur Trade." *Ethnohistory* 46, no. 1 (1999): 109–47.

White, Marian E. "Erie." In Trigger, *Handbook of North American Indians*, 412–17.

———. *Iroquois Culture History in the Niagara Frontier Area of New York State*. Ann Arbor: University of Michigan Press, 1961.

———. "Late Woodland Archaeology in the Niagara Frontier of New York and Ontario." In *The Late Prehistory of the Lake Erie Drainage Basin: A 1972 Symposium Revised*, ed. David M. Brose, 110–36. Cleveland: Cleveland Museum of Natural History, 1976.

———. "Neutral and Wenro." In Trigger, *Handbook of North American Indians*, 407–11.

White, Richard. *The Middle Ground: Indians, Empires, and Republics in the Great Lakes Region, 1650–1815*. New York: Cambridge University Press, 1991.

———. *The Roots of Dependency: Subsistence, Environment, and Social Change among the Choctaws, Pawnees, and Navahos*. Lincoln: University of Nebraska Press, 1983.

Widder, Keith R. "Effects of the American Revolution on Fur-Trade Society at Michilimackinac." In Brown, Eccles, and Heldman, *The Fur Trade Revisited*, 299–316.

———. *Reveille Till Taps: Soldier Life at Fort Mackinac, 1780–1895*. Mackinac Island, Mich.: Mackinac Island State Park Commission, 1972.

Zuckerman, Michael. "Through a Glass Darkly: Countryman's Radical American Revolution." *William and Mary Quarterly*, 3rd ser., 53, no. 2 (1996): 373–78.

Index

Albany, 94, 127–30, 132–33, 139, 194
Alcohol. *See* Liquor
Algonquian, 90, 128
Allemangel, 64, 212n6
Allen, William, 66
American Revolution, 108–9, 115–16, 154, 212n54, 233n59
Amherst, Sir Jeffrey, 99, 153, 178, 207n20, 225n26; on Devil's Hole attack, 142–43; on Indian gifts, 21–22; on Indian relations, 138–40
Askin, John, 113
Atkin, Edmond, 29, 31, 35, 53–54
Attyatawitsera, 151
Aubry, Charles, 164, 224n23, 229n12

Backcountry forts, 2, 11, 21, 28, 198, 200, 205n6; Indian accommodations of, 14–15; kinds of, 7–9
Bag' gat' iway (Indian ball game), 17
Balfour, Sir Henry, 99–100
Baptiste, 184
Beaver Island, 102
Berks County, 64, 81
Bethlehem, Penn., 60, 62, 72, 74, 79–81, 82–83, 215n26, 216n33; Indian refugees at, 64–66, 69–70
Bildanowan, 149
Black Boys (Penn. rebels), 166

Black Dog, 183–85, 199, 201
Blockhouses, 8–9, 11–12, 16, 81, 86, 175, 194, 196
Bloody Run, battle of, 123
Blue Mountain, 59–60, 62–65, 71, 74, 78, 79, 82; forts, 69; Kittatinny, 67f; region, 60, 61m, 64, 85, 213n7, 214n16
Bogaert, Harmen Meyndertsz van den, 7
Bougainville, Louis-Antoine de, 135
Bouquet, Colonel Henry, 122, 142, 148
Bowman, Hans, 83–84
Braddock, General Edward, 37, 63, 98
Bradstreet, Colonel John, 25, 151–52, 163, 166; at Detroit, 102–3; at Niagara, 145–46, 148–49
Brahm, William Gerard de, 43–46, 47m, 210n30
Brandy, 23, 96–97
Brant, Molly, 194
Brehant de Galinee, Rene de, 128
Brehm, Dederick, 114
British forts, 5, 7, 11, 17, 23, 26, 49, 129, 197; backcountry forts, 23, 26; and Indian neighbors, 1, 3, 5, 7, 9, 11, 13, 15, 17, 19, 21, 23, 25
Browning, William, 142–43
Bruyan, Jacques, 96
Bull, Commander John, 82–83
Burgoyne, General John, 110, 117

Burnet, Governor William, 133–34
Bushy Run, battle of, 123
Butricke, Ensign George, 172, 177

Cadillac, Antoine de la Mothe, 95, 97
Cadotte, Jean Baptiste, 101, 219n22
Cahokia, 160, 170–71, 175
Cahokia Indians, 161, 164, 182
Campbell, Captain James, 170, 173
Campbell, Lieutenant Colonel John, 103–4
Canaghquaeson, 12
Canajoharie, 193–94, 196–97, 200; local residents, 195–96; Mohawks, 193–94, 196–97
Cartier, Jacques, 94
Carver, Jonathan, 104
Catawbas, 58
Cayton, Andrew R. L.: *Contact Points*, 5, 205n4
Cayugas, 123, 127, 133
Charlestown, 8, 18, 29, 37, 39, 41, 54, 56–57, 209n20
Chartres Village, 177
Chenussio Senecas, 17, 25, 121, 123–24, 148, 150–55, 222n1, 224n22; and Devil's Hole attack, 142–45; as French allies, 131–32; as portage workers, 134–36; tensions with British, 138–39
Cherokees, 12, 16, 19, 24, 27–29, 30*m*, 31–32, 33–41, 42*m*, 43–46, 48–58, 161, 166, 175, 197, 206n10, 208n7, 209n20, 210n35, 211n52; British alliance with, 29, 46, 48, 54, 73; headmen, 34–35, 48, 51, 53; leaders, 24, 27–29, 31, 32, 33*f*, 34, 37–38, 45, 52, 55, 58, 207n3; Overhill, 19, 29, 35, 44, 48, 53–54, 56–57; rumored Iroquois alliance, 54; South Carolina alliance, 27, 29, 31; women, 12, 29, 40, 48–49, 205n9, 209n22, 210n35
Cherokee War, 24, 55
Chickasaws, 51, 58, 156, 161, 166, 184–86
Chinoniata, 135
Choctaws, 43, 55, 204n3

Chota, 27, 38–41, 44, 48–51, 54, 56; Virginia fort at, 39, 44, 48
Clark, George Rogers, 109, 111, 191, 233n59
Claus, Daniel, 153, 155
Clinton, George, 14, 194
Cole, Edward, 177–81, 185
Committee on Indian Affairs, S. Carolina (1755), 36
Conoquieson, 144
Cooper, James Fenimore, 1, 2, 3
Corn, 45, 49, 64, 80, 95, 103, 131; agriculture, 94, 100; crop failure, 115–17; Eastern Woodland trio crop, 91; and L'Arbre Croche, 88, 98; and Fort Michilimackinac, 111–14; French destruction of, 129; Indian women selling to forts, 13, 40–41, 48, 52, 104, 106, 118
Couagne, Jean Baptiste de, 122
Covenant Chain, 144–45, 196
Crawford, Hugh, 164
Creek Indians, 27, 46, 54
Croghan, George, 166–73, 177, 185
Cross Village, Mich., 119–20
Crown Point, 7, 205n5
Cumberland River, 175
Cuming, Andrew, 32, 33*f*

D'Abbadie, Governor Jean-Jacques, 162, 164
Dablon, Claude, 94–95
Dease, John, 117–18
Delawares, 60, 63–64, 66, 69, 85, 150, 175, 212n5, 214n18, 215n29, 225n23; at Easton, 72–74, at Fort Allen, 77–79, 81–83; attack settlements, 63–64; Minisinks, 77–79, 215n26; Munsees, 64, 73, 76, 78, 214n18
Delaware War (1755–1758), 24, 59, 69, 87
Demere, Paul, 32, 58, 211n54
Demere, Raymond, 6, 32, 38–46, 48–57, 209n25, 210n29
Demler, Lieutenant George, 147*f*
Denny, Governor William, 76–78, 80–84, 216n34

Detroit, 11, 90, 97–98, 109, 113, 115, 117, 139, 148, 170
Devil's Hole, 122, 142–45, 147f, 150, 152–53; Iroquois attack at, 122, 150, 152–54
Dinwiddie, Governor Robert, 36–39, 43, 48
Dobbs, Governor Arthur, 39
Dongan, Governor Thomas, 129
Dorchester, Lord, 118
Du Peron, Francois, 94

Eastern Woodland (region), 7, 13, 92; Adena culture, 91; peoples, 31, 70, 91, 96, 123, 140, 158, 227n3
Easton, Penn., 60, 64, 69–70, 72–74, 77–86, 214n18, 215n26, 216n33
Easton Conference, 72–73, 77–79, 84, 86
Edmonds, Walter. *Drums along the Mohawk*, 3
Elliott, John, 34, 53
Erie, Lake, 121, 126, 129, 138, 140–41, 149, 151
Erie Indians, 128, 224n23
Eyre, Lt. Col. William, 102

Farmar, Major Robert, 166, 168–71
Farquhar, Commandant Hugh, 138
Felicity (sloop), 112–13
Finger Lakes region, 127, 128–29
Five Nations Iroquois, 127, 129–30; and Iroquois Confederacy, 123, 130–31, 133, 135, 138, 144, 224n16
Forbes, General John, 83, 173–74, 180; Forbes campaign (1758), 50, 56, 83
Fort Allen, 9, 18, 24, 59, 66, 67f, 68f, 68, 70, 74–75, 79, 90, 199, 212n1, 214n16, 215n25, 217n34; Indian involvement with, 60, 69, 71–72, 78–79, 81–84, 86, 216n33; trading post at, 85
Fort Augusta, 8m, 16–17, 82, 84, 205n5, 217n41
Fort Chartres (Fort Cavendish), 6, 25, 20f, 26, 156–57, 159m, 160, 189f, 199, 227n1; British/French interests at, 157, 160, 162, 164, 166, 174, 178, 180–81, 188; Croghan expedition to, 166–67; demise of, 190–92, 232n42, 233n59; disease at, 172–73; Indian involvement with, 26, 161, 168, 170, 175, 177, 179–80, 182, 185, 190, 228n6; living conditions at, 172, 173, 188, 228n6; as news outlet, 183; provisioning at, 169–70; Village, 177, 230n21
Fort de Baude, 95, 97
Fort Detroit, 17, 95, 102, 106, 129, 132, 141, 168, 179, 233n59; Indian involvement with, 123, 139, 141, 145, 148, 161, 175; provisions at, 103, 106; siege of, 121–22
Fort Duquesne, 56, 63, 83
Fort Edward Augustus (La Baye), 17
Fort Erie, 142, 149, 151
Fort Franklin, 66, 81, 216n34
Fort Hamilton, 81, 216n34
Fort Hendrick, 193, 195–97
Fort Hunter, 194
Fort Johnson, 14, 23, 193
Fort Kaskaskia, 172, 230n21, 232n50, 233n59
Fort Lebanon, 78
Fort Le Boeuf, 123, 140, 162
Fort Ligonier, 72
Fort Littleton, 82
Fort Loudoun, 6, 9, 18, 24, 29, 30m, 33f, 42f, 47f, 50, 51, 57, 59, 90, 207n3, 211n54; construction of, 44–48; Cherokee influence at, 19, 24, 53–55, 58
Fort Mackinac, 113, 115, 118
Fort Miamis, 17
Fort Michilimackinac, 7, 17, 20f, 99–100, 102, 104, 109, 115–16, 119, 121, 149, 132, 219n23, 220n28; demise of, 148, 179; food and provisions at, 89–90, 94–95, 103, 113, 114–15, 117; French occupation of, 89, 97–98; Indian involvement at, 94–95, 98, 102, 106, 110, 118, 123, 197, 219n23; liquor at, 107–9; Roberts–Rogers conflict, 107–8

Fort Niagara, 7, 11, 17, 20f, 25, 102, 106, 114, 122, 124, 135–36, 137f, 138–41, 145–46, 225n24; British take control of, 136; conference at (1764), 148–55; as four fort system, 126–27; French at, 132–38; Indian involvement with, 121–22, 124, 132–36, 141, 143, 145, 197; and Little Niagara, 134, 138–39, 141
Fort Norris, 67f, 77, 81, 216n34
Fort Northkill, 78
Fort Orange (later Albany), 127
Fort Oswego, 102, 193; Post, 16, 106, 126, 133, 142
Fort Ouiatenon, 166–68
Fort Pitt (Pittsburgh), 11, 140, 166–67, 172, 175, 177–78, 180, 188, 190, 217n41; Indian attacks on, 17, 72, 122–23, 166; provisioning Fort Chartres, 169–70
Fort Presque Isle, 123, 135, 138, 140
Fort Prince George, 31, 36, 38–41, 43–44, 210n35
Fortress Louisbourg, 7
Fort Schlosser, 142, 145–46, 147f, 149, 153
Fort Toulouse, 49–50, 55
Fort Venango, 123, 140–41, 143, 224n23, 225n31
Fort William Henry, 1, 82, 98, 204n1
Fox Indians, 161, 166
Fox War (1716), 97
Franklin, Benjamin, 59–60, 65–66, 68f, 81, 87
Fraser, Lieutenant Alexander, 166, 170–71
French and Indian War. *See* Seven Years' War
French Farm Lake, 113
French forts, 9, 13, 19, 228n6; posts, 99, 129, 132, 139, 160–61, 167
French John, 54–55
French Maxim, 21, 102
Fur trade, 12, 18–19, 34, 110, 161; Atlantic, 123, 127; Fort Chartres, 160, 169, 173, 187; European, 88–89, 94, 155, 227n3; at Fort de Baude, 95; French/Indian kinship in, 107, 205n9, 219n17; Indian culture and, 90–91; Indian women in, 13, 92, 96, 101, 112; at James Bay, 95; at Fort Michilimackinac, 94–95, 97, 99, 104, 109, 111, 116; Odawas/Ojibawas and, 118; Iroquois and, 123

Gage, Sir Thomas, 15, 19, 156, 173–74 188, 228n8; and James Campbell, 103; demise of Fort Chartres, 156, 173, 188; on gift giving, 22, 162, 178–79, 187, 232n41; and Indian hostilities, 143–45, 162, 166, 169, 175, 177, 180, 186–87, 190–91, 206n14; and liquor, 23, 106; and Rogers/Roberts conflict, 107; and trade with Indians, 102, 106–7, 150, 153, 188; and William Johnson, 15, 107–8, 143, 145, 149–50, 152–53, 177, 179, 181
Geiger, Lieutenant, 77
Genesee River, 112, 128
German Flats, 16
Gibbs, Sergeant William, 43
Glasier, Beamsley, 109
Glen, Governor James, 27–29, 31–32, 34–37, 50, 52, 58
Gnadenhütten, 62, 64–66, 74
Godfroi, Jacques, 164
Gordon, Captain Henry, 173
Grand Island, 126
Grant, Ludovic, 31, 34–35
Great Lakes: Eastern Great Lakes, 123, 127, 129, 131; Northern Great Lakes, 89–90, 109, 118, 126; Western Great Lakes, 127, 142, 146, 148, 152, 205n9, 218n13
Great Lakes region, 5, 16, 90, 92, 94, 100, 102–3, 107, 109, 114–15, 119, 127, 139–41, 143, 217n3, 218n13, 219n17; French in, 94; Indian-British relations in, 98, 103, 124; Indian unrest in, 121, 123, 128, 148–49, 157–58; British military regime in, 124, 132; people of, 12, 63, 89, 92, 96–97, 99, 109, 132, 136, 142, 219n20; outposts in, 8, 97, 106–8, 116, 122, 124, 127, 132, 139, 141, 146, 148

Haldimand, Frederick, 110–11, 113–17
Hamilton, Major Isaac, 156, 190
Hamilton, Governor William, 111
Hananaa, 176, 186, 192
Harris, Captain, 80
Harrison, Commander Thomas, 39–40
Hays, Captain William, 64–66
Heckewelder, John, 70–71
Henry, Alexander, 100–102, 149
Hillsborough, Earl of, 19, 22, 174
Hiwassee Old Town, 49–50
Holmes, Ensign Robert, 17
Hopewell Culture, 91
Horsfield, Timothy, 75–77, 80, 83, 86, 212n6, 217n42
Hospitality, 60, 70–71, 213n13
Howard, Captain William, 103–4, 106–7
Huron, Lake, 94; people/culture of, 90, 94, 128, 148, 213n13

Illinois, 26, 109–12, 123, 156–57, 159*m*, 160–64, 166–78, 186–88, 190–92, 228nn4,6,8, 229n8, 233n59
Illinois Indians, 26, 146, 158, 161, 164, 166, 170, 197, 227n3, 228n7, 230n21, 231n40
Indian affairs, 6, 14, 19, 36, 98, 143, 171, 177, 179, 181; allies, 15, 19, 28, 36, 50, 57, 63, 83, 160, 173, 191; attacks, 11, 64, 111, 169–70, 177, 187, 213n7; trade, 11, 29, 84, 92
Indian Department, British (1758–77), 12, 85, 104, 108, 177–81; agents, 143, 162; commissaries, 106, 107
Indian uprising of 1763–64 (Pontiac's Rebellion), 123, 152, 154, 157–58, 176
Iroquois, 11–12, 14, 16, 71, 90, 121, 123–24, 128, 130, 135–36, 146, 151, 196, 224n22; as British allies, 129–30, 133–34, 138, 140, 143, 145, 223n11; decline of, 123; diplomacy, 25, 63, 69, 72, 121, 124, 129–31, 133, 195, 222n4, 223n12, 224n16; Fort Allen, 77, 79, 83; hostilities, 78, 90, 128, 140, 144; land agreement (1701), 129–30; land agreement (1726), 139;
neutrality, 131–33, 135–36, 223n11; trade/hunting, 128, 133
Iroquois Confederacy, 123, 131, 133, 135, 138, 144, 223n12, 224n16
Iroquois League, 127, 130, 233n7
Iroquois region, 95, 127–28, 138

James Bay, 95
Jamet, Commander John, 101
Jarron, Samuel, 56
Johnson, Sir William, 12–13, 19, 136, 178, 194; and Chenussio Indians, 150–52, 154; and Croghan, 167–68, 171; diplomacy, 77, 85, 122, 138, 145, 148–49, 190, 222n4; discussions with Gage, 15, 19, 107, 143, 145, 153, 177, 179, 180–81, 190; gift giving to Indians, 99, 143, 148, 179, 232n41; and Indian hostilities, 15–16, 21, 23, 98, 139, 142, 144, 146, 148–50, 167, 194–96; and Indian trade, 102, 106, 138, 150, 153; in King George's War, 14; and liquor, 107–9, 141, 149; and Niagara land cession, 151–52; at Niagara peace conference, 123, 145, 148, 152, 219n25, 222n4; and Nickas, 200
Joncaire, Chabert, de, the Elder, 131–32

Kaendae, 136
Kalm, Peter, 134
Kanadasego, 144
Kanadiohara, 16
Kanakarighton, 133–34
Kanuksusy, 69, 74, 76, 214n18
Kaskaskia, 156, 161, 166–67, 173, 175; posts, 160, 170, 190; residents, 173–74
Kaskaskia Indians, 174, 182–86
Kaskaskia River, 165*f*
Kaské, Charlot, 140, 161, 164, 229n8, 233n59
Kegeweskam, 88, 117
Keowee, 31, 40–41, 43, 44, 49
Kickapoos, 161, 166, 177, 182–83, 185–87
King George II, 27–28, 32–33, 38

King George's War, 14, 97, 194
King William's War, 95

La Belle-Famille, battle of, 136
L'Arbre Croche, 88, 98, 100, 102, 113–15, 117, 119; La Fourche, 102, 108–9; Odawa residents of, 101, 104, 108–9, 117, 119–20
Last of the Mohicans: book, 1, 3; movie, 3, 4, 204n13
Laudeviet, 184
Lehigh River (water gap), 8*m*, 59, 60, 62, 66, 83; region (township), 65–66; Valley, 60
Levancher, 164
Lewis, Major Andrew, 38–39, 44, 48
Liquor, 79, 96, 107; abuse of, 23, 75, 77, 108, 131, 149, 180; forts as a source of, 82, 107, 170; as gifts, 22–23, 83–84, 108, 110, 214n18; missionaries and, 96–97; regulation of, 78, 80; Teedyuscung and, 74, 76, 78–79; as trade item, 34, 75, 84, 108, 131, 187–88
Little Carpenter (Attakullakulla), 27–28, 31–32, 33*f*, 33–35, 37–41, 43–46, 48–49, 51, 53–58, 207n1, 210n30, 211n54
Little Ice Age, 92
Loftus, Major Arthur, 162, 229n9
Loquus, Gabriel, 83
Lord, Captain Hugh, 156
Loudon, Lord, 29, 194
Lower Castle, Mohawk (Tiononderoge), 194
Lower Landing, Niagara, 122, 127, 131–32, 142, 145–46, 147*f*
Lower towns, Cherokee, 31, 36, 43, 57
Lyttelton, William Henry, 32–33, 37–41, 43–44, 49, 52–54, 56–58

Mackinac: Fort, 89; Island, 98, 111, 113, 116–18, 219n17; people of, 103, 120; trade at, 90, 108, 110; Straits, 88–89, 93*f*, 94–95, 100, 105*f*, 118, 219n17
Maisonville, Alexander, 164, 166

Marquette, Jacques, 94
Matchekewis, 116, 201
McBeath, George, 115
McKee, Alexander, 116
Meis, Jacob, 69, 100
Menominee Indians, 110
Métis, 96, 98, 101, 200
Mexico, Gulf of, 126
Michigamea Indians, 161, 167, 182–85
Michigan, Lake, 17, 94, 98, 102, 107, 110–12, 114; people of, 111, 114, 119
Michigan (sloop), 121
Michilimackinac: American regime at, 118; British regime, 104, 118 French regime, 97, 99; Indians at, 97–98, 109–11, 149; outposts near, 24, 94–95, 97, 101–2, 106–7, 109, 113, 115, 117, 123, 132, 148, 179, 197; traders at, 106, 113
Middle towns, Cherokee, 39
Miller, Lieutenant, 74–77
Minavavana (Le Grand Saulteur), 100, 219n20
Missionaries, Jesuit, 94, 97, 213n13
Mississippi River, 25, 157, 160
Missouri Country, 179
Missouris, 161, 164, 170
Mohawk River, 193; Valley, 144
Mohawks, 7, 14, 123, 193–96, 200
Mompesson, Captain John, 114
Montcalm, Joseph de, 1, 98
Montour, Captain Andrew, 149
Montreal, 101, 123, 127, 129–30, 135–36, 138
Montresor, John, 122, 145–46, 147*f*, 149, 226n39
Moravian, 60, 62, 72, 79, 86; missionaries, 64–65, 69, 74
Morgan, George, 172–75, 181, 187
Morris, Governor Robert, 65–66, 72–77
Murray, William, 156, 214

Nanfan, Lieutenant Governor John, 129
Navy Island, 141

Neutrals, 128
New Netherlands, 128
New Orleans, 160, 162, 169–70, 172, 177, 229n8
Niagara Escarpment, 122, 126
Niagara Falls, 122, 126–27, 129
Niagara portage (Carrying Place), 123–24, 131, 135–37, 139, 141–42, 151–52, 154, 225n26
Niagara region, 126, 136, 139, 154; Indian presence in, 128, 134, 138–39, 153, 224n22; land cession in, 143; unrest in, 122, 127, 139–40, 142
Niagara River, 122, 126–28, 147f, 151; placement of forts near, 129, 132, 141, 145
Niagara Senecas, 136, 224n22
Niagara's House of Peace, 155
Niagara traders, 135
Nickas, 195–96, 200
Nipissings, 90, 98
Northampton County, Penn., 60, 62, 67f, 71, 78, 83–84, 216n34
Noyan, Pierre, 96

Oconostota, 41, 46, 50, 58
Odawas, 24, 89–90, 94–95, 116–20, 128, 140, 197, 224n23, 226n38, 228n8; at Mackinac Straits, 97–98; at L'Arbre Croche, 100–103, 108–10, 116–18; at Niagara conference, 148–49
Ohio River, 157, 163, 166–67, 178, 188, 190
Ohio Valley, 16–17, 25, 63, 101, 123, 206n16, 233n59
Ojibwas, 17, 88, 95, 98, 100–102, 108, 113, 123–24, 146, 179, 218n13, 219n20, 224n23; attack Michilimackinac, 101; as British allies, 116–17
Old Hop (Connecorte), 28, 31–32, 33f, 34–35, 37–41, 43–46, 48–58, 201, 207n1
One-Eyed Chief, 183

Oneidas, 12, 123, 127, 144, 223n7
Onondagas, 15–16, 123, 127, 129–30, 132–35
Ontario, Lake, 126, 128, 134, 136, 141, 193
Oquaga, 16
Orndt, Captain Jacob, 77, 79–83, 216n33, 217n36
Osages, 161, 164, 182, 184, 228n7
Oswego, 16, 133, 142; Fort/Post, 102, 106, 126, 193
Oughnour, Daniel, 122
Overhill region, 27–29, 30m, 31–32, 35–41, 42m, 43–44, 46, 48–50, 52–58, 209n20, 210n29, 211n54; fort, 31, 35–37, 40, 43, 50, 58; leaders, 37, 48, 50, 54, 55, 57; towns, 32, 42f, 43, 50, 55–56

Parkman, Francis, 2, 17
Parsons, William, 65
Paxinosa, 69
Pennsylvania backcountry, 63, 81–82; line of forts in, 65–66, 68
Peorias, 164, 184–85
Peters, Richard, 73–74, 86
Petuns, 128
Peyster, Arent Schuyler de, 110–11, 117
Pfister, Lieutenant Francis, 153
Philadelphia, 60, 64, 80, 85, 172, 217n42
Pierz, Father Francis, 119–20
Plains Indians, 158, 166
Point aux Ecors, 163
Pond, Peter (traveler), 109
Pontiac, 101–2, 121, 123, 148, 150, 161, 166, 177, 185, 198, 206n16, 228n8, 229n8, 233n59; death of, 177; and revitalization movement, 140–41
Pontiac's Rebellion (1763–64), 17. *See also* Indian uprising of 1763–64
Potawatomis, 90, 94–95, 98, 161, 164, 175, 177, 182–87, 190, 224n3
Pouchot, Captain Pierre, 136, 138
Poulous, 193–95

Proclamation of 1763, 16
Provincial governments, 18–19, 25

Quebec, 116, 123, 127
Queen Anne's War, 97

Ralston and Brown Stockade, 8*m*
Ratzer, Bernard, 147*f*
Reading, Penn., 60, 62, 75; militiamen, 75
Reed, Colonel John, 171, 173–74, 178–80
Regiment, Royal Irish, 181
Revanche (French merchant ship), 53
Revolutionary War, 113, 155, 197
Reynolds, Captain George, 69, 75–77, 215n25
Richter, Daniel K., 123, 223n11
Roberts, Benjamin, 107–8
Roberts, Kenneth: *Northwest Passage*, 3
Robertson, Captain Daniel, 115–17
Robertson, Samuel, 112–13
Rogers, Major Robert, 104, 107–8
Ross, Lieutenant John, 164, 165*f*, 166, 170, 174, 178, 181
Rum, 12; abuse of, 23, 41, 75, 80, 82, 99, 107–8, 114, 149; as "milk," 100; at Fort Allen, 59, 78; forts as a source of, 17, 41, 85; as gifts, 17, 21, 75, 109–10, 148, 219n20; Indian life and, 23, 73, 106, 108, 149; at Fort Loudon, 194; Poulous and, 192–95; Rogers/Roberts conflict and, 107–8; Teedyuscungand, 73, 78; as trade item, 53, 55–56, 75, 77, 80, 99, 107–8, 148; John Wilkins and, 182–86

Sadekanaktie, 129
Saginaw Bay, 98
St. Ignace, 94, 97
St. Joseph Island, 118
St. Lawrence River, 7, 94, 108, 126
St. Mary's River, 98, 118
Saluda conference, 36; 1755 agreement at, 52, 205n12
Saluda Old Town, 35, 37
Saratoga, 117

Saucier, Francois, 160
Sauks, 161, 166
Saulteurs/Saulteaux, 98–99
Sault Sainte Marie, 94, 110; post, 101
Savannah Indians, 43, 46, 48, 51–52, 54–55
Savannah River, 54–55
Savannah Tom, 55
Scioto, 164, 171
Senecas, 81, 121, 128; attacks on forts, 140–43; British relations with, 123–24, 134, 136, 138, 144–45, 148; French relations with, 128–29, 131–33, 135–36; hostilities, 122, 128–29, 133, 135, 139–44, 151–54, 186, 222n4; at Niagara, 123, 128; and wage labor, 131–33, 135, 143, 152
Settico, 57
Settlements, white, 63–64, 72–73
Settlers, 14–15; Indian relations with, 16, 21, 23, 31, 68, 78, 107, 139, 162, 164, 166, 170, 174, 197, 206n14, 212n6, 213n7; petitions from, 81–83; relationship with forts, 7, 18, 24, 36, 57–58, 60, 63, 68–69, 71, 85–86, 98, 158, 161, 171, 188, 194; and trade/agriculture, 15–16, 19, 119, 140, 168
Seven Years' War: in the backcountry, 20*f*, 86, 205n6; French ceded forts after, 9, 11, 19, 63, 98, 124, 127, 135; Indian and British relations during, 11, 12, 14, 42*f*, 50–51, 62, 140, 157–58, 194, 196; military readiness during, 10, 18–19, 160, 167; trade and food during, 110, 117, 154
Shamokin, 8*m*, 16, 63, 84, 205n5
Shawnees, 54, 69, 124, 164, 166–67, 171, 175, 177, 183, 224n23, 226n38
Shelburne, Earl of, 173
Shirley, William, 194
Shrubshoal, Lieutenant William, 39–40
Shurtleff, Mary Belle, 120
Silvy, Anointe, 94
Sinclair, Patrick, 111–15
Sinnot, Pierce, 164
Sioux Indians, 161

Six Nations Iroquois, 12, 31, 63, 127, 134, 143, 152, 222n4; as former Five Nations, 127, 223n7; and peace, 171; and rum, 23; and Teedyuscung, 76; and trade, 123, 136
Smallpox Conjurer, 52
Springs, Harbor, 119
Squash Cutter, 151
Standing Turkey, 51–52, 56, 58
Stedman, John, 152–53
Sterling, Captain Thomas, 167–68, 178
Stewart's Blockhouse, 8*m*
Stilliards (scales), 35
Stuart, John, 54, 164
Superior, Lake, 98
Suquehannock Indians, 128
Susquehanna Region/Peoples, 63, 68–69, 73, 78–79, 81, 84
Susquehanna River, 8*m*, 26, 60

Tacite, 32
Tatamy, 78
Tecumseh, 198
Teedyuscung (aka Gideon), 60, 214n18, 215n29; at Fort Allen, 73–74, 76–77, 80–81, 83–84, 87
Tellico, Great, 44–46, 49–52, 55–56; Mankiller of, 35, 49–50, 55
Tennessee River, 45
Teute, Frederika J.: *Contact Points*, 5, 205n4
Timberlake, Lieutenant Henry, 42*f*
Tioga, 69, 73–74, 77, 79–80
Tohaditkarawa, 150–51
Tomeroy, 164, 182–84, 186
Tomotley, 41, 43–46, 48–49
Traders: British, 60, 95, 103, 106–7, 119, 139, 144, 163, 186; French, 34, 98–99, 106–7, 124, 127–28, 131–32, 140, 170, 179, 187; at Michilimackinac, 106, 113
Trans-Appalachian West, 19, 180, 217n2
Treaty, Cherokee, 1730, 27

Treaty of Greenville, 1795, 188
Treaty of Paris, 1763, 17
Tunica Indians, 162
Tuscarora Indians, 123

Upper Castle, Mohawk, 193. *See also* Canajoharie

Vaudreuil, Marquis de, 135
Vincennes, 111, 169–70, 173, 175, 190

Wabash region, 26, 110, 169, 175–76, 182–83; Indians in, 163, 170, 176, 186, 190
Wabash River, 166, 190–91
Wackerberg, Lieutenant Andrew, 85–86
Wage labor, 131–33, 135, 153–55
Walking Purchase, 79, 215n29
Wall, Lieutenant Robert, 50
Wallace, Anthony F. C., 62, 123, 214n18, 215n22
Washington, George, 36, 38, 63, 155
Wayne, Captain Isaac, 68
Weiser, Conrad, 73, 76–79, 215n26, 216n34
Wetterhold, Captain Jacob, 75, 77, 216n34
Weyrick, Corporal Christian, 75
White, Richard: *The Middle Ground*, 4, 198, 204nn3, 4, 206n16, 207n19, 217n3, 228n8, 229n8
Wilkins, Colonel John, 6, 122, 143, 172, 174–76, 199, 232nn42, 50; Indian journal of, 181–90
Willanawa, 46
Williamsburg, 37, 48
Wyoming, 63, 74, 76–77

Yamasee War (1715), 29, 208n7
Young, James, 68–69
Young Chief, 183

Zeisberger, David, 70

Daniel Ingram is assistant professor of history at Ball State University.

www.ingramcontent.com/pod-product-compliance
Lightning Source LLC
Chambersburg PA
CBHW020049170426
43199CB00009B/225